The Book of Hebrews

By
M. L. Andreasen

TEACH Services, Inc.
New York

2008 09 10 11 12 13 · 5 4 3 2 1

Copyright © 2005 TEACH Services, Inc.
ISBN-13: 978-1-57258-292-7
ISBN-10: 1-57258-292-8
Library of Congress Control Number: 2004109725

Published by

TEACH Services, Inc.
www.TEACHServices.com

Contents

Contents

Preface

THE BOOK of Hebrews appeared at a critical time in the history of the early church. The destruction of Jerusalem was impending—all signs declared that the event could not be far off—and many of the believers felt that this meant the end of the world. At this we are not to wonder, for even in the minds of some of the apostles the destruction of Jerusalem and the end of the world were closely intertwined, as their question, "When shall these things be? and what shall be the sign of thy coming, and of the end of the world?" clearly shows. Matt. 24:3.

The disciples had been perturbed at Jesus' reactions when He visited the city and the temple for the last time. In the midst of the triumphant entry, when the people were jubilantly acclaiming Him King, He had wept over the city and said, "If thou hadst known, even thou, at least in this thy day, the things which belong unto thy peace! but now they are hid from thine eyes. For the days shall come upon thee, that thine enemies shall cast a trench about thee, and compass thee round, and keep. thee in on every side." Luke 19:42, 43. To this He added later, "All these things shall come upon this generation." Matt. 23:36.

This caused consternation among the disciples. It did not seem possible that God would forsake His city and His people. And how could an enemy, however strong, destroy the temple? Was it not built of massive stones, incapable of destruction? Perhaps Christ had not noticed how large these stones were. If He had He would be more cautious in His utterances. And so "his disciples came to him for to shew him the building of the temple" (Matt. 24:1), apparently unaware of the fact that He knew more about them than they could possibly know.

As they walked about, "one of his disciples saith unto him, Master, see what manner of stones and what buildings are here!" Mark 13:1. They fervently hoped that a view of the massiveness of the structure would make such an impression upon Him that He would not refer lightly to its destruction. Was not the temple God's dwelling place? Was it not built so solidly that nothing on earth could destroy it? It was embarrassing for them to have Christ make statements which they firmly believed could never come to pass.

We are not informed which of the disciples asked Him to consider "what manner of stones and what buildings are here"; but Christ promptly turned to him and said, "Seest *thou* these great buildings?" Then He added, "There shall not be left one stone upon another, that shall not be thrown down." Mark 13:2. These words were spoken with such finality that the disciples said no more. But they wondered.

This conversation had taken place as the company left the temple on the way to the Mount of Olives. Doubtless the disciples talked the situation over on the way to the garden, for it was a most important and astounding prediction that Christ had made. Therefore, when He was seated on the "mount of Olives over against the temple, Peter and James and John and Andrew asked him privately," saying, "Tell us, when shall these things be? and what shall be the sign of thy coming, and of the end of the world?" Mark 13:3; Matt. 24:3.

For reasons which we do not know, Christ did not in His answer as recorded in the twenty-fourth chapter of Matthew differentiate between the destruction of Jerusalem and the end of the world. It is evident, however, that the one event is symbolic of the other, and that the prophecy is of double application, referring to two events, which, though widely separated in time, have much in common. The disciples had asked two questions: the first, "When shall these things be?" referring to Christ's statement that not one stone should be left upon another in the destruction of the city and temple; the other, "What shall be the sign of thy coming, and of the end of the world?" Christ in His answer embraced both events.

The disciples must have been intensely interested in what Christ said about the destruction of Jerusalem. They had heard Him say that "the days shall come upon thee, that thine enemies shall cast a trench about thee, and compass thee round, and keep thee in on every side, and shall lay thee even with the ground, and thy children within thee; and they shall not leave in thee one stone upon another; because thou knewest not the time of thy visitation." Luke 19:43, 44. These statements came close to them, for they loved Jerusalem the city of the living God, and from Christ's saying they concluded the destruction would likely take place in their day.

There are grounds for believing that the disciples expected an early return of their Master. He had promised to come again, and had said, "I will not leave you comfortless [margin, "orphans"]: I will come to you." John 14:18. "A little while, and ye shall not see me: and again, a little while, and ye shall see me."

John 16:16. When in perplexity they wondered, "What is this that he saith, A little while? we cannot tell what he saith" (Verse 18), He asked them, "Do ye inquire among yourselves of that I said, A little while, and ye shall not see me: and again, a little while, and ye shall see me?" (Verse 19.) He then tells them of the sorrow that shall be theirs, but that their sorrow shall be turned into joy, and then gives them the promise, "I will see you again, and your heart shall rejoice, and your joy no man taketh from you." Verse 22.

"I will see you again." Cheering words. They hoped and prayed He would soon return. What could be more natural than this? But year after year passed, and Christ did not come. At the time when the book of Hebrews was written, thirty or more years had passed, and still no word had come from the Master. Had He forgotten His promise? Would He ever return? There was every indication that erelong Jerusalem would be besieged by the Roman armies in fulfillment of Christ's prediction: "When ye therefore shall see the abomination of desolation, spoken of by Daniel the prophet, stand in the holy place, (whoso readeth, let him understand:) then let them which be in Judaea flee into the mountains: let him which is on the housetop not come down to take any thing out of his house: neither let him which is in the field return back to take his clothes." Matt. 24:15–18. Was it not time for Christ to come? Surely the time must be near.

The apostles must have done much searching of the Scriptures during this waiting time. Those who had known Christ and walked with Him, who had carefully treasured every word He had uttered, rehearsed again and again what He had said, and wrote down an account thereof. These accounts were compared, with the prophecies, and light was thrown on much that had perplexed them. Christ *was* coming again; of that there could be no doubt. The Old Testament prophets so declared; and Christ had confirmed their statements. But apparently He was not coming immediately. They found by studying Christ's promises that the end could not come until the gospel had been preached in all the world; and this had not been done. (Matt. 24:14.) Also there were to be signs in the heavens; the sun, the moon, and the stars should witness to the fulfillment of prophecy, and these signs had not appeared, nor had the powers of heaven been shaken. (Verses 29, 30.) Apparently there were not a few things they had overlooked. Yet, certain things should come to pass in their own generation, according to Christ's words in Matthew 23:36: "All these things shall come upon this generation." But would He Himself come? They hoped He would, and prayed that He might.

We should not censure the early disciples for their hope in regard to the soon coming of Christ. They clung to the promises of His soon return, and passed by others that gave balance to Christ's promises. This attitude caused Paul to issue a warning in his second letter to the Thessalonian church, which evidently believed that the coming of Christ was just at hand. "Let no man deceive you by any means," he said—an echo of Christ's first statement in regard to the same subject, "Take heed that no man deceive you." Matt. 24:4. "That day shall not come," continued Paul, "except there come a falling away first, and that man of sin be revealed, the son of perdition." 2 Thess. 2:3.

This shows that Paul did not believe that Christ would come in his day. He knew that the man of sin was first to be revealed and that many long years would elapse before Christ should appear. And so he warned the church against entertaining a false hope.

Paul's letter brought light to them, but it also caused a certain measure of discouragement. The believers had hoped that the coming of the Lord was near at hand, and now they were told that the event was far off. The months and years following the receipt of the letter were trying ones. It appeared to the church that their hope had been taken away, and that which had buoyed them up and made persecution bearable had been removed.

If ever the church needed help and encouragement it did then. The apostles were passing away one by one, and soon the church would be left to fight its battles alone. Christ had promised not to leave them orphans. (John 14:18, margin.) But now it seemed that this very thing would happen. It was a critical time. And it was in this hour of perplexity that the book of Hebrews appeared with needed light and comfort.

That which particularly caused concern to the church was the *reason* for Christ's long absence. Paul had given them some information on this matter when he said to the Thessalonians that there must "come a falling away first, and that man of sin be revealed, the son of perdition." 2 Thess. 2:3. But this was evidently not a sufficient explanation. What was Christ *doing?* Was He sitting in idle expectation, waiting for certain things to happen before He could return; or was He doing some most important work that vitally affected their salvation, and the salvation of all mankind? If the latter was the case, if Christ was performing a service comparable to that of the earthly priest who, after the slaying of the sacrifice went into the holy place, there to minister the blood of the victim, then Christ's absence became understandable. All Israel well understood that the death of the sacrifice was not sufficient to forgiveness. There must be a ministration of the blood to make the offering efficacious. If Christ indeed was priest, if as victim He had died on Calvary and there shed His blood, was it not necessary that that blood be ministered? And was this what Christ was doing now in heaven?

It was to answer these questions that Hebrews was written. Christ is indeed priest and high priest. He has "not entered into the holy places made with hands [the earthly temple], which are the figures of the true; but into heaven itself, now to appear in the presence of God for us." Heb. 9:24. There in the heavenly temple He has "appeared to put away sin by the sacrifice of himself." Verse 26. And there, says Paul, "shall the blood of Christ, who through the eternal Spirit offered himself without spot to God, purge your conscience from dead works to serve the living God." Verse 14.

What the people needed was a clear conception of the work Christ was doing for them in the courts above. They needed an understanding of the heavenly sanctuary and its services. That would explain the delay in His return, and would restore their wavering faith.

The conditions and problems which the church then had to meet are not unlike those facing the church today. *They* were living at the time of the fulfillment of the first part of Christ's prophecy—the destruction of the city of Jerusalem and the temple. *We* are living at the time of the fulfillment of the second part of the prophecy—the coming of the Lord Jesus in the clouds of heaven. As there were extravagant and erroneous views held then; as there were those then who had but a faint conception of Christ's work in the sanctuary; so there are those now who likewise err. There is as much need today of a thorough study of the Scriptures as there was then, and more so.

The book of Hebrews was a great factor in stabilizing the apostolic church in the crisis hour before the fall of Jerusalem. It is to be hoped that a discussion of the mighty themes of the book of Hebrews will be of some help to the church of God today. As believers in the soon coming of Christ, we need to become firmly grounded in the faith once delivered to the saints. All need to have their eyes fastened on our great High Priest and the work He is doing in the sanctuary above, where "he ever liveth to make intercession for them." Heb. 7:25. And may it be the blessed privilege of many with "boldness to enter into the holiest by the blood of Jesus, by a new and living way, which he hath consecrated for us, through the veil, that is to say, his flesh." Heb. 10:19, 20. This was the prayer and hope of the author of Hebrews, and this also is the prayer and hope of the author of this volume.

—THE AUTHOR.

The Importance and Content of Hebrews

THE BOOK of Hebrews holds an important and unique place in the canon of the New Testament, as it deals chiefly with the ascended Christ and His session at the right hand of God. Were it not for this book, we would know but little of Christ's work in heaven and His present position; the ascension would be the last full glimpse we would have of Him until His return; His mediatorial work would be almost completely obscured; prophetic references in the Old Testament, to the cleansing of the sanctuary would have no New Testament confirmation; and the entire Aaronic priestly ministration would constitute a discarded Old Testament curiosity instead of a living representation of the redemptive work of Christ in the sanctuary above.

There were many things Christ could have told His disciples had they been spiritually prepared to receive them. Because of their dullness of comprehension He had to weigh and measure each "word unto them, as they were able to hear it." Mark 4:33. When He told them of His suffering, death, and resurrection, "they understood none of these things, and the saying was hid from them, neither knew they the things which were spoken." Luke 18:34.

Almost in reproach Christ had said to the disciples, "None of you asketh me; Whither goest thou?" John 16:5. This suggests that He would have been pleased to have them interested in His future work, and that He would have informed them concerning it had they

asked. But instead He was compelled to say, "I have
yet many things to say unto you, but ye cannot bear
them now." Verse 12. He therefore told them only the
things that they could bear, leaving for the future
other information which they needed but which only
time and further advancement in Christian knowledge would enable them to understand.

In the twenty-six books of the New Testament—leaving out for the present the book of
Hebrews—we have a connected and relatively
complete story of the life and teachings of Christ; of
the progress of the work on earth after His departure;
of the establishment and growth of the apostolic
churches and the great Christian doctrines; ending
in the last book of the Bible with a prophetic picture of
the struggle and eventual victory of the church in its
conflict with evil. But in this comprehensive account
one important phase is missing: we are told
little—almost nothing —of Christ after He disappeared from view at His ascension, nothing of His
mediatorial work at the right hand of the Majesty on
high. And yet, this was the very subject to which He
had reference when in perplexity He asked, "None of
you asketh me, Whither goest thou?"

On Calvary, Christ died and shed His blood for us.
This was in fulfillment of the sanctuary type in which
a lamb was slain to provide atonement. But the
slaying of the lamb did not in and of itself effect atonement. "It is the blood that maketh atonement," not
the death of the sacrifice. Lev. 17:11, R.V. The blood
of the passover lamb had to be put on the lintel and
doorposts before it availed for atonement. Must a like
ministration of the blood of Christ, the true Lamb of
God, also be observed? Hebrews answers this in the
affirmative, and presents Christ as high priest of the
heavenly sanctuary, who ministers His own blood,

thereby obtaining eternal redemption for us. "Neither by the blood of goats and calves, but by his own blood he entered in once into the holy place, having obtained [or "thereby obtaining,"] eternal redemption for us." Heb. 9:12.

Book of Hebrews Unique

The epistle to the Hebrews is the one book which argues the deity of Christ, presenting Him as the express image of the Father, the Creator and Upholder of all things, whom even the Father addresses as Lord and God. It is the one book that discusses Christ as apostle and high priest, comparing and contrasting His priesthood with that of Aaron's. It is the one book that interprets the sufferings and death of Christ as vital and necessary in His preparation for the priesthood, declaring that only thus could He become a merciful and faithful high priest. It is the one book that gives us the astounding information that "the heavenly things" must be cleansed with the blood of Christ, and thus assists us in rightly interpreting the cleansing of the sanctuary mentioned in Daniel as referring to the heavenly archetype. It is the one book that portrays Christ's entrance into the "holy places" in heaven through the greater and more perfect tabernacle of which He is minister, thereby establishing a parallel between the entrance of the high priest on earth and Christ's entrance in heaven. It is the one book in the New Testament that consistently uses sanctuary language throughout, such as: the first and second tabernacle; the holy and the most holy; sin offerings, burnt offerings, and sacrifices; the sprinkling of the altar with blood, and the carrying of the blood into the sanctuary; the veil; the priests and the high priest accomplishing the service; the burning of the body of the sin offering outside the camp—all of these references constituting a parallel between Christ's work and that of the Levitical priest, showing the connection between the lamb slain on the sanctuary altar and the true Lamb of God. Thus significance and even glory is given to the sacrificial system instituted by God.

Hebrews is the only book in the New Testament that discusses the seventh-day Sabbath in the light of God's rest at creation, informing us that there remains the keeping of a Sabbath to the children of God. It is the only book that connects the rest of the soul with the seventh-day Sabbath rest that God instituted in the Garden of Eden, which fact emphasizes the Sabbath as the true sign of sanctification. It is the only book which informs us that the God who once shook the earth when He spoke the Ten Commandments from Sinai, will "once more" shake not the earth only but also the heavens. It is the only book that presents Christ's second coming in the setting of the sanctuary doctrine, informing us that "unto them that look for him shall he appear the second time without sin unto salvation." It is the only book which for our encouragement discusses a group of people who, despite their faults and weaknesses, at last obtained a good report and had their names inscribed in the Lamb's book of life. It is the only book that presents the saints entering with Christ into the holies by a new and living way, and thus holds before them the possibility of the high honor and inexpressible glory of standing in the unveiled presence of God.

A Book for This Time

Hebrews thus occupies a very high and important place in the Scriptures. It is a book for this time, obscured for a while, but now coming into its own. Rightly understood, it furnishes the sanctuary setting for the preaching of the last message of mercy to the world, and thus greatly aids in preaching the Sabbath more fully.

This book has been long neglected by the people of God. We rightly place stress on Christ as our high priest, yet there is a tendency to neglect the only book in which this work is emphasized. In all the rest of the New Testament there is no discussion of His priestly work; in fact, outside of the book of Hebrews the term "high priest" is not even once mentioned as referring to Christ. On the other hand, in chapter after chapter in Hebrews is Christ as high priest the subject, and ten times the title is applied to Him directly; in seven other instances He is compared or contrasted with the high priests on earth, besides numerous incidental references. Deprived of this book, Seventh-day Adventists could not easily maintain their doctrine of Christ, or present Biblical confirmation for certain positions on the sanctuary question.

The book of Hebrews connects the sanctuary on earth with the sanctuary in heaven. The first half of the book gives a view and a review of the services on earth, making constant references to the higher service above. It compares and contrasts the qualifications of the priests on earth with the greater dignity and surpassing glory of our great Apostle and High Priest in heaven. It lays a solid foundation of precise knowledge in regard to the sanctuary service on earth, which is necessary to an adequate understanding of Christ's work in heaven. Again and again it stresses the parallels between the tabernacle and its services on earth, and the tabernacle and the services in heaven, presenting the former as a type of the latter.

Having thoroughly instructed his readers in the priesthood and service on earth; having in particular emphasized that the priests went daily into the first apartment, but that the high priest went into the most holy only once a year, the author of the book suddenly illuminates and vitalizes the earthly service by asserting that the Holy Spirit signifies something by this. (Heb. 9:8.) This is a most important statement, as it places the seal of approval of the third person of the Godhead upon that which otherwise might be considered only a discarded ritual. As the Holy Spirit played a significant part in the incarnation; as the Holy Spirit testified to the divinity of Christ at His baptism; as the Holy Spirit became Christ's special representative at His departure; so the Holy Spirit now calls attention to the sanctuary service and invests it with typical significance. This endorsement by the Holy Spirit of the sanctuary service should not be passed by lightly. It lifts it above the level of a Jewish ordinance to that of typical representation of the deep things of God in the plan of salvation.

Conditions in the Early Church

The number of believers at the time of the death of Christ was not large, "about an hundred and twenty," but it was greatly augmented on the day of Pentecost when "about three thousand souls" were converted and added to the church. (Acts 1:15; 2:41.)

The church in Jerusalem soon grew to be both large and influential. In addition to the apostles, a "great company of the priests were obedient to the faith," and also "certain of the sect of the Pharisees which believed." Acts 6:7; 15:5. Thirty years later there were still "many thousands of Jews" in the city, even though persecution had compelled a number to leave. (Acts 21:20.)

It might be expected that as soon as possible after the ascension a house of worship would be erected in Jerusalem to accommodate the believers. This, however, does not seem to be the case. We are told that at the hour of prayer Peter and John went up to the temple, and that "all that believed" continued "daily with one accord in the temple." Acts 2:44; 2:46. Even though smaller companies broke bread "from house to house," and during the time of persecution "many gathered together praying" in "the house of Mary the mother of John, whose surname was Mark," the church continued to use the temple as their meeting place, probably assembling in Solomon's porch, which was roomy enough to hold a large congregation. (Acts 2:46; 12:12.)

Rites and Ceremonies

From the record in the book of Acts it appears that not only did the church continue to worship in the temple but the believers also observed many of the rites and ceremonies of the Jews, including circumcision. (Acts 15:1.) In view of the fact that a great company of priests belonged to the church, this is not surprising; for naturally it would take time for these to adjust themselves to the new conditions. The apostles did not see clearly the changes which the conception of Christ as high priest necessitated in their relation to the temple. He had given no command abolishing the Mosaic law, nor had He spoken against the temple services. Although we have no record that He Himself observed the ordinances, He recognized their validity by admonishing the people to do whatever the scribes and the Pharisees bade them observe, as well as by telling the leper, "Go thy way, shew thyself to the priest, and offer the gift that Moses commanded." Matt. 23:2; 8:4. These statements would readily be seized upon by those who were inclined to "observe and do" all that Moses commanded as proof of the continued validity of the Mosaic ordinances.

Though the death and resurrection of Christ ushered in the new covenant era, it was apparently not God's intent to break finally with the Jews at that precise time. They had rejected Christ and crucified Him, but mercy was still extended to them; and for several years—at least until the end of the prophetic seventy weeks—the chief work of the apostles was confined to the Jews. The disciples were greatly encouraged when on the day of Pentecost thousands were converted, and also when numbers were daily added to the church. The "great company of priests" naturally made their influence felt in the church and enhanced its prestige, as did also the "sect of the Pharisees." This was evidently not the time for the church to take an antagonistic attitude toward the temple and its services. Thousands of Jews had been won to Christ in a few months. Might it be possible that still other thousands would accept the Messiah, and the Jews remain God's chosen people?

If any had such expectations they were doomed to disappointment. The Jewish nation was not ready to accept Jesus as their Messiah. They had crucified the Saviour, stoned Stephen, and beaten the apostles. (Acts 5:40; 7:58.) As persecution increased, Peter was put into prison and threatened with execution, and

James, the brother of John, was killed with the sword. (Acts 12:1–19.) The Jewish nation was turning away from the new doctrine. There was little hope that Israel would accept Jesus as their Messiah.

The death of Stephen seems to have been the turning point in the attitude of the Jewish people toward the Christian faith. "There arose on that day a great persecution against the church which was in Jerusalem." Acts 8:1, R. V. Many of the believers were scattered throughout Judea and Samaria—God's way of sowing the seeds of truth in those regions. It is significant that though the people were dispersed, the apostles remained in Jerusalem. (Verse 1.)

Paul

One of the chief persecutors of the Christians was Saul, a young Pharisee. He "laid waste the church, entering into every house, and dragging men and women committed them to prison." Acts 8:3, R. V. His own testimony is that he "compelled them to blaspheme; and being exceedingly mad against them...[he] persecuted them even unto strange cities." Acts 26:11.

This was the man whom God has selected to be "a chosen vessel...to bear...[His] name before the Gentiles, and kings, and the children of Israel." Acts 9:15. On the way to Damascus, where he was going to apprehend the Christians that he might bring them bound to Jerusalem (Acts 9:2), he was himself apprehended of God, thoroughly converted, and began immediately to tell others of the new-found Saviour. This aroused the hatred of the Jews, and he was compelled to flee for his life. Shortly after this he retired to Arabia, where he spent some time, perhaps years, in seclusion, and then quietly began his public work.

The next few years we hear little of Paul. That he must have been active is evident, for Paul could not long be idle. These were years of preparation for the work God had in mind for him. He must have done much studying and meditating during this time; for when he finally began active service, his whole religious conception was mature and his theology ripe. He had thought things through, and was ready for the work God had given him to do.

The First Church Council

It is in Antioch that we find Paul some years later working with Barnabas and others. Here he was ordained to the gospel ministry. (Acts 13:1–3.) After his ordination Paul started on his first missionary journey, which brought him in direct contact with the Gentiles. On this tour he met both success and opposition, was heralded as a god, and also stoned and left for dead. When he and Barnabas came back to Antioch they rehearsed to the church "all that God had done with them, and how he had opened the door of faith unto the Gentiles." Acts 14:27.

Paul's work among the Gentiles did not meet with the approval of those among the Jewish believers who were proponents of the ceremonial law. This was largely because he did not require the Gentiles to be circumcised and observe the law of Moses. When this became known to the church at Jerusalem, certain men of Judea came down to Antioch, who did not hesitate to tell the new believers, "Except ye be circumcised after the manner of Moses, ye cannot be saved." Acts 15:1. This caused "no small dissension and disputation," so much so that the church at

Antioch at last "determined that Paul and Barnabas, and certain other of them, should go up to Jerusalem unto the apostles and the elders about this question." Verse 2.

Paul agreed to this, and in due time he and Barnabas arrived in Jerusalem, where they met with the apostles and elders, and told them "all things that God had done with them." Verse 4. As they were recounting their work for the Gentiles, "there rose up certain of the sect of the Pharisees which believed, saying, That it was needful to circumcise them, and to command them to keep the law of Moses." Verse 5.

It was evidently the hope of the apostles that Paul's speech would have satisfied the people as they learned of the blessing that had attended the work of the two missionaries. But when the Pharisees gave their decision that "it was needful to circumcise them, and to command them to keep the law of Moses," there was no way of avoiding a public discussion.

As a result "the apostles and elders came together for to consider of this matter," and there was "much disputing." Verses 6, 7. That Paul and Barnabas were the center of the "disputing" there can be no doubt. Paul later speaks of his opponents as those "to whom we gave place by subjection, no, not for an hour." Gal. 2:5. Paul stood his g round. It was an interesting as well as a lively debate.

Finally Peter arose and said, "Men and brethren, ye know how that a good while ago God made choice among us, that the Gentiles by my mouth should hear the word of the gospel, and believe. And God, which knoweth the hearts, bare them witness, giving them the Holy Ghost, even as he did unto us; and put no difference between us and them, purifying their hearts by faith. Now therefore why tempt ye God, to put a yoke upon the neck of the disciples, which neither our fathers nor we were able to bear? But we believe that through the grace of the Lord Jesus Christ we shall be saved, even as they." Acts 15:7–11.

The substance of the speech was that he did not think the ceremonial law should be forced upon the Gentiles, as God had shown that He "put no difference between us and them, purifying their hearts by faith." Peter's was a compromise speech, and did not raise the question of the circumcision of the Jews. His recommendation was that the *Gentiles* only should not be circumcised.

After Peter had spoken, "the multitude kept silence" while Paul and Barnabas told them what "God had wrought among the Gentiles by them." Verse 12.

Decision of the Council

James, who presided at the meeting, now gave his decision. He stated that Peter had spoken in harmony with "the words of the prophets; as it is written, After this I will return, and will build again the tabernacle of David, which is fallen down; and I will build again the ruins thereof, and I will set it up: that the residue of men might seek after the Lord, and all the Gentiles, upon whom my name is called, saith the Lord, who doeth all these things." Verses 15–17.

He therefore gave it as his sentence "that we trouble not them, which from among the Gentiles are turned to God: but that we write unto them, that they abstain from pollutions of idols, and from fornication, and from things strangled, and from blood. For Moses of old time hath in every city them that preach him, being read in the synagogue every sabbath day." Verses 19–21.

As a result of this meeting, two men were sent with Paul and Barnabas to Antioch and a letter written by the apostles and elders saying, "Forasmuch as we have heard, that certain which went out from us have troubled you with words, subverting your souls, saying, Ye must be circumcised, and keep the law; to whom we gave no such commandment: it seemed good unto us, being assembled with one accord, to send chosen men unto you with our beloved Barnabas and Paul, men that have hazarded their lives for the name of our Lord Jesus Christ. We have sent therefore Judas and Silas, who shall also tell you the same things by mouth. For it seemed good to the Holy Ghost, and to us, to lay upon you no greater burden than these necessary things; That ye abstain from meats offered to idols, and from blood, and from things strangled, and from fornication: from which if ye keep yourselves, ye shall do well. Fare ye well." Verses 24–29.

Paul, in telling the story of his visit to Jerusalem, gives this additional information: "Fourteen years after I went up again to Jerusalem with Barnabas, and took Titus with me also. And I went up by revelation, and communicated unto them that gospel which I preach among the Gentiles, but privately to them which were of reputation, lest by any means I should run, or had run, in vain. But neither Titus, who was with me, being a Greek, was compelled to be circumcised." Gal. 2:1–3.

It is significant that Paul found it necessary to go to Jerusalem and counsel with the brethren about circumcision, and also to speak "privately to them which were of reputation, lest by any means I should run, or had run, in vain." Verse 2.

This decision of the council throws an interesting side light on conditions in the Jerusalem church. Not only did the believers continue to observe the ceremonial law many years after Christ, but a large element in the church held that the Gentiles should be circumcised as well as the Jews. The decision, however, concerned the Gentiles only. They were released from the obligation to observe the ceremonial law, while, by implication the Jews were to continue to observe it as heretofore. Paul thus gained only a partial victory. He could now freely go to the Gentiles, knowing that they would not be compelled to be circumcised.

While the status of the Gentiles was thus settled in this first church council, the underlying principle of the ceremonial law does not seem to have been recognized. Yet, even as it was, a great advance step was taken. The Gentiles were freed from the yoke of bondage "which neither our fathers nor we were able to bear." Acts 15:10. Once this step was taken, it could not be long before the principle would be seen to apply to the Jews as well as to the Gentiles.

The Second Jerusalem Council

The next years Paul spent in arduous labor in many parts of the Mediterranean field, working for Jew and Gentile alike. About the year 60, or a little later, he again visited Jerusalem to report the work he had done. When the brethren heard Paul's account "they glorified the Lord, and said unto him, Thou seest, brother, how many thousands of Jews there are which believe; and they are all zealous of the law: and they are informed of thee, that thou teachest all the Jews which are among the Gentiles to forsake Moses, saying that they ought not to circumcise their children, neither to walk after the customs. What is it therefore? the multitude must needs come together: for they will hear that thou art come. Do therefore this that we say to thee: We have four men which have a vow on them; them take, and purify thyself with them, and be at charges with them, that they may shave their heads: and all may know that those things, whereof they were informed concerning thee, are nothing; but that thou thyself also walkest orderly, and keepest the law. As touching the Gentiles which. believe, we have written and concluded that they observe no such thing, save only that they keep themselves from things offered to idols, and from blood, and from strangled, and from fornication." Acts 21:20–25.

Paul Arrested

There were in Jerusalem at that time "many thousands of Jews" which believed. These were all "zealous of the law." James and the elders therefore counseled Paul to take four men and with them perform some minor ceremonial requirements, not in themselves vital, but which would serve to show that Paul walked orderly and kept the law. We do not know the reason for Paul's compliance with this request. Perhaps he reasoned that "circumcision is nothing, and uncircumcision is nothing." 1 Cor. 7:19. In any event, Paul went with the men and performed the purification required by the law. As a result of some misapprehension on the part of the temple authorities in regard to the men accompanying Paul, he was arrested and placed in custody. (Acts 21:33.)

It is significant to find that nearly thirty years after the death of Christ there were thousands of Jews in Jerusalem who believed and yet were zealous for the ceremonial law, and that this element in the church was so influential that James, the elders, and even Paul, felt it necessary to yield to their prejudices. The Jerusalem church had not shaken itself loose from the Old Testament ideas of worship, and were still observing ordinances which Paul had discarded. Although this was not the case in other churches—at least not where Paul's influence prevailed—the example of the church at Jerusalem vitally affected believers elsewhere.

Under these circumstances it was natural that Paul should feel the need of the Jewish believers being given instruction that would make plain the temporal and provisional nature of the Levitical system, with an explanation of the new system that was to take its place. But Paul was now in prison and could not personally visit the church. The believers, and particularly the Jerusalem church, needed help, and it must not be long in forthcoming. Rome was on the march; there were wars and rumors of war; and it would not be long until the imperial armies would be at the gates. When the city should be taken, it would be too late; for, according to Jesus' prophecy, the believers would then have to flee, and the church would be scattered. (Luke 21:20, 21.) What was to be done must be done quickly.

Then suddenly, at exactly the right time, the book of Hebrews appeared, giving just the needed help. It came in the direct providence of God to save the church in Jerusalem. How did it come into existence? Who wrote it?

The Author of Hebrews

IN STATING our belief that Paul is the author of Hebrews, we well know that in the eyes of the critics we disqualify ourselves for further serious consideration. The ordinary arguments for or against the Pauline authorship of Hebrews have been exhaustively presented by others, and very little can be said that has not been said many times before. We are, however, convinced that too much weight has been given to internal evidence, to grammatical construction, to the use of phrases that arc said to be unPauline, and to the line of arguments used by the author and the form of their presentation. To us it seems precarious to assert that this or that phrase or word could not be Pauline for no other reason than that it does not occur in his other books. At best those arguments are negative, and it is always unwise to build a positive philosophy on uncertain, negative assertions.

The arguments in the book of Hebrews, and their general presentation, are exactly what was needed by the Jerusalem church at that time. Paul knew of the adherence of "thousands of Jews" to the Levitical system. He knew also that to get the apostles and elders as well as the people to turn from the now useless ceremonies, it was necessary that the provisional and temporary nature of the temple and its services be set forth. If Paul did not write Hebrews, someone wrote it who knew exactly what was needed, and who felt the urge of presenting to the church the true meaning of that which was passing away as well as that which was to take its place.

That the arguments and thoughts of the book of Hebrews bear the stamp of Paul is admitted even by many who do not believe Paul to be the author. When we consider the history of the early Christian church, and the attitude of the church in Jerusalem; when we know that Paul was in the midst of a controversy about the very questions with which the book of Hebrews deals; that he was an experienced writer; that, being in prison, he could not meet these problems in person; that he was the only apostle who could or did stand against the Judaizing teachings in the church and was not afraid to withstand to the face even Peter—how can anyone under these circumstances fail to believe that Paul would desire to express himself on a subject that loomed so large to him and which was so important?

Indeed, it would be most unlikely that Paul should repress the desire to write. He saw, as no one else, the typical nature of the ceremonial system. He knew, as no one else, the true nature of Christ's mediatorial work in heaven above. He understood, as no one else, the nature of the power that should exalt itself until its representative should at last sit in the temple of God showing himself that he is God. With this in view Paul, above all men, would feel the need of laying a firm foundation for an understanding of the mediatorial work of Christ that would at once show the uselessness of the Jewish sacrifices and also constitute the greatest defence against the false mediatorial system soon to be advocated by the one who should declare himself Christ's representative on earth. It would seem. that the best man—we might almost say the only man—to write such a document would be

Paul. He knew the problem. He had met the Judaizers face to face. He was the man best fitted to write such a treatise.

The Critics' Arguments

As already noted, the arguments which the critics advance against the Pauline authorship of Hebrews are chiefly concerned with the language of the epistle, which they say is much more beautiful and elegant than that of Paul's undisputed epistles. We do not believe that these arguments are conclusive. They could be so only on the supposition that it was not possible for Paul to write correct and beautiful Greek, and on the further supposition that he could not change his style with a change of subject matter. We do not believe that either of these arguments is valid.

In the stress and storm of a busy life Paul might dash off a communication that does not stand the test of correct grammatical construction, as appears to be the case with some of his epistles. But he was now in prison and had abundant time to write. Nor can it successfully be contended that Paul was unable to write correct Greek. He had the education, he knew Greek, and rash would be the person who would claim that Paul could not produce a treatise such as Hebrews if he should desire to apply himself to the writing of it. The difference between Paul's earlier and later writings shows that although Paul did not change his theology, his style underwent a change with the years.

To us it appears that the critics have given too little weight to the historical background. Clement, Barnabas, Luke, Apollos, might have written some kind of treatise dealing with the subject; but none of them had the experience that Paul had, nor could they have felt the need that Paul felt, especially after his last visit to Jerusalem. It must have grieved Paul that he had yielded to the demand of the church to observe an obsolete, though harmless, ordinance. As he sat in the lonely prison meditating upon the work he might be doing for the churches had he not been imprisoned, he must have felt as never before that he owed something to his Jewish brethren. Had not the Lord said that he was a chosen vessel to bear His name "before the Gentiles, and kings, and the children of Israel"? Acts 9:15. God had sent Paul to the Gentiles, but He had as truly sent him to the Jews. But thus far Paul had done little for Israel. He owed them a debt, and the time had come to pay it. He had failed when he last met with the church at Jerusalem. He must make amends.

Jerusalem's Destruction Near

Paul had the needed insight into the Mosaic ordinances and ceremonies rightly to evaluate them and give them their proper setting in the plan of salvation. He knew their transitory nature and that the time was past due for their abrogation. Not only did Paul know this, but he appears to be the only one of the leaders who had this clear vision. None of the other apostles sensed the crisis that would confront the church when the city and the temple should be destroyed. And that was only a short time in the future. It was high time not only that the church be warned but that it receive positive instruction in the deeper things of God regarding the ministration of their High Priest in heaven. This would be needed when all things earthly began to fail and their temple should be laid in ruins.

When Paul made his last visit to Jerusalem, the time was nearing when, according to Jesus' prophecy, the city and the temple would be destroyed. It was in October, A.D. 66, that the siege of Jerusalem began. At the time of Paul's last visit, just before the destruction, the church seemed unaware of the calamities soon to befall them. They still kept the feasts; they still sacrificed as in former years; they were still zealous for the ceremonial law. They had but a faint conception of Christ's work in the sanctuary above; they knew little of His ministry; they did not realize that their sacrifices were useless in view of the great sacrifice on Calvary.

It was high time that their eyes should be opened to heavenly realities. When their temple should be destroyed, it would be needful for them to have their faith anchored to something sure and steadfast that would not fail them. If their minds could be turned to the heavenly High Priest and sanctuary and to better sacrifices than those of bulls and goats, they would not be dismayed when a mere earthly structure should be destroyed. But if they had no such hope; if they had no vision of the sanctuary in heaven, they would be bewildered and perplexed as they should see the destruction of that in which they had trusted.

All this Paul understood better than any one else. He trembled as he thought of what would happen to the church when sudden destruction should come to the city and the temple. And he trembled even more at the thought of what would happen to his churches throughout the provinces when the Jerusalem believers should be scattered to the ends of the earth holding the views they now held in regard to ceremonial observances. He had just had a demonstration of how tenaciously they clung to circumcision and the Mosaic ordinances. When they were scattered by persecution, these believers would enter every church he had established, and teach the people that unless they were circumcised and kept the law of Moses they could not be saved. This had happened before, and the Jerusalem believers were still zealous for the law, as Paul had experienced. And when that time should come Paul would not be able to help.

This was a most dismal outlook. It seemed that the whole Christian church might split on the question of the ceremonial law. The Jerusalem teachers and believers, as they should disperse, would tend to create factions in every church in Christendom. The situation was critical. Paul was the only one who understood fully the issues involved. But he was helpless in prison. Can any doubt that he was anxious to communicate to the church the light God had given him, and thus save the church from division?

Paul's interest in the church in Jerusalem would be sufficient to impel him to write; but the added danger that would come to his churches as the believers were scattered at the destruction of Jerusalem would be an even stronger reason why he should write an epistle such as Hebrews. If the believers in Jerusalem once saw and understood Christ's work in the sanctuary above; if they understood that there was something better in store for them; if they understood that Christ was now serving as their high priest in the sanctuary in heaven, they would have a hope both sure and steadfast; and instead of being disheartened by the fall of their city, would see in it a fulfillment of Christ's prophecy; and as they were scattered to the provinces, they would be one with the believers in Paul's churches, would meet others of like precious faith, and rejoice in their common hope. Instead of creating dissension, they would be a strength to the churches.

It is difficult for us fully to appreciate the crisis that faced the early church. The only thing that could save the people from bewilderment and discouragement when the Roman armies laid their beautiful temple in ruins, was a clear conception of the true sanctuary and its services in heaven. That, and that only, could explain the experience they were to pass through. As verily as the people of God in 1844 could understand their disappointment and their future work only in the light of the sanctuary truth, so was this also the only hope of the apostolic church. An understanding of the sanctuary was their salvation. Light on this vital subject must come to them if they were to triumph victoriously.

And light did come. The book of Hebrews appeared in this crisis hour, containing the blessed truth of the sanctuary; of the greater and more perfect tabernacle; of Christ the high priest; of the new covenant; of the blood "that speaketh better things than that of Abel"; of the rest that remains for the people of God; and of the blessed hope that is as an anchor of the soul, both sure and steadfast, and which enters into that within the veil. (Heb. 6:19.)

The Date of Composition

Some critics summarily dispose of the arguments for Paul's authorship of Hebrews by the simple assertion that the epistle was written not before but after the fall of Jerusalem, sometime in the nineties or even later. It is, of course, clear that if Hebrews were written that late, Paul could not be its author; for he died in the sixties. The date of the composition of the epistle therefore becomes important.

There are several reasons why a late date cannot be accepted. We give three.

It would be most strange if in a treatise dealing with the abolition of the Levitical ordinances no mention whatever should be made of the destruction of the temple if this already had taken place. Not only was the fall of Jerusalem an important event in the history of Israel—*it was the supreme event,* in their minds comparable to the end of all things. That a writer should deal with the temple and yet make no reference to its destruction if it were already in ruins is incredible.

This becomes more evident as we consider that the author neglected one of the strongest arguments for his position by failing to make mention of such destruction if it had already taken place. If he could show that not only did God *intend* to abrogate the ceremonial ordinances but that they *were already effectively abolished* by the destruction of the temple, he would have had an unanswerable argument. Also, if at the time of the writing of the epistle the temple lay in ruins and Israel were scattered to the ends of the earth, the author would certainly not fail to mention this and show that God's displeasure had been signally demonstrated. He would thus buttress his argument for a new priesthood in place of that which had already ceased to function. The whole argument of the epistle would have taken a different direction, culminating in the indisputable fact that God had already destroyed their temple and scattered the people. It cannot be believed that an author of the standing of the writer of Hebrews would have omitted this most potent argument.

The second reason for our belief that Hebrews was written before the destruction of Jerusalem is found in the fact that the temple services are mentioned in Hebrews as still being carried on. A few illustrations out of many will suffice for our purpose. "The law *maketh* men high priests," can only refer to a present situation. Heb. 7:28. Had the author been looking back on a discarded practice he would have said, "The law *made* men high priests." Again, "There *are* priests that offer," would have been changed to "There *were* priests that offered." Heb. 8:4. "Who *serve* unto the example and shadow of heavenly things," would become, "Who served." The author observes that Christ "*suffered*" without the gate, while in the same connection he says that the blood of beasts "*is brought* into the sanctuary," and the bodies "*are burned* without the camp." Heb. 13:11, 12. Christ's suffering is put in the past tense; the ministry of blood and the disposition of sacrifice are put in the present tense. This is explicable only on the ground of Hebrews' being written before A.D. 70.

Still another argument concerns itself with the change of viewpoint in regard to ceremonial observances that came to the believers in Jerusalem before the fall of the city. At the time of Paul's last visit there were "many thousands of Jews" in the church. (Acts 21:20.) We do not know how many "many thousands" are, but two or three thousand cannot be considered "many thousands." Besides the common people there were "a great company of priests," and also "Pharisees which believed." (Acts 6:7; 15:5.) These were "all zealous of the law," so much so that Paul had to bow to their mandate and observe an obsolete ordinance. (Acts 21:26.) This shows that they still taught that "except ye be circumcised after the manner of Moses, ye cannot be saved." Acts 15: 1. These many thousands of believers were scattered everywhere at the time of the fall of the city, and it might reasonably be expected that, if they at that time still believed there was no salvation without circumcision, wherever they went they would carry their convictions with them; and being zealous of the law would create division and dissension in all the churches, and thus split Christendom.

But nothing of this kind took place. There was no division. Christendom was not split into Jewish and Gentile sections. There was only *one* church, and that church was not a circumcision church. Something had happened to the Jewish believers and zealots of the law, and that something must have taken place before A.D. 70. The appearance of the book of Hebrews gives the only reasonable solution.

Historians of the early church are under obligation to account for the sudden change in viewpoint of the Jerusalem church between the time of Paul's visit in the early sixties and the fall of the city in the year A.D. 70. A few years only intervened between the time of their zealous regard for the law and their turning to true apostolic Christianity. This miraculous change must have had a background. The only sufficient cause of which we know is the appearance of the epistle to the Hebrews. Those who believe in a late date for Hebrews are under obligation to produce their reasons for the preservation of the doctrinal unity of the church in view of the strong and ardent adherence to Jewish ceremonies of the Jerusalem church immediately before the fall of the city, and the opposite viewpoint held by the Pauline churches. The appearance of the book of Hebrews at precisely this time accounts for all the facts, and we know of no other efficient cause.

CHAPTER 1

OF THE BOOK OF HEBREWS

The Deity of Christ

SYNOPSIS OF CHAPTER

SOME OF the apostles were still living when the book of Hebrews was written in the early sixties of the first century after Christ. Many other Christians were living who had heard Christ preach and had seen Him as He walked from place to place throughout the land. Among them were some who had been present at the ascension and had heard the words of the angels: "Ye men of Galilee, why stand ye gazing up into heaven? this same Jesus, which is taken up from you into heaven, shall so come in like manner as ye have seen him go into heaven." Acts 1:11.

Jesus had promised to come again, and the disciples had hoped that His return would not be long delayed; but at the time the book of Hebrews was written thirty years had passed and no further word had come from Him. In vain they had scanned the heavens for some sign of their returning Lord. Why did He not come? What detained Him? Would He ever come?

The church had no clear understanding of Christ's mediatorial work, nor did they grasp the scope of God's plan, which involved the passing of centuries

1

and even millenniums before the end could come. True, Jesus had mentioned certain things which must first come to pass, but His words were only dimly comprehended. The believers preferred to cling to those sayings that seemed to promise an early return.

In view of the impending destruction of Jerusalem, which Christ had foretold and which He had said would occur in their generation, it was necessary that the people be fully informed in regard to Christ's high priestly work. A clear understanding of this not only would account for His prolonged absence but also explain the abolition of the ceremonial law and the cessation of the temple services. As these observances had been instituted by God Himself and were considered sacred, only God could abolish them. If Jesus, therefore, abrogated the ceremonial law, it was necessary that He be shown to be God. This the author does in the first chapter of the epistle.

Hebrews 1:1–3. "God, who at sundry times and in divers manners spake in time past unto the fathers by the prophets, hath in these last days spoken unto us by his Son, whom he hath appointed heir of all things, by whom also he made the worlds; who being the brightness of his glory, and the express image of his person, and upholding all things by the word of his power, when he had by himself purged our sins, sat down on the right hand of the Majesty on high."

The verses contain a summary of the entire epistle. They present the pre-eminent Son as the appointed heir of all things; the Creator; the express image of God; the upholder of all things; the Redeemer; the Priest-King, seated at the right hand of God. As prophet, He speaks for God; as priest, He purged our sins; as king, He shares the throne of the Majesty on high.

Verse 1. "God...spake in time past." Many critics do not accept the Old Testament writings as inspired. If they concede any inspiration at all, it is of an inferior kind. Such should consider the opening statement of Hebrews. God is there presented as the One who spoke in the Old Testament, even though the books bear the names of Job, Isaiah, and Malachi. The admonition, "See that ye refuse not him that speaketh," has an application here. Heb. 12:25. For if God spoke in the men of old, it is not Moses but God whom men reject when they discard the writings of the Old Testament. Of this, Christ says, "Had ye believed Moses, ye would have believed me: for he wrote of me. But if ye believe not his writings, how shall ye believe my words?" John 5:46, 47.

God spoke *in* the prophets, as the original reads, which suggests that God did not use these prophets as mere mechanical instruments, as one does in blowing a horn; but that while the Lord spoke, human lips framed the words and clothed them in human language.

God spake at "sundry times and in divers manners." There is no exact equivalent in English of the original expression, but the idea is clear that the revelations of old were fragmentary and of many different kinds. In visions and dreams; in disasters and war; in suffering and famine; by direct voice from heaven; by writing on a wall; by earthquake and fire; by the still, small voice; by priest and prophet; by king and peasant; by dumb beast and apostate prophet; by signs in the heavens and calamities on earth—through these and other means God spoke. Whatever way He chose to deliver His message, it was *God* who spoke. This places the writings of the Old Testament on a very high level.

Verse 2. God spake "by his Son," rather, "*in* his Son." The same God who formerly spake in the prophets has now spoken in His Son. This places Jesus in the prophetic line as one of the messengers and prophets of God.

The Son is said to have been "appointed heir." Some have taken this to mean that the time will come when the Father will resign His throne and relegate Himself to a secondary place, and the Son will take over the kingdom permanently. But this cannot be. There are certain powers which God has relinquished, and which are now exercised by the Son, but in the end the Son will subject Himself to the Father, that He—the Father—may be all in all. (1 Cor. 15:27, 28.)

See additional note on Hebrews 1:2 which appears on pages 28–30.

As the Son of God, Christ is Himself God, and as He is the Creator of all things, they are His by right of creation. When the Son, therefore, is said to have been appointed heir, the reference is to Him as the new Adam; and the inheritance referred to is the kingdom originally given to man, which Adam lost because of sin, and which Christ redeemed. "The earth hath he given to the children of men," of which Adam was the first representative. Ps. 115:16. When Adam sinned he lost his right to that which God had given him, and henceforth became a pilgrim and a stranger in the earth instead of its lord.

However, the moment Adam sinned, Christ stepped in. He took man's place, fulfilled the conditions of life laid down by God, redeemed Adam's disgraceful failure, and became the second Adam. Having fulfilled every requirement, He became and was appointed heir. As man unites with Christ he also becomes "an heir of God through Christ." Gal. 4:7. It was thus Abraham became "the heir of the world," and in like manner Christians become "heirs of God, and joint-heirs with Christ." Rom. 4:13; 8:17. The promise is, "Blessed are the meek: for they shall inherit the earth"; and at last the faithful shall hear the welcome words, "Come, ye blessed of my Father, inherit the kingdom prepared for you from the foundation of the world." Matt. 5:5; 25:34.

When the Son, therefore, is said to be appointed heir of all things, the meaning is simply that God has accepted Him as the second and new Adam, to take His place as head of the human race instead of the first Adam who fell, and that to Him shall come the dominion which Adam lost.

It was through Christ that God "made the worlds." The One who—took Adam's place and was appointed heir is the Creator of all things. In making the world God used the Son as His intermediary, not as one uses a tool, but as a fellow worker.

That Christ is Creator indicates a division of activity among the members of the Godhead. The Holy Spirit has His work to do; so has the Son, and so has the Father. In the plan of God He who was to be man's Redeemer was also his Creator.

Christ made not only this world but all worlds. "Without him was not any thing made that was made." John 1:3. "Worlds" has a larger signification than that of physical creation. It embraces also the spiritual and intellectual forces in the universe, such as are suggested by Paul's statement that "by him were all things created, that are in heaven, and that are in earth, visible and invisible, whether they be thrones, or dominions, or principalities, or powers: all things were created by him, and for him." Col. 1:6. Christ, the Creator of the physical worlds, is also the author of government, order, and law in heaven and on earth. "By him all things consist," or, as Meyer and Alford suggest, "In him the universe has its continuance and order." —Quoted in *Variorum Bible*, note on Col. 1:17.

Lightfoot says that "all the laws and purposes which guide the creation and government of the universe reside in him, the Eternal Word, as their meeting-point." —Quoted in M. R. VIincent, *Word Studies*, vol. 4, p. 381.

As we think of the magnitude of God's creation, of the millions and billions of worlds circling the throne of Deity, we get an enlarged conception of the greatness of God. Wonderful in wisdom, knowledge, and power must our God be. But if we apply to the universe what is said of this earth, and what evidently is a general principle—that "He created it not in vain, He formed it to be inhabited" (Isa. 45:18)—our conception takes on still greater proportions. If we conceive of many of these worlds as being inhabited, that in them are thrones and dominions and principalities and powers (Col. 1:16), that is, ordered government, and that these were created not only *by* Him but *for* Him, an expression that challenges our imagination, and then consider that this is this same God who so loved us that He came to this world to seek and to save that which was lost, we exclaim in amazement with the psalmist, "What is man, that thou art mindful of him? and the son of man, that thou visitest him?" Ps. 8:4.

The God who made the laws of the universe, who determined the laws of nature, also made the laws governing man's mental and physical nature. He is also the same God who gave the Ten Commandments as a guide of life.

It was according to a predetermined plan that the law which demands the life of the transgressor should have as its author the One who was later to suffer the penalty for man's transgression of it. Christ, who gave the law and required obedience to it, was willing to abide by the conditions that He had laid down for others, and upon man's failure, to take his place and suffer the penalty that He Himself had ordained. With these facts in mind we can never charge God with injustice. He does not require of anyone that which He is not willing to do Himself. This qualifies Him for being the final judge of mankind, the Arbiter of man's destiny.

Verse 3. The third verse presents Christ as "being the brightness of his glory." The participle "being" is an expression of eternal, timeless existence, and has the same sense as "was" in John 1:1, "In the beginning *was* the Word." The Word is Christ. (Verse 14.) He did not come into existence in the beginning. In the beginning He *was.* When He came to this world He *became* flesh. He had not previously been flesh. By way of contrast He did not *become* the brightness of the Father's glory. He always *was.* This constitutes the essential and eternal ground of His personality.

"Brightness" is variously translated outshining, outraying, reflection. It has the same relation to God's glory as the rays of the sun have to the sun. The rays cannot be separated from the sun, nor the sun from its rays. The two are inseparable.

So with the Father and the Son. The Son reveals the Father, is the outshining of the Father. Through and in Him we see God. As when we look at the sun we see not the sun but its light, so we see not the Father but the Son, God Himself being invisible, "dwelling in the light which no man can approach unto; whom no man hath seen, nor can see." 1 Tim. 6:16. The glory of God is the sum total of His attributes. (See Ex. 33:18; 34:6, 7.)

Man was created in the image of God, but Christ is "the *express* image" of the Father. As a seal impresses an exact image of itself upon the wax, so Christ is the exact counterpart of God. "Image" is a translation of the Greek *charakter,* from which we derive our "character." Originally *charakter* meant the tool used for engraving or marking. Later it came to mean the marking itself. The same development may be noted in some English words. Thus "seal" means an instrument used for making an impression upon the receiving medium, but it also means the impression itself. So "stamp" is both the instrument and the mark produced.

The Greek word *hupostasis,* translated "person," is the same word rendered "substance" in Hebrews 11:1; whereas in 2 Corinthians 11:17 and Hebrews 3:14 it is translated "confidence." Its root meaning is "that which stands under," as an underplacing, a substructure, a support, a foundation, that which can be built upon; and hence denotes firmness, steadfastness, assurance, confidence. It stands for reality as contrasted with imagination and fancy, and is used for the essence of things, the inmost nature of a person, the real self. Its meaning is well expressed by "standing" in Psalms 69:2: "I sink in deep mire, where there is no *standing.*" In Ezekiel 26:11 the same word is translated "ground."

When Christ, therefore, is said to be the express image of God's person, we attribute to Him more than mere outward likeness. He is the exact expression of the very inmost nature of God; that upon which men may confidently build; that in which they may with full assurance trust. As is the Father, so is the Son—one in essence, one in character, one in mind and purpose. "He that hath seen me hath seen the Father." John 14:9. "I and my Father are one." John 10:30.

Christ is said to be "upholding all things." The word for "upholding" denotes more than merely sustaining something so that it will not collapse. It means bearing forward to a destination. While it includes the idea of sustaining, it has the added meaning of movement, of guidance, of purposeful progress.

Christ is the one who upholds the universe and keeps the heavenly bodies in their appointed paths. Paul in another place says that "by him all things consist," or hold together. Col. 1:17. "Upholding" has a wider meaning than "consist," and embraces the concept of working to a purpose, of planning, of carrying to a predetermined conclusion. The picture is that of a workman bringing to completion a planned structure.

This definition changes the concept from that of a mere power upholding the physical universe to that of an intelligent Being who has a plan and is in the process of carrying it out. If in the "all things" that Christ is said to be upholding, we include things "visible and invisible, whether they be thrones, or dominions, or principalities, or powers," we must necessarily think of Christ as doing more than carrying a dead weight. Col. 1:16. His "upholding" includes the superintendence of a million worlds, with all their dominions and principalities and powers.

God's plan for the universe is not exhausted in creating a myriad of worlds and sending them spinning in space, nothing in particular being accomplished thereby. Paul hints of this when he

9

speaks of "the mystery which hath been kept in silence through times eternal." Rom. 16:25, R.V. In Ephesians 1:9, 10 he says that God has "made known unto us the mystery of his will, according to his good pleasure which he hath purposed in himself: that in the dispensation of the fulness of times he might gather together in one all things in Christ, both which are in heaven, and which are on earth; even in him." We may not be able to comprehend all that this includes; but it assures us that God has a plan, and that in due time it will be revealed.

Christ "by himself purged our sins." These words introduce Christ as High Priest. The word "our" is not found in the best manuscripts, and is to be omitted. The reading therefore is that Christ "by himself purged sins," or better, "made purification of sins." It is true that Christ purged "our" sins, but the. author here takes a more inclusive view, though later he will fully discuss, "our" sins. It may be remarked while the phrase "by himself" is thought by some to be a questionable reading, the Greek form for "purification of sins" is such that this thought must be included. What Christ did, He did by Himself. He had no helper but God. He trod the winepress alone. (Isa. 63:3.)

The phrase "purification of sins" in the Greek is in the middle voice, in which the action terminates on the subject. Therefore, when Christ is said to have made "purification of sins," its first meaning is that this refers to and reacts upon Himself. In His own life He overcame temptation. Though the sins of the world were laid upon Him, His own soul was not sullied by them. He repelled every suggestion to evil. Satan never got a foothold anywhere. A thousand attacks were made upon Him, but not one succeeded. This is the first meaning of "purification of sins."

Although, as noted, "by himself" is not included in the oldest manuscripts, the same idea is contained in the Greek middle voice, and may well be translated "by himself," or "for himself."

Of the phrase under consideration Westcott says that the genitive *purification of sins* "may express either (1) the cleansing *of* sins, i.e. the removal of the sins. Compare Matt. 8:3; Job 7:21 (Ex. 30:10), or (2) the cleansing (of the person) *from* sins. Comp. c. 9:14." —B. F. Westcott, *The Epistle to the Hebrews*, p. 15.

By His atonement Christ accomplished both the cleansing *of* sins and the cleansing of the person *from* sin. The purging of sins was finished on the cross; the purification of sinners is still in progress and will not be finished till the last soul is saved.

On the cross Christ finished His work as victim and sacrifice. He shed His blood, and thus provided a "fountain opened...for sin and for uncleanness." Zech. 19: 1. But His work as intercessor was not finished on the cross; nor is it yet finished. He is still our advocate with the Father, one who is "able also to save them to the uttermost that come unto God by him, seeing he ever liveth to make intercession for them." Heb. 7:25. Those who teach that Christ is not now our advocate, that He finished His work on the cross, have a very limited and imperfect view of the atonement.

Some aspects of the atonement may need further consideration. If Christ made purification of sins, and sin still exists, what is meant by "purification of sins"? This question becomes still more important when we learn that not only was Christ to make purification of sins *possible* but He was to *make an end of sins*, and that this was to be accomplished within the prophetic period of seventy weeks. Said the angel to Daniel, "Seventy weeks are determined upon thy people and upon thy holy city, to finish the transgression, and to *make an end of sins*, and to make reconciliation for iniquity, and to bring in everlasting righteousness, and to seal up the vision and prophecy, and to anoint the most holy." Dan. 9:24.

To make an end of sins means more than merely to forgive sins. It means the complete eradication of sin out of the life. It means sanctification, the uprooting of every evil, a life completely controlled by the Holy Spirit. This was Christ's work, and this He was to do within the allotted time mentioned by the angel.

Christ on earth gave a demonstration of what God can do when humanity is fully yielded to Him. In the body prepared for Him, He was tempted as men arc tempted. "He was oppressed, and he was afflicted;" hath borne our griefs, and carried our sorrows;" was "wounded for our transgressions" and "bruised for our iniquities." He was "despised and rejected of men," "poured out his soul unto death: and he was numbered with the transgressors"; "he bare the sin of many" and made "his soul an offering for sin." Because of this He was to "justify many: for he shall bear their iniquities." Isaiah 53.

This presents Christ as sin bearer. God "made him to be sin for us, who knew no sin." 2 Cor. 5:21. "His own self bare our sins in his own body on the tree." 1 Peter 2:24. He was "in all points tempted like as we are, yet without sin." Heb. 4:15. In the body prepared for Him, He gained the victory over every temptation, repelled every advance of Satan, triumphed over every obstacle, until Satan at last had no more arrows in his quiver to point at Him, "The prince of this world cometh," said Christ, "and hath nothing in me." John 14:30.

Christ voluntarily took our sins upon Him. Every temptation we have to meet, He met, until Satan's darts were exhausted. With no other help from God than we may have, He demonstrated that it is possible to resist sin and have constant victory over every temptation. His body temple, which Satan had attempted to defile, was stainless.

This part of His work He finished before the cross. He annulled sin in His own body, made it powerless and ineffective. Satan tried every evil device, and failed. Publicly Christ challenged Satan's emissaries, "Which of you convinceth me of sin?" and there was no answer. John 8:46. When He came to the end of His public ministry and faced Gethsemane and Golgotha, He confidently affirmed, "I have glorified thee on earth; I have finished the work which thou gavest me to do." John 17:4. Within the time allotted, and as far as He was concerned, He had made "an end of sin." This work He finished *before* the cross in the body given Him. This was the first phase of His atoning work.

The second phase of His work began in Gethsemane, and was completed when on the cross He exclaimed, "It is finished." John 19:30. In this second phase Christ bore the sins of men for the purpose of suffering for them and paying the penalty due to sin.

When Christ faced Gethsemane He sustained a different relation to the Father from that which He had sustained before. Hitherto He had relied on the Father's protection and care, and though severely tried, He was always conscious of the Father's love and care. But now He was to take the place of the transgressor, and suffer in his stead. He was to be treated as the sinner deserves to be treated, and at last be forsaken of God, till in anguish of soul He cried out, "My God, my God, why hast thou forsaken me?" Mark 15:34.

Would Christ be able to stand this ordeal? In past trials God had always come to His rescue. But now every hope and comfort must be removed. The knowledge that His sufferings would not be in vain had hitherto been a source of strength to Him. What if this incentive was taken away; what if *every* incentive was removed?

Satan had once challenged God, accusing Job of serving Him for ulterior motives. "Doth Job serve God for nought?" he had sneeringly asked. Job 1:9. To show the falsity of Satan's accusation, he was permitted to test Job. He applied every possible torture, but Job did not sin. At last Satan retired defeated. Job had stood the test and proved Satan's accusation false. "Though he slay me, yet will I trust him," he exclaimed. Job. 13:15.

Through a similar test Christ must pass. Every incentive must be taken away from Him. He must be tested as Job was tested, only more severely. And He was so tested. Gethsemane and Golgotha bear witness to both the severity and the outcome of the test. To all appearances Christ went into the grave forsaken of God and man. He trod the winepress alone. Hear these words:

"The Saviour could not see through the portals of the tomb. Hope did not present to Him His coming forth from the grave a conqueror, or tell Him of the Father's acceptance of the sacrifice. He feared that sin was so offensive to God that their separation was to be eternal. Christ felt the anguish which the sinner will feel when mercy shall no longer plead for the guilty race. It was the sense of sin, bringing the Father's wrath upon Him as man's substitute, that made the cup He drank so bitter, and broke the heart of the Son of God." —*The Desire of Ages*, p. 753.

However, it is not to be supposed that Christ died with a sense of defeat. He died a victor.

"Amid the awful darkness, apparently forsaken of God, Christ had drained the last dregs in the cup of human woe. In those dreadful hours He had relied upon the evidence of His Father's acceptance heretofore given Him. He was acquainted with the character of His Father; He understood. His justice, His mercy, and His great love. By faith He rested in Him whom it had ever been His joy to obey. And as in submission He committed Himself to God, the sense of the loss of His Father's favor was withdrawn. By faith, Christ was victor." —*Ibid.*, p. 756.

When Christ at last cried out, "It is finished," He had completed the second phase of His work. But there was still a third phase before Him, which included His session at the right hand of God and the demonstration which He must make in His saints on earth—a work closely connected with that which He was to do in the sanctuary above, and vital to our salvation.

Christ had demonstrated in His own body that it was possible to be completely victorious over sin; but the question would naturally arise as to whether His victory was merely a singular demonstration made possible by His unique relation to the Father or whether others could do what He had done? Could men overcome as He had overcome?

To complete Christ's work and make it efficacious for man, such a demonstration must be made. It must be shown that man can overcome as Christ overcame. The demonstration has long been in contemplation—even from eternity—but its execution has been delayed. The time has now fully come for the appearing of the sons of God. In the 144,000 the final demonstration will be made. They have followed, and they do follow, the Lamb whithersoever He goeth. (Rev. 14:4.) They stand without a mediator, face death, and remain true. "When He leaves the sanctuary, darkness covers the inhabitants of the earth. In that fearful time the righteous must live in the sight of a holy God without an intercessor." —*The Great Controversy*, p. 614. With Job they will say, "Though he slay me, yet will I trust him." They fully answer Satan's accusation of having ulterior motives for doing God's will. Satan's sneering challenge will be met by the saints of the last generation. When the answer is given, Christ has at last completed His work and stands glorified in His saints. Then the prophecy will be fulfilled: "Here is the patience of the saints: here are they that keep the commandments of God, and the faith of Jesus." Rev. 14:12.

There are thus three phases in Christ's work of atonement. In the first phase He met sin face to face and conquered it. In not one instance did He fail; not one stain of sin sullied His pure soul. His body-temple was holy, a fit place for God to dwell. This stage terminated before Gethsemane.

The second phase included Gethsemane and Golgotha. There the sins which He had met and conquered were placed upon Him, that He might bear them up to the cross and annul them, this being the meaning of "put away," in Hebrews 9:26. In the first phase He bore sins for the purpose of conquering them and eliminating them from the life. In the second phase He bore sins for the purpose of suffering and dying for them, that in His "death he might destroy him that had the power of death, that is, the devil." Heb. 2:14.

In the third phase Christ demonstrates that man can do what He did, with the same help He had. This phase includes His session at the right hand of God, His high priestly ministry, and the final exhibition of His saints in their last struggle with Satan, and their glorious victory. Then the death sentence, which was first pronounced upon the serpent in the garden, long delayed, will be carried out. This was made certain when Jesus repelled every advance of Satan on earth; it was made doubly certain when He died on the cross, and thus destroyed death and him that had the power of death; and it will at last be executed when Satan demonstrates that he has not changed, that he will kill the saints as he killed Christ, and that he does not hesitate to attack even the very city of God and God Himself. Then, finally, sin and sinners will be no more, and the complete end of sin will have come.

It is the first and second of these phases to which Hebrews 1:3 refers. These are included in the purging of sins. The third phase is now in progress in the sanctuary above and in the church below. Christ broke the power of sin in His lifework on earth. He destroyed sin and Satan by His death. He is now eliminating and destroying sin in His saints on earth. This is part of the cleansing of the true sanctuary.

When Christ had finished His work on earth, He "sat down on the right hand of the Majesty on high." "Sat down" does not here denote the mere act of sitting, but is a formal seating, as in an inauguration or installation into office. It is a word of delegated power; of investiture with authority; a formal

17

acknowledgment of the right to exercise office; a coronation. It marks the beginning of activity, not the end. The idea that Christ, having done His work on earth, sits down to rest, awaiting results, is wide of the truth. The Father installs and addresses Him as High Priest, gives Him the highest place by His right hand, and authorizes Him to function as mediator after the order of Melchisedec. In this is included the last phase of the atonement, which comprises Christ's work in the sanctuary above and His work in the church below. It is this phase of which Hebrews speaks when it says that Christ "is able also to save them to the uttermost that come unto God by him, seeing he ever liveth to make intercession for them." Heb. 7:25.

The induction, or coronation, of Christ took place consequent upon His ascension. He had fulfilled the conditions laid upon Him; He had lived a perfect life, and had overcome Satan; He had suffered and at last had died on Calvary; the blood had been shed, by and through which He was to enter the holy places in heaven; and now He was ready to begin His work as priest. By the coronation God recognized His right to the priesthood, seated Him at His own right hand, and the God-man takes His place beside the Father on the throne of the universe.

"The right hand of the Majesty on high" is the seat of honor, or authority. This seat was given Christ after He had made purgation of sin. He had finished the work given Him on earth to do. He had succeeded where Adam had failed, and had won for Himself the approval of God and the right to speak and act for mankind.

"If he were on earth, he should not be a priest, seeing that there are priests that offer gifts according to the law," and of course Christ had nothing to offer till after His death. Heb. 8:4. But if Christ were to be priest, "it is of necessity that this man have somewhat also to offer." Verse 3. This "somewhat" was not "the blood of goats and calves, but ... his own blood." Heb. 9:12. As soon as this blood was shed on Calvary, He had "somewhat" to offer. Now He could begin His priestly ministry, and God immediately upon His ascension to heaven installs Him at His own right hand. He is now a priest forever after the order of Melchisedec, and is ready to intercede for man in the holy places in heaven.

🙟 **Hebrews 1:4–14.** "Being made so much better than the angels, as he hath by inheritance obtained a more excellent name than they. For unto which of the angels said he at any time, Thou art my Son, this day have I begotten thee? And again, I will be to him a Father, and he shall be to me a Son?

"And again, when he bringeth in the firstbegotten into the world, he saith, And let all the angels of God worship him. And of the angels he saith, Who maketh his angels spirits, and his ministers a flame of fire.

"But unto the Son he saith, Thy throne, O God, is for ever and ever: a sceptre of righteousness is the sceptre of thy kingdom. Thou hast loved righteousness, and hated iniquity; therefore God, even thy God, hath anointed thee with the oil of gladness above thy fellows. And, Thou, Lord, in the beginning hast laid the foundation of the earth; and the heavens are the works of thine hands: they shall perish; but thou remainest; and they all shall wax old as doth a garment; and as a vesture shalt thou fold them up, and they shall be changed: but thou art the same, and thy years shall not fail.

"But to which of the angels said he at any time, Sit on my right hand, until I make thine enemies thy footstool? Are they not all ministering spirits, sent forth to minister for them who shall be heirs of salvation?"

The deity of Christ was the great stumbling block in the way of the Jews for accepting Christianity. Israel had long prided itself on its monotheism. Other religions had many gods; Israel had only One. "Hear, O Israel: The Lord our God is one Lord" (Deut. 6:4), had been the challenge to their heathen neighbors for more than a thousand years.

And now deity was claimed for Christ! How could this belief be harmonized with their Sacred Scriptures, which recognized only one God?

Under these conditions it became necessary to present proofs from the Scriptures of the Old Testament that Jesus was indeed divine. This Paul does in the section before us.

Verse 4. "Being made," better, "having become." This is in contrast to "being" in verse 3, which there means a permanent, unchangeable, eternal state. Here "having become" means a condition resulting from the incarnation, a change from one state to another.

"So much better than the angels." The remainder of the chapter is devoted to a discussion of the contrast between Christ and the angels. The author sets out to show that Christ is God essentially and in the highest sense. This He must be if He is to be our Saviour and if He is to purge us from our sins. Great as are the angels, and highly as the Jews esteemed them, no angel can ever be a Saviour. Only God can forgive sins; only God can save. The author therefore proceeds to show that Christ is "much better" than the angels.

"A more excellent name." Christ has by inheritance obtained a more excellent name. Although we are not here told what that name is, and though many names are given to Christ in the Bible, we are inclined to believe that "Jesus" is the name meant. This was the name given Him at birth; and as it was given Him in recognition of the fact that He should "save his people from their sins"; and as the angel who announced the name was only executing God's command, God in reality was the one who named Him. (Matt. 1:21.) It therefore seems likely that "Jesus" is the name here alluded to.

In His preincarnate state Christ was equal with God. He was with God and was God. (John 1:1.) But He did not hold His being on an equality with God a thing to be grasped "but emptied himself, taking the form of a servant, being made in the likeness of men; and being found in fashion as a man, he humbled himself, becoming obedient even unto death, yea, the death of the cross. Wherefore also God highly exalted him, and gave unto him the name which is above every name; that in the name of Jesus every knee should bow, of things in heaven and things on earth and things under the earth, and that every tongue should confess that Jesus Christ is Lord, to the glory of God the Father." Phil. 2:7–11, R.V.

In becoming man, Christ naturally became lower than the angels, though only for "a little while." Heb. 2:7, margin. After His humiliation and death, and because of it, God highly exalted Him and gave unto "him a name which is above every name: that at the name of Jesus every knee should bow." This name is the "more excellent name." "Angel" means "messenger," "servant"; "Jesus" means "Saviour"—in every way a more excellent name.

21

Verse 5. "Thou art my Son." Angels are never called sons of God individually, though they appear to be so called collectively. (Job. 2:1.) Nor are they begotten of God, but created. But not so Christ. He is God in His own right, not a created being.

Paul speaks of God's "Son Jesus Christ our Lord, which was made of the seed of David according to the flesh; and declared to be the Son of God with power, according to the spirit of holiness, by the resurrection from the dead." Rom. 1:3, 4. In his speech at Antioch, Paul said:

"We declare unto you glad tidings, how that the promise which was made unto the fathers, God hath fulfilled the same unto us their children, in that he, hath raised up Jesus again; as it is also written in the second psalm, Thou art my Son, this day have I begotten thee." Acts 13:32, 33.

These scriptures declare that the Son "*was made* of the seed of David *according to the flesh*—that is, He became truly man (Rom. 1:3)—and that He was "declared to be the *Son of God* with power." (Rom. 1:4.) The reading is not that Christ *became* the Son of God, or was *made* the Son of God, but He was declared *to be* the Son of God. He that was Son *became* flesh. (John 1:14.) Jesus did not become God, for He was already God. He was simply declared *to be* the Son of God.

When was the declaration made to man that Jesus is the Son of God? It was first made by the angel at the time of the birth of Jesus. "There is born to you this day in the city of David a Saviour, who *is* Christ the Lord." Luke 2:11, A.R.V. It was next announced by God Himself at the baptism: "Thou *art* my beloved Son; in thee I am well pleased." Luke 3:21, A.R.V. And after the resurrection He was "declared *to be* the Son of God with power...by the resurrection from the dead." Rom. 1:4.

"This day have I begotten thee." According to Acts 13:32, 33, previously quoted, this was by the resurrection from the dead. Christ is the eternal Son of God, but He sustained an added relationship to the Father when He was raised from the dead. As man He was a member of the human family. When He was raised from the dead and His work was accepted of God, He was the first man who in his own right could claim to have fulfilled the condition of life laid down by God, which in effect is, "Obey and live."

God had promised man life on condition of obedience. (Ex. 19:5; Luke 10:25–28.) Christ met the conditions laid down, and thus earned the *right* of life; and God, by raising Him from the dead, recognized and admitted this right. Whereas some believe that "begotten" refers to the eternal generation of Christ, it seems better to apply it to Christ's first coming to this world, especially in view of the "for" in verse 5, which points back to the fact that Christ by inheritance obtained a better name. As "inheritance" points to a definite event in time, it is better to consider "begotten" as belonging to the earthly experience of Christ.

Verse 6. "Let all the angels of God worship him." These words are not found in our present Hebrew Bible, but are recorded in the Greek Septuagint of Deuteronomy 32:43.

This command to the angels is confirmatory of the deity of Christ. As one of the Godhead, Christ was worshiped before He came to this earth. When He became man, the question would naturally arise among the angels as to their right to worship Him; for if He was man, and only man, He had no right to receive worship. The question therefore was this, Had

Christ in becoming man lost His Godhood? The Father Himself settled the question when He commanded the angels to worship Christ. Only God may be worshiped. (Rev. 22:8, 9.) Therefore, Christ is God.

God's command to the angels as regards the deity of Christ is final. He was God before the incarnation; He was God during the incarnation; and He is God after the incarnation. We can but believe that this command to worship Christ is recorded for the specific purpose of meeting the objection of some that Christ after becoming man is less than God. To worship any creature, however exalted, is idolatry; it is to substitute a created being for the Creator. When John fell down to worship an angel he was admonished, "See thou do it not: for I am thy fellow servant, and of thy brethren the prophets, and of them which keep the sayings of this book: *worship God.*" Rev. 22:9. When the Father commands the angels to worship Christ, He thereby emphasizes the deity of Christ. In this proclamation He says in effect: "My Son has assumed humanity. He has suffered, died, and been raised again. Let no one think that His Godhood has suffered any impairment. As He was God before, so He is God now. Let all the angels of God worship Him."

Therefore, let Christ's essential and unquestioned deity be doubted no longer. Christ is very God, and the Father not only has given permission to worship Him, but has commanded that He be worshiped.

Verse 7. "Who maketh his angels spirits." The angels are God's ministers. They are His servants, doing His will. As the wind and the waves obey His will, as the fire accomplishes His design, so God uses His angels as they are needed. Some see in this verse a reference to the cherubim and seraphim. "Spirits" is the same word elsewhere used for winds, and of the cherubim it is written: "And he rode upon a cherub, and did fly: yea, he did fly upon the wings of the wind." Ps. 18:10. "Seraphim" means burning, fire, shining ones. Hence the Revised Version translates, "Who maketh his angels winds, and his ministers a flame of fire." Paul's intent in quoting these statements is to show that angels are servants and that God uses them as His ministers. By contrast, the Son is shown to be God.

Verse 8. "Thy throne, O God." In these words the Father addresses the Son reverently, and calls Him God. This is the climax in the apostle's argument on the position and dignity of Christ. There can be no higher testimony to the deity of Christ than this apostrophe of the Father to the Son. In the most solemn manner Christ's Godhood is affirmed, and this by God Himself.

The reference to the throne and the scepter is significant. It indicates actual, not merely potential, possession of power. It indicates that the kingdom is not only future but present, and is in active operation. The throne and the kingdom are everlasting; and the scepter—the government—is in righteousness.

Verse 9. "Thou hast loved...and hated." This has special reference to Christ's earthly life, for this is the ground upon which the latter part of the verse is based. Because Christ loved righteousness and hated iniquity, God anointed Him.

We rightly stress love as an essential Christian virtue, but in our present state we need to develop hate as much as love. No man is safe who has not learned to hate sin.

A man may resist and even abstain from sin without hating it. It simply does not appeal to him, and is no temptation. Other phases of sin may appeal to him; but knowing it is sin, he refuses to countenance it. Such a man is to be commended for his resistance, but he cannot be said to be safe. Not until he has learned to hate sin, not only be indifferent to it, is he really safe. The man who hankers after sin, who finds it alluring or interesting, has not yet attained to Christ's standard. He must learn to hate sin as well as to love righteousness.

This Christ did. And because He both loved and hated, God anointed Him with the oil of gladness above His fellows. This anointing doubtless took place at the coronation of Christ, following His ascension, and constituted God's approval of Christ and His work, as well as an ordination for future service. It is to be noted that the name "Christ" means "the anointed One."

The "fellows" here mentioned are probably those who, like Christ, are anointed, whether prophet, priest, king, or cherub. These were all thus dedicated to their specific work. Even Lucifer was anointed. "Thou art the anointed cherub that covereth," God says of Him. Eze. 28:14. But of all these, Christ has the pre-eminence.

Verse 10. "Thou, Lord." In verse 8 the Father addressed the Son as God. Here He addresses Him as Lord. Jesus is both Lord and God. Peter says that "God hath made that same Jesus, whom ye have crucified, both Lord and Christ." Acts 2:36. This is another tribute of God to Christ's deity.

Verse 11. "Thou remainest." This statement also is in proof of the deity of Christ. As Creator, Christ existed before creation; and after creation perishes, He still remains. This argues the eternity of Christ.

Verse 12. "Thou art the same." As verse 11 asserted Christ's eternity, so this asserts His immutability, another attribute of deity.

Verses 13, 14. The angels stand about the throne in an attitude of reverence and worship, and have never been invited to sit at God's right hand. They are servants, ministering spirits, sent forth to minister to them who shall be heirs of salvation. "The heir, as long as he is a child, differeth nothing from a servant, though he be lord of all; but is under tutors and governors until the time appointed of the father." Gal. 4:1, 2. Man is now inferior to angels. But the time will come when he will grow up and claim his heritage.

In this first chapter the apostle. sets out to prove the deity of Christ, and successfully accomplishes his task. His purpose in writing the book requires him to establish beyond a doubt that Christ is God. He intends to show that the ceremonies that had been instituted by Moses at the command of God had been fulfilled and abolished by Christ. These ceremonies the Jews considered the very heart of their religion, and they were indissolubly connected with the temple. For any man to touch any of these ordinances, was to touch the apple of their eye. The Jews would strenuously contend that only the same God who had commanded. them to build the temple, and who had instituted the services, could of right make any change.

This point Paul would concede. His first work, therefore, is to prove beyond a doubt the deity of Christ. This he does, first by presenting Him as Creator and Redeemer, then by showing His surpassing superiority over the angels, and lastly by presenting the Father Himself as the chief witness to Christ's Godhood. As these proofs are all substantiated by quotations from the Old Testament Scriptures, which the Jews acknowledged as authority, the apostle has proved his point. Christ is God. The Scriptures say so, and God confirms it.

But Paul had more in mind than merely to establish a theological dogma. He quietly introduces God's command to the angels to worship Christ. The discerning Jew would readily conclude that if angels were commanded to worship Christ, man could do no less; and the Jew is therefore immediately confronted with the challenge of what he is to do with Christ. It is to this point Paul leads his readers. He brings them face to face with their duty as defined by God.

ADDITIONAL NOTES

Christ Appointed Heir

Hebrews 1:2

There are several statements in the New Testament that indicate that the Father for a time relinquishes certain powers to the Son, but that the Son will return these powers to the Father "when he shall have put down all rule and all authority and power." 1 Cor. 15:24. This, however, has nothing to do with the appointment of the Son as heir. This appointment was simply the Father's acknowledgment of the successful completion of Christ's work as the second Adam. The first Adam had failed. The second Adam takes his place as man, and is acknowledged by God as the rightful heir to the dominion first given to Adam. The second Adam displaces the first and is officially appointed heir.

This, however, is entirely distinct from the agreement between the Father and the Son as members of the

Godhead, whereby the Father for a time relinquished and the Son assumed certain powers for the quelling of the rebellion that had arisen because of Lucifer's apostasy.

For reasons not fully known to man, Christ was given the work of dealing with Lucifer and his angels. "There was war in heaven: Michael and his angels fought against the dragon; and the dragon fought and his angels." Rev. 12:7. As might be expected, Lucifer and his angels "prevailed not; neither was their place found any more in heaven. And the great dragon was cast out, that old serpent, called the Devil and Satan." Rev. 12:8, 9.

This controversy begun in heaven was continued when Christ became incarnate, and in the wilderness the two antagonists met face to face. In heaven Christ overcame Lucifer; and on earth, weak and emaciated though Christ was, the enemy retired defeated. The closing events of this controversy, when all Satan's rule and authority and power will be finally crushed and forever ended, are what Paul refers to in 1 Corinthians 15:23–28. These. verses read as follows:

"But every man in his own order: Christ the firstfruits; afterward they that are Christ's at his coming. Then cometh the end, when he shall have delivered up the kingdom to God, even the Father; when he shall have put down all rule, and all authority and power. For he must reign, till he hath put all enemies under his feet. The last enemy that shall be destroyed is death. For he hath put all things under his feet. But when he saith all things are put under him, it is manifest that he is excepted, which did put all things under him. And when all things shall be subdued unto him, then shall the Son also himself be subject unto him that put all things under him, that God may be all in all."

The problem in these verses is the use of the pronouns he, his, him. These are generally interpreted thus:

Verse 24: "Then cometh the end, when he [Christ] shall have delivered up the kingdom to God, even the Father;

when he [Christ] shall have put down all rule and all authority and power."

Verse 25: "For he [Christ] must reign, till he [Christ] hath put all enemies under his [God's] feet."

Verse 27: "For he [God] hath put all things under his [Christ's] feet. But when he [God] saith all things are put under him [Christ], it is manifest that he [God] is excepted, which did put all things under him [Christ]."

Verse 28: "And when all things shall be subdued unto him [God], then shall the Son also himself be subject unto him [God] that put all things under him [Christ], that God may be all in all."

According to verse 24, when the end comes Christ "shall have delivered up the kingdom to God, even the Father." This wording is clear and precise; the Son delivers up the kingdom to the Father. The wording in verse 27 is also clear: "He hath put all things under his feet." This can mean only that the Father has put all things under Christ's feet, in accordance with Christ's statements: "All power is given unto me in heaven and in earth." "Jesus knowing that the Father had given all things into his hands." "All things that the Father hath are mine." "The Father loveth the Son, and hath given all things into his hand." Matt. 28:18; John 13:3; 16:15; 3:35.

We are not now concerned with the exact time when the Father gave all things into the hands of the Son, nor the reason for it. Suffice it to say that in view of the incarnation and the suffering and death of Christ there was a certain work which the Son was to perform and which He had a right to do as mediator and judge. This included the putting "down of all rule and all authority and power" opposed to God. 1 Cor. 15:24.

When this is done, Christ will "also himself be subject unto him that put all things under him, that God may be all in all." Verse 28.

Angels

Hebrews 1: 13, 14

Angels were held in high esteem among the Jews, so much so that Paul at one time warned against angel worship. (Col. 2:18.) This tendency to reverence angels doubtless made Paul's argument in Hebrews very effective. If the Jews, or some of them, thought angels worthy of worship, God's command to the angels to worship Christ must have made a deep impression upon the Jews. If Christ were so much higher than the angels that they were required to worship Him, then He must indeed be none less than God Himself.

That angels—though they are but ministers, servants—are accorded a high place and entrusted with great responsibilities, is clearly taught in the Old Testament, as well as in the New.

Angels were present at creation as well as at the giving of the law. (Job 38:7; Acts 7:53.) *Cherubim guarded the way to the tree of life, and angels in the form of men visited and gave instruction to Abraham. (Gen. 3:24; 18:2, 16.) Angels were sent with messages to all the patriarchs and prophets. (Gen. 32:1; Num. 20:16; 1 Kings 19:5; Isa. 63:9; Dan. 9: 21, 22; Zech. 1:9; Acts 27:23, etc.) Angels accompany Christ when He comes (Matt. 25:31); angels gather together the tares at the end of the world, and also the elect (Matt. 13:41; Mark 13:27); an angel shall at last bind Satan and cast him into the bottomless pit (Rev. 20:1); the angels have immediate access to God (Matt. 18:10), and continually carry messages to and from heaven (John 1:51). They have charge of the elements (Rev. 14:18; 16:5) as Lucifer once had charge of the air (Eph. 2:2); and they will finally pour out the seven plagues (Rev. 16: 1). The Bible is filled with examples of the work and power of the angels, so much so that we can readily understand why Israel held them in such high honor.

An instance is recorded in the fourth chapter of Daniel which not only illustrates the great responsibilities with which God entrusts angels but also reveals God's method of government.

The story itself is so well known that we need to relate only the high points. In a dream Nebuchadnezzar saw a great tree that seemed to reach to heaven and cover the earth. The tree was fair and its fruit much, and all flesh was fed of it. Then an angel came down from heaven and commanded that the tree be hewn down but the stump be left in the earth. Further the angel said, "Let his heart be changed from man's, and let a beast's heart be given unto him, and let seven times pass over him." Dan. 4:16.

This dream caused the king great uneasiness, and when the wise men could not interpret it, Daniel at last came in; and to him the king related the dream, and said, "All the wise men of my kingdom are not able to make known unto me the interpretation: but thou art able; for the spirit of the holy gods is in thee." Verse 18.

Daniel immediately perceived the seriousness of the dream, and that it foretold trouble, but the king encouraged him to speak freely.

Daniel then gave the interpretation: The tree—"it is thou, O king, that art grown and become strong." Verse 22. That the tree is hewn down but a stump left in the earth, means that the king would lose his reason and be with the beasts of the field seven years, "till thou know that the most High ruleth in the kingdom of men, and giveth it to whomsoever he will." Verse 25.

Though this should come upon the king, there was mercy mixed with judgment. "Thy kingdom shall be sure unto thee, after thou shalt have known that the heavens do rule." Verse 26. That meant that if the king learned his lesson his kingdom should be restored to him. Daniel then made a personal plea to him: "O king, let my counsel be acceptable unto thee, and break off thy sins by righteousness, and thine iniquities by shewing mercy to the poor; if it may be a lengthening of thy tranquillity." Verse 27.

But the king took no heed. Though God gave him a year to think matters over, at last the judgment came, and

Nebuchadnezzar "was driven from men, and did eat grass as oxen, and his body was wet with the dew of heaven, till his hairs were grown like eagles' feathers, and his nails like birds' claws." Verse 33.

However, in his humiliating condition he turned to God and was accepted. He recounts his restoration thus:

"At the same time my reason returned unto me; and for the glory of my kingdom, mine honour and brightness returned unto me; and my counsellors and my lords sought unto me; and I was established in my kingdom, and excellent majesty was added unto me. Now I Nebuchadnezzar praise and extol and honour the King of heaven, all whose works are truth, and his ways judgment: and those that walk in pride he is able to abase." Verses 36, 37.

To be deprived of one's reason may be considered one of the worst things that can befall a man. Nebuchadnezzar was so deprived, as he himself records, "My reason returned unto me." Verse 36. Severe as the punishment was, it brought the desired result, for Nebuchadnezzar was truly converted.

How and by whom was this punishment apportioned? It was a holy one, an angel, that came down from heaven and announced the judgment. (Verse 23.) But more: "This matter is by the decree of the watchers, and the demand by the word of the holy ones." Verse 17. The angels were the ones who determined what should be done, and they also carried out the decree.

Each person has an accompanying angel (Matt. 18:10), who has the individual in charge and who within certain limitation decides what shall be done in specific cases. We conceive the relation to be somewhat the same as with a servant or nurse here who has charge of the little ones and decides all minor matters along agreed lines. This is doubt-less what Paul has in mind when he says "that the heir, as long as he is a child, differeth nothing from a servant though he be lord of all; but is under tutors and governors until the time appointed of the father." Gal. 4:1, 2.

So we are under the angels who have charge of us. They are "ministering spirits, sent forth to minister for them who shall be heirs of salvation." Heb. 1:14.

We can imagine Nebuchadnezzar's angel being greatly concerned over his charge. The king had possibilities for good, but he was becoming unmanageable, proud, and conceited. Several things had been tried. He had been brought in contact with Daniel and the three Hebrews. He had seen the power of God in saving the three young men in the fiery furnace. He had even been permitted to see with the three men in the furnace "the form of the fourth...like the Son of God." Dan. 3:25. But the effect of all this had passed away, and he was now taking honor to himself that belonged only to God. What could his angel do? What could any do?

Apparently Nebuchadnezzar's angel felt the need of counsel, for others were called in and the matter discussed. They agreed that something extraordinary must be done if Nebuchadnezzar was to be saved, and at last they determined upon the severe sentence that both his kingdom and his reason were to be taken from him. It appears that in this case they considered the matter to be so important that they carried their decision to God Himself and received His approval. Hence the sentence was signed "by the decree of the watchers, and the demand by the word of the holy ones"—that is, a group of angels in consultation had come to their conclusion—but later we are told that it was also "the decree of the most High." Verses 17, 24. The Lord concurred in the decree, and approved of what had been done.

This gives an interesting side light on the work of the angels, and also gives a view of the working of the government of God. Angels are not merely God's messengers. They are that, but more. They have responsibilities; they have decisions to make, and decrees to carry out. They are a vital part of the government of God.

CHAPTER 2

OF THE BOOK OF HEBREWS

The Humanity of Jesus

SYNOPSIS OF CHAPTER

THIS CHAPTER opens with a warning against indifference. It is the first of many admonitions scattered throughout the book, which evince the author's anxiety for the spiritual welfare of his readers. From the nature of the exhortations we learn that, unlike the Corinthians, the dangers threatening them were not moral delinquencies but a gradual drifting away from the things they had heard, coupled with a lack of desire to apply themselves to a serious study of the Word.

The larger part of the chapter is devoted to a discussion of the humanity of Christ. In the first chapter the author brought indisputable proof of the deity of Christ. In the second chapter he shows that it is needful for Christ to become man if He is to be a merciful and faithful high priest. How else could He deal gently with the weak and erring? He must be tempted in all points like as we are; for it is only by passing through the experiences to which men are subject that He can succor those who are weak.

Hebrews 2:1–4. "Therefore we ought to give the more earnest heed to the things which we have heard, lest at any time we should let them slip. For if the word spoken by angels was stedfast, and every transgression and disobedience received a just recompence of reward; how shall we escape, if we neglect so great salvation; which at the first began to be spoken by the Lord, and was confirmed unto us by them that heard him; God also bearing them witness, both with signs and wonders, and with divers miracles, and gifts of the Holy Ghost, according to His own will?"

This section contains a warning against the subtle sins of apathy and carelessness. Paul was greatly concerned about the spiritual condition of the people. There were troublous times ahead for the church. Persecution would soon break out anew; in a very few years the Roman armies would take the city, the temple would be destroyed, and the Christians would be compelled to flee for their lives. Despite this, the church was not fully awake. They were adrift with no sure anchor. Their condition was critical, and most serious of all, they did not sense their danger.

Verse 1. "Therefore" refers to the fact that God had sent His Son and through Him had spoken to them. This was an additional reason why they should give more earnest heed to the call of God.

"More earnest heed." Christ never preached for the sole purpose of imparting information. Wonderful as were the truths He revealed, His preaching had a deeper purpose than that of enriching the mind. He wanted to move men to action; He wanted them to give heed to what He said; He wanted them to be doers and not forgetful hearers of the Word.

This also is the intent of the apostle. He warns the church to give more earnest heed to what they have heard. He intimates that they are not entirely heedless; but he desires them to give *more* earnest heed to the things which belonged to their peace.

They already had the knowledge needed. They knew what to do. But they were not living up to the light they had. They must be stirred into action.

"The things which we have heard." The apostle is not presenting new light to them. This he will do later as he unfolds to them some of the deep things of God as they are able. But first he wishes them to give more earnest heed to the things that they know already. They were in a dangerous condition and must be aroused from their lethargy.

"Lest at any time we should let them slip," or more literally, "lest we be floated past them," or "drift away from them."

The picture is that of a boat's being carried along with the current, the occupants unaware of the fact that they are drifting. Before they realize it they are nearing the cataract, far past the old landmarks, and danger is at hand, and possibly destruction.

Drifting is one of the easiest and pleasantest means of locomotion, but it is also a most treacherous and dangerous one. No effort is needed to drift, and as one glides down the river toward sure death, the feeling is one of well-being and contentment, with accompanying delightful drowsiness. The downward movement is hardly perceptible, for as the boat moves down the river it seems to remain motionless. The water moves with the boat and appearances are deceitful. Unless one awakens in time, the danger is very real.

This was the condition of the church to which the author was writing. They were drifting spiritually, and did not sense their danger. Slowly they were nearing the precipice, and soon it would be too late.

For every one who falls into great sin, there are ten who are drifting. Even where one seems to leap suddenly into sin, it is often the case that, he has previously been drifting, unnoticed by others and perhaps by himself. Most open sin begins by slowly drifting. Therefore, let all beware.

"Float past," "drift away," "slip away." These are different renderings, and all of them significant. We are told that we ought to give the more earnest heed; that is, we must, we owe it, it is imperative. We are to be watchful lest we float past, or drift away from the moorings of the Word of God. In view of this danger, it behooves each one to examine himself, lest he be drifting without being aware of his peril. Carelessness in prayer, discontinuance of family worship, absence from church services, lukewarmness in spiritual or church activities, neglect of Bible study or private devotion, avoidance of the ordinances of the Lord's house, remissness in tithe paying and offerings—these and many other signs should be carefully watched. Our attitude toward them indicates if and how fast we are drifting. The apostle's admonition against drifting is as applicable today as when it was written.

Verse 2. "The word spoken by angels," rather "through" or "by means of" angels. This is doubtless a reference to the law that Paul said was "ordained by angels," and that Stephen says Israel had received "by the disposition of angels." (Gal. 3:19; Acts 7:53.) The word spoken was "stedfast"; that is, the transgression of the law, or neglect of its provisions, was severely punished.

The presence of angels at Sinai is alluded to in these texts: "The Lord came from Sinai, and rose up from Seir unto them; he shined forth from Mount

Paran, and he came with ten thousands of saints: from his right hand went a fiery law for them." Deut. 33:2. "The chariots of God are twenty thousand, even thousands of angels: the Lord is among them, as in Sinai, in the holy place." Ps. 68:17. What the functions of these angels were on this occasion we are not told beyond the information contained in the references from the New Testament above noted. The Jews believed that the fire, smoke, and storm at Sinai were caused by the angels, and cited Psalms 104:4 as proof. "Who maketh his angels spirits; his ministers a flaming fire."

The most likely explanation of the passage in Hebrews is that, Paul, knowing the high regard in which the Jews held angels, used this belief to emphasize the fact that if the word of angels was held in such high esteem, how much more should they heed the word of Christ, who is far above the angels.

Verse 3. "How shall we escape, if we neglect?" This question is so framed as to demand the answer, "We shall not escape." The danger here pointed out is not that of rejecting Christ and the gospel. Many do that to their eternal loss. But we are persuaded that many more neglect than reject. And it is against neglect that the apostle warns.

Comparatively few definitely and finally reject God's offer of eternal life. Most men intend at some time to attend to their religious duties. But they delay and neglect; and before they are aware of it the harvest is past, the summer is ended, and they are not saved. (Jer. 8:20.) It is always dangerous to neglect. Now is the accepted time.

How much evil has come into the world because of neglect and delay! An unpleasant task is left to the last moment; a confession is long overdue, but it is not forthcoming; a loved one is anxiously awaiting a letter, but the evil spirit of procrastination is at work, and the letter is not written. Young people may be convinced that the time has come when they should give their hearts to God, but they delay, and sometimes with fatal results. How often we intend to do a good deed, to say a kind word, to send a bouquet of flowers; but we delay and wait, and sometimes wait too long. It is well to be prompt. "To day if ye will hear his voice, harden not your hearts," is a message all should heed. Heb. 3:15.

"Began to be spoken by the Lord." The Lord is here said to be the first preacher of the gospel; and in a very real sense this is true, for it was He who in the Garden of Eden first proclaimed the good news to Adam and Eve when He said, "I will put enmity between thee and the woman, and between thy seed and her seed; it shall bruise thy head, and thou shalt bruise his heel." Gen. 3:15. This is the first gospel promise. Christ is the Lamb slain from the foundation of the world. (Rev. 13:8.)

"Confirmed unto us by them that heard him." Paul was not one of the twelve apostles, and we have no record that he ever heard Jesus speak except in his vision on the way to Damascus. He therefore rightly says *them* that heard, not *us* that heard. This, incidentally, excludes any of the twelve apostles from being the author of Hebrews.

The writer of this epistle was one who had not heard Jesus personally.

Verse 4. "God also bearing them witness." The first three of these witnesses—signs, wonders, miracles— are mentioned in Acts 2:22. The gifts are enumerated in 1 Corinthians 12:11, 28–31.

It may well be considered a rebuke to the church today that these signs are not more in evidence than they are. When Christ said, "These signs shall follow them that believe," He did not exempt any generation. Mark 16:17. We have many modern inventions, but none of these can make up for a loss of spiritual power. The church today is in danger of saying, "I am rich and increased with goods, and have need of nothing; and knowest not that thou art wretched, and miserable, and poor, and blind, and naked." Rev. 3:17.

There are those who assert that we are not now in need of the things which might have been appropriate and helpful in past ages. Why should we pray God for healing when we have such excellent medical institutions? Why should we ask God for rain when irrigation is much more dependable? Why ask God for wisdom when we already have, or can readily obtain, a college education? Why should we desire signs and wonders from God when the world is full of the wonderful things man has done? God may make Balaam's ass speak, but man can make a wax cylinder speak. God may transport Philip a short distance through the air, but man with his airplanes has long since exceeded that distance. God may make an axhead float, but man makes a fifty-thousand-ton steel ship float. True, there are some things God has done which man cannot do, or at least has as yet not done. But then, God has had longer experience than man. Give man a little time, and he will rival the Almighty, is his boast. There are those who believe that the time is near when God can be bowed out with thanks for past services. He may have been needed in the past, but we shall not need Him in the future. Except—

Except when we stand face to face with life's realities; when a loved one is on the deathbed, and no human hand can save; when buildings collapse, and death rains down from heaven; when we are lying on a raft in the ocean and human help is far off; when we grope in the darkness for light, and life and death are alike incomprehensible; when we search our souls for some sure anchorage in life's wild sea of mountainous waves; when the shadows lengthen and the sun is setting; when the evening star appears and we set out to sea and in bewilderment ask, "Whither?"

No, in the things that matter, we cannot get along without God. And most of all in a time such as this, when the old moorings loosen, when the foundations are giving away, when the storm is about to overtake us. And at this time, when anxious eyes are scanning the horizon in vain for the appearance of the sons of God, the church is not giving the trumpet a certain sound. The time is here, and overdue, when God's true church must stand out clear and distinct from the hundreds of sects and denominations that fill the land. The wayfaring man must no longer be left in doubt. The church must arise and shine.

In the early church God did mighty things for His people. As the apostles bore witness of the things they had seen and heard, God was "also bearing them witness." He furnished the power, and as they worked side by side with Him, three thousand were converted in a day. Signs and wonders accompanied the preaching, sinners trembled, hypocrites were exposed, the sick were healed, and many wonders were performed. And the church grew mightily.

Today the world is in need of the gospel more than ever before; the pure, unadulterated gospel of Christ and the early church. And at this very time the people of God are in danger of trusting to the wisdom of men rather than to the power of the Holy Spirit. Activity is substituted for spirituality; devices for an unction from on high. Statistics, goals, campaigns, and drives—are used to measure progress; but they can never measure the fruits of the Spirit. When God and the apostles bore witness in early time, men "were pricked in their heart, and said unto Peter and to the rest of the apostles, Men and brethren, what shall we do?" Acts 2:37. When they were told, "Repent, and be baptized," they responded, and thousands joined the church. Nor did they apostatize soon after. "They *continued stedfastly* in the apostles' doctrine and fellowship." Verse 42.

As a result of this work, "fear came upon every soul: and many wonders and signs were done by the apostles." Verse 43. It is to this the author of Hebrews refers when he mentions that in this work God was "also bearing them witness, both with signs and wonders, and with divers miracles, and gifts of the Holy Ghost, according to his own will."

When we contrast Pentecost with some of the popular revivals today, we can better see the need of the church. At Pentecost there was little appeal to emotions, no hymns to break down resistance, no elaborate organization to get results. But there was a man, a man filled with the Holy Ghost, a poor, weak man who a few weeks previously had cursed and sworn and denied his Lord, but who had repented and found the forgiveness he was now offering to others; and above all there was "God also bearing them witness," and the result was that men cried out in anguish for help. God was working.

We are not decrying organization, altar calls, gospel songs, or emotional appeals. Let all that can successfully use them do so, and may God bless them. But it is our profound conviction that the church needs greater power than it now has, and that when it gets this power, there will not be as many devices as there are now to get results, and that those who are converted will be better grounded than they are now. For that power we long, for that power we pray—power to change hearts and move men; power to end apostasy; power to hold the young people in the love of the truth; power to turn the hearts of the fathers to the children, and the children to their fathers; power to anoint for service; power to evangelize the world; power to make an end of sin and transgression, and to bring in everlasting righteousness. The *time* for the latter rain has come, but the rain is not here. "Raindrops around us are falling, but for the showers we plead."

Hebrews 2:5–8. "For unto the angels hath he not put in subjection the world to come, whereof we speak. But one in a certain place testified, saying, What is man, that thou art mindful of him? or the son of man, that thou visitest him? Thou madest him a little lower than the angels; thou crownedst him with glory and honour, and didst set him over the works of thy hands: thou hast put all things in subjection under his feet. For in that he put all in subjection under him, he left nothing that is not put under him. But now we see not yet all things put under him."

Christ is here presented as being lower than the angels, though crowned with glory and honor. He is shown to be very man, as truly as in the first chapter He was shown to be very God. His humanity enables Him to be the kind of high priest men need.

It is an ever-present source of comfort to the Christian to know that Christ understands our sorrows and perplexities, and sympathizes with us. If Christ had not become man, the question might easily have arisen, How can we know that God loves and cares for us when He never experienced the trials we encounter, has never been poor or forsaken, and has never known what it is to be alone and face an unknown future? He asks us to be faithful to death, but He has never faced the issues we face. If He were one of us and one with us, He would know how hard it is to meet certain trials. But if He has never been man, does He really know all our sorrows, and can He sympathize with us when we stray?

To this we unhesitatingly answer that God as God, *does* know, and that it was not for His sake, but for ours, that He became poor; it was not for His but for our sake that He suffered and died. We needed the demonstration that Christ came to give, or we would never have known the deep love of God for suffering humanity; nor would we have known the suffering which sin has brought to the heart of God. "All heaven suffered in Christ's agony; but that suffering did not begin or end with His manifestation in humanity. The cross is a revelation to our dull senses of the pain that, from its very inception, sin has brought to the heart of God." —*Education*, p. 263.

Verse 5. Not "unto the angels." God has not put the world to come in subjection unto the angels. Because of sin man fell very low in the scale of values. When Christ identified Himself with humanity and became man, a new dignity became ours. We are now closely united with God in a fellowship that is even closer than that which the angels know. In this new relationship God did not put man in subjection to angels. We deal directly with Christ without any intermediary.

Verse 6. "What is man?" This quotation is taken from the eighth psalm, in which man is discussed. Compared with creation in general, with angels, with God, man is so puny and insignificant that it seems God would never notice him. Yet God is mindful of him, and even visits him—doubtless primarily a reference to the incarnation. Man has a definite place in the thoughts of God. Hear these words: "I know the thoughts that I think toward you, saith the Lord, thoughts of peace, and not of evil, to give you an expected end." Jer. 29:11. For "expected end" the margin has, "to give you a future and a hope." This is God's plan for us.

Verse 7. "A little lower than the angels," or as the margin reads, "a little while inferior to." That man in many respects is now inferior to angels is evident. That he is potentially greater is equally clear.

Angels excel in strength; move with a speed greater than that of light; and possess powers not given to man. (Ps. 103:20; Dan. 9:21; Isa. 37:36; 2 Kings 19:35.) They pronounce and execute judgment upon the great of earth; protect and encamp about the saints of God; and have power to bind even Satan. (Dan. 4:13, 17; Ps. 34:7; Rev. 20:2.)

On the other hand, there are things of which they are deprived, but which man possesses. Angels are unitary beings without family life as we know it, with all its endearing ties. Angels have no fathers or mothers, brothers or sisters, sons or daughters. They do not marry; hence, are strangers to some of the deepest experiences of life. Angels have never known the joys of childhood, nor have they ever brought a new life into the world; they have never felt the exaltation of motherhood or fatherhood; nor, by way of contrast, have they ever passed through the deep waters, anxiously watching by the bedside of one of their own little ones, and seen life slowly ebb away. The deep and exalted experiences of conjugal love, of father and mother love, as well as of their sorrows, are not vouchsafed the angels.

Angels are not commissioned to preach the gospel, nor have they been permitted to suffer and die for their faith. They have never faced imprisonment or torture, nor have they known the surpassing joy of being lifted from the mire of sin into the kingdom of God. Conversion is a closed book to them as far as personal experience is concerned, and they have never heard the sweet news of sins forgiven. As far as we can judge, the most profound and sacred of life's experiences as we know them here are denied them. They have, at present, wisdom far beyond that of man; but in some respects man is even now superior to them.

While angels possibly have compensating powers and opportunities of which we know nothing, potentially man is destined to a higher place in the plan of God than the angels. Without pursuing this subject any further, we merely call attention to the fact that angels are ministering spirits, servants, while we are children and heirs. The heir, as long as he is a child, is under the jurisdiction of the servants. When he grows older he becomes lord of the house. (Heb. 1:14; Gal. 4:1, 2.)

Instead of "a little lower than the angels," some versions read, "a little lower than God," or "but little lower than God." We prefer the reading, "a little lower than the angels," as being more consonant with the apostle's argument, even though "little lower than God," is a permissible translation.

"Glory and honour." This distinctly points to the experience of Adam and Eve recorded in the first chapter of Genesis. God did not create man to be a servant or a slave. He made him to be king, and bestowed glory and honor upon him. This, though he lost his first estate because of sin, is prophetic of the high destiny which God has in mind for him. Men may degrade men, use and misuse them, and attempt to erase the image of God in the soul. Men may even degrade and misuse themselves, entirely contrary to God's plan. But God has something great in store for them. The day of redemption will reveal this fully.

Verse 8. "All things in subjection." In God's original plan man was set "over the works of thy hands"; that is, he was made ruler of the earth, and was told to "subdue it; and have dominion over the fish of the sea, and over the fowl of the air, and over every living thing that moveth upon the earth." Gen. 1:28.

Scholars are not agreed as to the extent of this original dominion, some contending that it included power over nature and the elements as Christ had power over them while He was on earth; others holding that all that is meant is to affirm that man was given dominion over, and was superior to, brute creation. The reader must decide for himself this not too important question.

"We see not yet." Man does not now have dominion over the earth. He is constantly face to face with powers over which he has no control. But God intends that the dominion that he lost by sin shall be restored to him according to the promise recorded by the prophet: "Unto thee shall it come, even the first dominion." Micah 4:8. This, we understand, is the meaning of "not yet," which thus really constitutes a promise of that which shall be.

Hebrews 2:9–18. "But we see Jesus, who was made a little lower than the angels for the suffering of death, crowned with glory and honour; that he by the grace of God should taste death for every man. For it became him, for whom are all things, and by whom are all things, in bringing many sons unto glory, to make the captain of their salvation perfect through sufferings. For both he that sanctifieth and they who are sanctified are all of one: for which cause he is not ashamed to call them brethren, Saying, I will declare thy name unto my brethren, in the midst of the church will I sing praise unto thee. And again, I will put my trust in him. And again, Behold I and the children which God hath given me. Forasmuch then as the children are partakers of flesh and blood, he also himself likewise took part of the same; that through death he might destroy him that had the power of death; that is, the devil; and deliver them who through fear of death were all their lifetime subject to bondage. For verily he took not on him the nature of angels; but he took on him the seed of Abraham. Wherefore in all things it behoved him to be made like unto his brethren, that he might be a merciful and faithful high priest in things pertaining to God, to make reconciliation for the sins of the people. For in that he himself hath suffered being tempted, he is able to succour them that are tempted."

The sufferings of Christ have always been a fruitful field for study and contemplation. In the verses before us we are introduced to some of the deeper aspects of redemption. It was by the grace of God that Christ tasted death for every man. This in itself is a remarkable statement, and even more so is the assertion that "it became" God to permit Him to do this. Through suffering Christ was made perfect—another notable expression—and His death became the means through which Satan, who had the power of death, was to be destroyed. In all things it behooved Christ to be made like unto His brethren, that He might be a merciful and faithful high priest. Having suffered being tempted, He is able to succor them that also are tempted and bring them needed help.

This section will repay careful study. We would call the attention of the reader to the additional notes at the end of the chapter, where certain phases of the subject are considered more exhaustively.

Verse 9. "But we see Jesus." The "but" here denotes contrast. Man does "not yet" have dominion, "but we see Jesus." He had dominion, even while He was here on earth. He sent Peter to catch a fish, and in the fish's mouth was found the coin needed for the occasion. (Matt. 17:27.) He told the disciples to let down the net, and they caught a multitude of fish. (John 21:6.) He commanded the winds and the waves, and they obeyed Him. (Matt. 8:26.) He cursed the fig tree, and it withered. (Matt. 21:19.) He exorcised demons, healed the sick, and raised the dead. (Mark 5:13; Matt. 8:14, 15; John 11:43, 44.) He multiplied the loaves and the fishes, walked on the water, and rebuked Satan. (Mark 8:1–9; Matt. 14:25; 4:10, 11.) There was no situation of which Jesus was not the master. "We see not yet" man in possession of these powers, "but we see Jesus." He is prophetic of the possibilities of man.

"A little lower than the angels." When Jesus became man He was made a little lower than the angels, or as the margin reads, "a little while inferior to." Thus Jesus in a very real sense took our nature without losing His Godhood, though He relinquished the independent use of the prerogatives of Deity. At no time did He exercise His divine powers except as

He received commandment from God. (John 14:31; 5:19.) As man He was at all times subject to God.

"For the suffering of death." The Authorized Version affirms that Jesus became man that He might suffer and die. He was made "a little lower than the angels for the [purpose of] suffering of death." The Revised Version affirms that it was as a reward for His suffering and death that Christ was crowned with glory and honor. The differences in interpretation depend on the meaning of the preposition which in the Authorized Version is translated "for," and in the Revised, "because of." As the Greek construction is not decisive, and as both translations are possible, we accept both. It is true, as the Authorized Version says, that Christ became man that He might die. It is also true, as the Revised Version says, that as a reward for His faithfulness He was crowned with glory and honor. Both views have able defenders. In cases where two interpretations are possible and both true, we see little point in engaging in controversy.

"By the grace of God." Christ's sufferings are not here considered as punishment laid on Him, for it was by "the grace of God" that He tasted death for every man—a significant expression. Some of the older manuscripts instead of "by the grace of God" have "apart from God," which suggests that Christ in His death suffered alone without the sustaining presence of God. This would give point to His despairing cry, recorded in Matthew 27:46: "And about the ninth hour Jesus cried with a loud voice, saying, Eli, Eli, lama sabachthani? that is to say, My God, my God, why hast thou forsaken me?"

"Taste death for every man." This does not mean, as some suggest, that He merely tasted lightly of

51

death and did not suffer the full measure. Gethsemane shows that He drank the cup to the dregs and tasted death as no other man ever tasted it.

Verse 10. "It became him." It was befitting Him; it was characteristic of Him. "Him" here is the Father, as "captain" unquestionably is Christ.

When the apostle says that it became God to make Christ perfect through suffering, he is in effect passing moral judgment upon the atonement. As he views God's plan for the redemption of man, he approves of what God is doing, saying that it is morally fitting for God to do this, that it is in harmony with His character. Such an opinion voiced by man might seem the height of presumption; for who is man that he should weigh the actions of God and pronounce judgment upon them? True, the apostle approves of God's plan; but the right to approve carries with it the right to disapprove. The apostle indeed is bold to subject God to human appraisal; also, it seems that God runs a serious risk in thus permitting man to evaluate His work.

In this as in all matters we may believe that God knows what He is doing. He is so sure of His ground that He does not hesitate to permit man to express his view of the moral fitness of His actions. He knows that the enlightened judgment of mankind will sustain Him. And so He confidently permits the apostle to say that it was befitting God to make His Son perfect through suffering, which is merely another way of saying that in view of the entrance of sin and in order to its complete eradication, it was right and fitting that Christ should come to this world and share the experiences of mankind.

For God thus to take man into His confidence is one of the comforting attributes of God. Note the invitations given, and the confidence of God in man expressed in these statements: "Come now, and let us reason together, saith the Lord." Isa. 1:18. "Consider what I say." 2 Tim. 2:7. "1 speak as to wise men; judge ye what I say." 1 Cor. 10: 15. God lays His case before men and appeals to their judgment. This also is befitting God, characteristic of Him.

"Perfect through sufferings." This does not mean that Christ was not previously perfect. Christ was perfect as God. He was perfect as man. By His sufferings He became perfect as *Saviour.* The thought is that of reaching a prescribed goal, of finishing a race, of completing a task. Before Christ came to earth, the path He must tread was plain before Him; every step was clear. To reach the goal, He must go all the way. He could not stop short of His ultimate destination; He must persevere to the end. It is the finishing of this course that is involved in the text before us, not any moral shortcoming. It is as a man running a race, reaching the three-quarter mark and running strong, showing no sign of weakness. But he has not finished. Not until the race is completed will he receive the crown. It is the last quarter that counts. When finally he finishes he has attained, and will receive the award. He has then perfected his course.

"Perfect" here means "to reach the standard set; to attain to maturity of growth and the full development of physical, intellectual, and spiritual powers; to reach the position or condition aimed at, and enjoy the privileges thus earned."

Suffering serves a definite purpose in the plan of God. If Christ had come to this earth and had done the perfect will of God; if He had failed in nothing but lived blamelessly before God and man; yet He would not have met God's standard or man's need without suffering. It is not what man does in the strength of manhood or with the plaudit of the multitude that counts. It is in adversity, in pain, in agony of body and mind, that true strength and nobility are measured. It was in the wilderness, in the garden, on the cross, that Christ's greatness revealed itself. Not until He had experienced to the full the meaning of drinking the cup, was He perfected. It is to His lifework, culminating in the cross, that He refers when He says, "I do cures to day and to morrow, and the third day I shall be perfected." Luke 13:32.

Verse 11. "He that sanctifieth" is Christ. "They who are sanctified" are His brethren. The "one" is God. Though Christ is Son in a different sense from us, yet we have one Father. God's intent is to bring many sons to glory. Christ is the captain who leads His men to battle. They follow where He leads, and for this reason "he is not ashamed to call them brethren." They are proud of their Captain, and He is proud of them. Note how tenderly Christ speaks of His brethren:

"And he stretched forth his hand toward his disciples, and said, Behold my mother and my brethren! for whosoever shall do the will of my Father which is in heaven, the same is my brother, and sister, and mother." Matt. 12:49, 50.

"Jesus saith unto her, Touch me not; for I am not yet ascended to my Father: but go to my brethren, and say unto them, I ascend unto my Father, and your Father; and to my God, and your God." John 20:17.

Christ is not ashamed of us if we are not ashamed of Him. But "whosoever shall be ashamed of me and my words, of him shall the Son of man be ashamed, when he cometh in his own glory, and the glory of the Father, and of the holy angels." Luke 9:26, R.V.

Sanctification is here presented not as a theory but as a life, that which makes Christ and His brethren one. Said Christ, "For their sakes I sanctify myself, that they also might be sanctified through the truth." John 17:19. Christ sanctified Himself for a purpose; this purpose He declares to be "that they also might be sanctified." He sets the example that others may follow.

"For which cause he is not ashamed." The author is speaking of sanctification. Recounting his own experience, he says:

"Not as though I had already attained, either were already perfect: but I follow after, if that I may apprehend that for which also I am apprehended of Christ Jesus. Brethren, I count not myself to have apprehended: but this one thing I do, forgetting those things which are behind, and reaching forth unto those things which are before, I press toward the mark for the prize of the high calling of God in Christ Jesus, Let us therefore, as many as be perfect, be thus minded: and if in any thing ye be otherwise minded, God shall reveal even this unto you." Phil. 3:12–15.

Paul did not claim to have attained, to be already perfect, but he did "follow after." And Christ was not ashamed of him. Nor will He be ashamed of any who are "thus minded." It is not how far we have come in the Christian pathway that alone counts: it is the direction in which we are facing. As captain, Christ leads the way. He is not ashamed of those who follow Him. They all have the same mind and are advancing toward the same goal; some have advanced farther than others, but "whereto we have already attained, let us walk by the same rule, let us mind the same thing." Phil. 3:16.

Verse 12. Of those who walk by the same rule and mind the same things, Christ is proud. With such He will worship, and to them He will declare God's name, singing praise to Him "in the midst of the church."

These statements are quoted from Psalms 22:22, and present Christ to us as worshiping with His brethren in the church. He is completely one with us, and His voice is raised with ours in giving praise to God for His wonderful goodness. What a picture! And how much greater must be the reality!

Verse 13. These two quotations are taken from Isaiah 8:17, 18, the first from the Septuagint Version. They both stress the fact that Christ is one with us. As we are to put our trust in God, so He put His trust in the Father, thus giving proof of His—humanity and of His oneness with mankind. It is a perfect picture of His complete fellowship with us. He has the same trust and faith which He demands of us.

In the second quotation the metaphor is changed from brethren to that of children. This is an especially endearing term, which Christ used to express His deep solicitude and love for His own. (Luke 13:34; Matt. 18:2.) How beautiful and significant are the words which Christ addressed to the disciples, some of whom were much older than He, "Children, have ye any meat?" John 21:5.

"The children which God hath given me." In His high-priestly prayer Christ eight times in six verses refers to the disciples as being given Him of God. (John 17:2, 6, 9, 11, 12, 24.) He did not ascribe honor to Himself, but gave God the glory for the result of His lifework. His burden was that they might be faithful. He was encouraged by the fact that "those that thou gavest me I have kept, and none of them is lost, but the son of perdition." John 17:12.

How well it would be if parents could have the happy privilege of someday appearing before God and being able to say, "Behold, I and the children whom the Lord hath given me." Isa. 8:18. How much better than to be asked the dread question, "Where is the flock that was given thee, thy beautiful flock?" Jer. 13:20.

But let no one despair. The promise in Proverbs 22:6 shall yet be fulfilled: "Train up a child in the way he should go: and when he is old, he will not depart from it." The good news that there is hope that "thy children shall come again to their own border," and "shall come again from the land of the enemy" may find unexpected fulfillment. Jer. 31:16, 17.

Verse 14. "Children are sharers." (R.V.) The apostle is still considering Christ's complete humanity. As children are sharers in flesh and blood, so also is Christ. That He might enter into all the experiences of mankind, He subjected Himself to death; but this death had a purpose. He did not die because He had filled His days and dissolution was approaching. As He had a work to do in life, so He had a work to do in death. He died that He "might bring to nought him that had the power of death, that is, the devil." (R.V.)

Satan is here said to have "the power of death." This is not true in the absolute sense. He has the power of death only as death results from sin. His kingdom is a kingdom of death, and in it he rules. "Through one man sin entered into the world, and death through sin." Rom. 5:12, R.V. As the originator of sin, Satan is the cause of death. As sin rules in our lives, so death rules, and so Satan rules. By causing men to sin, he causes death. Only in this way does he have the power of death.

"Through death...destroy him that had the power of death." The Bible records but two exceptions to the general rule that all must die: Enoch and Elijah. (Gen. 5:24; 2 Kings 2:11.) Men are under the dominion of sin, and hence are brought under death. When Jesus died on the cross, Satan triumphed; for it appeared that even the Son of God acknowledged Satan's power of death and became subject to it. But God had another purpose.

Of old the question had been asked, "Shall the prey be taken from the mighty, or the lawful captive delivered?" Isa. 49:24. To this the answer had been given: "Even the captives of the mighty shall be taken away, and the prey of the terrible shall be delivered: for I will contend with him that contendeth with thee, and I will save thy children." Verse 25. On this Christ comments: "No man can enter into a strong man's house, and spoil his goods, except he will first bind the strong man; and then he will spoil his house." Mark 3:27.

Christ was the one who entered the strong man's house, bound him, and took away his prisoners, and in this way fulfilled the scripture that the "captives of the mighty shall be taken away, and the prey of the terrible shall be delivered." Christ entered death—the very stronghold of Satan—and wrested from him his prey. When Satan thought he had Christ in his power, when the tomb was sealed and Christ locked in, Satan exulted. But Christ burst the bonds of death and walked forth from the grave, for "it was not possible that he should be holden of it." Acts 2:24. Not only did Christ rise Himself, but "the graves were opened, and many bodies of the saints which slept arose, and came out of the graves after his resurrection." Matt. 27:52, 53. And "when he ascended up on high, he led captivity captive." Eph. 4:8. And so, though the "strong man armed keepeth his palace, a stronger than he shall come upon him, and overcome him." Luke 11:21. The stronger man, Christ, entered the realm of death, and in death overcame him who had the power of death, delivered "the prey of the terrible" (Isa. 49:25), took away his captives, and spoiled his house (Matt. 12:29); "and having spoiled principalities and powers, he made a shew of them openly, triumphing over them in it" (Col. 2:15).

Long before this, "Michael the archangel, when contending with the devil he disputed about the body of Moses, durst not bring against him a railing accusation, but said; The Lord rebuke thee." Jude 9. But this time, when Jesus entered Satan's domain to despoil it, there was no disputing. He simply entered the strong man's house, took away from him the keys, broke the bonds of death, delivered "the prey of the terrible," and loosened Satan's strangle hold. As a first fruit He took some along to heaven, led captivity captive, and showed them openly in triumph. Henceforth, death for the believers is but a sleep; they rest in peace until God calls them. For many it will even be a blessed sleep. (Rev. 14:13.) Christ "hath abolished death." 2 Tim. 1:10. He has "the keys of hell and of death." Rev. 1: 18. (See also 1 Cor. 15:51–57.)

Verse 15. "Fear of death." Those living in this age and in favored lands but faintly comprehend the bondage of those who live in "fear of death." Heathen and pagans are steeped in superstition and dread. The worship of many of these consists in pacifying evil spirits, on the supposition that the good spirits will not harm them, but the evil might do them untold injury. This results in devil worship. Their life is one of constant fear: fear of enemies, fear of evil spirits, fear of death.

But it is not heathen only who live in fear. In lands of civilization thousands are lying on beds of sickness and pain, fearing the outcome; millions are anxiously looking for the things that are coming upon the earth, living in constant apprehension, in veritable bondage, from which Christ alone can deliver them. If they only knew that Christ has taken the sting out of death, removed its poisonous fang, and changed death to a sleep, they would rejoice.

The fear of death grips not only the old and infirm but also many in the prime of life. This fear increases as years are added. But this need not be. To the true Christian the twenty-third psalm is real. "Though I walk through the valley of the shadow of death, I will fear no evil."

The fear of the future comes to many a man while he is still young. He may be threatened with financial disaster; he may be fearing a serious operation; he may be facing death on the battlefield; he may be entangled in legal involvements. All such God invites to come to Him, be relieved of their fear, and find comfort. Even though some may be motivated by mere physical fear, God will hear their cry; and many are those who have found in prayer not only present consolation but an abiding hope. May we not believe that God uses certain experiences to turn men's hearts to Him? And as men turn to God, fear dissolves and faith takes its place.

We suppose, however, that this reference to the fear of death applies primarily to those millions of dear souls who are in bondage of sin and are longing for deliverance. They fear the present; they fear the future; they fear life; they fear death. Is there any hope or comfort or deliverance? The answer is that Christ has destroyed the power of Satan, has abolished death, and has delivered, and will deliver, all from the fears that have bound them.

Verse 16. "He took on Him." According to our translation, Christ did not take upon Himself the nature of angels, but that of men. However, a better rendering is, "Christ did not extend help to angels, but to man." When angels sinned, they did so in full knowledge of the consequences. When they took the step that separated them from God, there was no more that God could do for them. All the light of heaven had been theirs; every entreaty had been made; but all appeals had been rejected. God had done all that could be done. Their step was irrevocable. Their sin was unpardonable.

Verse 17. "It behoved him." The word "behoove" has in it the idea of moral obligation.. In the following verses the same Greek word is variously translated "ought," "owe," "bound to," "must needs," "debtor," "debt due." "Ye also *ought* to wash one another's feet." John 13:14. "How much *owest* thou?" Luke 16:5, 7. "We are *bound to* give thanks." 2 Thess. 2:13. "Then *must* ye needs go out." 1 Cor. 5:10. "He is a *debtor.*" Matt. 23:16. "Till he should pay the *debt.*" Matt. 18:30. "Pay all that was *due.*" Verse 34.

Commentators express wonder at the audacity of mere man telling God what He ought to do. The author, of course, would not do this if he did not know that he is expressing God's own viewpoint.

God need not have created. He could have omitted creation, and avoided all obligations. But if He did create, if He called into being moral creatures, certain responsibilities rested upon Him. As the father of a family has obligations because of his being the head

61

of the house, so also God has responsibilities. It is not correct to say, as some do, that because God did not create Satan a sinful being, He is relieved of all obligations. True, God did not create Satan, but He did create Lucifer, who became Satan, and because of this creation, certain necessities rest upon God. This He would be the last to deny or avoid. He is in no way responsible for sin, but there are some things which He is obligated to do because of sin's existence. It is this the author has in mind when He uses the word "behoove."

What is it that He "must" or "ought" to do? "It behoved him to be made like unto his brethren" "in all things." What does this mean? It means that He must become man so completely and fully that it can never be said that He is a stranger to any temptation, any sorrow, any trial or suffering which men must and do pass through. Although this does not mean that His experiences must be identical with ours in every respect—for not one or a thousand lifetimes would be sufficient for that—it does mean that the trials must be representative, and in principle include all that man must suffer, and that in severity they must fully measure up to all that men have to bear.

The reason Christ must thus suffer is "that he might be [or "become," A.R.V.] a merciful and faithful high priest." The two characteristics of mercy and faithfulness are necessary to a just ministry. Mercy alone might be too lenient, and might ignore justice. Faithfulness provides a balance to mercy, as it considers the rights and duties of both the offender and the offended. As high priest Christ must be kind and understanding toward the offender, but He must also be true to justice and not ignore the law. Faithfulness will keep the nice balance between unconditional mercy and unrelenting justice. The high priest must consider the sinner, but he must also consider the one sinned against. He must be faithful to his trust as well as merciful to the transgressor.

As all sin is primarily sin against God, the reconciliation which the high priest is to effect must include first of all man's reconciliation to God. This involves God's standard of righteousness, His law. Without due regard to its demands, no true reconciliation can be effected. This is involved in Christ's being a "merciful and faithful high priest in things *pertaining to God.*" He must be just to all parties concerned.

"*Make reconciliation.*" This was the work of the priests, and particularly of the high priest. It is noteworthy that the word "reconcile" either in the Old or in the New Testament is never used in the sense of reconciling God to man, but always of reconciling man to God.

Verse 18. "Suffered being tempted." This phrase gives an insight into the nature of Christ's temptations. The body given Him was not such that He was unaffected by temptations, so that for Him in reality there were no temptations. There are good people whose disposition is such that certain temptations that are very severe to others are no temptation to them. But this was not Christ's experience; for if it had been, He would not have experienced the terrific struggle of a poor sinner who is mightily tempted to yield. Christ must be tempted in all points like as we are! He must actually suffer being tempted.

How much Christ suffered in resisting temptation, the wilderness, Gethsemane, and Golgotha reveal. In the first two cases the temptation was so overwhelming that He would have died under the impact had not an angel been sent to strengthen Him. The cup was not removed despite His prayer. He must drink it. To these experiences the apostle doubtless refers when he says, "Ye have not yet resisted unto blood, striving against sin." Heb. 12:4. Christ *did* resist unto blood. The temptations and sufferings of Christ are our ground for believing that "he is able to succour them that are tempted," or better, that "are being tempted," or that "are under temptation." Christ's heart broke under the strain.

Says the psalmist, "God is our refuge and strength, a very present help in trouble." Ps. 46:1. The idea of "a very present help in trouble," is the meaning conveyed in the statement that Christ is able to succor them that are tempted. The tense in the original implies that Christ stands ready to supply immediate help to those who are in the midst of temptation, or who are continuously tempted. This is a most precious promise.

ADDITIONAL NOTES

Suffering and Death of Christ

In any evaluation of the sufferings of Christ consideration must be given to the spiritual aspects of the agony rather than the mere physical. As far as bodily suffering is concerned—others have suffered as much or more, and exhibited a courage that must command admiration.

But mere physical agony does not explain the heart-rending cry that came from the lips of the Saviour, "My God, my God, why hast thou forsaken me?" Matt. 27:46. Only spiritual distress can account for this, a feeling of being forsaken, being left alone, and that in the crisis hour. We hear no complaint as the nails are driven into His hands; we hear no complaint as the cross is rudely thrust into the ground; we hear no complaint as He is spit upon, scourged, reviled; the thing that occupied His mind was the hiding of God. Martyrs were upheld in their last hour by the assurance of the love and care of God. But not so Christ. He was alone, and apparently forsaken. To Him, God seemed far off.

We do not get the full picture, however, of the sufferings of Christ if we confine ourselves to the cross. Note these extracts from the writings of Mrs. E. G. White:

"Those who think of the result of hastening or hindering the gospel think of it in relation to themselves and to the world. Few think of its relation to God. Few give thought to the suffering that sin has caused our Creator. All heaven suffered in Christ's agony; but that suffering did not begin or end with His manifestation in humanity. The cross is a revelation to our dull senses of the pain that, from its very inception, sin has brought to the heart of God. Every departure from the right, every deed of cruelty, every failure of humanity to reach His ideal, brings grief to Him. When there came upon Israel the calamities that were the sure result of separation from God,—subjugation by their enemies, cruelty, and death,—it is said that 'His soul was grieved for the misery of Israel.' 'In all their affliction He was afflicted;...and He bare them, and carried them all the days of old.'" —*Education,* p. 263.

"His whole life was a sacrifice of Himself for the saving of the world. Whether fasting in the wilderness of temptation or eating with the publicans at Matthew's feast, He was giving His life for the redemption of the lost." —*The Desire of Ages,* p. 278.

"God suffered with His Son. Angels beheld the Saviour's agony. They saw their Lord enclosed by legions of satanic forces, His nature weighed down with a shuddering, mysterious dread. There was silence in heaven. No harp was touched. Could mortals have viewed the amazement of the angelic host as in silent grief they watched the Father separating His beams of light, love, and glory from His beloved Son, they would better understand how offensive in His sight is sin....

"Christ's agony did not cease, but His depression and discouragement left Him. The storm had in no wise abated, but He who was its object was strengthened to meet its fury. He came forth calm and serene. A heavenly peace rested upon His blood-stained face. He had borne that which no human being could ever bear; for He had tasted the sufferings of death for every man." —*Ibid.*, pp. 693, 694.

"All heaven and the unfallen worlds had been witnesses to the controversy. With what intense interest did they follow the closing scenes of the conflict. They beheld the Saviour enter the garden of Gethsemane, His soul bowed down with the horror of a great darkness. They heard His bitter cry, 'Father, if it be possible, let this cup pass from Me.' Matt. 26:39. As the Father's presence was withdrawn, they saw Him sorrowful with a bitterness of sorrow exceeding that of the last great struggle with death. The bloody sweat was forced from His pores, and fell in drops upon the ground. Thrice the prayer for deliverance was wrung from His lips. Heaven could no longer endure the sight, and a messenger of comfort was sent to the Son of God." —*Ibid.*, pp. 759, 760.

From these quotations we learn that the suffering of God did not begin or end with Christ's manifestation in humanity, but that suffering has been God's portion since the inception of sin. In this suffering we cannot differentiate between the suffering of the Father and that of the Son. As truly as the one suffered, so did the other. When Isaac was bound on the altar and the father stood ready to plunge the knife into the heart of the son, we cannot believe that Isaac only suffered. No more can we believe that Jesus only suffered. For the Father to hear the fearful words, "my God, my God, why hast thou forsaken me?" and not be able to answer, "Son, I have not forsaken thee; I am right here," must have caused the Father agony that can only be compared to what the Son suffered when no answer came back. We refuse, to judge who suffered more.

With this in mind the author previously quoted tells us that what happened in Gethsemane filled Jesus "with a bitterness of sorrow that exceeded the last great struggle with death." In our evaluation of the sufferings of Christ, we must not omit Gethsemane.

What did happen in Gethsemane? It was there the separation of Father and Son took place. In the darkness, and alone, they parted. The Son had made the supreme decision. He would drink the cup, bitter though it be. But His human nature succumbed. He fell dying to the ground, and would have died had not superhuman strength been given Him for the purpose of additional suffering. Had He died there, He would not fully have tasted death. He endured all that humanity could endure; His body could bear no more. But He was not permitted to die, welcome though that would be, as that would be the end of suffering. He must live beyond the point where He naturally would have died; He must consciously come to the moment of death and taste to the full what death means—separation from the Father. When He rose from the struggle "He *had* tasted the sufferings of death for every man." On the cross He died. In Gethsemane He tasted death. Note this further extract, also from Mrs. E. G. White:

"In the garden of Gethsemane, Christ suffered in man's stead, and the human nature of the Son of God staggered under the terrible horror of the guilt of sin, until from His pale and quivering lips was forced the agonizing cry, 'O my Father, if it be possible, let this cup pass from Me': but if there is no other way by which the salvation of fallen man may be accomplished, then 'not as I will, but as Thou wilt.' Human nature would then and there have died under the horror of the sense of sin, had not an angel from heaven strengthened Him to bear the agony. The power that inflicted retributive justice upon man's substitute and surety, was the power that sustained and upheld the suffering One under the tremendous weight of wrath that would have fallen upon a sinful world. Christ was suffering the death that was pronounced upon the transgressors of God's law. It is a fearful thing for the unrepenting sinner to fall into the hands of the living God. This is proved by the history of the destruction of the old world by a flood, by the record of the fire which fell from heaven and destroyed the inhabitants of Sodom, But never was this proved to so great an extent as in the agony of Christ, the Son of the Infinite God, when He bore the wrath of God for a sinful world. It was in consequence of sin, the transgression of God's law, that the Garden of Gethsemane has become pre-eminently the place of suffering to a sinful world. No sorrow, no agony, can measure with that which was endured by the Son of God. Man has not been made a sin bearer, and he will never know the horror of the curse of sin which the Saviour bore. No sorrow can bear any comparison with the sorrow of Him upon whom the wrath of God fell with overwhelming force. Human nature can endure but a limited amount of test and trial. The finite can only endure the finite measure, and human nature succumbs: but the nature of Christ had a greater capacity for suffering; for the human existed in the divine nature, and created a capacity for suffering to endure that which resulted from the sins of a lost world. The agony which Christ endured broadens, deepens, and gives a more extended conception of the character of sin, and the character of the retribution which God will bring upon those who continue in sin. The wages of sin is death, but the gift of God is eternal life through Jesus Christ to the repenting, believing sinner." —*Ministry*, May, 1938, pp. 38, 39.

A man who dies does not necessarily by that fact taste death. Most people who die are unaware of what is taking place. Few are able to evaluate their own, reactions as the end draws near, and most of them are unconscious some time before the event. But even such as are conscious of their state lose that consciousness at the moment death takes place, when of all times they should be alert if they are really to taste death. Thus in a certain sense it may be said—though this seems a contradiction—that no man who has died has ever fully tasted death. This can only be done by being conscious at the moment of dissolution.

In the same sense it may be said that no man who has died has ever tasted suffering to the full. However much he has endured, when death comes, the suffering ends. A person of weak bodily resistance is not able to endure as much physical suffering as one with a stronger constitution, and hence will succumb earlier. But however strong a person may be, he can withstand only a certain amount of suffering and torture, and then he dies. Were he given superhuman strength, and thus enabled to live beyond the point where he ordinarily would have died, he could more truly be said to have suffered to the full.

It should also be had in mind that the moment of death is not all that is included in death as punishment. Though death is the climax of the punishment, it is also the end of suffering.

A man is sentenced to be hanged three weeks from the time the sentence is pronounced. Those three weeks are a vital part of his punishmnt. Every day he is one day nearer the fatal date, and his anxiety and torture daily increase. When at last the moment arrives, when the trap springs, when the neck is broken, his sufferings are over. Death is both the climax of, and the release from, suffering. No evaluation of the sufferings of death is adequate that takes into account only the moment of death. What goes before must be given due consideration.

If we apply this to the case of Christ's death, we find that no evaluation of His sacrifice and suffering is adequate if Gethsemane is left out. The garden experience is closely connected with Golgotha; the two cannot be separated. On the cross Christ suffered and died; in Gethsemane He also suffered and in some respects reached depths lower than on the cross, With this in mind, note again the extract previously quoted: "As the Father's presence was withdrawn, they saw Him sorrowful with a bitterness of sorrow exceeding that of the last great struggle with death." —*The Desire of Ages*, p. 759.

The Bible Doctrine of the Trinity*

Samuel T. Spear

"The Bible, while not giving a metaphysical definition of
the spiritual unity of God, teaches His essential oneness in
opposition to all forms of polytheism, and also assumes
man's capacity to apprehend. the idea sufficiently for all
the purposes of worship and obedience. John 17:3; 1 Cor.
8:6. The same Bible as clearly teaches that the adorable
Person therein known as Jesus Christ, when considered in
His *whole* nature, is truly divine and truly God in the most
absolute sense. John 1:1–18; 1 John 5:20; Rom. 1:3, 4;
9:5; Titus 2:13.

"There is, however, a sense in which the Christ of the
Bible, while essentially divine, is, nevertheless, in some
respects *distinct* from and *subordinate* to God the Father.
He is spoken of, and frequently speaks of Himself, as the
Son of God, as the only-begotten of the Father; as being
sent by God the Father into this world, and as doing the
will of the Father. He is never confounded with the Father,
and never takes His place. 'My Father' is a phrase that was
often on His lips. He not only prayed to the Father, but He
described Himself as always doing the things that please
Him. John 8:29. He said to Mary Magdalene, after His
resurrection, 'Go to My brethren, and say unto them, I
ascend unto My Father, and your Father; and to My God,
and your God.' John 20:17. He said to the disciples in the
upper room, just before His death, 'I go unto the Father; for
My Father is greater than I.' John 14:28. There is no difficulty in finding in His ministry abundant references to God
the Father as in some respects *distinct* from and *superior* to
Himself, and, hence, involving the idea of His own
subordination.

---

*   From the New York *Independent* of November 14,
       1889. Published by the Pacific Press as No. 90 of
       Bible Students' Library.

"The same fact appears in the writing of the apostles. Paul said to the Corinthians, 'And ye are Christ's; and Christ is God's.' 1 Cor. 3:23. He also said to them, 'And the head of the woman is the man; and the head of Christ is God.' 1 Cor. 11:3. He further said to this church: 'And when all things shall be subdued unto Him, then shall the Son [Christ] also Himself be subject unto Him that put all things under Him, that God may be all in all.' 1 Cor. 15:28. God is said to have 'raised Him [Christ] from the dead, and set Him at His own right hand in the heavenly places,' to have 'highly exalted Him,' after His resurrection, and to have 'given Him a name which is above every name.' Eph. 1:20; Phil. 2:9. These and the like passages do, beyond all question, make a distinction between God the Father and Jesus Christ, and to the former do assign some kind of superiority which implies subordination in the latter. No such superiority is ever assigned to Christ in respect to God the Father.

"These facts—namely, the absolute unity of the Godhead, excluding all multiplicity of gods, the absolute divinity of the Lord Jesus Christ and the subordination of Christ in some respect to God the Father—when taken together, have led biblical scholars to consider the question which relates to the method of harmonizing them. What shall be said on this point? The following observations are submitted in answer to this question:

"1. All the facts above stated rest on the same authority, and, hence, no one of them can be denied without denying this authority or misinterpreting the language used.

"2. The Bible, while committing itself to the facts, does not assume even any *apparent* disharmony between them, and does not, in express terms, supply any specific theory for harmonizing them. In one class of passages we have the unity of the Godhead; in another class, the absolute divinity of Christ; in still another class, a distinction between God the Father and Christ, and the subordination of the latter to the former; and there is no effort in any of these passages, or anywhere else in the Bible, to harmonize the different statements. So the matter stands in the word of

God; and if Christians were to confine their thoughts to simply what that word says, they would never raise any curious questions in regard to the subject, which is, perhaps, on the whole, the best course to pursue.

"3. It is not necessary, for the practical purposes of godliness and salvation, to speculate on the point at all, or know what biblical scholars have thought and said in regard to it. It is enough to take the Bible just as it reads, to believe what it says, and stop where it stops.

"4. If, however, as some are inclined to do, we undertake to explain the different statements of the Bible relating to the subject, then we must not, on the one hand, adopt any theory of the trinity of the Godhead, of which the divinity of Christ is one element, that involves the supposition of three gods instead of one, and, on the other hand, we must not adopt any theory of the unity of God, or in respect to Christ, that logically excludes the divinity of the latter. All the statements of the Bible must be accepted as true, with whatever qualifications they mutually impose on one another. The whole truth lies in them all when taken collectively.

"The Arian, who regards Christ as more than human but less than divine, and also the Socinian, who regards Him as simply human, are alike at fault in reasoning from those passages that set forth His subordination to the Father, and in omitting to give due and proper force to those that teach His absolute divinity. Neither accepts the whole testimony of the Bible in respect to Christ. This leads both to false though not identical conclusions. Christ is not, as the Socinian affirms, simply a man, and, in His higher nature, is not, as the Arian declares, less than divine. He is a *theanthropic*Christ, being divine and human at the same time and is, hence, properly designated as the God-man. Great as may be the mystery of the fact, it is, nevertheless, a fact according to His own teaching and that of the apostles.

"5. The subordination of Christ, as revealed in the Bible, is not adequately explained by referring it simply to His human nature. It is true that, in that nature, He was a created and dependent being, and in this respect like the race whose nature He assumed; and yet the Bible statement of His subordination extends to His divine as well as His human nature. Paul tells us that God 'created all things by Jesus Christ,' and that He is the person, or agent, 'by whom also He [God] made the worlds.' Eph. 3:9; Heb. 1:2. Neither of these statements can have any relation to the humanity of Christ, and yet in both God is represented as acting in and through Christ, and the latter represented as the medium of such action. So, also, God is described as sending forth His Son into the world, as giving 'His onlybegotten Son' for human salvation, and as not sparing 'His own Son', but delivering 'Him up for us all.' Gal. 4:4; John 3:16; Rom. 8:32. These statements imply that this Son, who is none other than Christ Himself, existed prior to His incarnation, and that, at thus existing, He was sent forth. given, not spared, but delivered up, by God the Father. The act. assigned to God the Father in thus devoting 'His own Son' to the work of human redemption, relates to Him as He was before He assumed our nature in the person of Jesus of Nazareth, and supposes in the Father some kind of *primacy* in making this devotement.

"We learn also from Paul that when this Son, having been incarnated on earth, and having been subsequently exalted in heaven, shall have had all things put under Him, 'then shall the Son also Himself be subject unto Him that put all things under Him, that God may be all in all.' 1 Cor. 15:28. This implies subordination on the part of the Son to God the Father; and this subordination, whatever may be its exact nature, obviously relates to the higher nature of Christ, and not simply to His humanity. It was in this higher nature that He descended into the vale of humiliation, and it was in this nature that God 'highly exalted Him.' Phil. 2:9.

"Christ, when, after His resurrection, giving to His apostles their final commission, said to them, 'All power is *given* unto Me in heaven and in earth.' Matt. 28:18. The Greek word translated power means authority; and Christ here speaks of this authority as being delegated to Him. By whom was it delegated?—Evidently by God the Father, in respect to whom Christ said on another occasion, 'All things are delivered unto Me of My Father.' Matt. 11:27. In another passage we have these words: 'The Father loveth the Son, and hath given all things into His hand.' John 3:35.

"These scriptures, taken together, show that the subordination of Christ to God the Father, as stated in the Bible, is not limited simply to His human nature, but extends also in some sense to His higher nature. This is the view expressed by Dr. Meyer, in his comment on the words, 'And ye are Christ's; and Christ is God's.' 1 Cor. 3:23. He says that it is 'precisely on the *divine* side of His being that Christ is, according to Paul, the Son of God, and therefore, not subordinate *simply* in respect to His manhood.'

"6. The conclusion from all the Scriptures put together is that there is in the Godhead some *essential and imminent distinction as to the mode of subsistence and operation,* in virtue of which Christ is properly spoken of as *subordinate* to God the Father, and also spoken of as divine and equal to the Father in power and glory, and that this distinction, whatever it is, does not conflict with the doctrine of the divine unity as taught in the Bible. This fact in regard to the Godhead makes its appearance in the great plan for human salvation. God, in this plan, is brought before our thoughts under the *personal* titles of Father, Son, and Holy Ghost, with diversity in offices, relations, and actions toward men. These titles and their special significance, as used in the Bible, are not interchangeable. The term 'Father' is never applied to the Son, and the term 'Son' is never applied to the Father. Each title has its own permanent application, and its own use and sense.

"The distinction thus revealed in the Bible is the basis of the doctrine of the tri-personal God....This doctrine, as held and stated by those who adopt it, is not a system of tritheism, or the doctrine of three Gods, but is the doctrine of one God subsisting and acting in three persons, with the qualification that the term 'person,' through perhaps the best that can be used, is not, when used in this relation, to be understood in any sense that would make it inconsistent with the unity of the Godhead, and hence not to be understood in the ordinary sense when applied to men. Bible trinitarians are not tritheists. They simply seek to state, in the best way in which they can, what they regard the Bible as teaching.

"Our Saviour, in prescribing the formula to be observed in baptism, directed that converts to Christianity should be baptized 'in the name of the Father, and of the Son, and of the Holy Ghost.' Matt. 28:19. Here we have the distinct element of threeness in three personal titles of the Godhead; and while this implies some kind of distinction between the persons thus designated, the language places them all on the same level of divinity. The baptismal formula, as given by Christ, is a strong argument in favor of this distinction; and yet no trinitarian ever understood Christ as here asserting or implying anything inconsistent with the essental unity of the Godhead.

"Paul believed in the unity of the Godhead; yet in his Epistle to the Ephesians, he says: 'For through Him [Christ] we both [Jews and Gentiles] have access by one Spirit [the Holy Spirit] unto [God] the Father.' Eph. 2:18. Here, in form at least, is a manifest assumption of *tri-personality.* There is a difference, considered with reference to this 'access' between the personalities mentioned. The access is *through* the one first named, *by* the second, and *unto* the third. The doctrine of the Trinity, as elsewhere derivable from the Bible, is here incidentally implied as existing in the apostle's mind. Indeed, the element of *threeness*, in some sense not contradictory of essential unity, is clearly taught in the Scriptures with reference to God.

"This *threeness*, moreover, does not, as claimed by those who hold the Sabellian theory, appear to be simply a threefold manifestation of God, as if one were to speak of Him as the Creator, the moral Governor, and providential Ruler of the world. Such a theory does not fairly express the natural and proper import of Bible language, and cannot be applied to that language without rendering it either tautological or absurd. We might say of a man that be is a father, a citizen, and a judge at the same time; yet no candid person, if acquainted with the Bible, would ever think of saying that this is analogous to the use of the titles Father, Son, and Holy Ghost, as employed in the Bible with reference to God. These titles, upon their face, appear to have a *personal* character, and are manifestly so used. The only reason why they must be qualified in such use grows out of the fact that the unity of the Godhead is also revealed in the Bible. If tri-theism were the doctrine of that book, then these titles, without any. qualification, would appropriately express the fact.

"7. All efforts to explain the precise *nature* of the distinction in virtue of which the God of the Bible is in some respect *tri-personal*, and in virtue of which Christ, while essentially divine, is, in some respect, *subordinate* to God the Father, must end in total failure, and hence had better be omitted altogether. The subject matter involved does not lie within the domain of human thought, and must be left among the things which we cannot know, and with which we should not perplex ourselves.

"The theory of the *eternal generation* of the Son by the. Father, with the cognate theory of the *eternal procession* of the Holy Ghost from the Father, or from the Father and the Son, while difficult even to apprehend, and while at best but a mystical speculation, is an effort to be wise, not only above what is written, but also beyond the possibilities of human knowledge. It is quite as great a mystery as that which it seeks to explain, and really explains nothing.

"So, also the theory of a threefold consciousness of the *triune* God—one consciousness for God the Father, another and a different consciousness for God the Son, and a third and a different consciousness for God the Holy Ghost—is another speculation in respect to which we do not, and in this world, at least, never can know enough either to affirm or deny. The exact mode in which the revealed Trinity is a fact is and must be to us a perfect mystery, in the sense of our total ignorance on the point. We do not, in order to believe the revealed fact, need to understand this mode.

"8. The Christian doctrine of the Trinity—whether, as to its elements, taken collectively or separately—so far from being a dry, unpractical, and useless dogma, adjusts itself to the condition and wants of men as sinners. Paul said to the Ephesians that there is 'one Spirit, even as ye are called in one hope of your calling,' and then added that there is 'one Lord,' Jesus Christ, connecting with Him 'one faith' and 'one baptism,' and then, ascending to the climax of thought, added again that there is 'one God and Father of all, who is above all, and through all, and in you all.' Eph. 4:4–6. What Christian head or heart will object to this statement of the Trinity?

"To the Corinthians the apostle said: 'The grace of our Lord Jesus Christ, and the love of God, and the communion of the Holy Ghost, be with you all. Amen.' 2 Cor. 13:14. Who finds fault with the Trinity of the Godhead as set forth in this benedictive prayer? To the same church he also said: 'But to us there is but one God, the Father, of whom are all things, and we *in* Him; and one Lord Jesus Christ, *by* whom are all things, and we *by* Him.' 1 Cor. 8:6. The phrase 'of whom are all things, and we in Him,' as applied to the 'one God the Father,' and the phrase '*by* whom are all things, and we *by* Him' as applied to the 'one Lord Jesus Christ,' differ from each other; and this difference in the preposition used implies a distinction between God the Father and the Lord Jesus Christ. God the Father appears in this language as the *primal* source, and Christ appears as the *medium.* So, also, the apostle said to the Ephesians: 'And be ye kind one to another, tender-hearted, forgiving one another, even as God for Christ's sake hath forgiven you.' Eph. 4:32. Here the forgiveness comes from God, who is one of the personalities of the Trinity; but it comes 'for Christ's sake,' and through Him, who is another personality in the same Trinity. Who has any objection to the doctrine as thus

77

appearing? Who cavils with it when he asks the Father to forgive him for Christ's sake?

"The truth is that God the Father in the *primacy* attached to Him in the Bible, and God the Son in the redeeming and saving *work* assigned to Him in the same Bible, and God the Holy Ghost in His office of regeneration and sanctification—whether considered collectively as one God, or separately in the relation of each to human salvation—are really omnipresent in, and belong to, the whole texture of the revealed plan for saving sinners. In this plan there is nothing superfluous, and nothing that is not adapted to the *felt* wants of man. The simple-minded Christian, when thinking of these wants, and contemplating the divine Trinity, as he finds it in the Bible, has no difficulty with the doctrine. It is a light to his thoughts, and a gracious power in his experience. Content with the revealed facts, and spiritually using them, he has no trouble with them. He does not attempt metaphysically to analyze the God he worships, but rather thinks of Him as revealed in His word, and can always join in the following Doxology.—

> "'Praise God, from whom all blessings flow!
> Praise Him, all creatures here below!
> Praise Him above, ye heavenly host!
> Praise Father, Son, and Holy Ghost!'

"It is only when men speculate outside of the Bible and beyond it, and seek to be wiser than they can be, that difficulties arise; and then they do arise as the rebuke of their own folly. A glorious doctrine then becomes their perplexity, and ingulfs them in a confusion of their own creation. What they need is to believe more and speculate less."

Extracts From the Writings of Mrs. E. G. White on the Divinity of Christ

"It will be profitable to contemplate the divine condescension, the sacrifice, the self-denial, the humiliation, the resistance the Son of God encountered in doing His work for fallen men. Well may we come forth from contemplation of His sufferings exclaiming, Amazing condescension! Angels marvel, as with intense interest they watch the Son of God descending step by step the path of humiliation. It is the mystery of godliness. It is the glory of God to conceal Himself and His ways, not by keeping men in ignorance, of heavenly light and knowledge, but by surpassing the utmost capacity of men to know. Humanity can comprehend in part, but that is all that man can bear. The love of Christ passes knowledge. The mystery of redemption will continue to be the mystery, the unexhausted science and everlasting song of eternity. Well may humanity exclaim, Who can know God? We may, as did Elijah, wrap our mantles about us, and listen to hear the still, small voice of God." —*Bible Echo*, April 30, 1894, p. 133.

"Laying aside His royal robe and kingly crown, Christ clothed His divinity with humanity, that human beings might be raised from their degradation, and placed on vantage ground. Christ could not have come to this earth with the glory that He had in the heavenly courts. Sinful human beings could not have borne the sight. He veiled His divinity with the garb of humanity, but He did not part with His divinity. A divine-human Saviour, He came to stand at the head of the fallen race, to share in their experience from childhood to manhood. That human beings might be partakers of the divine nature, He came to this earth, and lived a life of perfect obedience." —*Review and Herald*, June 15, 1905, p. 8.

"Jesus could give alone security to God; for He was equal with God. He alone could be a mediator between God and man; for He possessed divinity and humanity. Jesus could thus give security to both parties for the fulfillment of the prescribed conditions. As the Son of God He gives security to God in our behalf, and as the eternal Word, as One equal with the Father, He assures us of the Father's love to usward who believe His pledged word. When God would assure us of His immutable counsel of peace, He gives His only begotten Son to become one of the human family, forever to retain His human nature as a pledge that God will fulfil His word." —*Ibid.*, April 3, 1894, p. 210.

"But while God's Word speaks of the humanity of Christ when upon this earth, it also speaks decidedly regarding His pre-existence. The Word existed as a divine being, even as the eternal Son of God, in union and oneness with His Father. From everlasting He was the Mediator of the covenant, the One in whom all nations of the earth, both Jews and Gentiles, if they accepted Him, were to be blessed. 'The Word was with God, and the Word was God.' Before men or angels were created, the Word was with God, and was God.

"The world was made by Him, 'and without Him was not any thing made that was made.' If Christ made all things, He existed before all things. The words spoken in regard to this are so decisive that no one need be left in doubt. Christ was God essentially, and in the highest sense. He was with God from all eternity, God over all, blessed forevermore.

"The Lord Jesus Christ, the divine Son of God, existed from eternity, a distinct person, yet one with the Father. He was the surpassing glory of heaven. He was the commander of the heavenly intelligences, and the adoring homage of the angels was received by Him as His right. This was no robbery of God....

"There are light and glory in the truth that Christ was one with the Father before the foundation of the world was laid. This is the light shining in a dark place, making it resplendent with divine, original glory. This truth, infinitely mysterious in itself, explains other mysterious and otherwise unexplainable truths, while it is enshrined in light, unapproachable and incomprehensible." —*Ibid.*, April 5, 1906, p. 8.

"Wondrous combination of man and God! He might have helped His human nature to withstand the inroads of disease by pouring from His divine nature vitality and undecaying vigor to the human. But He humbled Himself to man's nature. He did this that the Scripture might be fulfilled; and the plan was entered into. by the Son of God, knowing all the steps in His humiliation, that He must descend to make an expiation for the sins of a condemned, groaning world. What humility was this! It amazed angels. The tongue can never describe it; the imagination can not take it in. The eternal Word consented to be made flesh! God became man! It was a wonderful humility." —*Ibid.*, Sept. 4, 1900, pp. 561, 562.

"Jesus Christ 'counted it not a thing to be grasped to be equal with God.' Because divinity alone could be efficacious in the restoration of man from the poisonous bruise of the serpent, God Himself, in His only begotten, assumed human nature, and in the weakness of human nature sustained the character of God, vindicated His holy law in every particular, and accepted the sentence of wrath and death for the sons of men. What a thought is this!

"In Him was life; and the life was the light of men. It is not physical life that is here specified, but immortality, the life which is exclusively the property of God. The Word, who was with God, and who was God, had this life. Physical life is something which each individual receives. It is not eternal or immortal; for God, the life giver, takes it again. Man has no control over his life. But the life of Christ was unborrowed. No one can take this life from Him. 'I lay it down of myself,' He said. In Him was life, original, unborrowed, underived. This life is not inherent in man. He can possess it only through Christ. He can not earn it; it is given him as a free gift if he will believe in Jesus as his personal Saviour. 'This is life eternal, that they might know Thee, the only true God, and Jesus Christ whom Thou has sent.' This is the open fountain of life for the world." —*Signs of the Times*, April 8, 1897, p. 214.

" 'Before Abraham was, I am.' Christ is the pre-existent, self-existent Son of God. The message He gave to Moses to give to the children of Israel was, 'Thus shalt thou say unto the children of Israel, I AM hath sent me unto you.'

"The prophet Micah writes of Him: 'But thou, Bethlehem Ephratah, though thou be little among the thousands of Judah, yet out of thee shall He come forth unto me that is to be ruler in Israel; whose goings forth have been from of old, from everlasting.' Micah 5:2.

"Through Solomon Christ declared: 'The Lord possessed me in the beginning of His way, before His works of old. I was set up from everlasting, from the beginning, or ever the earth was. When there were no depths, I was brought forth; when there were no fountains abounding with water. Before the mountains were settled, before the hills was I brought forth....When He gave to the sea His decree, that the waters should not pass His commandment: when He appointed the foundations of the earth: then I was by Him, as one brought up with Him: and 1 was daily His delight, rejoicing always before Him.' Prov. 8:22–25, 29, 30.

"In speaking of His pre-existence, Christ carries the mind back through dateless ages. He assures that there never was a time when He was not in close fellowship with the eternal God. He to whose voice the Jews were then listening had been with God as one brought up with Him." —*Ibid.*, Aug. 29, 1900, pp. 2, 3.

"The apostle would call our attention from ourselves to the Author of our salvation. He presents before us His two natures, divine and human. Here is the description of the divine: 'Who, being in the form of God, thought it not robbery to be equal with God.' He was 'the brightness of His glory, and the express image of His person.'

"Now, of the human: 'He was made in the likeness of man: and being found in fashion as a man, He humbled Himself, and became obedient unto death.' He voluntarily assumed human nature. It was His own act, and by His own consent. He clothed His divinity with humanity. He was all the while as God, but He did not appear as God. He veiled the demonstrations of Deity which had commanded the homage, and called forth the admiration, of the universe of God. He was God while upon earth, but He divested Himself of the form of God, and in its stead took the form and fashion of a man. He walked the earth as a man. For our sakes He became poor, that we through His poverty might be made rich. He laid aside His glory and His majesty. He was God, but the glories of the form of God He for a while relinquished. Though He walked among men in poverty, scattering His blessings wherever He went, at His word legions of angels would surround their Redeemer, and do Him homage. But He walked the earth unrecognized, unconfessed, with but few exceptions, by His creatures. The atmosphere was polluted with sin and curses, in place of the anthem of praise. His lot was poverty and humiliation. As he passed to and fro upon His mission of mercy to relieve the sick, to lift up the depressed, scarce a solitary voice called Him blessed, and the very greatest of the nation passed Him by with disdain.

"Contrast this with the riches of glory, the wealth of praise pouring forth from immortal tongues, the millions of rich voices in the universe of God in anthems of adoration. But He humbled Himself, and took mortality upon Him. As a member of the human family He was mortal, but as a God He was the fountain of life to the world. He could, in His divine person, ever have withstood the advances of death, and refused to come under its dominion; but He voluntarily laid down His life, that in so doing He might give life and bring immortality to light. He bore the sins of the world, and endured the penalty which rolled like a mountain upon His divine soul. He yielded up His life a sacrifice, that man should not eternally die. He died, not through being compelled to die, but by His own free will. This was humility. The whole treasure of heaven was poured out in one gift to save fallen man. He brought into His human nature all the life-giving energies that human beings will need and must receive." —*Review and Herald,* July 5, 1887, p. 417.

"But although Christ's divine glory was for a time vailed and eclipsed by His assuming humanity, yet He did not cease to be God when He became man. The human did not take the place of the divine, nor the divine of the human. This is the mystery of godliness. The two expressions human and divine were, in Christ, closely and inseparably one, and yet they had a distinct individuality. Though Christ humbled Himself to become man, the Godhead was still His own. His Deity could not be lost while He stood faithful and true to His loyalty. Surrounded with sorrow, suffering, and moral pollution, despised and rejected by the people to whom had been intrusted the oracles of heaven, Jesus could yet speak of Himself as the Son of man in heaven. He was ready to take once more His divine glory when His work on earth was done." —*Signs of the Times*, May 10, 1899, p. 306.

"In contemplating the incarnation of Christ in humanity, we stand baffled before an unfathomable mystery, that the human mind cannot comprehend. The more we reflect upon it, the more amazing does it appear. How wide is the contrast between the divinity of Christ and the helpless infant in Bethlehem's manger! How can we span the distance between the mighty God and a helpless child? And yet the Creator of worlds, He in whom was the fullness of the Godhead bodily, was manifest in the helpless babe in the manger. Far higher than any of the angels, equal with the Father in dignity and glory, and yet wearing the garb of humanity! Divinity and humanity were mysteriously combined, and man and God became one. It is in this union that we find the hope of our fallen race. Looking upon Christ in humanity, we look upon God, and see in Him the brightness of His glory, the express image of His person." —*Ibid.*, July 30, 1896, p. 5.

"As legislator, Jesus exercised the authority of God; His commands and decisions were supported by the sovereignty of the eternal throne. The glory of the Father was revealed in the Son; Christ made manifest the character of the Father. He was so perfectly connected with God, so completely embraced in His encircling light, that He who had seen the Son, had seen the Father. His voice was as the voice of God." —*Review and Herald*, Jan. 7, 1890, p. 1.

"In Christ, divinity and humanity were combined. Divinity was not degraded to humanity; divinity held its place, but humanity by being united to divinity, withstood the fiercest test of temptation in the wilderness." —*Ibid.*, Feb. 18, 1890, p. 97.

The Right and Cost of Free Moral Agency

The author's use of the words "became him" and "behoved" in verses 10 and 17 raises the question of man's free agency. That God has given man the right to think, is evident from the author's own use of this right. The importance of the subject becomes apparent as we consider that were it not for the right of freedom of thought and choice, there could be no sin and no need of a Saviour, and the death of Christ would never have taken place. The question might rightly be raised if the right to think and determine one's actions is worth the cost. God answers this question in the affirmative in having given these rights to man.

It is evident that in the creation of intelligent beings God created serious problems for Himself, problems that arose simply because God decided to create. Creation was not a necessity laid upon God. He created because He wanted to create. This being so, God must necessarily accept the consequences of His action, foresee them, and prepare for them. He cannot be taken by surprise, or He would not be God. To emphasize: God need not create, but if He does create He must foreknow and prepare for all eventualities. This necessity is laid upon Him and He accepts the responsibility. Though He is not responsible for sin, He must in creation so adjust matters that it will be met and conquered. And as sin primarily is not a physical phenomenon but a mental attitude, it is with minds He must deal, minds that He Himself has created, and to which He has given free moral agency.

In the right to think, lies God's problem, if so it may be called. God, having given men this right, cannot abridge that right without calling in question His own integrity. Should He in any way attempt to force men's thinking, He would in that act deny Himself. He must at all cost respect the right that He has given man. It is His most precious gift to mankind, in fact, the one thing that raises men above the brute creation. Take that right away, abridge it in any way, and men cease to be men.

This right to think has had serious consequences to man, but more so to God. In the exercise of that right, religions and philosophies have been permitted to arise and flourish, diametrically opposed to all that God stands for. Governments have been established that are contrary to God's order, but which He nevertheless recognizes, because of the basic right to think which He has given man. It is upon this premise that Paul can say that "the powers that be are ordained of God." Rom. 13: 1. A case in point is the Roman government in the time of Paul. It was oppressive and not in any sense Godlike. But God, having given men the right to think, respects that right and also their right to act upon it.

This presents a real problem. If God's nature does not permit Him to direct men's thinking by force, His only recourse is to attempt to change their minds by persuasion and argument. This compels Him to use arguments that will appeal to the reason which He has given men. Only thus can His cause prosper.

That God appeals to men's reason is forcibly stated in the words of Paul: "I speak as to wise men; judge ye what I say." 1 Cor. 10:15. God was so sure of His case that He could have Paul say, "I will leave the decision with you. I have presented the case. You be the judge." In these words Paul recognized men's right to think for themselves. Through Paul, God appealed to men's judgment, their intellect. He felt His argument so conclusive that He could safely leave the decision to them.

When false philosophies, perverted thinking, and erroneous theories invade men's minds and determine their action, God's only recourse is to set before them the truth. If men will not hear, God lets them experiment with their theories, to demonstrate how they work. In such experiments men and governments are now engaged. Through trial and error God would have men come to the conclusion that the golden rule cannot be improved upon, and that God's plan is not only a good plan but the only one that will work. When a sufficient number have so decided, God will set up a kingdom that will never perish. This kingdom will be established on the right of men to think and make their own decisions. God in the beginning founded such a kingdom, but because of sin it has been delayed some thousands of years.

We are wont to think of the tremendous cost this has been to men; and it must be admitted that the cost has been enormous. We believe, however, that God counted the cost before He created, and that He decided that the right to think, the right of free moral agency, was worth the cost. Before questioning the justice of this decision, let us consider its cost to God, for one cannot arrive at a just estimate of the value of free moral agency until the entire cost is taken into consideration.

What has been the cost to God of giving men freedom to think and act? As Paul might say, Much in every way.

The incarnation was a foreseen result of creation. As God foresaw and foreknew the coming of sin, so He also knew that there was but one way to restore man. And that was the way of the cross. Sin meant suffering and death even to the Godhead. Was creation, was free moral agency, worth such a price?

Sin started with Lucifer, an exalted angel. According to the Bible, he was a cherub, anointed to this position by God Himself. (Eze. 28:14.) The expression "Thou art the anointed cherub" seems to indicate that he was the only one so anointed, or perhaps the highest of the anointed ones. Were this not the case, the expression would be, "Thou art an anointed cherub." We therefore believe that he was an exalted angel, perhaps the highest of created beings.

Under the symbol of the king of Tyre, Lucifer is said to have been "wiser than Daniel." Though he was created perfect, his "heart was lifted up" and he became proud. He came at last to the place where he said, "I am God." (Eze. 28:3, 17, 9.) He was cast out of heaven because of his pride and usurpation of power after he had attempted by war to gain the coveted position. "There was war in heaven: Michael and his angels fought against the dragon; and the dragon fought and his angels, and prevailed not; neither was their place found any more in heaven. And the great dragon was cast out, that old serpent, called the Devil, and Satan, which deceiveth the whole world: he was cast out into the earth, and his angels were cast out with him."

Isaiah adds this information concerning Lucifer's revolt: "How art thou fallen from heaven, O Lucifer, son of the morning! how art thou cut down to the ground, which didst weaken the nations! For thou hast said in thine heart, I will ascend into heaven, I will exalt my throne above the stars of God: I will sit also upon the mount of the congregation, in the sides of the north: I will ascend above the heights of the clouds; I will be like the most High." Isa. 14:12–14.

This leaves no question as to Lucifer's intention. He would rule "the stars of God," the angels. He would be "like the most High." He would sit "in the sides of the north," God's dwelling place. The climax was his proclamation, "I am God." Eze. 28:9.

Although we are not in possession of the details that led to Lucifer's open rebellion against God, some things are clear.

The war in heaven, according to the record in the twelfth chapter of the book of Revelation, was closely connected with Christ's work as Redeemer. The birth of Jesus is there recorded, as also the attempt of the adversary "to devour her child as soon as it was born." Verse 4. But the "child was caught up unto God, and to his throne." Verse 5. The phrase "and to his throne" is significant. When Christ ascended to heaven, He "sat down on the right hand of the Majesty on high." Heb. 1:3. But this is exactly the place Lucifer planned to occupy. He wanted to be "a god," "like the most High." (Eze. 28:2; Isa. 14:14.) And now Christ occupied that place, and Lucifer was cast down.

The controversy between Christ and Lucifer began in heaven before the creation of this world. When Adam and Eve were in the garden, Lucifer had already become Satan, and appeared in the guise of a serpent to tempt them. We do not know how long before the creation of this earth

Lucifer fell, but as rebellion takes time to ripen into revolt, it must have been some time before. In any event, Satan's plan was fully developed before man's fall. That his hatred and rebellion were directed against Christ is evident from God's statement that the seed of the woman "shall bruise thy head, and thou shalt bruise his heel." Gen. 3:15. By this we know that the controversy was between Christ and Satan, and that it began before the creation of this world.

The controversy, with the eventual incarnation of Christ and His ensuing death, could have been avoided by the simple expedient of not creating; or if there must be creation, of creating beings not possessed of moral attributes or endowed with freedom of thought and free moral agency. But for reasons best known to Himself, God proceeded with creation, well knowing what it would cost Him.

There were other considerations involved in creation; among them, and perhaps chiefly, the question of God's right to govern and lay moral obligations on His creatures. How had God acquired such powers, and what right had He to enforce obedience? Satan claimed He had simply taken these powers to Himself. According to him, God happened to be first on the scene, and as there was no one to dispute Him, had proclaimed Himself God. Now He refused to share with others, and when Lucifer decided to be God also, an attempt was made to cast him out of heaven. God was arbitrary, and did not consider Himself subject to the laws that He had laid on others.

The following are quotations from the writings of Mrs. E. G. White:

Satan "tried to falsify the word of God, and pervert His plan of government before the angels. He claimed that God was not just in laying rules and laws upon the inhabitants of heaven. He represented that God was not self-denying, and that Christ was not self-denying; why, then, should the angels be required to be self -denying?" —*Review and Herald*, March 9, 1886, p. 145.

"In heaven he complained against the law of God, declaring it unnecessary and arbitrary. He misrepresented the Lord Jehovah, and the high Commander of heaven. He claimed that he was above law, and maintained that right was upon his side; but he has fully made manifest that the principles he advocated were evil and injurious." —*Ibid.*, April 25, 1893, p. 257.

"Satan had accused God of requiring self-denial of the angels, when He knew nothing of what it meant himself, and when He would not Himself make any self-sacrifice for others. This was the accusation that Satan made against God in heaven; and after the evil one was expelled from heaven, he continually charged the Lord with exacting service which He would not render Himself. Christ came to the world to meet these false accusations, and to reveal the Father." —*Ibid.*, Feb. 18, 1890, p. 97.

"To dispute the supremacy of the Son of God, thus impeaching the wisdom and love of the Creator, had become the purpose of this prince of angels." —*Patriarchs and Prophets*, p. 36.

"Lucifer in heaven desired to be first in power and authority; he wanted to be God, to have the rulership of heaven." —*Review and Herald*, Jan. 16, 1913, p., 52.

"He [Satan] carried the matter to God, declaring that it was the sentiment of many of the heavenly beings that he should have the preference to Christ." —*Ibid.*, Feb. 4, 1909, p. 8.

"Satan claimed to be able to present laws which were better than God's statutes and judgments."—*Ibid.*, June 17, 1890, p. 370.

It would have been embarrassing for God to meet these charges if He had not already—long before—provided for their answer. God, knowing the end from the beginning, created the universe with redemption in mind. He knew that when He created thinking beings they would inquire into the reason for things, and that every act of His would need to be justified before men. As men are judged by their character as shown by their acts, so in turn God's creatures would judge their Creator. The ideas of right and justice which He had instilled in men would be the standard of their judgment of God. And by that judgment He would have to abide. How now, would God meet Satan's charges, or better, how had God already—in fact, from eternity—had the answer ready? For we hold it unworthy of God to make any adjustment in His plan because of charges made against Him. These charges must have been foreseen and provided for. To wait until circumstances and charges demanded a change would be unlike God.

And so we find a plan of God, kept in silence from times eternal, which in due time was revealed to man. (Col. 1:26.) This plan met all possible charges and revealed God as One who would never ask His creatures to do anything or take any place that He Himself was not willing to do or take. This plan, as already noted, included the incarnation—not merely a temporary incarnation which, while it would demonstrate God's willingness to suffer, would not permanently affect God—but an incarnation that was permanent, and that would ever remain a proof of God's willingness to share all that He has or is.

Satan's claim to equality with God, to be God, involved the charge that God had usurped authority that was not His, and that having once attained power He was unwilling that anyone else should share with Him. He indeed had power, but it was usurped power, Satan claimed, and He did not reign by the consent of the governed. If any should decide, "We will not have this man to reign over us" (Luke 19:14), God would put down the rebellion by force and continue to rule. His word and His practice did not agree.

God, as before stated, foresaw all this. He therefore—from eternity—had developed a plan that would make it possible for Him to become one with us, humble Himself to become man, and be subject to all that men are subject to. If men should then become so impressed with His worth that they of themselves would choose Him as their ruler, He would rule by the consent of the governed.

If, further, He should decide to share the throne with His creatures, make them heirs of God and joint heirs with

Christ, have them sit down with Him on His throne as Christ was sat down with the Father on His throne—then in a very real sense He would not rule *over* but *with* His people, and all would be priests and kings.

God, having all this in mind and every step arranged for, was not in the least disturbed by Satan's charges. Nor did He hasten to meet Satan's challenge. At the set time the incarnation would take place, not before. Satan used the intervening four thousand years to taunt God and make men believe that God had no intention of giving up any part of His power. But his assertions and claims only served to emphasize God's predetermined counsel when the time at last came to act. To Paul, and in a smaller degree to others of the apostles, God made known His plan, which had been hid from ages and generations. (Eph. 3:1–3.) This plan effectively met every one of Satan's charges and showed them all groundless. God stood justified.

All this "became" God. (Heb. 2:10.) It was befitting of Him so to arrange matters that His creatures would not only be satisfied with the existence He had given them, but be inexpressibly thankful for the privilege of life. His intent is that their life shall measure with His and be a happy and satisfying one. "In thy presence is fulness of joy; at thy right hand there are pleasures for evermore." Ps. 16:11.

It not only "became" God to do what He has done and is doing for man, but it "behoved" Christ to be made in all things like His brethren. And so Christ came to this world, ruled as it was by Satan, put Himself voluntarily under His dominion, and not only demonstrated that under the most cruel and forbidding circumstances men could be true to God, but also gave Satan an opportunity to demonstrate what he would do if he had the chance. What would Satan do? He would take the Son of God, revile Him, spit on Him, scourge Him, put a crown of thorns on Him, nail Him to a tree, and there let Him die, though He had done no evil, nor was there any malice in Him.

In this demonstration Satan's real character was revealed; just as in the incarnation was also revealed what God would do for man—live for him, die for him, love and care for him, forgive him his sins and trespasses, and at last give him a place with Him on the throne. He demonstrated that there was nothing He would not do for men; that there was no place too lowly for Himself; that He was willing to share, to give, to suffer. He held it not a thing to be grasped to be God. He was willing to give up all and take His place with men.

Far from being impious to think God's thoughts after Him, it is a blessed privilege that God has given men minds that can, at least to some small degree, fathom and appreciate what God is doing. We should be thankful that God not only permits but urges us to think. The cost of this privilege, to God, has been beyond our capacity to fully comprehend. But God, having given us this right, believes it is worth the cost.

In view of the cost to God, the cost to man of freedom of choice is infinitesimal. In fact, viewed in the light of eternity, the cost is only gain. Paul expressed it in these words: "For I reckon that the sufferings of this present time are not worthy to be compared with the glory which shall be revealed in us." Rom. 8:18.

CHAPTER 3

OF THE BOOK OF HEBREWS

Christian and Moses

SYNOPSIS OF CHAPTER

THE THIRD chapter divides naturally into two parts, verses 1 to 6 and 7 to 19. The first section compares and contrasts Christ and Moses; the second begins the discussion of Israel in the wilderness which subject is continued in the fourth chapter.

Moses held a place of high esteem with Israel. He had given them the law that came to be known as the law of Moses. He had been in the mount with God, and had interceded for the people. He had built the sanctuary, and to him God had spoken face to face. The rabbis taught that the soul of Moses was equivalent to all the souls, of Israel. They also thought it significant that the title *Moses, our Rabbi*, had the numerical value in Hebrew of 613, which is the same as the numerical value of the letters in *Lord God of Israel*.

The latter part of the chapter discusses Moses and Israel. Moses led Israel out of Egypt into the wilderness, where they wandered forty years. He never brought them into the Promised Land for which they started. That, however, was the fault of the people.They murmured and complained, and failed to enter because of unbelief.

Hebrews 3:1–6. "Wherefore, holy brethren, partakers of the heavenly calling, consider the Apostle and High Priest of our profession, Christ Jesus; who was faithful to him that appointed him, as also Moses was faithful in all his house. For this man was counted worthy of more glory than Moses inasmuch as he who hath builded the house hath more honour than the house. For every house is builded by some man; but he that built all things is God. And Moses verily was faithful in all his house as a servant, for a testimony of those things which were to be spoken after; but Christ as a son over his own house; whose house are we, if we hold fast the confidence and the rejoicing of the hope firm unto the end."

These verses contrast and compare the work of Christ with that of Moses. In doing so, the apostle does not speak slightingly of Moses, but commends him for his faithfulness. Both Christ and Moses built a house, and both were faithful in their work. Christ, however, was the greater of the two, for He was the Son in the house while Moses was servant. As the author has previously shown Christ to be better than the angels, so he now shows Him to be greater than Moses.

Verse 1. "Consider the Apostle and High Priest." *Jesus* is the earthly name of the Saviour, and when used in the New Testament, generally refers to His incarnate state. Christ, or the Messiah, refers to His divine nature. Jesus represents Him as the Son of *man*; Christ as the Son of *God*. When the two names are used together as in verse 1 of chapter 3, reference is to the God-man, our Saviour and Lord, Christ Jesus.

In this verse we are admonished to consider Him specifically in His positions as apostle and high priest. An apostle is one who is sent. This is the only place where Christ is called by that name, though in many places He is spoken of as being sent. (John 5:24; 6:44; 17:3.)

Verse 2. "Faithful...as also Moses was." The author presents Christ as the antitype of Moses, comparing and contrasting Him with the great leader of Israel. Though Moses was neither an apostle nor a high priest in the strict sense, yet he served as both. He was called of God to do his work. He was God's messenger with a divine commission, chosen by God Himself as verily as ever an apostle was. He built the tabernacle; he instituted the sanctuary service and instructed Aaron; he offered the first sacrifices, and superintended Aaron's work. He was in this sense. a high priest, and more.

The stress in this verse is on the faithfulness of both Moses and Christ "to him that appointed" them. The record of Christ's life emphasizes this point. At no time did Christ do His own will or speak His own words. "I seek not mine own will, but the will of the Father which hath sent me." John 5:30. "The word which ye hear is not mine, but the Father's which sent me." John 14:24. His very name is "the faithful and true witness." Rev. 3:14.

So also was Moses faithful in the work given him to do. He was "faithful in all mine house," that is, God's house. (Num. 12:7.) In building this house God Himself furnished the pattern, and told Moses, "Look that thou make them after their pattern, which was shewed thee in the mount." Ex. 25:40. The record reads: "According to all that the Lord commanded Moses, so the children of Israel made all the work.

And Moses did look upon all the work, and behold, they had done it as the Lord had commanded, even so had they done it: and Moses blessed them." Ex. 39:42, 43.

In like manner Christ could say, "The works which the Father hath given me to finish, the same works that I do, bear witness of me, that the Father hath sent me." John 5:36. "The Son can do nothing of himself, but what he seeth the Father do: for what things soever he doeth, these also doeth the Son likewise." John 5:19. And when His work was done, He announced, "I have finished the work which thou gavest me to do." John 17:4. Thus Moses and Christ were both faithful in their respective spheres.

Verse 3. "More glory." Christ has more glory than Moses, inasmuch as the builder is greater than the house. It is patent, of course, that however glorious a house may be, the one who produced it is greater.

The author here considers Christ a builder, and Moses the house, a figure which he later modifies.

Verse 4. "He that built all things is God." The church is the house of God, and as such Moses was part of the house. Christ is the builder of this house, and as He that built all things is God, this is an indirect pronouncement that Christ is God.

Verse 5. "Moses...servant." The figure is here changed, in that Moses is no longer the house but a servant in the house. As such he was faithful, as the record bears out.

"A testimony." Moses' building of the house was a testimony of the things that were to be spoken after; that is, it was symbolic of the true tabernacle and the true service of which Christ was to be minister. Moses himself acknowledged that One should come like unto him, when he announced, "The Lord thy God will raise up unto thee a Prophet from the midst of thee, of thy brethren, like unto me; unto him ye shall hearken." Deut. 18:15.

Verse 6. "Christ...Son." Christ is Son over His house, whose house are we, but only if we "hold fast the confidence and the rejoicing of the hope firm unto the end." The word here used means more than confidence. It is confidence bordering on boldness; not boldness in the sense of undue forwardness, but a holy boldness grounded in confidence.

No child is overawed by the fact that his father holds high office, if right relations exist between father and son. We find the child of a king approaching his father with boldness and without fear, holding his hand or climbing upon his knees while officials bow deeply and show great deference to the king.

God wants us to approach Him in confidence, and not in slavish fear; and He holds this confidence in such high esteem that He considers it a sign of sonship. If we are indeed children and not servants, we will show a holy boldness.

Of this Paul says in Romans: "For as many as are led by the Spirit of God, they are the sons of God. For ye have not received the spirit of bondage again to fear; but ye have received the Spirit of adoption, whereby we cry, Abba, Father. The Spirit itself beareth witness with our spirit, that we are the children of God: and if children, then heirs; heirs of God, and joint-heirs with Christ; if so be that we suffer with him, that we may be also glorified together." Rom. 8:14–17.

In Galatians he presents the same subject: "Wherefore thou art no more a servant, but a son; and if a son, then an heir of God through Christ." Gal. 4:7.

Paul here decries the servant spirit, the spirit of bondage. It is not this spirit we have received, he says, but the spirit of adoption—which in Galatians is called "the Spirit of his Son"—"whereby we cry, Abba, Father." "Abba" is the Aramaic for father, expressing in a peculiar sense and in a high degree the love and confidence of the child in his parent. It is used from childhood as an endearing term. It is noteworthy that Christ used it in the dark hour of the garden when He said, "Abba, Father, all things are possible unto thee; take away this cup from me: nevertheless, not what I will, but what thou wilt." Mark 14:36.

Some Christians exhibit too much of the servant spirit and have a pronounced inferiority complex that they confuse with humility. Christ was meek and humble of heart, but there was no affected humility in Him, none of the servant spirit. See Him that night when "he riseth from supper, and laid aside his garments; and took a towel, and girded himself. After that he poureth water into a bason, and began to wash the disciples' feet, and to wipe them with the towel wherewith he was girded." John 13:4, 5. Never was He greater than when on this occasion He stooped to serve. He knew who He was and whence He came. He knew "that the Father had given all things into his hands, and that he was come from God, and went to God." John 13:3. And it was in the consciousness of His greatness that He rose to serve. Behold the One to whom all power in heaven and earth had been given, who knew that He came from God and went to God. See Him kneel to serve, not in the spirit of servitude or with a feeling of inferiority. No, with all the graciousness of heaven, with all the majesty of His presence, He kneels, not to receive a favor, but to bestow one. What wonderful condescension, what surpassing humility, what impressive dignity! He served, but not in the spirit of servility.

The story is told of two clergymen, a Christian pastor and a Jewish rabbi, who, on the way to an interview with the President of the United States, discussed how they should approach him. The rabbi suggested that he would like to do what Jacob did of old when he appeared before Pharaoh and blessed him. This was agreed to, and when the two men appeared before the President, instead of the usual introductory ceremony, the rabbi lifted his hands in blessing, saying, "The God of Abraham, Isaac, and Jacob bless and keep thee." The President rose, and with bowed head received the blessing. The whole atmosphere was immediately changed. The two men had come to ask a favor. Now they bestowed one.

Christians are children of the Most High God. They have a right to stand in their God-given dignity as ambassadors of the King of heaven. Although they are to be meek and humble, they are not to be servile. They need not hide their identity. They are not to be ashamed of their faith. They are children of the great King, and are to exhibit a quiet, confident spirit, the mark of the true child of God.

Later on in the book of Hebrews we are exhorted with "boldness to enter into the holiest by the blood of Jesus," something the high priest on earth could never do. Heb. 10:19. Again, we are urged to come "boldly unto the throne of grace," and in the last book of the Bible, those "that do his commandments" have a "right to the tree of life, and may enter in through the gates into the city." Heb. 4:16; Rev. 22:14. For such the gates are not merely opened a little bit, gates ajar, as we sing. No, they are swung wide open. "Open ye the gates, that the righteous nation which keepeth the truth may enter in." Isa. 26:2. They have a right to the tree of life. They belong in the kingdom. They enter with boldness.

Sonship, however, is to be distinguished by more than boldness. We are to hold not only "the *hope* firm," but "the *rejoicing* of the hope firm unto the end." God is not satisfied with having His children sorrow and bowed down as a bulrush. That is a reflection on Him, as it is a reflection on an earthly father to have his children habitually unhappy and downcast. We give false testimony about God when we are gloomy and despondent. God wants us to be cheerful, and not by our demeanor to give a wrong impression of God. This is one of the signs that should distinguish the heir from the servant.

Hebrews 3:7–19. "Wherefore (as the Holy Ghost saith, Today if ye will hear his voice, harden not your hearts, as in the provocation, in the day of temptation in the wilderness: when your fathers tempted me, proved me, and saw my works forty years. Wherefore I was grieved with that generation, and said, They do alway err in their heart; and they have not known my ways. So I sware in my wrath, They shall not enter into my rest.)

"Take heed, brethren, lest there be in any of you an evil heart of unbelief, in departing from the living God. But exhort one another daily, while it is called To day; lest any of you be hardened through the deceitfulness of sin. For we are made partakers of Christ, if we hold the beginning of our confidence stedfast unto the end; while it is said, To day if ye will hear his voice, harden not your hearts, as in the provocation. For some, when they had heard, did provoke: howbeit not all that came out of Egypt by Moses. But with whom was he grieved forty years? was it not with them that had sinned, whose carcases fell in the wilderness? And to whom sware he that they should not enter into his rest, but to them that believed not? So we see that they could not enter in because of unbelief."

This section deals with Israel's wanderings in the wilderness. It recounts Israel's failure to enter God's rest, and points out the reasons for this failure.

The apostle has two purposes in mind in recounting the wilderness experience, both of which are important.

The first is to show the superiority of Jesus over Moses and Joshua. Neither Moses nor Joshua brought Israel into the rest that God had planned for them. Moses himself did not enter Canaan but died on the border; so he did not lead Israel in; and though Joshua brought them into the land, he did not bring them into the rest. That which neither Moses nor Joshua could do, Christ has done and is doing. This argument is in line with the general purpose of the author to show Christ's superiority over all others.

The fact that Israel did not enter the land because of unbelief furnishes the apostle an opportunity to admonish his readers not to fail as did Israel. A leader has now appeared who will bring them into the true rest of God. They must not fail to follow Him, and thus make their calling and election sure. This is his second purpose.

Verse 7. "The Holy Ghost saith." This quotation is taken from Psalms 95:7–11. While we attribute the psalms to David, Inspiration attributes them to the Holy Spirit. This should give added weight to the words.

"To day," as it is used here and in the following chapter, is the today of God's call, the day of salvation; it is *this* day, *any* day, *every* day, on which the call sounds. In Israel's day it was today; in Christ's day it was today; in our day it is today. It is the ever-present today. The day did not close in the wilderness, though many died there because they did not heed the call. It did not close in Christ's day, though many rejected Him. It has not closed today, though the last call of mercy is about to sound. It is still *today* for those who will hear and heed.

Verse 8. "Harden not your hearts." The first time Israel murmured against Moses and provoked God, was at Marah, three days after they had crossed the Red Sea. (Ex. 15:23–26.) When they arrived thirsty at this place, they could not drink the water, for it was bitter. God showed Moses a tree and told him to cast it into the water; and immediately after he had done this the water became sweet.

The statement, "There he proved them"! (verse 25), indicates that God purposely brought them to the bitter water to test them. He wanted to strengthen them for the trying days ahead, in which they would need faith in God; and so He permitted them to be deprived of water that they might learn to trust Him. He had just saved them from Pharaoh's army, and had parted the Red Sea for them. When they came to the bitter water, God would have been pleased to have them say, "The God who caused us to pass dryshod through the Red Sea, who slew Pharaoh's army, will not permit us to die of thirst. Let us wait and be patient. God is testing us. He will send us water when He sees best."

Instead of showing faith, they murmured against Moses and Aaron. They had not learned to trust God. They had little or no faith. God could not use them as His instruments when they revealed such lack of confidence in Him. Must God show them still more miracles before they would believe Him?

A little later when they lacked food, God rained manna from heaven for them. They were told to gather "a certain rate every day, *that I may prove them*, whether they will walk in my law, or no." Ex. 16:4. Thus God again tested them; but they did not stand the test.

The third test came when Israel "pitched in Rephidim: and there was no water for the people to drink." Ex. 17:1. By this time they should have known that God was testing them. But they cried for water, raising the old complaint against Moses: "Wherefore is this that thou hast brought us up out of Egypt, to kill us and our children and our cattle with thirst?" Verse 3. So God gave them water by having Moses smite the rock. (Verses 5, 6.)

It is this last experience to which Hebrews refers in the text before us. God did not rebuke them the first and the second time, but the third time when "they tempted Jehovah, saying, Is Jehovah among us, or not?" they went too far. Ex. 17:7, A.R.V. God was provoked, and Hebrews calls it "the provocation." (Heb. 3:8.) God had done much for them, but they had not learned their lesson.

Verse 9. "Your fathers tempted me...forty years." At the close of their wilderness wanderings, nearly forty years after the experiences mentioned above, Israel came into the wilderness of Zin, and again lacked water. It would seem after this long time they should have learned to trust God; but instead, they cried as before, "Why have ye brought up the congregation of the Lord into this wilderness, that we and our cattle should die there?" Num. 20:4. And so God gave them water. Once more they had failed to stand the test. "This is the water of Meribah; because the children of Israel strove with the Lord, and he was sanctified in them." Num. 20:13.

Verse 10. "I was displeased." (A.R.V.) This is a very mild statement. God had reason to be more than displeased. For forty years they had seen His works. Every week manna had rained down from heaven. (Ex. 16:4.) Their garments had miraculously been preserved: "Your clothes are not waxen old upon you, and thy shoe is not waxen old upon thy foot." Deut. 29:5. "Neither did thy foot swell." Deut. 8:4. Despite the manna from heaven and the very personal miracle of the preservation of their garments, they had not learned their lesson. "They do alway err in their heart," said God, "and they have not known my ways."

Verse 11. "They shall not enter." God had borne with them long. He could do no more for them. They had erred, not only in act but "in their heart." And so reluctantly God sware, "They shall not enter into my rest."

"My rest." Israel's chief ambition was to enter the Promised Land. God had promised them rest from their enemies; they were tired of their wilderness wanderings, and they thought that their entrance into Canaan would solve their difficulties. Hence, and naturally, all their hopes centered in Canaan, their promised home.

But God had more in mind for them than merely entering the Promised Land. He wanted them to enter into His rest. It was an invitation comparable to that given by Christ when He said, "Come unto me, all ye that labour and are heavy laden, and I will give you rest." Matt. 11:28. To enter into the land of Canaan would never give them the rest God had in mind. *His* rest is the rest of the soul, when the burden of sin is rolled away and the man set free. It was to this rest He called Israel.

But Israel did not respond. A few, indeed, did enter by faith, but the large majority refused, and died in the wilderness. God rejected that generation; and of the thousands who at last entered Canaan, only a few entered God's rest.

Verse 12. The apostle now takes occasion to issue a warning, based on Israel's example. "Take heed," he says, "lest there be in any of you an evil heart of unbelief." An "evil heart of unbelief" was the real difficulty with Israel in the wilderness. That was the reason they did not enter into God's rest. The danger was the same in Paul's day, and it is no less real in our time. Despite the lessons of the past, we quickly lose faith when help does not come at the time and in the manner in which we think it should come. In this respect we are even less believing than they; for we have added evidence of God's might and care, such as they did not have. Our lack of faith stands in marked contrast to the faithfulness of Christ and Moses as recorded in the first part of the chapter.

Verse 13. "Exhort one another day by day." (A.R.V.) We are in need of constant reminders of God's goodness and our duty, lest we forget. We need to take advantage of every means God has provided for the building up of the church of God: stated periods of public worship, prayer and meditation, study and communion, family worship, missionary endeavor, work for the unfortunate and shut-ins, hospital and prison work, attendance at the ordinances of God's house, and any other means that will encourage others and strengthen our own faith.

"The deceitfulness of sin." Most people are aware of the allurement and fleeting pleasure of sin. It often looks attractive, and men are lured into the snare. Its deceitfulness is not always immediately apparent. Wine may be pleasant to the taste and give a sense of exhilaration and delight. But the reaction reveals its deceitfulness; and with regret man discovers the temporary loss of self-direction and sanity. Other sin may be attractive and give promise of pleasure; and the self-hypnosis may last for a while. But as a man sows, so he shall also reap; and the awakening to the reality of the harvest—ruined health, broken home, disgrace, contempt of right-thinking people, loss of friends and possessions, condemnation of conscience, loss of eternal life—comes as a terrific shock. Self-destruction seems to many the only way out—a most cowardly and selfish means of climaxing a life of sin, and bringing further disgrace and loss to loved ones. It is well that we be exhorted daily, lest we become hardened through the deceitfulness of sin.

Verse 14. "Partakers of Christ," or "with Christ." It is not in the remote future that we are to become partakers with Christ. Union with Christ here and now is a most precious experience, and the highest attainment possible for a Christian.

This verse parallels verse 6, where we are admonished to hold fast our confidence and the rejoicing of our hope firm unto the end. In this place we are told to hold fast not only our confidence but "the beginning of our confidence." As our faith, confidence, and boldness were strong in the beginning, when we were in our first love, so we are to continue steadfast. We are not to lose our first love or our first confidence.

These admonitions were written to the members of the church of Jerusalem, and have there their primary application. They had shared with others the things they had, and many had laid all their earthly possessions at the feet of the apostles. (Acts 2:44, 45; 4:32–35.) They expected Christ to come soon.

But many years had passed since then, and there was still no sign of Christ's immediate coming. He had gone to prepare a place for them. But why did He tarry? Moses was with God forty days in the mount; but Christ had been gone nearly forty years. Their faith was waning. They needed the admonition to hold on; but more than this, they needed a clear conception of Christ's work so that they would not wait in idle expectation, but intelligently co-operate with Him in His work.

Israel had not entered into God's rest though they had entered Canaan, and in Paul's day the church in Jerusalem was in the same danger. It was high time to wake up. God wanted His church to enter by faith with Christ "within the veil; whither the forerunner is for us entered, even Jesus." Heb. 6:19, 20. But few were ready to heed the call.

Verse 15. This verse is a repetition of verse 8 by way of emphasis. God is anxious that Israel shall not harden their hearts. This may be done as Pharaoh hardened his heart in final impenitence; but there are other minor hardenings, which, while they may not immediately result in the loss of the soul, nevertheless do much harm, and of which we need to beware.

It is dangerous to steel the heart against calls for help to the needy, the poor, the outcast. Some may feel that not all money collected is used wisely, and may restrict their giving. But such an attitude tends to dry up the milk of human kindness in one's own heart, and thus does definite harm.

Constant contact with sickness and suffering have a tendency to make people less sympathetic than they should be. This is a danger that threatens all, especially physicians and nurses. They know that suffering is often the result of transgression of some kind, and that the sufferer is merely reaping what he has sown. This is often true, but no Christian can afford because of this to kill or deaden the impulse of sympathy and tenderness.

Some decide that they will control themselves at all times, and under no circumstances give way to tears, nor will they exhibit any special enthusiasm or joy. Such are inhibiting themselves, and after a while become incapable of responding properly to that which normally would call for deep feeling. They are cheating themselves, and not living to the full measure of their capacity. They become dull and uninteresting as they grow older; young people do not enjoy their company, and erelong they are relegated to a quiet seat in the corner. Life has left them behind.

There are those who tend to be careless in speech, in property rights, in personal habits. We need not particularize, but small habits have a tendency to harden into permanent conduct. When God warns us not to harden our hearts, He has reference to more than the final, unforgivable sin. Let each examine himself.

Verse 16. "Some...did provoke." Of the prominent ones who entered the land, Caleb and Joshua are mentioned. (Num. 26:65.) Others, of less eminence, were Eleazar, the priest, and Phinehas, his son. (Josh. 17:4; 22:13, 31, 32; Num. 25:7.) A study of the records reveals that others of the priests also were faithful.

Verses 17, 18. "Grieved forty years." From the first to the last, Israel was consistently disobedient. Forty years God bore with them, but to little purpose. They were anxious to enter Canaan and have rest from their wilderness wanderings, but they were not willing to conform to the conditions of entering into God's rest. At last God was compelled to reject them as unfit for the kingdom.

Verse 19. "They could not enter in because of unbelief." Though God had sworn that they should not enter, it was not an arbitrary decree. They simply were not able to enter: they *could not* enter. Their unbelief made it impossible.

CHAPTER 4

OF THE BOOK OF HEBREWS

The Sabbath

SYNOPSIS OF CHAPTER

PAUL WAS anxious that Israel's experience should not be repeated by his readers. As Israel wandered forty years in the wilderness, so nearly forty years had now elapsed since Christ's ascension. The Israel of Paul's time was no more ready to enter into God's rest then than was Israel in the time of Moses. The great events that Jesus had foretold were imminent: their glorious city and the temple were about to be laid in ruins. God had waited nearly forty years for the people to adjust themselves to the new order; the new covenant had been ratified by the blood of Christ; the old had been done away with; and it was time that its symbol, the temple, should be taken away. But Israel still clung to the old ceremonies. A generation had passed since the Aaronic priesthood had become ineffective, but the Jews still adhered to it. Thus far they had not "entered in."

To the apostle the parallel between Israel at the time of the ratification of the old covenant and Israel at the time of the establishment of the new covenant was clear, and also ominous. Would Israel repeat the failure of the fathers? There was every indication that they would. But God would not let them do this without one last appeal to save them from making this fatal mistake. Paul therefore recounts to them Israel's experience, and tells them to beware lest they also should seem to come short.

Israel's failure properly to regard the Sabbath was one chief cause for their rejection by God, as is evident from a reading of the twentieth chapter of Ezekiel. This was not because of their failure to observe the day itself, but rather because of their failure to understand what the Sabbath symbolized—conversion, complete dedication to God, sanctification, rest, fellowship, holiness.

Hebrews 4:1–5. "Let us therefore fear, lest, a promise being left us of entering into his rest, any of you should seem to come short of it. For unto us was the gospel preached, as well as unto them: but the word preached did not profit them, not being mixed with faith in them that heard it. For we which have believed do enter into rest, as he said, As I have sworn in my wrath, if they shall enter into my rest: although the works were finished from the foundation of the world. For he spake in a certain place of the seventh day on this wise, And God did rest the seventh day from all his works. And in this place again, If they shall enter into my rest."

The apostle discusses God's rest that Israel failed to enter, and connects it with the seventh-day Sabbath. This New Testament reference to the Sabbath of creation and its intimate relation to holy living, makes this section a noteworthy contribution to Christian doctrine and sanctification. It is not the question of a day merely, but of a life—a life of dedication and holiness. This life Israel of old rejected, and with it also its sign of sanctification, the Sabbath. There is danger that men may do the same thing today.

Verse 1. "Promise being left." The present tense here used marks a present and continuous leaving behind, and also a present and continuous invitation and admonition to enter. The promise had continually been held out, but each generation had rejected the promise, and thus closed its probation. Paul's generation was about to do the same, but while there was still time, God would make one more attempt. The door was still open, and the promise was still left, but there was no time to lose. They were in danger of coming short of it, as had Israel of old. This God would prevent if He could.

"His rest," not rest in general, not even *the* rest, but His, God's, rest. Of this we shall hear more.

Verse 2. "The gospel," the glad tidings. This was preached to us, and it has been preached to them. The reading of this verse is interesting. It is not, "Unto *them* was the gospel preached as well as unto us," but the reverse: "Unto *us* was the gospel preached, as well as unto *them.*" Through types and ceremonies, in sacrifices and rituals, the fathers received a knowledge of the gospel.

"Did not profit them." They received little profit from the preaching, because the word was not "mixed with faith." This becomes more emphatic when we learn that the reading is not the word *preached*, but the word *heard*, or the word "of hearing": "The word of hearing [margin] did not profit them, not being mixed with faith."

This statement throws a solemn responsibility on preachers, but equally so on hearers. Success in preaching does not depend upon the speaker only. It may, indeed, not depend upon him at all. Even Christ was limited by the receptiveness of the hearers. "He did not many mighty works there because of their unbelief." Matt. 13:58. It is possible for the hearers completely to nullify the preaching. It is well to have this in mind. There are times when the pulpit is less to blame than the pew.

We are wont to throw the blame on the preacher for the meager results that preaching brings. This may be the place where the blame belongs, for there are too many mediocre preachers, men with no vital message to communicate to others, men who themselves have not been touched by the celestial flame, who preach tame, dull, lifeless discourses that weary both God and men. Doubtless there are many men today who should be preaching instead of following the plow, but there are a large number of preachers who would do more good for humanity if they would engage in some other line of work than preaching.

Although this is true, it is equally true that the responsibility for unsatisfactory results does not always rest upon the minister. And it is this phase of the question with which our text deals. It puts the blame squarely on the hearers. They did not mix faith with hearing. They heard the words, perhaps, but their faith was lacking.

Noah persuaded only seven people to go with him into the ark: That was a small result indeed for such a time. Yet few would blame Noah, though he would not long remain on the pay roll were he preaching today. We conceive that this admonition of Paul's in regard to preaching and hearing would do much good if heeded today. We most certainly need better and more efficient preachers. But we just as certainly need better hearers. It would be well for each to apply this to himself personally.

Verse 3. "We which have believed do enter." The last verse in the third chapter affirms that Israel "could not enter in because of unbelief." Here the author states that "we which have believed do enter." This shows that the rest was still open, for at the very time when Paul was writing, some were entering. *They* could not enter because of unbelief. *We* which believe *do* enter.

The rest that the believer enters is here called *the rest* in the original, not merely *rest* or *a* rest. It is unfortunate that the definite pronoun *the* is left out, for it points clearly to *His* rest in verse 1, which is God's rest. The point which the apostle makes is that the door is still open, and "we which have believed do enter," or better, *are entering.* God has not cast away His people. As proof of this the apostle says that some are now entering in. Moses did not bring Israel in. Joshua did indeed lead Israel into Canaan, but not into God's rest. God, therefore, had made call after call to each succeeding generation. Even in Paul's day His house was not yet filled. There was room for others to enter; and they did enter, they *were* entering in.

"If they shall enter." This is the same construction that in chapter 3, verse 11 is rendered "They shall not enter." It is merely an emphatic way of stating that a certain thing shall not be done; and wherever this statement is found, as here in verse 5, it should read, "They shall not enter." It is confusing to the ordinary reader to find an identical expression translated two different ways.

The thought in this part of verse 3 is therefore this: "We which have believed are entering into God's rest. But of the others who believe not, God has sworn that they shall not enter into his rest."

115

"Although the works were finished." From the very beginning of the creation of this world God had in mind to provide rest for His people. This is evident from the fact that after the six days of creation God rested and invited men to rest with Him. God did not call Adam and Eve into being merely to present to them a life of labor and continued work. Hence, the very next day after their creation, the second day of their life, He invited them to rest and spend the day with Him. They had had one day of labor; now came the day of rest. In these two days they had a complete taste of life as God intended it for them. They could now choose intelligently and evaluate God's wonderful gift of life. God had given them a sample of what He had in store for them. This was done not a thousand years after creation but as soon as "the works were finished from the foundation of the world."

Paul here uses this fact to prove that God from the very beginning had in mind to provide His creatures with fullness of life, a complete, satisfying life, a life that combined just the right proportions of labor and rest. In their wilderness wanderings during those forty years, they saw but little promise of rest. Year after year went by, and still they were on the march. In Egypt they had homes, settled abodes, where they could rear their children and live in comparative peace, even though they had to work hard. They had their fleshpots and were not dependent upon manna from heaven for their sustenance. Altogether, as they compared their present position with that in Egypt, they were clear that Egypt held many advantages over the wilderness. If this were all God had to offer them, they had better go back to Egypt again. God had promised them rest, but there was no rest in sight.

Why did not God lead them into the Promised Land? For the reason that they were not spiritually prepared. The moment they were ready God could take them in, but not before. Their entrance was dependent upon their spiritual condition.

This was the crux of the situation. God would give them rest from their wanderings, rest from their enemies, as soon. as they had rest in their souls. The assurance had been given them, "My presence shall go with thee, and I will give thee rest." Ex. 33:14. This was the rest that Jesus meant when He said, "Come unto me, all ye that labour and are heavy laden, and I will give you rest. Take my yoke upon you, and learn of me; for I am meek and lowly in heart: and ye shall find rest unto your souls." Matt. 11:28, 29. This was the call that came to Israel at the time of the captivity: "Stand ye in the ways, and see, and ask for the old paths, where is the good way, and walk therein, and ye shall find rest for your souls. But they said, We will not walk therein." Jer. 6:16.

"Rest for your souls." This was the rest into which God would bring them, the rest in which God was chiefly interested and the people least. The people were chiefly interested in getting into the land of Canaan and finding rest from their wanderings. But the condition for this rest was rest in God, rest for their souls.

Continually came the thought to the mind of the children of Israel in the wilderness, Will God ever bring us into the Promised Land? We have been in the wilderness ten, twenty, thirty years, and we are as far from Canaan as ever. Are we all to die here? Will we never get in? Will we never gain our rest?

Paul is answering these questions in the verse before us. Yes, God will bring you in. He will give you rest. This, indeed, has been God's purpose from the time "the works were finished from the foundation of the world." After His work was finished He rested. The rest was as definitely a part of His program as the work. Yield yourselves to the fashioning hand of God, and He will give you rest—rest for your souls, and rest from your wanderings.

This argument Paul is now applying to his own generation. The Jews had been God's chosen people; but, despite this, it seemed to them that they had suffered more than any other nation. True, they were in the land, but they certainly had not had rest from their enemies. And now a crisis was approaching. They doubtless did not know what we now know: that this was their last opportunity. The last call was about to sound. Would they heed the call of Jesus and come to Him that they might find rest for their souls?

But was it not too late now? No, says Paul, some are entering; "we which have believed do enter." That meant that others might enter also.

Verses 4, 5. "The seventh day." The rest of the soul, in which God is vitally interested, is closely connected with the Sabbath. Rest in God means oneness with God, a complete dedication of the whole being to Him, every obstacle to perfect communion removed. The rest of the soul means entire sanctification, a yielding of all to the Master, a sinking into God.

Of this experience the Sabbath is the sign. "I gave them my sabbaths," says God, "to be a sign between them, that they might know that I am the Lord that sanctify them." Eze. 20:12. He says further that "they shall be a sign between me and you, that ye may know that I am the Lord your God." Verse 20.

In these verses God combines sanctification and the Sabbath, saying that the latter is a sign of the first. These are companion statements to those in the fifty-sixth chapter of Isaiah: "Blessed is the man that doeth this, and the son of man that layeth hold on it; that keepeth the sabbath from polluting it, and keepeth his hand from doing any evil." Isa. 56:2. To "the eunuchs that keep my sabbaths, and choose the things that please me, and take hold of my covenant," God says, "Even unto them will I give in mine house and within my walls a place and a name better than of sons and of daughters: I will give them an everlasting name, that shall not be cut off." Verses 4, 5. And lest any think that this has reference to the Jews only, God adds: "The sons of the stranger, that join themselves to the Lord, to serve him, and to love the name of the Lord, to be his servants, every one that keepeth the sabbath from polluting it, and taketh hold of my covenant; even them will I bring to my holy mountain, and make them joyful in my house of prayer: their burnt offerings and their sacrifices shall be accepted upon mine altar; for mine house shall be called an house of prayer for all people." Verses 6, 7.

These statements all make it clear that the Sabbath is closely connected with true Christianity, with rest in God, with sanctification, so closely that God calls it a sign of sanctification.

As God rested the first Sabbath with His own in the Garden of Eden, perfection met the eye everywhere. There was nothing to hurt or destroy in all God's holy mountain. And as "God did rest the seventh day from all his works," He saw a finished creation; the whole world united in His praise, and everywhere were harmony and love. The Sabbath was the perfect setting for this occasion, the pearl of all days, the day for which the other days had been a preparation. And so "on the seventh day God ended his work which he had made; and he rested on the seventh day from all his work which he had made. And God blessed the seventh day, and sanctified it: because that in it he had rested from all his work which God created and made." Gen. 2:2, 3.

"God blessed the seventh day, and sanctified it," and "did rest the seventh day from all his works." Gen 2:3; Heb. 4:4. This day which He in the beginning sanctified and upon which He rested, became the sign of sanctification, of holiness, of rest in God. Hebrews calls it "his rest," "my rest," "that rest." (Heb. 3:18; 4:1, 3, 5, 11.)

With this background it can easily be understood why God should call attention to the seventh day when He speaks of entering into His rest, as in the fourth verse before us. The Sabbath is so closely connected with rest in God, with sanctification, that He could not do otherwise.

"In this place again." The author is here repeating what He said before, that the disobedient shall not enter. It is an affirmation of the statement in Hebrews 3:18, "To whom sware he that they should not enter into his rest, but to them that believed not."

Hebrews 4:6–11. "Seeing therefore it remaineth that some must enter therein, and they to whom it was first preached entered not in because of unbelief: again, he limiteth a certain day, saying in David, To day, after so long a time; as it is said, To day if ye will hear his voice, harden not your hearts. For if Jesus had given them rest, then would he not afterward have spoken of another day. There remaineth therefore a rest to the people of God. For he that is entered into his rest, he also hath ceased from his own works, as God did from his. Let us labor therefore to enter into that rest. lest any man fall after the same example of unbelief."

We do not know the number upon which God has decided as necessary that His house may be filled. God's command is to "go out into the highways and hedges, and compel them to come in, that my house may be filled." Luke 14:23. His house was not filled in the time of Israel, for "they to whom it was first preached entered not in because of unbelief." Verse 6. It was not filled in the time of David, for then "would he not afterward have spoken of another day" in which they might enter. Verse 8. It was not filled in the apostle's day, else there could be no invitation to labor "to enter into that rest." Verse 11. It is true now as it was then, that there "remaineth therefore a rest to the people of God." Verse 9. There is still room, room for all, but the door will not remain open forever. In the parable of the ten virgins the fateful words are recorded, "And the door was shut." Matt. 25:10.

Verse 6. "Some must enter therein." This has reference to the rest of God, the true rest of the soul. As noted before, though Israel entered Canaan, few of them entered into God's rest.

But some must enter. God will have His house filled. Men's unbelief may compel God to change His method of working, but in the end God's eternal plan will be carried out.

Verse 7. "He limiteth a certain day," rather "appoints." This day is "to day if ye will hear his voice." In the original " certain day" and "to day" are in apposition, "to day" defining what is meant by "certain day."

Verse 8. "If Jesus had given them rest." It is unfortunate that the word "Jesus" is used, when it should be "Joshua," as is noted in the margin. Of this Alford says, "Our translators, in retaining 'Jesus' (the Greek form of *Joshua*) here, have introduced into the mind of the ordinary English reader utter confusion. It was done in violation of their instructions, which prescribed that all proper names should be rendered as they were commonly used." —*The New Testament for English Readers*, vol. 2, p. 640.

The apostle here meets the objection that would arise in the minds of some, that though Moses did not lead the people into the Promised Land, Joshua did, and that therefore God's purpose was fulfilled when Joshua led Israel into Canaan.

But this is the very thing that the apostle affirms is not what God had in mind. As stated before, it was not enough for Israel to enter the *land*. God wanted them to enter His *rest*. At the time the psalm from which this quotation is taken, was written, Israel was already in Canaan, and had been there many years; but though they were in the land, they had not entered God's rest. Hence, God made another call, "in David."

"Another day." If Joshua had given them rest, God's intent would have been fulfilled. But Joshua did not give them rest. He merely led them into Canaan. That Joshua did not give them rest is indicated in the "if." "*If* Joshua had given them rest." This statement is conclusive proof that God by "rest" means more than entering Canaan; for there was no if in regard to entering Canaan. *They were there already,* and in David's time, when this psalm was written, they had been there hundreds of years. But

Joshua had not given them *rest.* God therefore invites them to enter *today.*

Verse 9. "There remaineth therefore a rest to the people of God." The Greek word for "rest" in this verse is different from the word for "rest" in the other places. Here it is *sabbatismos,* a word that derives from *Sabbath,* and may be translated "keeping of Sabbath," or "Sabbathkeeping." The text therefore reads, "There remaineth therefore a keeping of Sabbath to the people of God."

"There remaineth." Neither Moses nor Joshua nor David had succeeded in bringing Israel into the rest of God. There remains therefore a keeping of Sabbath, or as Franz Delitzsch translated it, "There remaineth therefore still a Sabbath-rest for the people of God."

In explanation of this Delitzsch says: "The promise is still open, its fulfilment not yet exhausted: there is still reserved for the people of God, still to be expected by them, as a church of believers, a σαδδατιομός, the keeping of a Sabbath, the enjoyment of a Sabbath rest. So it is, and must be; for the Sabbath of God, the Creator, is destined to become the Sabbath of all creat ion."—*Commentary on the Epistle to the Hebrews,* vol. 1, p. 197.

"Remaineth" means that it is left, left over, not appropriated. This is exactly the meaning here. It is not a new Sabbath; it is the same Sabbath as in Eden, as in the time of Moses, Joshua, and David, as in the time of Jesus and Paul. It is the same Sabbath that has always been and that remains.

Farrar says: "Since the word used for 'rest' is here a different word from that which has been used through the earlier part of the argument (χατάπαυσις) it is a pity that King James's translators, who indulge

in so many needless variations, did not here introduce a necessary change of rendering, The word
means 'a Sabbath rest,' and supplies an important
link in the argument by pointing to the fact that 'the
rest' which the author has in view is God's rest, a far
higher conception of rest than any of which Canaan
could be an adequate type. The Sabbath, which in 2
Macc. xv. 1 is called 'the Day of Rest,' is a nearer type
of Heaven than Canaan." —*The Epistle of Paul the
Apostle to the Hebrews*, p. 68.

Verse 10. "For he that is entered into his rest." This
verse has been interpreted in two ways, depending
upon the meaning of the first "he." Some take "he" to
refer to Christ, that is, He, Christ, has entered into
God's rest. Others take "he" to refer to man in
general, so that the meaning would be, "Whoever has
entered into God's rest." There is nothing in the
context that shows to whom "he" refers. We are therefore left to determine for ourselves its meaning.

As has been noted before, where there are two
interpretations of a text, and neither of them does
violence to sound exegesis, ordinarily each of them
contains something of value. This is true of the
interpretation of "he" in the present instance. If by
"he" is meant Christ, then it is true that He entered
into God's rest, and ceased from His labors, as God
did from His. Whether we take God's rest here to
mean the rest which is the heritage of the saints and
into which they enter upon conversion—the same
rest to which God has issued so many calls as
recorded in this section of Hebrews—or we take it to
mean the rest mentioned in verse 4, where "God did
rest the seventh day from all his works," Christ
entered into just such rest. (Matt. 11:28, 29; Luke
4:16.)

If on the other hand we take "he" to mean man in general, the interpretation would be: "Whoever enters into God's rest, whoever is genuinely converted, hath also ceased from his own works as God did from his." The word "ceased" is the same word that is translated "rest" or "rested" in the other instances where it occurs in this section—as in verse 4, "God did rest," and is the same word that is translated "rest" in the verse before us; so that the reading therefore would be: "He that is entered into God's rest, he also hath rested from his own works as God did from his."

If we ask how God rested from His works' we find the answer in verse 4: "God. did rest the seventh day from all his works." As we incorporate this answer into our interpretation of the text, we get this result: "He that is entered into God's rest, he that is truly converted, rests on the seventh day as God did." The Sabbath is God's sign of sanctification. (Eze. 20:12.) But a sign is of little value without the reality for which it stands. Whoever, therefore, keeps the Sabbath holy, must himself be holy. This is the same as resting from, or ceasing from, our own works.

We can but believe that God had a purpose in linking the Sabbath with true conversion and sanctification. The story of Israel's disobedience, as recorded in the twentieth chapter of Ezekiel, clearly reveals that failure to keep the Sabbath holy loomed large in their rejection by God. This, however, as has been noted before, meant more than the keeping of a day. The day was important, but it was nevertheless only the outward sign of an inward experience, a sign of holiness, a sign of sanctification. Their failure to recognize and observe the Sabbath revealed an inward state of rebellion, a disinclination to obey

God, which necessitated a purge of the rebels. (Eze. 20:38.)

Many years, many centuries, God bore with Israel. And now, in Paul's day, just before the destruction of Jerusalem, He makes one last plea. He rehearses the story of the failings of their fathers, tells the children why the fathers failed to enter into the true rest of God, and pleads with them not to follow in their fathers' footsteps, but to turn to God while it is yet called today.

This plea, though addressed to the apostolic church, is also an appeal to every nominal Christian wherever found to turn to God and enter into His rest. It is an appeal for a complete return to the Father's house, a return to His rest, a return to God's glorious Sabbath.

Verse 11. "Let us labour therefore to enter into that rest." Let us be diligent, eager, earnest, in our effort to enter into God's rest.

"After the same example." Vaughan comments on this: "Lest any one fall (by placing his foot) in the mark left by the step of the Exodus generation." This enforces the lesson previously impressed, that we are to beware lest we follow the footsteps of those who grieved God by their disobedience.

Hebrews 4:12–16. "For the word of God is quick, and powerful, and sharper than any twoedged sword, piercing even to the dividing asunder of soul and spirit, and of the joints and marrow, and is a discerner of the thoughts and intents of the heart. Neither is there any creature that is not manifest in his sight: but all things are naked and opened unto the eyes of him with whom we have to do. Seeing then that we have a great high priest, that is passed into the heavens, Jesus the Son of God, let us hold fast our profession. For we have not an high priest which cannot be

126

touched with the feeling of our infirmities; but was in all points tempted like as we are, yet without sin. Let us therefore come boldly unto the throne of grace, that we may obtain mercy, and find grace to help in the time of need."

Verse 12. "Word of God." When it is said that the Word of God is quick and powerful, the specific reference is to the writings of the Old Testament, as the New Testament had not yet been written and made a part of the canon. This emphasizes what is said in the first chapter, that it was God who spoke through the prophets of old.

Delitzsch translates verses 12 and 13 as follows: "For full of life is the word of God, and full of energy, and more cutting than any two-edged sword, and penetrating even to a dividing asunder of soul and spirit, as well as the joints and marrow, and passing judgment on the thoughts and intents of the heart. Nor is any creature hidden from it: but all things are bare and exposed to the eyes of him with whom we have to do." —*Commentary on the Epistle to the Hebrews*, vol. 1, p. 202.

There are those who hold that "the word of God" here means Christ personified. However, it seems more natural to refer it to the spoken and written Word of God, particularly the latter.

The Word of God is no dead record of the past, but a living force, as the word "quick" indicates. God is "the living God," and His Word is the living Word. (Heb. 3:12.) Although this is true of the Word of God in general, it has here specific reference to what has just been said of God's rest and warnings to those who "seem to come short of it." (Verse 1.) A. T. Robertson, in *Word Pictures*, says it has reference to what has been "quoted about the promise of rest and God's rest, but true of any real word of God." —*Volume 5*, p.

363. Lange's *Commentary* says: "It is clear from the context that the passage is designed to justify and enforce the preceding warning (ver. 11) terminating emphatically and designedly with its suggestive ἀπειθείας [apeitheias (unbelief or disobedience)]." —*Hebrews*, p. 93. Vincent, in *Word Studies*, has the same opinion, putting it in these words: "The message of God which promises the rest and urges to seek it, is no dead, formal precept, but is instinct with living energy."—*Volume 4*, p. 426. Delitzsch is very clear. Quoting verses 12 and 13, he comments: "We may take it for granted, and as undeniable, that the only logical connection of these two verses with what precedes, as well as with what follows, is to be found in their expressing the living and inexorable energy of that word which, as it formerly brought death upon Moses' contemporaries through their disobedience to its injunctions, so now imposes on the church of Jesus Christ the duty of earnest striving after the promised salvation." —*Commentary on the Epistles to the Hebrews*, vol. 1, p. 202.

When the author therefore says that the Word of God is living and active, or energetic, we understand this to be true of the whole Word of God, but that it is here cited to enforce what has been said of God's rest and the punishment that came to those who were disobedient.

It is to be expected that unbelievers would scoff at God; but how can we account for so-called Christians making light of God's Word and His commandments, and in particular the commandment dealing with the seventh day? It is this very Word and commandment that are here under consideration, and which the apostle affirms are living and active. God knew that some who would read these admonitions and warnings would disregard the commandments as being a dead letter of the law. It is for such, and for all, that He affirms that the fourth commandment is still living and active.

This also is the significance of the first "for" in verse 12. Let all beware, he says, not to follow in the footsteps of the Exodus people who were disobedient, for the Word of God is still living and powerful, and the commandment is not outdated. They suffered because of their disobedience. The Word is no less powerful now than then.

In making this application of the words under consideration, we are not straining a point to support our view on the Sabbath and the law of God. From the quotations cited it can be seen that we do not stand alone in this interpretation. In fact, to have these verses state a general theory and not make any application to the subject under discussion, seems entirely without reason. The author has brought illustrations from the experience of Israel to show how they failed to enter into God's rest; how they were disobedient and grieved God. He has connected the rest of God with the seventh day, a most pertinent point, as it was the pollution of the Sabbath that was one of the reasons for Israel's rejection by God, as recorded in Ezekiel. He has pleaded with his people not to follow the example of the wilderness people but to enter God's rest while it is still called today, reminding them that there remains a keeping of Sabbath to the people of God. And now, lest any think that the warning and admonitions have no present application, that the seventh-day Sabbath is a dead letter, he reminds us that the Word is living and active, that it is sharp and piercing as a two-edged sword, and not an ineffective, ceremonial requirement.

"Powerful" is the Greek word *energes*, whence we derive the English word "energy." God's Word is alive, living, as God is living; and it is also active, powerful, energetic. These words almost personalize the Word, and endow it with characteristics that we ordinarily associate with personality. They remind us of the two witnesses in Revelation 11 who had power to shut heaven, who could turn water to blood and smite the earth with plagues. (Verses 13–16.)

The Word is not only living and energetic but sharper than any two-edged sword. A sharp sword will lay open the joints and marrow, and so the Word will pierce into the innermost recesses of the soul and spirit, and lay bare the thoughts and intents of the heart.

As a surgeon cuts into human tissue and decides what shall be removed, so the Word of God judges the thoughts and motives of the heart with unfailing accuracy. The word "discerner" in the original is a verbal adjective blending the ideas of divining, discriminating, judging. This is what the Word does to men's motives and thoughts. It not only acts as judge of our actions but lays bare the hidden, springs and motives that men may attempt to conceal.

Verse 13. What has been predicated of the Word is now attributed to God. The picture is a striking and powerful one. Nothing is hid from God. Everything is as an open book to Him. The soul stands naked in His presence.

This view of God is terrifying, or comforting, according to the relation men sustain to the judge of all. The hypocrite, the proud, the impure, the selfrighteous, tremble at the thought of the all-seeing eye of God. The trusting, the earnest and honest, the downtrodden and humble soul rejoices that God knows and understands all. No man can ever deceive God. He weighs men's actions and motives in the balances of the sanctuary. And His decisions are just.

Verse 14. "A great high priest, that is passed into the heavens." Rather, "through the heavens." Christ is here presented as being at the "right hand of the Majesty on high." Heb. 1:3. He is here called "Jesus the Son of God," a combination of the human and the divine, coupled with the title "Son." This text is used by some as proof of the restoration to Christ of all the attributes which He had as God, so that in His humanity He now exercises all the prerogatives formerly reserved for the Godhead.

"Let us hold fast," cling tenaciously to, keep on holding on. "Profession" means confession, faith, doctrine.

Verse 15. "High priest." The preceding verse mentions the "great" high priest. The greatness of Christ is the subject throughout the epistle. He is greater than angels, than Moses, than Joshua. And now He is presented not only as an apostle and high priest (chapter 3:1), but as a *great* high priest. Is He greater than Aaron, who was a great priest indeed? This the author will soon discuss. In the meantime he assures us that though Jesus is great, He is still one who can be touched with the feelings of our infirmities; for He has been tempted in all points like as we are, but without sin.

Too often men lose the fellow feeling they formerly possessed when elected to high position or place. Thus the chief butler, when restored to royal favor, completely forgot his fellow prisoner, though Joseph had befriended him. (Genesis 40.) This being a common human failing, we are assured that Jesus is not like that; that He has not lost His contact with us, though He is seated at God's right hand.

"Cannot be touched with the feeling of our infirmities." This means not merely that Christ feels kindly toward us and pities us, but that He suffers with us and is one with us in all things.

"Weaknesses" might be a better word than "infirmities." Christ suffers with us as we suffer, but He does more. Many of our difficulties are a result of infirmities, not of outright rebellion or wicked stubbornness, but a lamentable weakness that makes us give in instead of resisting, and causes all manner of difficulty. Even this condition Christ understands. He may not be able to excuse us, but we may be assured that He feels with us and understands; for He Himself was tempted in all points like as we are, or as a literal translation might give it, "in the way of resemblance."

Was Christ ever weak? Physically, yes. Go with Him to the wilderness, and there find Him battling to the death with evil while weakened from a forty-day fast, His bodily powers gradually diminishing as the temptations increase. A person in the strength of manhood can resist much more than one bodily weakened. Christ was weakened physically to the point of complete exhaustion, but not for a moment did He yield. He was at no time morally weak.

Weakness may be comparatively innocent, though often it is caused by sin. But let all know that whatever may be the condition, or cause of failure, Christ understands. He has had temptations "in the way of resemblance" to ours, and He has the remedy.

Real life is measured not by a sequence of events but by an attitude toward principles. "He that is faithful in that which is least is faithful also in much," is a principle of wide application. Luke 16:10. It is not necessary for one man to be tempted in the precise way or in every detail as another man in order to be able to understand and sympathize. But he must meet temptations and trials that are typical of mankind. Christ did this. The sharp rebuke to Peter, "Get thee behind me, Satan," is most revealing as to Christ's inner temptations, perhaps unsuspected by others. (Matt. 16:23.) Everything about Christ intimates an unusual acquaintance with men's problems and an understanding sympathy. This could be attained only through an identification of trials in all conditions of life.

Verse 16. "The throne of grace." This expression in Christian terminology has always been closely connectcd with prayer, and hence with the mercy seat. It was at the mercy seat the high priest supplicated God for forgiveness on the Day of Atonement. We are invited to come there to find grace to help in time of need.

ADDITIONAL NOTES

The Rest of God

When God had taken Israel out of Egypt, He said to Moses, "My presence shall go with thee, and I will give thee rest." Ex. 33:14.

To Moses and to Israel this was good news. At that time Israel was in the wilderness, and had no settled place of abode. As year after year passed and they were still in the desert far from Canaan, their hearts longed for rest—the rest that would come to them after their journeyings were ended and each man could sit under his own vine and fig tree.

This rest, however, could not be obtained by simply entering the land. Enemies were occupying Canaan;

giants were there: the Amorites, Amalekites, Perizzites, Philistines, and others. Even though Israel should enter Canaan, there were long years of fighting ahead. Simply crossing Jordan would not bring them the promised rest.

In God's plan, however, this was provided for. Said God:

"For mine Angel shall go before thee, and bring thee in unto the Amorites, and the Hittites, and the Perizzites, and the Canaanites, the Hivites, and the Jebusites; and I will cut them off....I will send My fear before thee, and will destroy all the people to whom thou shalt come; and I will make all thine enemies turn their backs unto thee. And I will send hornets before thee, which shall drive out the Hivite, the Canaanite, and the Hittite, from before thee. I will not drive them out from before thee in one year; lest the land become desolate, and the beast of the field multiply against thee. By little and little I will drive them out from before thee, until thou be increased, and inherit the land." Ex. 23:23–30.

These promises were given on conditions, "If thou shalt indeed obey his voice, and do all that I speak; then I will be an enemy unto thine enemies, and an adversary unto thine adversaries." Verse 22.

Israel, however, was more interested in entering the Promised Land than in fulfilling the conditions for entrance. The promises they remembered; the conditions they forgot. As a result God permitted them to wander forty years in the wilderness, hoping that they would at last find themselves, fulfill the conditions, and enter. But they learned little from their wandering, and most of them died in the wilderness and never saw the Promised Land.

To this experience reference is made in Hebrews, where God says that Israel shall not enter into His rest. He calls attention to the seventh-day Sabbath, and links it with Israel's refusal to enter into His rest, admonishing them not to "fall after the same example of unbelief." Heb. 4:11. As the history of Israel's experience is studied, it is clearly seen that the Sabbath was closely bound up with Israel's

entrance into the Promised Land, and that their failure to
enter was largely caused by their pollution of the Sabbath.

GOD's TRUE REST

God's rest is a spiritual experience into which the soul
enters upon conversion. In the unregenerate man there is
unrest and strife, an evil conscience makes life a burden;
the heart is filled with wicked thoughts; worldly ambitions
hold sway; envy and pride bring heartache and sorrow;
impurity dominates the mind; and man is at war with his
fellow men, with himself, and with his God. Then comes
the blessed day of surrender. The soul casts itself upon the
mercy of God and is accepted. The former things pass
away, all things become new, and all things are of God. He
enters a new world, becomes a new man, has a new name,
is a different person. At last there is peace in his heart—his
sins are forgiven. At last his soul is at rest; he has found
God. Gone are the accusations of conscience; gone his
wicked ambitions, his envy and pride, his love of the world,
his love of sin. He is a completely new creature. He has
entered God's rest. He has heeded Christ's call, "Come
unto me all ye that labour and are heavy laden, and I will
give you rest. Take my yoke upon you, and learn of me; for I
am meek and lowly in heart: and ye shall find rest unto
your souls. For my yoke is easy, and my burden is light."
Matt. 11:28–30.

This is the rest that was promised to Israel when God
said to Moses: "My presence shall go with thee, and I will
give thee rest." Ex. 33:14. It was of this rest Jeremiah
spoke when he said, "Stand ye in the ways, and see, and
ask for the old paths, where is the good way, and walk
therein, and ye shall find rest for your souls. But they said,
We will not walk therein." Jer. 6:16. Isaiah says, "The Lord
shall give thee rest from thy sorrow, and from thy fear, and
from the hard bondage wherein thou wast made to serve."
Isa. 14:3.

This call to rest has sounded throughout all time and is
still sounding. Many have heeded it, but more have
rejected it. The call rings out in every generation: "Go out

into the highways and hedges, and compel them to come in, that my house may be filled." Luke 14:23.

The writer of Hebrews connects this rest with God's rest at creation when "the works were finished from the foundation of the world....And God did rest the seventh day from all his works." Heb. 4:3, 4. The connection between the rest into which God invites the believer and His own rest at creation, though close, may not be immediately apparent; a little reflection, however, will make it clear.

When God had finished His six days' work at creation, that which had been planned from eternity at last found visible expression. The earth stood forth in its pristine beauty, the angels rejoiced, the sons of God shouted for joy, and the morning stars sang together. With what amazement and wonder the angels watched the gradual unfolding of the wisdom and the power of God as "he spake, and it was done; he commanded, and it stood fast." They saw light infiltrate the darkness, and beauty begin to take form. When, as the climax, God took lifeless clay and out of it formed a man; when out of the man He took a rib and builded it into a woman; when the man and the woman met one the perfect complement of the other; when the angels understood that what had been created was for the sake of the beings just formed; when they began to fathom though as yet only vaguely—that all this had a bearing on sin, which so mysteriously had appeared in the universe and which threatened to disrupt the previous harmony of heaven; when they realized that God in His goodness had permitted them to witness the supreme divine prerogative of the Godhead, the creation of life, and that they themselves would be called upon to have some part in the unolding drama of the eradication of sin from the universe, their joy knew no bounds. Christ, by whom God had made the worlds, had been exalted before their eyes. (Heb. 1:2.) They had seen Him create; they had seen Him breathe life into a lifeless form and create a man in His own image, a candidate for immortality, capable of reaching even greater heights than those of which they themselves were capable. Wonderful was their God, and equally wonderful was the One whom they had just seen reveal the power of the Godhead.

The day following the creation of man was the greatest of all days. God understood, of course, what the angels but dimly comprehended, and man not at all—the meaning and cost of creation. He saw the future. He knew of sin and the dark days coming; but He also knew that the supreme step had been taken that would eventuate in the complete vindication of God and the final cleansing of the universe from sin. He looked forward to the time when one pulse should beat throughout creation, one song of harmony rise from every tongue, when the family in heaven and earth should unitedly raise their voices in praise to Him that sitteth upon the throne and to the Lamb.

THE FIRST SABBATH

That first Sabbath on earth was the climax of the creation experience. When God's family of heaven and earth met that day in Eden, all gained a deeper conception of the beauty of life and what it may hold. God, during the six days, had given a demonstration of work and activity; now He gives a demonstration of communion, love, social life, worship. Here was the day for which all the other days had been made, the crown, the glory, the pearl of all days. On this day God set His seal of approval. He blessed and sanctified it.

When the first Sabbath came to earth, only God had worked the six previous days. The angels had looked on in wonder and admiration, but they had not created. Man had been brought into existence on the sixth day. So neither angels nor man had worked six days. Adam had indeed worked on the day of his creation in naming all the animals. But he had worked at most only part of one day. In a special sense, therefore, the first Sabbath in Eden was God's Sabbath, for He was the only one who had worked six days. It was His holy day, His day of rest. Hence, the strength and appropriateness of the Bible statements: "The seventh day is the Sabbath *of the Lord*." Ex. 20:10.

"*My* holy day." Isa. 58:13. "*My* rest," Heb. 3:11; 4:3, 5. "*His* rest," Heb. 3:18, 4:1, 10.

"On the seventh day God ended his work." Gen. 2:2. The word "ended" does not convey the exact meaning of the original, which would more nearly be "finished." Indeed the preceding verse says that "the heavens and the earth were finished," and "finished" is the same word that in the second verse is translated "ended."

God did more than merely end His work on the seventh day. A person may stop his work without finishing it. God not only stopped His work; He finished it. And He finished it on the seventh day. Had God finished His work on the sixth day, there would have been no Sabbath for mankind. But God included the Sabbath in the creation week, and thus made His finished work include both work and rest. Having worked six days and rested the seventh, God says to man, "I have worked six days and rested the seventh; now *you* work six days and rest the seventh, for the seventh day is the Sabbath of the Lord." It is noteworthy that two thousand years after creation, God in speaking of the Sabbath does not say that the seventh day *was* the Sabbath of the Lord, but that it *is*. In this Christ concurs when He affirms that the Son of man *is*, not *was*, Lord of the Sabbath.

God's ideal of perfect life, perfect communion, perfect love, joy, and peace, found expression in that first Sabbath in Eden. As we have noted, in a peculiar and distinct sense it was *His* Sabbath, *His* rest. That the first Sabbath left a deep impression upon God Himself, we know from the way in which He refers to it later. When, for example, in Hebrews He invites and pleads with Israel to enter His rest, He definitely points back to the Edenic Sabbath to define what He means by His rest, stating that "my rest" was the one He entered into when "the works were finished from the foundation of the world," and that then "God did rest the seventh day from all his works." Heb. 4:3, 4. Had God only meant rest in general He would have so stated it. The fact that He picks out the seventh day and specifically mentions that this is the day on which He rested in the beginning, and that it is "his rest" to which He invites all to enter, is significant. And that this is recorded in the New Testament in Hebrews, more than thirty years after the death of Christ, is equally significant. Christians would do well to ponder this.

Let the mind dwell upon the first Sabbath. God has finished His work and as He contemplates it, finds it "very good." God states this very modestly, for the earth and what He had made must have been surpassingly beautiful. As God beheld His creatures; as He saw Adam in his perfection of strength and manhood, and Eve in her loveliness; as He saw angels and men, sons of God, cherubim and seraphim; as He saw "the whole family in heaven and earth" in sweet communion and fellowship, He saw life as He meant it to be—ideal, pure, complete, satisfying. And so, as He drank in the whole scene, He rested and was refreshed. (Ex. 31:17.) The ideal and the climax had been reached. Of this the prophet says, "He will rejoice over thee with joy; he will rest in his love; he will joy over thee with singing." Zeph. 3:17.

Adam never forgot that first Sabbath. As long as he lived he recounted to his children and his children's children to the seventh generation the glory of that first Sabbath. And as Adam forgot not, so God did not forget. Ever fresh in His mind is the memory of earth's first glorious Sabbath. Men may forget the Sabbath, but God never. The Sabbath stands as a memorial of that which once was and again shall be.

The Sabbath thus became to Adam symbolic of rest with God, of perfect communion, of oneness with God. It was the one commandment that God chose to honor by joining man in its observance; or perhaps better, inviting man to join Him in its observance. It is the one command that was communicated to man not only by way of law but also by God's example. Among the ten it stands unique, symbolic of God's idea of perfection, of holiness, of rest, of ideal existence with God.

It is this idea of the seventh-day Sabbath that is introduced in Hebrews to symbolize God's rest. From the "foundation of the world" God spoke of the seventh day as His rest. (Heb. 4:3, 4.) It is evident from this reading that God connects the seventh day—the original seventh day "from the foundation of the world," when He had finished His work—with entering into His rest.

There are three distinct ways in which "rest" is used in this chapter: first, entering the land of Canaan, which was Israel's understanding of rest; second, rest from sin, resting in God, having His peace in the heart, rest for the soul, true conversion; and third, the perfect symbol and sign of that rest, the Sabbath, instituted by God Himself—not a spurious or new sabbath, but the original seventh day of creation, which "remaineth" and which God blessed and sanctified and gave to man as a sign of sanctification. (Eze. 20:12, 20.)

ISRAEL's EXPERIENCE

It is interesting in this connection to call to mind Israel's experience with the Sabbath, which forms the ground for God's statements in the fourth chapter of Hebrews. This history clearly reveals that the seventh-day Sabbath was closely bound up with Israel's entrance into Canaan, gives point to the introduction of the Sabbath into the argument in Hebrews, and is highly significant in view of the warning that we are not to "fall after the same example of unbelief." Heb. 4:11.

This history is recorded in the twentieth chapter of Ezekiel, and should be studied in this connection.

Ezekiel lived and prophesied at the time of the invasion of Judea by Nebuchadnezzar about the year 600 B.C. The king of Babylon had already been to Jerusalem once, and had carried some of the Jews into captivity, but the city and the temple had so far been spared. It was a time not unlike that in which the Jews found themselves when the book of Hebrews was written, and the Romans were about to come and finally destroy the temple.

At this critical time certain of the elders of Israel came to inquire of the Lord, and sat before Ezekiel, the prophet.

(Eze. 20:1.) The Lord promptly informed, them that He would not be inquired of by them. Instead, He had something He wanted to tell the people. "Cause them to know the abominations of their fathers," He commands the prophet. Verse 4. He then proceeds to recount His experience with the fathers, and how they had rebelled against Him and rejected His counsel. He does this for the purpose of showing that the calamities that had overtaken them were a result of their rejection of Him, and that their only hope was in a return to God.

God begins by saying that He first made Himself known to Israel in Egypt when He decided to bring them into the Promised Land, a land that flowed "with milk and honey." (Verse 6.) He had asked them to cast away their idols and other abominations, "but they rebelled against me, and would not hearken unto me: they did not every man cast away the abominations of their eyes, neither did they forsake the idols of Egypt: then I said, I will pour out my fury upon them, to accomplish my anger against them in the midst of the land of Egypt." Verse 8.

God therefore considered leaving them in Egypt and not delivering them; but instead of doing this, He was merciful to them for His name's sake, and brought them out of Egypt into the wilderness. (Verse 10.) There He spoke to them from heaven and gave them statutes and judgments, "which if a man do, he shall even live in them. Moreover also I gave them my sabbaths, to be a sign between me and them, that they might know that I am the Lord that sanctify them." Verses 11, 12.

But as they had rebelled against God in Egypt, so they now rebelled in the wilderness. "They walked not in my statutes, and they despised my judgments, which if a man do, he shall even live in them; and my sabbaths they greatly polluted." Verse 13.

God again considers the advisability of terminating His relations with Israel "because they despised my judgments, and walked not in my statutes, but polluted my sabbaths: for their heart went after their idols." Verse

16. But again He spared them and did not "make an end of them in the wilderness." Verse 17.

Many years Israel wandered in the desert, until most of the generation that had left Egypt were dead. God then spoke to the children and gave them the same promises He had given their fathers, with the warning: "Walk ye not in the statutes of your fathers, neither observe their judgments, nor defile yourselves with their idols: I am the Lord your God; walk in my statutes, and keep my judgments, and do them; and hallow my sabbaths; and they shall be a sign between me and you, that ye may know that I am the Lord your God." Verses 18–20.

But the children did no better than their fathers. They also rebelled against God; "they walked not in my statutes, neither kept my judgments to do them, which if a man do, he shall even live in them; they polluted my sabbaths." Verse 21.

God could do no more for them. He had tested both the fathers and the children, and all had failed. So God decided to "scatter them among the heathen, and disperse them through the countries; because they had not executed my judgments, but had despised my statutes, and had polluted my sabbaths, and their eyes were after their fathers' idols." Verses 23, 24.

In view of these experiences, God told Ezekiel to tell the elders that He would not be inquired of by them, for they had not turned from the sins of the fathers. However, God would not cast them off entirely. If they would heed His voice, He said, "I will cause you to pass under the rod, and I will bring you into the bond of the covenant: and I will purge out from among you the rebels, and them that transgress against me." Verses 37, 38. Having thus purged His people of the rebels, God said, I will again "accept them, and there will I require your offerings, and the firstfruits of your oblations, with all your holy things. I will accept you with your sweet savour, when I bring you out from the people, and gather you out of the countries wherein ye have been scattered; and I will be sanctified in you before the heathen." Verses 40, 41.

As Israel did not repent, God's threat that He would scatter them among the heathen was partly fulfilled in Ezekiel's day. A few years after this interview Nebuchadnezzar came to Jerusalem for the last time, destroyed the city and the temple and carried the people into captivity. (2 Chron. 36:13, 20.) God had repeatedly sent messengers to them but they had "despised his words, and misused his prophets, until the wrath of the Lord arose against his people, till there was no remedy." Verse 16.

No remedy! Dreadful words. And so Israel went into Babylonian captivity. But God once more restored them. After seventy years they were permitted to return, rebuild the temple and the city, and were given their last probation. But again they did no better. As formerly, they "despised his words, and misused his prophets," and as a last hope, God sent His own Son to them. It is to this Christ refers in the parable of the vineyard.

"There was a certain householder, which planted a vineyard, and hedged it round about, and digged a winepress in it, and built a tower, and let it out to husbandmen, and went into a far country: and when the time of fruit drew near, he sent his servants to the husbandmen, that they might receive the fruits of it. And the husbandmen took his servants, and beat one, and killed another, and stoned another. Again, he sent other servants more than the first: and they did unto them likewise. But last of all he sent unto them his son, saying, They will reverence my son. But when the husbandmen saw the son, they said among themselves, This is the heir; come, let us kill him, and let us seize on his inheritance. And they caught him, and cast him out of the vineyard, and slew him. When the lord therefore of the vineyard cometh, what will he do unto those husbandmen?" Matt. 21:33–40.

When the Jews had thus pronounced their own doom, Christ confirmed it by saying, "Therefore say I unto you, The kingdom of God shall be taken from you, and given to a nation bringing forth the fruits thereof." Verse 43.

When Paul wrote Hebrews, the climax was approaching. For the last time the temple was about to be destroyed, never to be rebuilt. The kingdom was to be taken from the Jews and given to another nation that would bring forth fruit. The last call was being given in Paul's appeal—after that there would be "no remedy."

It is this long history of unbelief and disobedience to which reference is made in the third and fourth chapter of Hebrews. With this in mind it becomes clear why the apostle discusses the seventh-day Sabbath. This is the specific commandment that is mentioned in the account of Israel's shortcomings, and it is likewise the specific reason given by God for rejecting them and bringing His wrath upon them. Six times God emphasizes "my sabbaths" in the twentieth chapter of Ezekiel, which indicates the importance God attached to the observance of the Sabbath. (Eze. 20:12, 13, 16, 20, 21, 24.)

ISRAEL'S LAST CALL

The question may be raised: Were not the Jews careful to observe the Sabbath after their return from the captivity? To this it must be answered that they were more than careful. They went to such extremes on the other side as to pervert entirely God's intent in regard to the Sabbath.

In the time of Christ the Sabbath among the Jews had become a yoke of bondage, an intolerable burden. Instead of being a sign of sanctification, it had become a sign of intolerance, bigotry, Pharisaism, and spiritual pride. It had completely lost its meaning as a symbol of the rest of God, and had become a symbol of their own righteousness.

Under these circumstances what did God do? He sent His Son to restore to them the true meaning of the Sabbath and its observance. But they rejected the Son and at last killed Him. Well might God ask, almost in despair, as He appeals to their own judgment: "And now, O inhabitants of Jerusalem, and men of Judah, judge, I pray you, betwixt me and my vineyard. What could have been done more to my vineyard, that I have not done in it?" Isa. 5:3, 4. God could do no more.

But there was still a remnant left in Jerusalem. Before the final destruction of the city and the temple He sent a message to them. He called to their attention the history of the failure of their fathers and why God rejected them, emphasizing their disregard of the Sabbath. Then He warned them not to "fall after the same example of unbelief." Heb. 4:11. He called specific attention to the seventh-day Sabbath, the Sabbath of creation, when "God did rest the seventh day from all His works." Heb. 4:4. This statement He connects closely with the call to repentance, thus associating the rest to which He calls His people—rest in God, true conversion—with the seventh-day Sabbath rest.

This matter of the Sabbath as presented in the book of Hebrews is significant in view of the fact that God was about to take away the vineyard from Israel and give it "to a nation bringing forth the fruits thereof." Matt. 21:43. God knew that the time would come when this new "nation" would go even further than the Jews bad done, completely reject the Sabbath and bring in a spurious sabbath, and attempt to substitute it for God's own day. For this reason, forty years after the crucifixion, when the temple was about to be destroyed and the new "nation" about to take over, God called attention to His Sabbath, the seventh-day Sabbath, linked it with true conversion, and thus established Sabbathkeeping on New Testament ground, a sign of the new birth, of true sanctification.

God now is gathering a company of men and women who will enter into a new covenant relation with their Creator; He is calling—and has called ever since men left their first Eden home—for them to return, that Eden may be restored; He is calling them to enter into the rest prepared for them from the foundation of the world.

This call to enter into God's rest is nothing less than a call to holiness, to consecration, to sanctification. Without holiness no man can see God, much less dwell with Him. It was evident that Israel could not attain to the rest of God by merely changing residence. They needed a change of heart. For this reason God could not accept the disobedient and rebellious people that come out of Egypt. We are warned not to fall after the same example of disobedience.

CHAPTER 5

OF THE BOOK OF HEBREWS

Christ's Qualifications as High Priest

SYNOPSIS OF CHAPTER

TO THE JEWS, a gentle and compassionate high priest was a novelty. In Christ's time the sacred office had fallen to low levels. Arrogancy, pride, and an overbearing attitude were common traits among the leaders. The remark of the Pharisees, "This people who knoweth not the law are cursed," well describes their estimate of the lower classes. John 7:49.

When Paul, therefore, put compassion for the weak and erring as one of the qualifications for the high priestly office, it must have made a deep impression on the people; for they needed compassion and understanding, and the fact that Christ had these qualifications would. predispose them in favor of a change of priesthood.

In the fifth chapter the author stresses Christ as the ideal priest. In Him, Israel would have their heart's desire, and would be assured of a compassionate and changeless high priest, who would not in time be superseded by one less worthy.

Hebrews 5:1–10. "For every high priest taken from among men is ordained for men in things pertaining to God, that he may offer both gifts and sacrifices for sins:

who can have compassion on the ignorant, and on them that are out of the way; for that he himself also is compassed with infirmity. And by reason hereof he ought, as for the people, so also for himself, to offer for sins. And no man taketh this honour unto himself, but he that is called of God, as was Aaron. So also Christ glorifieth not himself to be made an high priest; but he that said unto him, Thou art my Son, to day have I begotten thee. As he saith also in another place, Thou art a priest for ever after the order of Melchisedec. Who in the days of his flesh, when he had offered up prayers and supplications with strong crying and tears unto him that was able to save him from death, and was heard in that he feared; though he were a Son, yet learned he obedience by the things which he suffered; and being made perfect, he became the author of eternal salvation unto all them that obey him; called of God a high priest after the order of Melchisedec."

Verse 1. High priests are taken from among men and ordained for men. (Ex. 28: 1.)

"Things pertaining to God," has reference to all things wherein man's relation touches God, such as sin, forgiveness, mediation, prayer, thanksgiving.

"Gifts and sacrifices." Gifts are thought to refer to unbloody offerings, sacrifices to bloody. Priests are not to lord it over men but to serve them. They are not only to accept gifts and sacrifices but to offer them.

Verse 2. "Compassion" means to feel gently toward, to suffer with. The word denotes an even temper, "the mean difference between passionateness and indifference." This disposition the priest is to maintain in view of the fact that he himself is not perfect, and needs compassion.

"The ignorant." Men often show contempt for the ignorant when they need pity. The high priest must be no respecter of persons. He must treat all alike.

"The ignorant, and ... them that are out of the way," the erring, are primarily such as sinned ignorantly and erred in minor matters.

Verse 3. "He ought," he must, he is bound to, offer for himself. This should tend to make him compassionate. He must have no feeling of superiority, knowing that he is a sinner as are others. He is one with the people, and must offer for his own sins, as well as for the people's.

Verse 4. One important consideration in the office of high priest is the call. This must come from God. If a man thus receives a call from God, he is divinely fitted to exercise the prerogatives of his call, and men must give him due honor.

Verse 5. In the century before Christ the selection of candidates for the high priesthood became irregular, and was no longer confined to the house of Aaron. Wicked men sought the honor, and often obtained the office by the most dishonest means. Originally the office was for life, and descended from father to son, but now each high priest served only a few years, when he was displaced to make room for another who perhaps had obtained the office by bribery or even assassination. In the 125 years before Christ there was a total of twenty-nine high priests. The wise high priest would hold his office only long enough to fill his coffers. To continue to serve exposed him to removal by violent means. This custom explains why there were several high priests living contemporaneously at the time of Christ. They had resigned or been forcibly removed to make room for others.

Conditions such as these make more pertinent the statement that Christ did not glorify Himself to become high priest. "It is my Father that honoureth me." John 8:54. Christ did not appoint Himself. The Father appointed Him.

This fact refutes the concept some have that the Father is a hard, cruel master, unwilling to forgive, and who will exact the last farthing. On the contrary God appointed Christ mediator, thus indicating His interest in the salvation of man. "God was in Christ, reconciling the world unto himself, not imputing their trespasses unto them; and hath committed unto us the word of reconciliation." 2 Cor. 5:19.

The following quotations emphasize the fact that Christ did not appoint Himself high priest, and also that "the exercise of it waited for the ascension," which was the coronation:

"When Jesus *rose* 'the first-begotten from the dead,' He was fully constituted the high-priestly administrator of the 'everlasting covenant.' When He ascended to God's right hand, He clothed Himself 'with honour and majesty' and entered upon His administration." —*Bishops' Commentary*, note on Hebrews 5:6.

"The resurrection was the virtual investiture of Christ with the priesthood. The exercise of it waited for the ascension, which was to the resurrection as the coronation is to the accession of a sovereign." —C. J. Vaughan, *The Epistle to the Hebrews*, p. 92.

Verse 6. The two quotations in which God declares Christ to be Son and also high priest, are from Psalms 2:7 and 110:4. The first states the fact that Christ is the Son of God, the second appoints Him to the high priesthood.

Christ, as the Son of God, had the right of approach to the Father. Even as the Son of *man*, being perfect, He could not be denied access. But He awaited the appointment of the Father, and did not glorify Himself in assuming the office which He might have claimed as His right. It is significant that it was *Christ*, the anointed one, who had a right to the office, who did not glorify Himself. (Heb. 5:5.) On the other hand the Father "glorified his Son *Jesus*," thus exalting humanity, and establishing Jesus, the Son of man, as mediator. (Acts 3:13.)

Verse 7. This is a distinct reference to Gethsemane. It was there that He "offered up prayers and supplications with strong crying and tears," though the experience on the cross must be added to this. (Matt. 26:36–44; Luke 22:39–44; Mark 14:32–41; Matt. 27:46; Mark 15:34; Luke 23:46.)

"Was heard." This statement has occasioned some difficulty because of the fact that Christ was not saved from death, and hence it may seem that His prayer was not heard.

This text does not say that Christ asked to be saved from death, but only that He prayed to Him who is *able* to save Him from death, and the accounts in the Synoptics clearly state that Christ prayed that "if it were possible, the hour might pass from him." Mark 14:35. In Matthew He is quoted as praying, "O my Father, if this cup may not pass away from me, except I drink it, thy will be done." Matt. 26:42. These statements can only be understood in the light of Christ's desire to be spared from death, if it were possible and consistent with God's will. How, then, can it be said that He was heard, when His petition was not granted?

Had Christ in His prayer per-emptorily demanded that He be saved from death, then it must be admitted that His request was denied. But Christ did not demand *this*. When He added the words of

151

submission, "Thy will be done," He cleared the way for God to do as He thought best, and pledged Himself to accept God's decision. As Christ's will was also God's will, whatever the Father should decide would likewise be Christ's decision. In this way He *was* heard, and in this way every prayer is heard that ascends to God in submission to His will.

We often make it unnecessarily hard for God to hear us because of our unwise prayers. The potter, a good man, prays for sunshine and warm weather that his pots may dry. The farmer, a good man, prays for rain that he may get a good harvest, Four mariners sailing in four different directions all pray for a favoring wind. It is quite impossible for God to please all these, and quietly He wishes that men would learn to pray in Christ's way. "If I send rain," God says, "my good potter will think that I have not heard his prayer; and if I send dry weather, then my good farmer will think I have forsaken him. And as for my sailors, I have the same difficulty. If they would only think the matter through, they would know that I cannot please all. I wish they would have this in mind and give me some leeway."

What a wonderful thing it would be if we all could learn this lesson. As Christians we should know that we are not all-wise, that sonic things which we very much desire may not be for our good, and we should have enough faith in God to say, "Lord, I very much desire this thing, and it seems to me that it might be pleasing for Thee to grant it. However, I have learned that there are things I desire that may not be good for me. But I have faith in Thee, Lord. Thou knowest what is best. I leave this matter with Thee. Thou knowest the end from the beginning. So, Lord, Thy will be done."

Let no Christian think that his prayer is not heard. Every earnest prayer *is* heard, even though it be not answered favorably. "No" is as definite an answer as "Yes;" though often the answer is neither "Yes" or "No," but "Wait." God may be reluctant to say no, perhaps, and is waiting for us to adjust ourselves so that we will pray, "Thy will be done." The moment we do so, God is released, and relieved. Now He can do what ought to be done, and have our co-operation. Submission to the will of God is the great secret of effective prayer.

There is another view of the prayer of Christ in Gethsemane, which to our mind better explains both the agony of Christ in the garden and the statement that His prayer was heard. It is inherent in the answer to the question, "For what did Christ really pray?" Was it to be saved from temporal death, or was it the greater question of separation from the Father, as is suggested in His despairing cry on the cross, "My God, my God, why hast thou forsaken me?" Mark 15:34. We believe it to be the latter.

Christ foresaw and foretold His death. He had counted the cost. Hear Him say, "Now is my soul troubled; and what shall I say? Father, save me from this hour: but for this cause came I unto this hour." John 12:27. In view of this statement, it is clear that more was involved in His prayer in the garden than salvation from temporal death. For that very hour He had come. What He wanted was not salvation from death but victory *over* death, assurance of a resurrection, assurance that the separation from the Father was not to be eternal. And in that He was heard.

This view finds confirmation in the fact that in the Greek "save...from death" is literally "save out of death." Although it is often translated merely by *from,* here it seems most fitting to read *out of*. This then would not mean that Christ prayed to be saved *from* death—He expected to go down into the dark—but that He asked to be saved *out* of it. In this view there is no difficulty with John 12:27, which otherwise seems unexplainable.

"In that he feared." The meaning is, "because he feared." Fear here means reverent fear, the fear of God, piety. Hence it is variously translated, "for his piety," "because he feared God," "for his reverence," "because he had God in honor." The meaning is that Christ was heard because of His life of piety, because He feared and reverenced God.

This verse, taken in connection with verse 3, has been made the basis of the idea that Christ so identified Himself with humanity that it became necessary for Him, "as for the people, so also for himself, to offer for sins." The high priest of old did so, as He could not offer for others till he had offered for himself. While no one contends that Christ in any way was sinful, the question concerns itself with the degree to which Christ became and was one with us. Was He *made* sin to the extent that He was treated as a sinner, and needed to take the steps necessary for a sinner to take? Did the sins He carried for us become *His* sins? The high priest offered for himself, and here Christ is presented as praying for Himself to be saved from death, or out of death. Is the parallel here presented that we may give it reverent study?

We are not attempting a solution, for many factors are involved that cannot adequately be discussed here. We would refer the interested reader to the chapter on "Gethsemane" in the book *The Desire of Ages*, where he will find much of value in regard to this question. We caution the reader, however, to reserve decision until he is in possession of all available facts.

In any event, all are agreed that nothing must be imputed to Christ that in any way appears to detract from His dignity as the Son of God and the Sinless One. If we find Him praying to be saved from death we must find the ground of His prayer in something deeper than fear of what thousands and millions of martyrs have joyfully hailed. We must be able to evaluate such statements as these: "Christ was now standing in a different attitude from that in which He had ever stood before....As the substitute and surety for sinful man, Christ was suffering under divine justice. He saw what justice meant. Hitherto He had been as an intercessor for others: now He longed to have an intercessor for Himself."—*The Desire of Ages*, pp. 686, 687.

Verse 8. "Learned he obedience." Christ had always been obedient, and did not need to relearn it. Yet here He is said to learn by suffering. It had not hitherto been a matter of suffering for Christ to be obedient; but in His earth life He found increasing difficulty and attendant suffering in adhering to the divine pattern. Obedience was becoming costly to Him. It meant Gethsemane and Golgotha. (Phil. 2:8.) It was the hard way of learning obedience, but He did not shrink.

That Christ knew the cost of obedience is suggested in His saying, "Thinkest thou that I cannot now pray to my Father, and he shall presently give me more than twelve legions of angels?" Matt. 26:53.

Verse 9. "Being made perfect," or "having been made perfect," or "perfected." This presents the conception of having reached the goal aimed at, having finished the task. This goal was reached when

He "became obedient unto death, even the death of the cross." Phil. 2:8. He had demonstrated His obedience to the point of death, and was perfected. He could now ask us to be likewise obedient; and so He became the author, or cause, of eternal salvation to all them that obey Him. Having learned the cost of obedience Himself, He had the right to ask others to go where He had led the way.

Verse 10. "Called" is a different word, in the original, from the word translated "called" in verse 4. In the fourth verse it has the simple meaning of being called or appointed to an office. In verse 10 it means "named" or "addressed" or "saluted," as in recognition of an earned position or a title of honor. The application is to Christ's taking His position at the right hand of God and being formally addressed by God as high priest. It is the recognition by the Father of the position, which Christ had earned. God expresses approval of the new ministry in which Christ is henceforth to serve.

"Order." The Greek word for "order" is defined as "regular arrangement; fixed succession (of rank or character); official dignity."

Hebrews 5:11–14. "Of whom we have many things to say, and hard to be uttered, seeing ye are dull of hearing. For when for the time ye ought to be teachers, ye have need that one teach you again which be the first principles of the oracles of God; and are become such as have need of milk, and not of strong meat. For every one that useth milk is unskilful in the word of righteousness: for he is a babe. But strong meat belongeth to them that are of full age, even those who by reason of use have their senses exercised to discern both good and evil."

These verses contain an exhortation to cast off the sluggishness that afflicted the believers and made it impossible for the author to do for them all he would like.

Verse 11. "Of whom," both of Melchisedec and Christ. Paul realizes the difficulty of his subject, for the understanding of which spiritual perception is needed. It is evident that he is well acquainted with his readers, or he would not speak to and of them as he does. They are "dull of hearing," and this makes it hard for him to present his subject. His difficulty is twofold: a hard subject and dull hearers.

Verse 12. "Ye ought to be teachers." These were not new converts, or this could not be true. But they had apparently not progressed as far and as rapidly as it was their privilege.

"Teach you again." They had been taught before, but they had forgotten their lessons, and needed to be taught again. What they had forgotten was "the first principles of the oracles of God."

Paul's hearers are not the only ones who are guilty of sluggishness. Many today ought to be teachers when they are still in need of being taught. Old and young waste time on that which is not essential, fail to improve their opportunities, and need to learn again the first principles of Christianity, when by this time they ought to be teachers. This is a lamentable condition.

"Milk," "strong meat." Paul is taking the church to task. He is not making light of the Word by calling it milk; he is not belittling it in any way. But he feels constrained to say that they are satisfied with too light food. By this time they should be able to digest strong meat, but instead of this they are satisfied with baby food. There is, indeed, a "sincere milk of the word," but it is for "newborn babes," and it is to be given them that they "may grow thereby." 1 Peter 2:2. A little babe is wonderful, but a sixty-year-old babe is not. Such a one needs to be weaned, and to masticate and assimilate his own food, and not depend upon others to do it for him. Yet even today there are those who depend almost entirely on the preacher for spiritual sustenance, and who shun anything that requires study on their part. They glory in "the sincere milk of the word," and are like babes in arms that must be cared for and carried. God wants us all to grow up into the full stature of manhood in Christ, and "henceforth be no more children, tossed to and fro, and carried about with every wind of doctrine." Eph. 4:14. He wants us to grow "till we all come in the unity of the faith, and of the knowledge of the Son of God, unto a perfect man, unto the measure of the stature of the fulness of Christ." Eph. 4:13.

Verse 13. "Unskilful." "He is a babe." As men become skillful in a trade or profession, so God wants us to become skillful in the use of the Word. Babe is ordinarily used as an endearing term, but here it is a term of reproach. Here it applies to the laity, but we fear that in some cases it may apply to ministers also; at least when what they *are* is contrasted with what they *should* and *might* be. But let each apply this to himself.

Verse 14. The author is evidently preparing his readers for some serious counsel. He speaks of strong meat and tells them that this is for full-grown men, whom he defines to be such as "by reason of use have their senses exercised to discern both good and evil."

This exhortation was designed to stir up the church members to a greater degree of interest in that which the apostle wishes them to know. He thinks the time has come for the church to take a forward step, throw off their infantile habits, and become adults. Children can be kept interested by the use of devices and all manner of incentives to interest. Adults should have outgrown such, should lay aside childish things and all juvenile and adolescent contrivances and methods, and as men, do the work given them to do. Paul's admonitions are present truth.

ADDITIONAL NOTES

Extracts From the Writings of Mrs. E. G. White on Bible Study

The fifth chapter of Hebrews closes with a rebuke to the church for not being more diligent in their study of the Scriptures. They had had enough experience so that Paul could say that by now "ye ought to be teachers" but instead of this "ye have need that one teach you again which be the first principles of the oracles of God." Heb. 5:12.

In view of this rebuke, which we doubt not is as applicable now as then, it may be well to read again some warnings and admonitions sent to us to encourage us to greater faithfulness in Bible study.

ON BENDED KNEES

"Ignorance will not excuse young or old, or release them from the punishment due for the transgression of God's law, because there is in their hands a faithful presentation of that law and of its principles and its claims. It is not enough to have good intentions; it is not enough to do what a man thinks is right, or what the minister tells him is right. His soul's salvation is at stake, and he should search the Scriptures for himself. However strong may be his convictions, however confident he may be that the minister knows what is truth, this is not his foundation. He has a chart pointing out every way-mark on the heavenward journey, and he ought not to guess at anything, but to know what is truth. He should search the Scriptures on bended knees; morning, noon, and night, prayer should ascend from secret places, and a continual prayer should arise from his heart that God will guide him into all truth." —*Bible Echo*, May, 1886.

SINK THE SHAFT DEEP

"Let all seek to comprehend, to the full extent of their powers, the meaning of the word of God. A mere superficial reading of the inspired word will be of little advantage; for every statement made in the sacred pages requires thoughtful contemplation. It is true that some passages do not require as earnest concentration as do others; for their meaning is more evident. But the student of the word of God should seek to understand the bearing of one passage upon another until the chain of truth is revealed to his vision. As veins of precious ore are hidden beneath the surface of the earth, so spiritual riches are concealed in the passage of Holy Writ, and it requires mental effort and prayerful attention to discover the hidden meaning of the word of God. Let every student who values the heavenly treasure put to the stretch his mental and spiritual powers, and sink the shaft deep into the mine of truth, that he may obtain the celestial gold,—that wisdom which will make him wise unto salvation." —*Fundamentals of Christian Education*, pp. 169, 170.

"The Bible contains all the principles that men need in order to be fitted either for this life or for the life to come. And these principles may be understood by all. No one with a spirit to appreciate its teachings can read a single passage from the Bible without gaining from it some helpful thought. But the most valuable teaching of the Bible is not gained by occasional or disconnected study. Its great system of truth is not so presented as to be discerned by the careless or hasty reader. Many of its treasures lie far beneath the surface, and can be obtained only by diligent research and continuous effort. The truths that go to make up a great whole must be searched out and gathered up 'here a little and there a little.'" —*Signs of the Times,* Sept. 19, 1906, p. 7.

"The study of the Bible demands our most diligent effort and persevering thought. As the miner digs. for the golden treasure in the earth, so earnestly, persistently, must we seek for the treasure of God's word.

"In daily study the verse-by-verse method is often most helpful. Let the student take one verse, and concentrate the mind on ascertaining the thought that God has put into that verse for him, and then dwell upon the thought until it becomes his own. One passage thus studied until its significance is clear, is of more value than the perusal of many chapters with no definite purpose in view, and no positive instruction gained." —*Education,* p. 189.

"Jesus did not disdain to repeat old, familiar truths, for He was the author of these truths. He was the glory of the temple. Truths which had been lost sight of, which had been misplaced, misinterpreted, and disconnected from their pure position, He separated from the companionship of error; and showing them as precious jewels in their own bright luster, He reset them in their proper framework, and commanded them to stand fast forever. What a work was this! It was of such a character that no finite man could comprehend or do it. Only the divine Hand could take the truth which, from its connection with error, had been serving the cause of the enemy of God and man, and place it where it would glorify God, and be the salvation of humanity. The work of Christ was to give again to the world the truth in its original freshness and beauty. He represented the spiritual and the heavenly, by the things of nature and experience. He gave fresh manna to the hungry soul, presented a new kingdom which was to be set up among men." —*Fundamentals of Christian Education,* p. 237.

"True, earnest, self-sacrificing Christians will understand more and more of the mystery of godliness. The Spirit of Christ abides with them. They are co-laborers with

Christ, and to them the Saviour reveals His purposes. There is seen in them none of the surface-work which leaves the character dwarfed, feebled, and sickly. Daily they grow in grace and in the knowledge of God. They recognize the mercy which administers reproof and reaches out the hand to restrain evil. In word and deed they say, 'Lord, to whom shall we go? Thou hast the words of eternal life.'" —*Signs of the Times*, May 15, 1901, p. 308.

"No one can search the Scriptures in the Spirit of Christ without being rewarded. When a man is willing to be instructed as a little child, when he submits wholly to Christ, he will find the truth in His Word. If men would be obedient, they would understand the plan of God's government. The heavenly world would open its treasures of grace and glory for exploration. Human beings would be altogether different from what they are now; for by exploring the mines of truth, men would be ennobled. The mystery of redemption, the incarnation of Christ, His atoning sacrifice, would not be, as they are now, vague in our minds. They would be, not only better understood, but altogether more highly appreciated." —*Ibid.*, Sept. 12, 1906, p. 523.

"God intends that to the earnest seeker the truths of His Word shall be ever unfolding. While 'the secret things belong unto the Lord our God,' 'those things that are revealed belong unto us and to our children.' The idea that certain portions of the Bible cannot be understood has led to neglect of some of its most important truths. The fact needs to be emphasized, and often repeated, that the mysteries of the Bible are not such because God has sought to conceal truth, but because our own weakness or ignorance makes us incapable of comprehending or appropriating truth. The limitation is not in its purpose, but in our capacity. Of those very portions of Scripture so often passed by as impossible to be understood, God desires us to understand as much as our minds are capable of receiving. 'All Scripture is given by inspiration of God,' that we may be 'throughly furnished unto all good works.'" —*Ibid.*, April 25, 1906, p. 264.

"The central theme of the Bible, the theme about which every other in the whole book clusters, is the redemption plan, the restoration in the human soul of the image of God. From the first intimation of hope in the sentence pronounced in Eden to that last glorious promise of the Revelation, 'They shall see His face; and His name shall be in their foreheads,' the burden of every book and every passage of the Bible is the unfolding of this wondrous theme,—man's uplifting,—the power of God, 'which giveth us the victory through our Lord Jesus Christ.'

"He who grasps this thought has before him an infinite field for study. He has the key that will unlock to him the whole treasure-house of God's word." —*Education*, pp. 125, 126.

"Every one should seek to understand the great truths of the plan of salvation, that he may be ready to give an answer to every one who asks the reason of his hope. You should know what caused the fall of Adam, so that you may not commit the same error, and lose heaven as he lost paradise. You should study the lives of patriarchs and prophets, and the history of God's dealing with men in the past; for these things were 'written for our admonition, upon whom the ends of the world are come.' We should study the divine precepts, and seek to comprehend their depth. We should meditate upon them until we discern their importance and immutability. We should study the life of our Redeemer, for He is the only perfect example for men. We should contemplate the infinite sacrifice of Calvary, and behold the exceeding sinfulness of sin and the righteousness of the law. You will come from a concentrated study of the theme of redemption strengthened and ennobled. Your comprehension of the character of God will be deepened; and with the whole plan of salvation clearly defined in your mind, you will be better able to fulfill your divine commission." —*Review and Herald*, April 24, 1888, p. 258.

"What was it that Jesus withheld because they could not comprehend it? It was the more spiritual, glorious truths concerning the plan of redemption. The words of Christy which the Comforter would recall to their minds after His ascension, led them to more careful thought and earnest prayer that they might comprehend His words and give them to the world. Only the Holy Spirit could enable them to appreciate the significance of the plan of redemption. The lessons of Christ, coming to the world through the inspired testimony of the disciples, have a significance and value far beyond that which the casual reader of the Scriptures gives them. Christ sought to make plain His lessons by means of illustrations and parables. He spoke of the truths of the Bible as a treasure hid in a field, which, when a man had found, he went and sold all that he had, and bought the field. He represents the gems of truth, not as lying directly upon the surface, but as buried deep in the ground; as hidden treasures that must be searched for. We must dig for the precious jewels of truth, as a man would dig in a mine." —*Ibid.*, Oct. 14, 1890, p. 625.

"The great plan of redemption, as revealed in the closing work for these last days, should receive close examination. The scenes connected with the sanctuary above should make such an impression upon the minds and hearts of all that they may be able to impress others. All need to become more intelligent in regard to the work of the atonement, which is going on in the sanctuary above. When this grand truth is seen and understood, those who hold it will work in harmony with Christ to prepare a people to stand in the great day of God, and their efforts will be successful. By study, contemplation, and prayer, God's people will be elevated above common, earthly thoughts and feelings, and will be brought into harmony with Christ and His great work of cleansing the sanctuary above from the sins of the people. Their faith will go with Him into the sanctuary, and the worshipers on earth will be carefully reviewing their lives, and comparing their characters with the great standard of righteousness. They will see their own defects; they will also see that they must have the aid of the Spirit of God if they would become qualified for the great and solemn work for this time which is laid upon God's ambassadors." —*Testimonies*, vol. 5, p. 575.

"The science of Redemption is the science of all sciences; the science that is the study of the angels, and of all the intelligences of the unfallen worlds; the science that engages the attention of our Lord and Saviour; the science that enters into the purpose brooded in the mind of the Infinite,—'kept in silence through times eternal;' the science that will be the study of God's redeemed throughout the endless ages. This is the highest study in which it is possible for man to engage. As no other study can, it will quicken the mind, and uplift the soul...

"The theme of redemption is one that angels desire to look into; it will be the science and the song of the redeemed throughout the ceaseless ages of eternity. Is it not worthy of careful thought and study now?...

"As the life of Christ and the character of His mission are dwelt upon, rays of light will shine forth more distinctly at every attempt to discover truth. Each fresh search will reveal something more deeply interesting than has yet been unfolded. The subject is inexhaustible. The study of the incarnation of Christ, His atoning sacrifice and mediatorial work, will employ the mind of the diligent student as long as time shall last; and, looking to heaven with its unnumbered years, he will exclaim, 'Great is the mystery of godliness.'

"In eternity we shall learn that which, had we received the enlightenment that it was possible to obtain here, would have opened our understanding. The themes of redemption will employ the hearts and minds and tongues of the redeemed through the everlasting ages. They will understand the truths which Christ longed to open to His disciples, but which they did not have faith to grasp. Forever and forever new views of the perfection and glory of Christ will appear. Through endless ages the faithful householder will bring forth from his treasures things new and old."—*Signs of the Times*, April 18, 1906, p. 246.

"The incarnation of Christ, His divinity, His atonement, His wonderful life in heaven as our advocate, the office of the Holy Spirit,—all these living, vital themes of

Christianity are revealed from Genesis to Revelation. The golden links of truth form a chain of evangelical truth, and the first, and staple, is found in the great teachings of Christ Jesus."—*Fundamentals of Christian Education,* p. 385.

"As men seek for earthly treasure, so are they diligently to search for the truth. The truth is to be regarded of higher value than anything else within the reach of man, and the searcher for truth must be willing to purchase it at any sacrifice or cost to himself. The word of God is the mine of truth, and the Lord would have us individually search the Scriptures, that we may become acquainted with the great plan of redemption, and take in the grand subject as far as it is possible for the human mind, enlightened by the Spirit of God, to understand the purpose of God. He would have us comprehend something of His love in giving His Son to die that He might counteract evil, remove the defiling stains of sin from the workmanship of God, and reinstate the lost, elevating and ennobling the soul to its original purity through Christ's imputed righteousness." —*Review and Herald,* Nov. 8, 1892, p. 690.

ATTITUDE IN STUDY

"Those who desire to know the truth have nothing to fear from the investigation of the word of God. But upon the threshold of investigation of the word of God, inquirers after truth should lay aside all prejudice, and hold in abeyance all preconceived opinion, and open the ear to hear the voice of God from His messenger. Cherished opinions, long-practiced customs and habits, are to be brought to the test of the Scriptures; and if the word of God opposes your views, then, for your soul's sake, do not wrest the Scriptures, as many do to their soul's destruction in order to make them seem to bear a testimony in favor of their errors. Let your inquiry be, What is truth? not, What have I hitherto believed to be truth? Do not interpret the Scriptures in the light of your former belief, and assert that some doctrine of finite man is truth. Let your inquiry be, What saith the Scriptures? Let God speak to you from His living oracles, and open your heart to receive the word of God." —*Ibid.*, March 25, 1902, p. 177.

"You should not search for the purpose of finding texts of Scripture that you can construe to prove your theories; for the word of God declares that this is wresting the Scriptures to your own destruction, You must empty yourselves of every prejudice, and come in the spirit of prayer to the investigation of the word of God." —*Fundamentals of Christian Education*, p. 308.

"If you search the Scriptures to vindicate your own opinions, you will never reach the truth. Search in order to learn what the Lord says." —*Christ's Object Lessons*, p. 112.

HOW TO STUDY

"How shall we search the Scriptures? Shall we drive our stakes of doctrine one after another, and then try to make all Scripture meet our established opinions? or shall we take our ideas and views to the Scriptures, and measure our theories on every side by the Scriptures of truth? Many who read and even teach the Bible, do not comprehend the precious truths they are teaching or studying.

"Men entertain errors, when the truth is clearly marked out, and if they would but bring their doctrines to the word of God, and not read the word of God in the light of their doctrines, to prove their ideas right, they would not walk in darkness and blindness, or cherish error. Many give the words of Scripture a meaning that suits their own opinions, and they mislead themselves and deceive others by their misinterpretations of God's word." —*Review and Herald*, July 26, 1892, p. 465.

"As we take up the study of God's word, we should do so with humble hearts. All selfishness, all love of originality, should be laid aside. Long-cherished opinions must not be regarded as infallible. It was the unwillingness of the Jews to give up their long-established traditions that proved their ruin. They were determined not to see any flaw in their own opinions or in their expositions of the Scriptures;

but however long men may have entertained certain views, if they are not clearly sustained by tile written word, they should be discarded. Those who sincerely desire truth will not be reluctant to lay open their positions for investigation and criticism, and will not be annoyed if their opinions and ideas are crossed. This was the spirit cherished among us forty years ago." —*Ibid.*

"I would say to my brethren and sisters, Keep close to the instruction found in the word of God. Dwell upon the rich truths of the Scriptures. Thus only can you become one in Christ. You have no time to engage in controversy regarding the killing of insects. Jesus has not placed this burden upon you. 'What is the chaff to the wheat? These side issues which arise are as hay, wood, and stubble compared with the truth for these last days. Those who leave the great truths of God's word to speak of such matters are not preaching the gospel. They are dealing with the idle sophistry which the enemy brings forward to divert minds from the truths that concern their eternal welfare. They have no word from Christ to vindicate their suppositions.

"Do not spend your time in the discussion of such matters. If you have any question as to what you should teach, any question as to the subjects upon which you should dwell, go right to the discourses of the Great Teacher, and follow His instructions....

"Erroneous theories, with no authority from the word of God, will come in on the right hand and on the left, and to weaklings these theories will appear as truth which makes wise. But they are as nothingness. And yet many church members have become so well satisfied with cheap food that they have a dyspeptic religion. Why will men and women belittle their experience by gathering up idle tales and presenting them as matters worthy of attention? The people of God have no time to dwell on the indefinite, frivolous questions which have no bearing on God's requirements." —*Ibid.*, Aug. 13, 1901, pp. 517, 518.

SANCTUARY TO BE STUDIED

"Those who would share the benefits of the Saviour's mediation should permit nothing to interfere with their duty to perfect holiness in the fear of God. The precious hours, instead of being given to pleasure, to display, or to gain seeking, should be devoted to an earnest, prayerful study of the Word of truth. The subject of the sanctuary and the investigative judgment should be clearly understood by the people of God. All need a knowledge for themselves of the position and work of their great High Priest. Otherwise, it will be impossible for them to exercise the faith which is essential at this time, or to occupy the position which God designs them to fill. Every individual has a soul to save or to lose. Each has a case pending at the bar of God. Each must meet the great judge face to face. How important, then, that every mind contemplate often the solemn scene when the judgment shall sit and the books shall be opened, when, with Daniel, every individual must stand in his lot, at the end of the days." —*The Great Controversy*, p. 488.

"In the future, deception of every kind is to arise, and we want solid ground for our feet. We want solid pillars for the building. Not one pin is to be removed from that which the Lord has established. The enemy will bring in false theories, such as the doctrine that there is no sanctuary. This is one of the points on which there will be a departing from the faith. Where shall we find safety unless it be in the truths that the Lord has been giving for the last fifty years?" —*Review and Herald*, May 25, 1905, p. 17.

"The sanctuary in heaven is the very center of Christ's work in behalf of men. It concerns every soul living upon the earth. It opens to view the plan of redemption, bringing us down to the very close of time, and revealing the triumphant issue of the contest between righteousness and sin. It is of the utmost importance that all should thoroughly investigate these subjects, and be able to give an answer to every one that asketh them a reason of the hope that is in them.

"The intercession of Christ in man's behalf in the sanctuary above is as essential to the plan of salvation as was His death upon the cross." —*The Great Controversy*, pp. 488, 489.

"The significance of the Jewish economy is not yet fully comprehended. Truths vast and profound are shadowed forth in its rites and symbols. The gospel is the key that unlocks its mysteries. Through a knowledge of the plan of redemption, its truths are opened to the understanding. Far more than we do, it is our privilege to understand these wonderful themes. We are to comprehend the deep things of God. Angels desire to look into the truths that are revealed to the people who with contrite hearts are searching the word of God, and praying for greater lengths and breadths and depths and heights of the knowledge which He alone can give." —*Christ's Object Lessons*, p. 133.

"Satan is striving continually to bring in fanciful suppositions in regard to the sanctuary, degrading the wonderful representations of God and the ministry of Christ for our salvation into something that suits the carnal mind. He removes its presiding power from the hearts of believers, and supplies its place with fantastic theories invented to make void the truths of the atonement, and destroy our confidence in the doctrines which we have held sacred since the third angel's message was first given. Thus he would rob us of our faith in the very message that has made us a separate people, and has given character and power to our work." —*Special Testimonies*, Series B, no. 7, p. 17 (Nov. 20, 1905).

RESULTS OF BIBLE STUDY

"Strict integrity should be cherished by every student. Every mind should turn with reverent attention to the revealed word of God. Light and grace will be given to those who thus obey God. They will behold wondrous things out of His law. Great truths that have lain unheeded and unseen since the day of Pentecost, are to shine from God's word in their native purity. To those who truly love God the Holy Spirit will reveal truths that have faded from the mind, and will also reveal truths that are entirely new, Those who eat the flesh and drink the blood of the Son of God will bring from the books of Daniel and Revelation truth that is inspired by the Holy Spirit. They will start into action forces that cannot be repressed. The lips of children will be opened to proclaim the mysteries that have been hidden from the minds of men. The Lord has chosen the foolish things of this world to confound the wise, and the weak things of the world to confound the mighty." —*Fundamentals of Christian Education,* p. 473.

"Just as soon as there is the diligent study of the Bible that there should be, we shall not fail of noting a marked difference in the characters of the people of God." —*Review and Herald,* April 9, 1889, p. 226.

CHAPTER 6

OF THE BOOK OF HEBREWS

Steadfastness in the Faith—The Covenant Oath

SYNOPSIS OF CHAPTER

THE APOSTLE continues the exhortation that he began in chapter five. His readers are sluggish, and have been living on milk when they should be having more substantial nourishment. He therefore proposes to leave behind some of the first principles of the gospel and go on to the deeper things of God.

Beginning with verse 4, he issues a solemn warning against the peril of apostasy. From his first statements it would appear that he is addressing his readers particularly, but in verses 8 and 9 he assures us that he is persuaded of better things of them. The impression is left, however, that while they may not be in immediate need of his correction, there is sufficient ground in their attitude to justify him in warning them.

In the last section, verses 13 to 20, he discusses the oath that God made to Abraham, showing the immutability of God's counsel and giving steadfastness to the hope set before them.

Hebrews 6:1–3. "Therefore leaving the principles of the doctrine of Christ, let us go on unto perfection; not laying again the foundation of repentance from dead works, and of faith toward God, of the doctrine of baptisms, and of laying on of hands, and of resurrection of the dead, and of eternal judgment. And this will we do, if God permit."

These verses are closely connected with the preceding exhortation to leave childish things behind, and act like mature men and women. They have been children long enough, and it is high time that they grow up. The apostle enumerates six fundamental doctrines upon which Christianity is built, but which he intends to leave and not discuss. He is not discarding these doctrines, but wants to build a superstructure upon them. The man who continues to lay foundations, will never have a finished building. Paul wants to complete the structure.

Verse 1. "Leaving," not in the sense of forsaking, but having laid the foundation; he leaves off building it, and begins to erect the house.

"Repentance." This is mentioned as the first foundation principle. This doctrine was prominent in the Old Testament. Hear the prophet speaking, "Repent, and turn yourselves from all your transgressions; so iniquity shall not be your ruin." Eze. 18:30. "Repent, and turn yourselves from your idols." Eze. 14:6. "Turn ye, turn ye from your evil ways; for why will ye die, O house of Israel?" Eze. 33:11. John the Baptist prepared the way for Christ by preaching "the baptism of repentance." (Mark 1: 1–4.)

"Faith toward God" is second in the list of fundamental doctrines. The eleventh chapter of Hebrews is a commentary on the need of faith, and how the men of old exercised it. Repentance and faith are so familiar to New Testament readers that we need say little concerning them. They arc the first steps in Christian living, without which no progress can be made in our approach toward God.

Verse 2. "The doctrine of baptisms." Some have stumbled over the fact that the plural is here used, when Paul elsewhere emphasizes the fact that there is only one baptism. (Eph. 4:5.) The same plural word is used in Hebrews 9:10, where it is translated "washings," and has reference to the many acts of purifications in the Jewish ritual. This, however, could not be its meaning here, as Paul would not consider these washings a fundamental doctrine either of Christianity or of the Jewish faith.

The simplest explanation seems to be that the two baptisms in the Christian church, baptism by water and baptism of the Spirit, are here meant. John the Baptist says of this, "I indeed have baptized you with water: but he shall baptize you with the Holy Ghost." Mark 1:8. After His resurrection Jesus said, "John truly baptized with water; but ye shall be baptized with the Holy Ghost not many days hence." Acts 1:5. (See also Acts 11: 16; 1 Cor. 12:13; John 3:5.) In view of these statements we are justified in believing that baptism by water and baptism of the Spirit are the two baptisms indicated by the use of the plural.

"Laying on of hands." In the Old Testament the laying on of hands was a commanded ordinance. Thus the Levites were ordained by the laying on of hands to "execute the service of the Lord." Num. 8:10, 11. So also was Joshua ordained. "The Lord said unto Moses, Take thee Joshua the son of Nun, and lay thine hand upon him." "And he laid his hands upon him, and gave him a charge, as the Lord commanded." Num. 27:18, 23. (Deut. 34:9.)

In the New Testament the same custom was followed. (Acts 8:17.) It was by the "laying on of the apostles' hands the Holy Ghost was given." Verse 18. This custom, which in many places has fallen into disuse, is worthy of study by the people of God. It is here enumerated among the fundamentals of Christianity.

"Resurrection of the dead." "That the dead are raised, even Moses shewed at the bush, when he called the Lord the God of Abraham, and the God of Isaac, and the God of Jacob." Luke 20:37. (See also Ps. 16: 9, 10; Isa. 26:19; Dan. 12:2.)

In like manner the New Testament stresses the resurrection. Paul sums up the importance of the resurrection when he says, "But if there be no resurrection of the dead, then is Christ not risen: and if Christ be not risen, then is our preaching vain, and your faith is also vain." 1 Cor. 15:13, 14.

"Eternal judgment." From earliest times men knew that a judgment was coming. "And Enoch also, the seventh from Adam, prophesied of these, saying, Behold, the Lord cometh with ten thousands of his saints, to execute judgment upon all." Jude 14, 15. (See also Ps. 9:3–8, 15, 16; Dan. 7:9 ff.)

In the New Testament likewise the judgment occupies a prominent place. (See Matt. 12:41, 42; 25: 31–46; Luke 11:31, 32; 2 Cor. 5:10.)

It will be noted that these six foundation principles are the same in the New Testament as in the Old. "The foundation of God standeth sure." 2 Tim. 2:19. It is a matter of comfort to know that while certain changes resulted from the incarnation, the foundation principles are the same, that they stand sure, and that God did not save men in the Old Testament on a different basis from that in the New. It is still true that there is only one name given among men whereby we may be saved.

If some should be disposed to question the statement that all these foundation principles are the same in both dispensations, and cite baptism as an example, we would not argue the question. However, we would call attention to the fact that baptism is not a strictly New Testament ordinance only, and that it was in use before Christ. John baptized as a forerunner of Christ, and we have good reason to believe that he was not the first, but that for a long time previously a kind of baptism had been in use among the Jews. The proof of this is not germane to our discussion, so we will merely refer the interested reader to any Biblical encyclopedia dealing with the subject.

Verse 3. Paul will "leave" these principles for the present, hoping and believing that they are well understood. He intends to present some of the deeper truths, the "strong meat," which will bring him to the work of Christ as high priest, and to a study of the sanctuary in heaven, the true tabernacle. Before entering this field, however, he digresses to consider the fate of such as reject the Word of God after they have once been enlightened, and to issue a warning.

Hebrews 6:4–12. "For it is impossible for those who were once enlightened, and have tasted of the heavenly gift, and were made partakers of the Holy Ghost, and have tasted the good word of God, and the powers of the world to come, if they shall fall away, to renew them again unto repentance; seeing they crucify to themselves the Son of God afresh, and put him to an open shame. For the earth which drinketh in the rain that cometh oft upon it, and bringeth forth herbs meet for them by whom it is dressed, receiveth blessing from God: but that which beareth thorns and briers is rejected, and is nigh unto cursing; whose end is to be burned. But, beloved, we are persuaded better things of you, and things that accompany salvation, though we thus speak. For God is not unrighteous to forget your work and labour of love, which ye have shewed toward his name, in that ye have ministered to the saints, and do minister. And we desire that every one of you do shew the same diligence to the full assurance of hope unto the end: that ye be not slothful, but followers of them who through faith and patience inherit the promises."

This section deals with the awful fate of those who renounce the faith and fall away from God. Of such it is said that it is impossible to renew them again to repentance. It is unfortunate that the English translation does not make clear that this fate is reserved for those only who persist in rebellion and refuse to repent.

Two things need to be guarded against in an exegesis of these verses. First, is the idea that all who fall away from the faith are beyond repentance and are irrevocably lost. This teaching has been the cause of much discouragement, and perhaps even loss of souls. The other danger is just as real. If there is hope for all who repent, and all will eventually be saved, why be unduly alarmed? If there is no such thing as unpardonable sin, why should we be concerned about it? This also is false doctrine. There is an unpardonable sin, and we need to beware of it. This will be discussed under the particular verses involved.

Verse 4. "it is impossible." The question at issue is the possibility of restoring such as have had a deep Christian experience and have fallen away. Can they be restored to Christian fellowship and again receive mercy?

That the author is not discussing the ordinary Christian, but those of an advanced experience, seems clear. They have once been enlightened and "have tasted of the heavenly gift." "Being enlightened," is the ordinary expression for one who accepts Christ. (Eph. 1:18; John 1:9.) "Tasted of the heavenly gift" means the blessing of sins forgiven, and probably also includes some special gift of the Spirit.

They have also been "partakers of the Holy Ghost"; that is, received the Spirit. It is clear from this that these have been genuinely converted, and have made definite progress in the Christian life.

Verse 5. "Tasted the good word of God." This includes an appreciation of the Word and the promises of God.

"The powers of the world to come." In the early apostolic age many miracles were wrought, deliverances effected, sick healed, and even the dead restored to life. To taste of these powers is to have part in them, either as the subject of some healing or other miracle, or of having performed them. It means that these persons had witnessed the mighty power of God in doing that which it is beyond the power of mere man to perform.

Verse 6. "If they shall fall away." This is an unfortunate translation, for it teaches that those who have witnessed or have had a part in these powers of God, who have seen mighty works performed and then have fallen away, are not capable of restoration. "They crucify to themselves the Son of God afresh, and put him to an open shame."

These words have been a source of much perplexity to those who fear they have passed the bounds of mercy, committed sin against the Holy Ghost, and that there is no hope for them. Let such carefully consider the following:

As noted above, the translation of the text in the King James Version is unfortunate for it conveys the unwarranted idea that all who fall away after having had certain experiences are lost forever. The margin of the Revised Version comes nearer giving the correct meaning when it says that it is impossible to renew men to repentance "the while they crucify"; that is, *as long as they continue to crucify.* The thought is that there is no hope for them unless they turn from their evil ways; no hope for them as long as they continue to resist the call of God.

The matter of sin against the Holy Ghost will not be discussed here except to say that ordinarily this is manifested in continued resistance to the call of God and the wooing of the Spirit. It consists in a hardening of the heart, till there is no longer any response to the voice of God. Hence, a person who has sinned against the Spirit has no remorse, no feeling of sorrow for sin, no desire to turn from it, and no conscience that accuses him. If one has a sincere desire to do right, it may confidently be believed that there is still hope for him.

This should be a source of comfort to the discouraged soul, but it is by no means to be used as an incentive to carelessness. God desires to comfort the disconsolate, but He also wants to warn His people not to follow Israel of old in their unbelief. The history of their disobedience is written for our warning. Says God, "I will therefore put you in remembrance, though ye once knew this, how that the Lord, having saved the people out of the land of Egypt, afterward destroyed them that believed not." Jude 5. And Christ in the parable warns of those who "have no root, which for a while believe, and in time of temptation fall away." Luke 8:13.

Verse 7. "The earth...drinketh in the rain." The picture here is that of the earth, which receives rain from heaven, and in return brings forth herbs and food for man. This is an illustration of' the human heart, which receives the blessed rain and dew from heaven, the good Word of God, and in return should produce fruit to the glory of God.

Verse 8. "Thorns and briers." If, on the other hand, the earth receives rain from heaven, and brings forth only thorns and briers, it is rejected, and "is nigh unto cursing; whose end is to be burned."

This is a most forceful illustration, and one that cannot be misunderstood. God blesses us, and He expects us to bring forth fruit. If with all the blessings He has given us and with all the light that has illuminated our path, we still refuse to bring forth fruit, or if we fall away, there is only one end for us: oblivion and separation from God.

This should give us pause. God is good, and even though we have gone astray, He will still receive us unless we continue in evil. He will send the rain "oft," but not always. There is a line beyond which we may not pass. It is well for all to beware.

Verse 9. The apostle has spoken sharply to his readers by way of warning and admonition. Now he soothes them. He is persuaded that they have no intention of rejecting God's call, but will attend to the "things that accompany salvation."

Verse 10. "Work and labour of love." Men are not saved by works, yet God is not unrighteous to forget those who have ministered and do minister in what some may count minor capacities. To minister to the saints may seem a small matter for the apostle to mention when there are many weighty matters to engage his attention. A night's lodging, food and drink for the wayfarer, hospitality and kindness—these are all recorded in the book of God. And God is not unrighteous to forget such acts of kindness. (Matt. 10:42; 25:31–40.)

Verse 11. "To the full assurance of hope." It is a good thing to begin; it is a better thing to finish. However good a beginning may be, it is useless unless it is persevered in unto the end. "The hands of Zerubbabel have laid the foundation of this house; his hands shall also finish it." Zech. 4:9. God's promise is that "he which hath begun a good work in you will perform it until the day of Jesus Christ." Phil. 1:6. Too many begin but do not finish.

The believers to whom the epistle is addressed had been zealous in entertaining the saints, and Paul wants them to continue their ministrations. The wording, however, goes beyond that of mere ministration, and includes that of showing "the same diligence to the *full assurance of hope.*" By this the apostle means that they are to be as diligent in their desire for salvation as they are in other matters. There must be no stopping short, no falling away, no slacking in their race for the prize.

Verse 12. "Not slothful." Slothfulness is the opposite of diligence. To many, religion is an easy-going occupation that can be attended to at leisure. It is not first on their program but near the end of the list. Everything else must be done first, and God may have what is left. This needs to be reversed.

Young people at times decide that religion can wait till they get older; when they have had all that can be obtained from life here, it is time enough to attend to more serious matters. Others take their religion lightly, and follow the line of least resistance. God wants all to be diligent, "not slothful in business;

fervent spirit; serving the Lord." Rom. 12:11. He wants us to be "followers of them who through faith and patience inherit the promises."

Hebrews 6:13–20. "For when God made promise to Abraham, because he could swear by no greater, he sware by himself, saying, Surely blessing I will bless thee, and multiplying I will multiply thee. And so, after he had patiently endured, he obtained the promise. For men verily swear by the greater: and an oath for confirmation is to them an end of all strife. Wherein God, willing more abundantly to shew unto the heirs of promise the immutability of his counsel, confirmed it by an oath: that by two immutable things, in which it was impossible for God to lie, we might have a strong consolation, who have fled for refuge to lay hold upon the hope set before us: which hope we have as an anchor of the soul, both sure and stedfast, and which entereth into that within the veil; whither the forerunner is for us entered, even Jesus, made an high priest for ever after the order of Melchisedec."

That God condescended to make an oath is a remarkable illustration of His willingness to help us in every way, even at great cost to Himself. Many years had God waited for Abraham to attain to the point where faith overshadowed all else. And now the moment had come. Abraham doubted no more. His obedience was absolute, his faith was without the slightest admixture. Now God could use him. It is interesting to note that Abraham lived long enough after this to begin to see the fulfillment of the promise in the birth of his grandchildren, Jacob and Esau.

An anchor is symbolic of that which holds, hence of surety and security. The Christian has such an anchor that will hold in any storm of life that may come. It is sure and steadfast, for it is itself anchored in Christ.

Verses 13,14. "God made promise." The first promise God made to Abraham in regard to an heir was shortly after He told him to get out "of thy country, and from thy kindred, and from thy father's house, unto a land that I will shew thee." Gen. 12: 1. The promise was contained in the words: "I will make of thee a great nation, and I will bless thee." Verse 2. At that time Abraham was seventy-five years old. (Verse 4.)

Some years went by, and Abraham was yet child- less. God then came to him "in a vision, saying, Fear not, Abram: I am thy shield, and thy exceeding great reward." Gen. 15:1. Abraham reminded God that he was childless, and as by this time there was little hope that a child would be born to Sarah, he suggested that perhaps one born in his house might be appointed heir. To this God answers, "This shall not be thine heir; but he that shall come forth out of thine own bowels shall be thine heir." Verse 4. God then gave him a view of the heavens, asked him to number the stars if he were able, and then said, "So shall thy seed be. And he believed in the Lord; and he counted it to him for righteousness." Verses 5, 6.

However, Abraham was not fully satisfied, and when he asked how he might know that he should inherit the land, God said, "Take me an heifer of three years old, and a she goat of three years old, and a ram of three years old, and a turtledove, and a young pigeon. And he took unto him all these, and divided them in the midst, and laid each piece one against another: but the birds divided he not." Verses 9, 10.

This was a usual way of making a covenant. The animals were taken, and cut in two from head to tail. Then the pieces were placed against each other, each piece opposite and a little distance from the corresponding piece, and the contracting parties walked between the pieces. (See Jer. 34:18, 19.) And so at night, "when the sun went down, and it was dark, behold a smoking furnace, and a burning lamp that passed between those pieces. In the same day the Lord made a covenant with Abraham, saying, Unto thy seed have I given this land, from the river of Egypt unto the great river, the river Euphrates." Gen. 15:17, 18. The smoking furnace and the burning lamp were symbols of the presence of God.

When after some years Sarah bare no child—and as she by this time was seventy-five years old, there was little hope that any child would ever be born to her—she suggested that perhaps her maid, Hagar, might bear Abraham a child and this child become the heir. Ten years had gone by since God had first promised them an heir, and Abraham doubtless believed with Sarah that this was the way out. In due time, therefore, a child was born to Hagar, Abraham at the time being eighty-six years old.

Thirteen years more passed, and Abraham was now ninety-nine years old, and his wife eighty-nine. God at this time visited Abraham, and told him not to call his wife Sarai, "but Sarah shall her name be. And I will bless her, and give thee a son also of her: yea, I will bless her, and she shall be a mother of nations; kings of people shall be of her." Gen. 17:15, 16. This was too much for Abraham, and he "fell upon his face, and laughed, and said in his heart, Shall a child be born unto him that is an hundred years old? and shall Sarah, that is ninety years old, bear?" Verse 17. "And God said, Sarah thy wife shall bear thee a son indeed; and thou shalt call his name Isaac: and I will establish my covenant with him for an everlasting covenant, and with his seed after him....But my covenant will I establish with Isaac, which Sarah shall bear unto thee at this set time in the next year." Verses 19, 21.

A little later God again visited Abraham and inquired after Sarah, and was told, "Behold, in the tent." Gen. 18:9. God then renewed the promise, "I will certainly return unto thee according to the time of life; and lo, Sarah thy wife shall have a son. And Sarah heard it in the tent door, which was behind him. Now Abraham and Sarah were old and well stricken in age; and it ceased to be with Sarah after the manner of women. Therefore Sarah laughed within herself, saying, After I am waxed old shall I have pleasure, my lord being old also? And the Lord said unto Abraham, Wherefore did Sarah laugh, saying, Shall I of a surety bear a child, which am old? Is any thing too hard for the Lord? At the time appointed I will return unto thee, according to the time of life, and Sarah shall have a son. Then Sarah denied, saying, I laughed not;. for she was afraid. And he said, Nay; but thou didst laugh." Verses 10–15.

Verse 15. "And so, after he had patiently endured, he obtained the promise." Twenty-five years Abraham waited before the promised son was born. It cannot be said that during this time either Abraham or Sarah showed much faith. True, in the beginning Abraham believed God, and it was counted to him for righteousness; but as the years went by, his faith grew dimmer, and a year before the child was born he laughed outright at God.

The supreme trial came to him after Isaac was practically grown. "God did tempt Abraham, and said unto him....Take now thy son, thine only son Isaac, whom thou lovest, and get thee into the land of Moriah; and offer him there for a burnt offering upon one of the mountains which I will tell thee of." Gen.

22:1, 2. The story is too well known to need repetition. When at last they came to the mount, and Isaac was bound on the altar, "Abraham stretched forth his hand, and took the knife to slay his son." Verse 10. A voice from heaven stayed his hand, and he was told not to lay his hand on Isaac, but that God had provided an offering instead of his son. A ram caught in the thicket was then taken and offered to God. (Verse 13.) Then it was that the angel of the Lord called to Abraham and said, "By myself have I sworn, saith the Lord, for because thou hast done this thing, and hast not withheld thy son, thine only son: that in blessing I will bless thee, and in multiplying I will multiply thy seed as the stars of the heaven, and as the sand which is upon the sea shore; and thy seed shall possess the gate of his enemies; and in thy seed shall all the nations of the earth be blessed; because thou hast obeyed my voice." Verses 16–18.

Verses 16, 17. The confirmation of God's word by an oath mentioned in Hebrews is the one recorded in the twenty-second chapter of Genesis. It was at least forty years from the time the promise was first given to Abraham as he came out of Chaldea until the oath of confirmation was given, when Abraham accounted that God was able to raise Isaac up, "even from the dead; from whence also he received him in a figure." Heb. 11:19. (Gen. 12:2; 22:13.)

It was a different Abraham who stood with hand raised ready to slay his son, from the one who had laughed at God's promise some fifteen or more years earlier. He had learned much since then, and not the least during those three days after he received the command to take his only son and offer him. Abraham had learned to trust God unhesitatingly. No longer did he trust to the flesh; no longer did he depend upon his own devices. He did not know all that was involved in God's command, but he accounted that God was able to raise Isaac from the dead, if need be. He had learned to trust God fully. He was worthy of becoming the father of the faithful. The supreme test had been given him. And he had not failed.

"The immutability of his counsel." The promise that God gave to Abraham was not exhausted in the birth of Isaac. He was indeed a son of promise, a child of a man "as good as dead," and a woman "past age." (Heb. 11:11, 12.) He was not the promised seed, however, but only a link, though a necessary one, in the long line that at last brought forth the man child who was also miraculously conceived. When God told Abraham that "in thy seed shall all the nations of the earth be blessed," Paul takes this statement to mean Christ. (Gen. 22:18.) "He saith not, And to seeds, as of many; but as of one, And to thy seed, which is Christ." Gal. 3:16. Abraham had waited many years for Isaac to be born. At times his faith nearly failed him. The promise seemed impossible of fulfillment. But in due time the child was born.

From the time the promise was first given to Abraham to the time Christ came to the earth was about two thousand years—as far on the other side of Christ as we are on this. To God's people this must have seemed a long time. If the Messiah was to come, why did He wait? Had God forgotten His promise?

Abraham's long wait for his son was prophetic of the long wait of God's people until the true Son should come. God had reason for waiting, as He had reason for waiting in the time of Abraham. "When the fullness of the time was come [and not before], God sent forth his Son." Gal. 4:4. God's purposes know neither haste nor delay, and not until the time is ripe does God act.

Verse 18. "Two immutable things." God's promise and His oath. God's word in itself is immutable. No oath can add anything to what God has said, nor make it surer. That God confirmed it with an oath is entirely for our sake. Men use an oath for confirmation, and so God condescends to do the same, to help us in our faith. This oath must have been a definite help to the people living before Christ. If any doubt should come up in their minds, they could fall back on the fact that not only had God promised but He had *confirmed it with an oath.* He would therefore surely keep His word. Thus the oath would help strengthen their faith.

"Strong consolation." This in the view of the oath. God could do no more. He had promised and He had sworn. There can be nothing stronger than this.

"Fled for refuge." The illustration is taken from the practice of a person who, believing himself to be in danger, fled to the temple as a place of refuge, and laid hold on the horns of the altar. This was considered an inviolable place, and he was safe, at least for the time being.

An example of this is recorded in I Kings 2:28 ff. Joab feared for his life, and so "fled unto the tabernacle of the Lord, and caught hold on the horns of the altar. And it was told King Solomon that Joab was fled unto the tabernacle of the Lord; and, behold, he is by the altar." Solomon then commanded one of his servants to "go, fall upon him." So the servant "came to the tabernacle of the Lord, and said unto him, thus saith the king, Come forth." Verse 30. When he failed to come out at the king's command, the servant fell on Joab and killed him. (Verse 34.)

It is this custom of taking hold of the horns of the altar that is presented in Hebrews. We have sinned. Our only hope is to flee for refuge to the sanctuary. There we may lay hold of the horns of the altar and find refuge, not temporary and insecure as in the case of Joab mentioned above, but a hope that never fails.

Verse 19. "An anchor of the soul." An anchor is that which holds a ship in the storm, and keeps it from drifting on the rocks. There are times when anchors slip, not having anything solid on the ocean floor to fasten to. But not so in this case. This anchor is "sure and stedfast" and enters "into that within the veil."

"Anchor" is not mentioned in the Old Testament, and the use of it here as an illustration is new. But it is a most apt one. In the storms of life we need an anchor, something to tie to, something that will hold us. The Christian hope is such an anchor. It goes within the veil, and it will hold.

Verse 20. "The forerunner." A forerunner is more than a guide who points the way. He is one who goes ahead of others and leads them. We may go with Christ and follow Him wherever He goes.

ADDITIONAL NOTES

An Anchor of the Soul

Note these expressions of assurance given in the latter part of chapter six: "God made promise"; "he sware by himself"; "surely blessing I will bless thee"; "the immutability of his counsel"; "two immutable things"; "impossible for God to lie"; "a strong consolation"; "lay hold upon the hope"; "an anchor of the soul"; "sure and stedfast"; "within the veil"; "Jesus, made an high priest for ever."

These expressions all denote strength and security. God here attempts to put into human language the impossibility of His promise failing us. Always God's word should be sufficient to assure us of the immutability of His counsel. But to this He adds an oath—a most unusual thing, to say the least—to make His promise doubly sure. And all this, the author says, constitutes an anchor of the soul both sure and steadfast; and this anchor as a hope is itself anchored within the veil, where Jesus is for us entered. This line of reasoning thus brings us from the promise made to Abraham that dark night when God's presence passed between the pieces, to Jesus within the veil in the sanctuary in heaven. (Gen. 15:17.)

It may well be asked why God should feel impelled to confirm His word with an oath. In no other case are we told that God did this. Why was the promise made to Abraham so important that God should think it necessary to confirm it? Is not His promise enough?

Though Abraham believed God, and it was counted to him for righteousness (Gen. 15:6), his faith was not at first of the strong, sturdy, unwavering kind, but rather as a grain of mustard seed. This caused him later to laugh at God when he was told that a son should be born. (Gen. 17:17.) Abraham needed something that he could hold on to when the dark days should come and the promise of the seed seem impossible of fulfillment. God's promise should indeed have been enough for him. But God, loving and pitying Abraham, in His great mercy gave him something which he could never forget and which he would remember and cling to in the days when his faith might falter.

As Abraham sat watching the pieces of the slaughtered animals, he doubtless wondered what would take place. As the sun went down, "a deep sleep fell upon Abram; and, lo, an horror of great darkness fell upon him." Gen. 15:12. Then, suddenly, a light approached and "a smoking furnace, and a burning lamp ... passed between those pieces." Verse 17. "In the same day the Lord made a covenant with Abram." Verse 18.

This covenant concerned "the seed," which God had already promised to Abraham. (Gen. 12:7; 13:15; 15:18.) Of this Paul says: "He saith not, And to seeds, as of many; but as of one, And to thy seed, which is Christ." Gal. 3:16.

The ceremony that Abraham had witnessed was the solemn taking of an oath, in which the contracting parties "cut the calf in twain, and passed between the parts thereof." Jer. 34:18. By this act they signified that should they break their covenant they were worthy of being dismembered as the calf had been; that is, it was a blood covenant in which the participants staked their life on the faithful performance of the agreement.

This must have made a deep impression upon Abraham, an impression that would grow and deepen with the years. It is doubtful that he understood all that was included in the "seed," though he probably saw it "afar off"; for Christ tells us, "Your father Abraham rejoiced to see my day: and he saw it, and was glad." John 8:56. This is confirmed by Abraham's answer to Isaac's question: "Where is the lamb for a burnt offering?" "My son," said Abraham, "God will provide himself a lamb for a burnt offering." Gen. 22:7, 8.

The covenant concerns "the seed." It was this that was so tremendously important that God confirmed it with an oath. It is in "the seed," in Christ, that we have "a strong consolation"; He is our hope, "which hope we have as an anchor of the soul." And this hope enters "into that within the veil; whither the forerunner is for us entered, even Jesus." Heb. 6:19.

In saying this, the author combines the Christian hope with the sanctuary. He would not in this place need to make any reference to the veil or to Christ's entrance into the holy places did he not have the purpose of connecting the hope and the anchor with "that within the veil."

The promise given to Abraham long ago as to the seed was fulfilled in Christ. This was a promise not merely that a

Son should be born, but as announced by the angel, "Unto you is born this day in the city of David a *Saviour,* which is Christ the Lord." Luke 2:11. And again: "Thou shalt call his name JESUS, for *he shall save his people* from their sins." Matt. 1:21. That is, it was not merely that a son should be born to fulfill the promise of the seed, but that this Son should be the Saviour.

The covenant that God made with Abraham was, of course, the new covenant. In this all Christians are interested, for it is indeed the Christian's hope; and this "hope we have as an anchor of the soul, both sure and stedfast; and which entereth into that within the veil." Heb. 6:19.

An anchor is an implement fastened to a ship by a cable, which, being cast overboard, lays hold of the earth or the rocks by a kind of hook, and thus holds the ship in place and saves it from being dashed to pieces on the rocks. An anchor cannot fasten itself to the water. Unless the cable is long enough to reach bottom so that the prongs of the anchor can fasten themselves to the earth or projecting rocks, it is of little use.

This is the picture here presented. The two cables, God's promise and oath, will hold. But the anchor itself must be fastened to something that is sure and steadfast, that will not slip or permit it to drag, but will hold it securely. And whatever that is, it is "within the veil; whither the forerunner is for us entered, even Jesus." Heb. 6:19, 20. In Christ, as the Rock of Ages, the anchor is fastened. It will surely hold.

Some have been much exercised over the question of which veil is here meant, the first or the second. The text does not tell us, which it doubtless would have if this question had been important. It simply says "the veil," not further defining it. It is not the veil that is emphasized, but that which is "within the veil," which in the next verse is said to be our forerunner, even Jesus. It is Christ who is at the other end of the line; it is He who holds the anchor. If He is in the first apartment, that is where our hope and anchor are. If He is in the second apartment, that is where they are. That may be why "veil" is not further defined. Wherever Christ is, there is our anchor and hope.

It is worthy of note that Paul here takes occasion to place the anchor in the sanctuary. In these holy places are the candlestick, the shewbread, the altar of incense—the light, the bread, and perpetual intercession. There are the ark, the mercy seat, the law, the Shekinah, the angelic ministry—and greatest of all, there is "Jesus, made an high priest for ever after the order of Melchisedec." Heb. 6:20. It is here the anchor is fastened. And it will not slip; it will not drag; it will hold.

In the fourth chapter of Hebrews the apostle in a most remarkable way connects the seventh-day Sabbath with the true rest of God. In the sixth chapter he just as significantly connects the new covenant, the Christian's hope and anchor, with the sanctuary. It seems that he is anxious to impress upon the believers the fact that not only is there a sanctuary but also there is Christ within the veil, and that from the sanctuary we may receive hope and strong consolation, and that above all we may know that as long as Christ in the sanctuary holds the cables, the anchor will hold.

With some conception of this, the poet writes:

> "Will your anchor hold in the storm of life,
> When the clouds unfold their wings of strife?
> When the strong tides lift, and the cables strain,
> Will your anchor drift, or firm remain?
>
> "If 'tis safely moor'd, 'twill the storm withstand,
> For 'tis well secured by the Saviour's hand;
> And the cables, pass'd from His heart to thine,
> Can defy the blast, through strength divine.
>
> "It will firmly hold in the straits of Fear,
> When the breakers tell that the reef is near;
> Though the tempest rave and the wild winds blow,
> Not an angry wave shall our bark o'erflow.
>
> "It will surely hold in the floods of death,
> When the waters cold chill our latest breath;

On the rising tide it can never fail,
While our hopes abide within the veil.

"When our eyes behold, in the dawning light,
Shining gates of pearl, our harbor bright,
We shall anchor fast to the heavenly shore,
With the storms all past forevermore,

"We have an anchor that keeps the soul
Steadfast and sure while the billows roll;
Fastened to the Rock which cannot move,
Grounded firm and deep in the Saviour's love."

—W. J. KIRKPATRICK

CHAPTER 7

OF THE BOOK OF HEBREWS

Christ Superior to Melchisedec

SYNOPSIS OF CHAPTER

IN THE FIRST chapter of the epistle the apostle presented Christ as God; in the second chapter he showed that He was also man. In chapter three he compared Moses and Christ, and showed that Christ is superior to Moses. In chapter four he stressed the fact that while Joshua brought the children of Israel into the land, he did not bring them into God's rest, which work is left for Christ to do. In the fifth chapter the author began a discussion of the qualifications of Christ for the office of high priest, but interrupted his description to admonish his hearers that it is time for them to be weaned from milk and begin to take solid food. He continued his exhortation in the sixth chapter, where he warns them to beware of falling away from the faith. In the latter part of the chapter he takes up the thread where he left off in the fifth chapter, and gradually leads up to his subject again, which is Christ, a priest after the order of Melchisedec. This subject he continues in the seventh chapter, in which he enumerates seven points wherein Christ and His priesthood are superior to Melchisedec and his priesthood.

Hebrews 7:1–3. "For this Melchisedec, King of Salem, priest of the most high God, who met Abraham returning from the slaughter of the kings, and blessed him; to whom also Abraham gave a tenth part of all; first being by interpretation King of righteousness, and after that also King of Salem, which is, King of peace; without father, without mother, without descent, having neither beginning of days, nor end of life; but made like unto the Son of God; abideth a priest continually."

All we know historically of Melchisedec is contained in three verses in Genesis and in one verse in the Psalms. (Gen. 14:18–20; Ps. 110:4.) Of most other people mentioned in the Bible there is some intimation of their origin and family, but of Melchisedec we know nothing. As the Jews held Melchisedec in high honor, it is possible they had access to information that we do not have.

Verse 1. We are here introduced to Melchisedec, who was king of Salem as well as a priest of the most high God. Abraham had just rescued Lot, and had also taken some booty. On the way home he met Melchisedec, who blessed him.

Verse 2. The fact that Abraham paid him tithe indicates that Abraham recognized his right to receive tithes, and that hence he was known to him.

There has been much discussion as to who Melchisedec was. Of this the Bible gives no further information than that found in Genesis 14:18–20, and the references in the epistle to the Hebrews. There are some who believe that He was Christ; others, the Holy Spirit; others, Shem; still others, a supernatural being from another world. We take it for granted that if it were important for us to know, God would have given light on the question. In the absence of any such information we may well leave speculation out, and accept him as one of the contemporaries of Abraham, king of one of the small principalities of that time.

"King of righteousness." This may mean that as king he reigned in righteousness, or, as others hold, that he was chief among righteous persons. Likewise "King of peace," or "King of Salem," may mean that he reigned in Salem—which means peace—or that he was a peaceful king. The impression left is that he was a priest of the most high God, and that in addition he was also king, and that both his reign and his personal character justified the attributes of King of righteousness and King of peace.

Verse 3. "Without father, without mother." It is these words that have given rise to the speculation that Melchisedec was some supernatural being, as he must of necessity be if he was actually without father and mother, without beginning of days and without end of life, which assertion can be literally true of the persons of the Godhead only. However, it is not necessary to take this view of the wording.

The Jews were very particular in recording and preserving their genealogies. This was especially true of the priests. No one could serve as priest unless he belonged to the family of Aaron of the tribe of Levi, and this he must be able to prove without any doubt whatsoever. If there was a break in the line somewhere, he would be counted out and thus lose the privileges accorded the priests. For this reason every Jew, and particularly the priests, preserved very carefully all genealogical records.

Of Melchisedec we have no genealogy. There is no record of his birth or of his death. As far as the Bible is concerned, he had neither father nor mother, beginning of days or end of life. Significantly it is added that *he was* made like unto the Son of God, not that he *was* like Him. Even though it is difficult to determine just what is meant by "made," the reading suggests that in God's intent he was to be a type of Christ, and that God directed events to that end. For this reason his genealogy was not preserved, nor is there any other record of either his birth or his death, nor of father or mother. All this fits into the Messianic picture, making it possible for God to use him as a type of the true Priest to come.

We accept the view that Melchisedec was an ordinary human being whom God chose, because of his character and qualifications, to represent Christ. He could not be a divine being, one of the Trinity, for a high priest must be "taken from among men" in order to be able to serve. (Heb. 5:1.) Even Christ could not be high priest until He had become incarnate, had partaken of our human nature and trials, had suffered and learned obedience. Nor could Melchisedec be an angel or some other celestial being, for these are not men, and only a man can be high priest. We are therefore confined to consider Melchisedec an ordinary human being. If so, all we know of him is that he was King of righteousness and King of Salem, and that Abraham paid him tithe. With that we must let the matter rest.

Hebrews 7:4–10. "Now consider how great this man was, unto whom even the patriarch Abraham gave the tenth of the spoils. And verily they that are of the sons of Levi, who receive the office of the priesthood, have a commandment to take tithes of the people according to the law, that is, of their brethren, though they come out of the loins of Abraham: but he whose descent is not counted from them received tithes of Abraham, and blessed him that had the promises. And without all contradiction the less is blessed of the better. And here men that die receive tithes; but there he receiveth them, of whom it is witnessed that he liveth. And as I may so say, Levi also, who receiveth tithes, payed tithes in Abraham. For he was yet in the loins of his father, when Melchisedec met him."

In this section four points are mentioned wherein Melchisedec's priesthood is superior to Aaron's: (a) because Abraham paid him tithe (verses 4–6); (b) because Abraham received Melchisedec's blessing (verse 7); (c) because Melchisedec is a type of One who never dies (verse 8); and (d) because even Levi paid him tithe (verses 9, 10).

Verse 4. "Consider how great this man was." It is the greatness of Melchisedec which the author wishes to stress; for if he can show how great Melchisedec was, then he can easily show that Christ is even greater.

"Even the patriarch." Abraham is here called "the patriarch" to heighten the effect. Melchisedec was so great that "*even* the patriarch" paid him tithes. In doing so, Abraham acknowledged the superior priestly authority of Melchisedec.

Verse 5. "Commandment to take tithes." The Levites had not only permission to receive tithes but a commandment to do so. This constituted them a divinely ordained order. However, they were not the first to take tithes. Melchisedec did so before them. If they were divinely ordained, so was Melchisedec. And the fact that "even the patriarch Abraham" paid Melchisedec tithes shows that he had the highest endorsement that any man could have. If the Levites were authorized by God to receive tithes, Melchisedec was even more so.

Verse 6. "Descent is not counted." Abraham was the friend of God, greater than the Levites. To him were given the promises; he was the father of the faithful. If he recognized Melchisedec, his descendants could not fail to do so also. Melchisedec had the authority of God and the recognition of Abraham. These factors cannot be disregarded in any true estimate of the greatness of Melchisedec.

Verse 7. Melchisedec blessed Abraham. Without contradiction the less is blessed by the greater. As Abraham with bowed head received the blessing of Melchisedec, he recognized his spiritual superiority and authority.

Verse 8. "Here." "There." Here men that die receive tithes. There One receives tithes of whom it is witnessed that He lives.

In these words the author goes beyond Melchisedec to the One whom he represents. Of Christ it is affirmed that "he ever liveth." Verse 25.

Verses 9, 10. "Levi also." Abraham is considered the father of the faithful, and in this sense whatever he did his posterity did in him. Thus even Levi paid tithe to Melchisedec, which is another strong proof of the greatness of Melchisedec.

Hebrews 7:11–19. "If therefore perfection were by the Levitical priesthood, (for under it the people received the law,) what further need was there that another priest should rise after the order of Melchisedec, and not be called after the order of Aaron? For the priesthood being changed, there is made of necessity a change also of the law. For he of whom these things are spoken pertaineth to another tribe, of which no man gave attendance at the altar. For it is evident that our Lord sprang out of Juda; of which tribe Moses spake nothing concerning priesthood. And it is yet far more evident: for that after the similitude of Melchisedec there ariseth another priest, who is made, not after the law of a carnal commandment, but after the power of an endless life. For he testifieth, Thou art a priest for ever after the order of Melchisedec. For there is verily a disannulling of the commandment going before for the weakness and unprofitableness thereof. For the law made nothing perfect, but the bringing in of a better hope, did; by the which we draw nigh unto God."

The fifth point of superiority of the Melchisedec priesthood over that of Aaron is the fact that Aaron's priesthood never made anything perfect, "but the bringing in of a better hope did." (Verses 11, 19.)

The discussion in this section concerns principally the need of a change in the law of the priesthood, necessitated by the weakness and unprofitableness of the whole arrangement.

Verse 11. "What further need." The complaint against the Levitical system was the fact that it could never "make the comers thereunto perfect." This shows plainly that God's intent and purpose was the perfection of the worshipers. Had the Levitical priesthood accomplished this, there would have been no need of another priesthood. But the fact that the priesthood did not effect perfection, and the further fact that God wanted this done, compelled the institution of another priesthood that would accomplish the perfection God had in mind.

On the other hand, if God desired perfection, and if the Levitical system did not or could not produce this, then it was imperative that the new plan should accomplish perfection. If not, there would be no point in changing the priesthood. For this reason much is said in the epistle about perfection. Our new High Priest must produce perfection in Himself and in others, else nothing is gained by the change. Thus, in a very real way Christ is on trial in the kind of men He produces.

Verse 12. "A change also of the law." The law provided that Aaron should be priest and that his sons should serve after him. As Christ did not belong to the tribe of Levi, and as only members of this tribe could be priests, it is evident that there must be a change in the law if Christ is to serve.

Verses 13, 14. "Another tribe." Christ came of the house of David and the tribe of Judah. (Rom. 1:3; Mark 10:47, 48; Micah 5:2; Matt. 1:1; Luke 3:33.) Of this tribe "no man gave attendance at the altar." Only men of the tribe of Levi could do that. This is evident, the writer says, and all Jews would agree with him.

Verse 15. "Far more evident." The apostle has been arguing that there must be a change of the law if there is to be a change of the priesthood. He has shown that Christ is not of the tribe of Levi, yet He is priest, and that therefore the law which says that only men of the tribe of Levi can be priests, must be changed. However, he finds his greatest proof in the prophecy that another priest is to arise after the similitude of Melchisedec. If this is to be, then it is not only evident, but far more evident, that the old Levital law has been abrogated.

Verse 16. "An endless life." Better, "an indissoluble life," one that cannot cease, that cannot be loosed or undone, that continueth ever.

"Carnal commandment" is not here used as a term of reproach, but merely to show the inferior quality of the priesthood under the Levitical ordinances as contrasted with the priesthood of Christ. The eldest son of a priest followed his father in office. This did not always make for the best kind of priests. Also, the length of service for the Levites was not long, at most thirty years, from the age of twenty to fifty, and for the strictly priestly functions the time of service was only twenty or twenty-five years. (1 Chron. 23:24–27; Num. 4:47; 8:24, 25.) The strenuous work of the priests compelled their retirement at fifty, when a man ordinarily should be at his best.

Contrast this with the indissoluble life of Christ. He is a priest forever, "after the power of an endless life."

Verse 17. "Thou art a priest for ever." To this statement the author returns again and again, and on this he bases his argument. No mere man could be a priest forever. The Levitical priests served only a few years. If, therefore, one is to come who is to serve forever, he must be more than a man, more than a Levite. Hence, it is "far more evident" that there must be a change of the priestly law if that kind of priest is to officiate.

As stated above, the law appointed sons to be priests in their father's place, but the son did not always follow in the footsteps of his godly father. Hence, men held holy office who were utterly unfit for this sacred work. As opposed and contrasted with this, Christ is appointed high priest after the power of an endless life. He has no successor who might prove unworthy. The priesthood is not to be given to another. He ever liveth to make intercession for His people, and He is always accessible. This appointment is by God Himself, who testifies that Christ is "a priest for ever after the order of Melchisedec."

Verse 18. "A disannulling of the commandment." The author is still speaking of the law of the Levitical priesthood. It was both weak and unprofitable. Not that it was so originally, for God Himself had instituted it. But it was with the law as with the first covenant, which was good in itself, but which failed because of the people's attitude toward it. The sacrificial law, given to teach abhorrence for sin, was made an instrument for the encouragement of sin. Israel came to believe that their sacrifices paid for their transgression. In this they were encouraged by some of the priests, and the whole service became an abomination. There was nothing for God to do but to abolish both the service and the priesthood.

Verse 19. "The law made nothing perfect." The law provided for sacrifices according to the nature of the offense. Thus a man might offer his sacrifice, bring it to the tabernacle, confess his sin, and go away forgiven. The next day he might sin again, repeat the same service, and be forgiven, and so the next day and the next, throughout the whole year. There was no end to the sacrifices. Even on the Day of Atonement the services were not final in character. As soon as the work on the day was accomplished, another yearly round was begun, and when that was finished, still another, and so year after year. Elsewhere Paul states that the law could "never with those sacrifices which they offer year by year continually make the comers thereunto perfect. For then would they not have ceased to be offered?" Heb. 10:1, 2. The complaint here is that there was no end to the sacrifices, and the reason given is that the law could not make the transgressors perfect, else the offerings would have ceased.

What the law could not do, the bringing in of a better hope did. This hope centers in Christ, for He is the one who takes the place of the Levitical priesthood, which was weak and unprofitable. Hence, we read of Christ that "by one offering he hath perfected for ever them that are sanctified." Heb. 10:14. What the law could not do, Christ did.

Hebrews 7:20–28. "And inasmuch as not without an oath he was made priest: (for those priests were made without an oath; but this with an oath by him that said unto him, The Lord sware and will not repent, Thou art a priest for ever after the order of Melchisedec:) by so much was Jesus made a surety of a better testament. And they truly were made priests, because they were not suffered to continue by reason of death: but this man, because he continueth ever, hath an unchangeable priesthood. Wherefore he is able also to save them to the uttermost that come unto God by him, seeing he ever liveth to make intercession for them. For such an high priest became us, who is holy, harmless, and undefiled, separate from sinners, and made higher than the heavens; who needeth not daily, as those high priests, to offer up sacrifice, first for his own sins, and then for the people's: for this he did once, when he offered up himself. For the law maketh men high priests which have infirmity; but the word of the oath, which was since the law, maketh the Son, who is conse-crated for evermore."

The sixth point of superiority of the Melchisedec priesthood over the Aaronic is its being founded upon an oath, even the oath of God. (Verses 20, 21.) The seventh and last point in its unchangeable priest-hood in contrast to the constant changes in the Levitical.

In verse 22 the author introduces the idea of the covenant of which Christ is the surety and mediator. He does not in this place discuss it further, but only introduces the subject to prepare the reader for what he later has to say. He does, however, present Christ as one who is able to save to the uttermost and who ever liveth to make intercession for us. Christ being holy, harmless, and undefiled, a surety is provided for us that is adequate and will stand the test of God.

Verses 20, 21. "The Lord sware and will not repent." Twice before in Hebrews we are told that God sware: when He assured Abraham of the seed that should come, and when He sware that Israel should not enter into His rest. (Heb. 3:11; 6:13.)

Oath taking is always a solemn occasion. In this case God swears and "will not repent." "Thou art a priest for ever after the order of Melchisedec." We may well ask why this should be made such a solemn occasion, and why it was necessary for God to say that He would not repent of making Christ a priest after the order of Melchisedec. Priests were inducted without an oath. Why an oath in this case, and why the statement that God will not repent of it? On the surface this gives the impression of being a most unusual occasion, and that much was involved. What is the reason for this?

That much was involved in Christ's appointment to the office of high priest is evident. The cost to God is indicated in the statement that He will not repent of it. Great as has been the cost of sin to man, this is nothing compared to its cost to God. But despite this cost, God will not repent of it. Let us briefly consider this cost.

1. The plan of redemption involved the death of the Son of God. Unless we conceive of God as being entirely unlike us, this cost must have been immense. "I might give myself," one father said upon hearing the story of the cross, "but I could never give my son."

2. The cost to the Son of God was equal to that of the Father. He must become incarnate, be subject to His own creatures and from them suffer every indignity, and at last be hanged on the tree as a criminal. He must take our place as subject, while man takes the place of ruler and judge.

3. The plan of salvation would eventually involve a reorganization of the universe. Man would become an

heir of God and joint heir with Christ. He would be given a place on Christ's throne, as Christ sits on the Father's throne. The human race would be elevated to become kings and priests, and though eventually God receives the kingdom and becomes all in all, there will ever be a sharing of power and responsibility that will raise man greatly above the angels, and make him a partaker of the divine nature.

The plan of redemption was not something thrust on God to which He had to submit because of Satan's charges and rebellion. Rather, every step in the plan of God for the salvation of man was planned by Him beforehand, even from the days of eternity. God was not forced into a corner because of sin. His original plan involved man's elevation and his sharing the throne, and all this was included in Christ's appointment as high priest. This appointment was confirmed by an oath, and to this God adds that He will not repent. This gives us security for all eternity to come.

Verse 22. "By so much." "So much" includes what we have briefly sketched. Man was and is the gainer; the cost to God is above our comprehension; but God does not repent of what He has done. The eventual outcome will show the exceeding greatness and goodness of God.

"A surety." "Surety" here has the meaning of one becoming responsible for, or guaranteeing the performance of, some agreement. In the "better testament" Christ is the surety both on God's part and on man's. By His death He gave assurance to man that God will go the whole way in fulfilling His part of the agreement; by His life He gave assurance to God that man will fulfill his part. Being both God and man, He could do this.

"Testament" is the same word used elsewhere for covenant. There has been much discussion in regard to its correct use, but we may safely assume that when God chooses a word that means both covenant and testament, or either, He chooses it because this word expresses what He has in mind. As we proceed we shall find that God's covenant is also a testament, and the testament is a covenant, and that as the original word means both testament and covenant, God uses the right expression to convey both conceptions.

Verses 23, 24. "An unchangeable priesthood." These verses are clear in their meaning. The Levitical priests died, and could not continue their work. Whenever a high priest died, another priest would have to carry on. This change was disadvantageous, in theory at least, in that the same high priest who was responsible in the daily service could not complete his work in the services of the Day of Atonement. It happens at times that an attorney-at-law in charge of a case at court, because of illness or death, is unable to continue, and another must take his place. The second man may be as good as the first, but he does not know or understand fully the background as did the first, and the client feels uneasy.

This is the picture given us here. The Levitical priests could not continue by reason of death. But Christ can continue. He has an unchangeable priesthood. He "ever liveth to make intercession."

Verse 25. Save "to the uttermost." All would be happy if the gates of heaven were open just wide enough so they could. barely press in, but this is not Christ's idea of salvation. He wants the gates swung wide open, and His people to come in as those who have a right to enter. "Blessed are they that do his commandments, that they may have right to the tree of life, and may enter in through the gates into the city." Rev. 22:14.

Some approach God with slavish fear. This is not pleasing to God. "Ye have not received the spirit of bondage again to fear; but ye have received the Spirit of adoption, whereby we cry, Abba, Father. The Spirit itself beareth witness with our spirit, that we are the children of God: and if children, then heirs; heirs of God, and joint-heirs with Christ, if so be that we suffer with him, that we may be also glorified together." Rom. 8:15–17.

As the Christian contrasts his condition with that of the believers in olden time, he better understands his privileges. Though the cities of refuge were a wonderful blessing, and doubtless saved many lives from the avenger of blood, there is no comparison between that salvation and the salvation provided in Christ. Christ can and does save to the uttermost those who come to Him. He ever lives to make intercession.

What is meant by the statement that Christ can save to the uttermost?

1. He can wash away sins of the deepest dye. "Though your sins be as scarlet, they shall be as white as snow; though they be red like crimson, they shall be as wool. If ye be willing and obedient, ye shall eat the good of the land." Isa. 1:18, 19.

2. He can save fornicators, idolaters, adulterers, effeminate, abusers of themselves with mankind, thieves, covetous, drunkards, revilers, extortioners. (1 Cor. 6:9–11.) A man's station in life will neither help nor hinder him. Christ saves poor and rich alike.

3. He can save man, body, soul, and spirit, and purify mind, will, heart, memory, conscience, imagination. His salvation is an eternal salvation. He saves "to the uttermost."

Verse 26. "Holy." It became us to have a high priest that is holy, harmless, and undefiled. It was fitting and needful that we should have such a one.

The word here used for "holy" has distinct reference to character. It means one who is dedicated; consecrated, sanctified, completed, perfected. Christ is all this. In no respect does He come short. He challenged men to convince or convict Him of sin, and none accepted the challenge. He was wholehearted for God and man.

"Harmless." Guileless, innocent, not vindictive, not planning any harm to anyone, not corrupting by example. On the positive side it means doing good to others, planning for their well-being, setting a right example.

"Undefiled." Chaste, pure, not corrupted or corruptible, no stain of any kind, not adversely influenced by surroundings. It suggests not merely holiness and purity in itself, but the added thought of having passed through experiences that might have a tendency to leave a stain but did not do so.

"Separate from sinners." Christ had the capacity of mingling with sinners and yet being separate from them. He had the ability to be alone in a crowd. Note how Luke puts it: "It came to pass, as he was alone praying, his disciples were with him." Luke 9:18. The American Revised Version says, "As he was praying apart, the disciples were with him." The reading here is very distinct. The disciples did not *come* to Him as He was praying alone; they were *with* Him, yet He was apart from them. In like manner Christ was with sinners and yet apart from them. He could isolate Himself in a crowd; He could pray apart, while His disciples were with Him. He knew how to master circumstances.

"Higher than the heavens." This is Christ in His exaltation. He is higher than anything created, whether it be thrones or principalities, dominions or powers. He is at the Father's right hand. It is this kind of high priest that becomes us.

Verse 27. "Who needeth not daily." Some think that this should read "yearly" instead of "daily," for we have no record that the high priest brought a sin offering daily. There was indeed an offering commanded to be offered daily by Aaron and his successors, but this appears to be a meal offering, and not a sin offering. (Lev. 6:20–22.) The difficulty is therefore with the statement that the high priest of old presented a sin offering daily, and that Christ did not need to do this.

This difficulty vanishes, however, when we consider that whatever services the priests performed, they did as deputies of the high priest. They officiated in his place, and what they did was counted as though the high priest himself did it. They were merely helpers, and as they offered sin offerings daily, the high priest can be said to offer daily.

When the tabernacle was first built in the wilderness, the high priest performed all the services that were later done by the priests. He lit the lamps in the holy place; he changed the shewbread; he offered the incense and officiated at the altar. (Ex. 30:7, 8; Lev. 24:5–9; Lev. 1:5.) When others took part, they merely served as his assistants, and did his work for him. He had the right to officiate at any time and in any capacity. Illustrative of this is the fact that throughout the history of the temple it was the custom of the high priest to officiate in the daily service the week preceding the Day of Atonement. We therefore accept the statement that the high priest *daily*, in the persons of the priests, offered for his own sins.

"For his own sins." On the Day of Atonement the high priest offered first for his own sins and then for the sins of the people. (Lev. 16:11, 15.) This was necessary. Being sinful, he could not appear before God in the most holy place unless and until he had brought an offering for himself. Christ did not need to do this. He was sinless.

The question has been raised as to the meaning of the statement, "This he did once." What is meant by "this"? Did Christ offer for His own sins once, as did the high priest, and then for the people? Christ had no sin of His own. The only sins He had were those He bore for us. He was *made* to be sin. When, therefore, He offered Himself once, He provided for all the sins He carried. Those sins were our sins, which He bore in His body on the tree. They were *His* sins only as He had taken upon Himself the responsibility for them.

Verse 28. The priests had infirmity. Christ had none. The law made sinful men high priests. The oath made Christ high priest. If the law of heredity had been invoked, Christ could never have been high priest, for only the sons of Aaron could hold this office. As it is we have a High Priest consecrated forevermore, because God went outside the rank of the priestly succession to choose His own Son. This is significant in view of the stress some churches place upon apostolic succession. Had this principle been followed, Christ would not now be a high priest consecrated for evermore. He would have been ruled out as ineligible.

ADDITIONAL NOTES

The Ceremonial Law

One of the chief weaknesses of the Levitical system was the fact that it provided only for the forgiveness of unintentional sins. In each case for which a sin offering was brought, it was specifically provided that it was only for sins done in ignorance. "If a soul shall sin through ignorance;" "if the whole congregation of Israel sin through ignorance;" "when a ruler hath sinned, and done somewhat through ignorance;" "if any one of the common people sin through ignorance." Lev. 4:2, 13, 22, 27. In each case, as noted, only sin done through ignorance was provided for. Thus, after a man had brought the required sin offering, he was still in uncertainty as to sins he had committed knowingly. For such there was no sacrifice. As he left the sanctuary, the burden of sin was not entirely lifted. Only minor sins, sins committed unwittingly, were forgiven; but the sins that really held him down were those he knew were wrong. In his heart he must have felt that though sins done in ignorance were deplorable, they did not begin to compare with sins that he had deliberately planned and executed. He could but feel that God would in some way cover his ignorant transgression. What did concern him were the deliberate and willful sins. For them there was no provision in the Mosaic system. But these were the very sins that counted. These were the sins that touched the conscience. And for them Moses had no forgiveness.

For this reason the gospel must have made a strong appeal to those in Israel who were concerned about sin. In Antioch, Paul summed up his message in these words: "Be it known unto you therefore, men and brethren, that through this man is preached unto you the forgiveness of sins: and by him all that believe are justified from all things, from which ye could not be justified by the law of Moses." Acts 13:38, 39.

In general, only sins of ignorance were provided for in the law of Moses, but now Paul proclaims forgiveness for "*all things*, from which ye could not be justified by the law of Moses." Here he states what the Jews already knew, that they could not be justified from all sins by the law of Moses. The good news was that "through this man is preached unto you the forgiveness of sins," and that through Christ they could be justified from "*all* things." The sacrifices and gifts that were offered daily on the altar could not satisfy as "pertaining to the conscience," but only sanctified "to the purifying of the flesh." Heb. 9:9, 13. By way of contrast, "how much more shall the blood of Christ, who through the eternal Spirit offered himself without spot to God, purge your conscience from dead works to serve the living God." Verse 14.

As noted above, however much a man might be forgiven his "unwitting" sins, his conscience would not be clear. For the real sins, those he had committed knowingly and wittingly, were not covered by any sacrifice he could offer. Every Jew must have felt this deficiency keenly and longed for some remedy that would affect the conscience. And this remedy was provided in Christ. He brought in a better hope.

Lest any should think that only sins done unwittingly could be forgiven in Old Testament times, let us hasten to assert that there was a Saviour in the time of Moses as well as now. All that Paul contended was that there were many things from which they could not be justified *by the law of Moses*. He never for a moment meant to say that there was not full and free forgiveness for all kinds of sins—one excepted—then as well as now. His only contention was that there was no provision for willful sin *in the law of Moses*. And that is true.

How, then, were willful sins forgiven at that time? The same as now. Though your sins were as scarlet, though they were red like crimson, forgiveness could be had. (Isa. 1:18.) But *forgiveness could not be had by offering a sacrifice*. If God had said, "If a man commit adultery with his neighbor's wife, and do that which is evil, let him bring to me a lamb without blemish," God would set a value on sin, and men would receive the idea that sin would be forgiven at a price. That would completely destroy moral values and do untold harm. It was such a conception that led Tetzel in the days of Luther to sell indulgences, which people perverted into liberty to commit sin at a price. In the Old Testament, adultery was punishable by death. (Lev. 20:10.)

God could not afford to give man the idea that purposeful sin could be condoned or winked at in any way. David knew better. When he had sinned his grievous sin he stated, "Thou desirest not sacrifice; else would I give it: thou delightest not in burnt offering. The sacrifices of God are a broken spirit: a broken and a contrite heart, O God, thou wilt not despise." Ps. 51:16, 17.

Remember, this was in Old Testament times. David knew that God would not accept a sacrifice for that kind of sin. But he also knew that God would not despise "a broken and a contrite heart." Sins, real sins, were forgiven then as now, by repentance. There has been no change.

In Galatians, Paul asks a searching question: "Wherefore then serveth the law?" Gal. 3:19. Other versions more graphically translate: "Why then the law?" As applied to the ceremonial law we may partially answer the question by saying that it did serve a very definite purpose. It taught men that sin meant death. It taught men that when they sinned, an innocent animal must die, and that they were the cause of its death, and hence had to slay the animal themselves. From this they would most certainly receive the idea that even sin done in ignorance was serious, and that when they sinned, an innocent victim must die in their stead. However, they would also be aware of the fact that after they had done all that the ceremonial law required, they were still not forgiven all their sins. Their conscience would call to mind many things for which no sacrifice could be brought. What were they to do about these sins? Here the prophetic message came to their aid. Isaiah—and the other prophets—directed their attention away from sacrifices of bulls and goats, to the Lamb of God who "was wounded for our transgressions" and "bruised for our iniquities: the chastisement of our peace was upon him; and with his stripes we are healed. All we like sheep have gone astray; we have turned every one to his own way; and the Lord hath laid on him the iniquity of us all." Isa. 53:5, 6. The command of God was clear, "Thou shalt make his soul an offering for sin....He shall bear their iniquities.....He bare the sin of many, and made intercession for the transgressor." Verses 10–12.

This put a spiritual application on the sacrifices made. Sinners saw instinctively that the Son of God was the real Lamb: that no lamb of the flock could pay for a man's sin. Thus considered, they understood that the whole service was symbolic and pointed to the death of the Messiah to come, in whom alone true forgiveness could be had.

The establishment of cities of refuge also helped to instruct the people in God's plan of saving sinners. If a man committed a murder in olden times, the avenger of blood had a right to avenge the crime by killing the murderer. (Num. 35:19.) However, if the slaying was accidental and not premeditated, God had provided a temporary refuge. "I will appoint thee a place whither he shall flee," was God's dictum. Ex. 21:13. Originally this was the sanctuary, but in later times six cities of refuge were established in Israel where one who had committed an unintentional murder might flee. This was because it would be impossible for many to make the long journey to Jerusalem to escape the avenger of blood. These cities of refuge were conveniently located to accommodate all Israel. The relief, however, was only temporary. If they were found guilty of a premeditated act, they were taken from the city and slain.

This arrangement was a merciful provision for one who had unwittingly sinned, but it did not automatically save him. Innocent or guilty, he had to stand trial.

"And they shall be unto you cities for refuge from the avenger; that the manslayer die not, until he stand before the congregation in judgment." Num. 35:12. "The congregation shall judge between the slayer and the revenger of blood according to these judgments: and the congregation shall deliver the slayer out of the hand of the revenger of blood, and the congregation shall restore him to the city of his refuge, whither he was fled: and he shall abide in it unto the death of the high priest, which was anointed with the holy oil." Verses 24, 25.

Even after a man had been declared innocent of intentional murder, he still was not safe, for the avenger of blood might at any time kill him if he strayed beyond the city limits. This was the law governing such a case:

"If the slayer shall at any time come without the border of the city of his refuge, whither he was fled, and the revenger of blood find him without the borders of the city of his refuge, and the revenger of blood kill the slayer; he shall not be guilty of blood: because he should have remained in the city of his refuge until the death of the high priest: but after the death of the high priest the slayer shall return into the land of his possession." Verses 26–28.

Thus the man was saved, if innocent of deliberate sin, but it was an unsatisfactory and incomplete salvation. He was guiltless and had been so declared, but yet he could not return to his home. He must stay in the city of refuge until the death of the high priest, whether that be a day or twenty years. His life was saved, but he was not free. Any misstep out of the city, and the avenger of blood would get him. And, of course, if he was guilty of premeditated murder, he was executed. In consideration of this, we agree with the author of the book of Hebrews, that we need a "better hope." We need One who can "save them to the uttermost that come unto God by him." Heb. 7:25.

The whole economy of Israel was at best imperfect, but it did point to something better. This something better is what the book of Hebrews presents. The author is intent upon making clear the difference between what was provided in the sanctuary service of old and what Christ can and will do. His argument could not fail to make a deep impression upon his readers. They well knew the shortcomings, of their religious system, and many were longing for consolation in Israel.

CHAPTER 8

OF THE BOOK OF HEBREWS

The Two Covenants

SYNOPSIS OF CHAPTER

BEGINNING with a discussion of Christ's work as high priest in the true tabernacle not made with hands, the author turns, in verse 6, to a consideration of the old and the new covenant. Finding fault with the people, God announces that He will make a new covenant based on better promises than the old covenant. In this covenant He will write the law in the heart, and will also be merciful to their unrighteousness, and their sins and iniquities He will remember no more.

Hebrews 8:1–5. "Now of the things which we have spoken this is the sum: We have such an high priest, who is set on the right hand of the throne of the Majesty in the heavens; a minister of the sanctuary, and of the true tabernacle, which the Lord pitched, and not man. For every high priest is ordained to offer gifts and sacrifices: wherefore it is of necessity that this man have somewhat also to offer. For if he were on earth, he should not be a priest, seeing that there are priests that offer gifts according to the law: who serve unto the example and shadow of heavenly things, as Moses was admonished of God when he was about to make the tabernacle: for, See, saith he, that thou make all things according to the pattern shewed to thee in the mount."

In these verses the apostle is summing up what he has said before. Christ is at the right hand of God; He is a minister of the sanctuary and the true tabernacle, and offers gifts and sacrifices. If He were on earth He would not be priest, for He is not of the tribe of Levi. His ministry is the true ministry, of which the service on earth was only a shadow.

Verse 1. "This is the sum." The author has laid the foundation. He is now ready to build on it, but before doing so, he presents a summary of what he has said.

"We have such an high priest," not an ordinary high priest, but one who is "set at the right hand of the throne of the Majesty in the heavens." His high place indicates His authority. For a further discussion of this, see notes on Hebrews 1:3.

Verse 2. "A minister of the sanctuary, and of the true tabernacle, which the Lord pitched, and not man." The earthly sanctuary was a shadow; the real sanctuary is in heaven. That Christ is here called a minister of the sanctuary signifies that He does more than hold the title merely. He ministers. He serves. He is high priest.

Verse 3. It is evident that if Christ is to minister He must have "somewhat also to offer," or He could not serve. Ordinarily priests offered "gifts and sacrifices." "Of necessity" Christ must also offer something.

Verse 4. The question as to when Christ became priest has been much discussed. Did He become priest at His baptism, His ascension, or at some other time? According to the text we are here considering, a priest could not begin to serve until He had "somewhat...to offer." As Christ ministers His own blood, He could not begin to minister until that blood was shed. This does not mean that He was not priest before, for one must be made a priest before He can minister; but the exact time when He became priest we do not know. At Calvary He was both priest and victim. As Aaron and his sons were selected some time before their dedication, and spent the intervening time in preparation and in getting acquainted with their duties, so it may well be that Christ became priest on earth at the beginning of His teaching ministry, that the intervening years were years of preparation, and that He was officially installed after His ascension.

That His earthly life was a preparation for His assuming the office of high priest has been asserted earlier in this epistle. Our High Priest "can have compassion on the ignorant, and on them that are out of the way; for that he himself also is compassed with infirmity." Heb. 5:2. He has been "touched with the feeling of our infirmities" and "was in all points tempted like as we are, yet without sin." Heb. 4:15. "In all things it behoved him to be made like unto his brethren, that he might be a merciful and faithful high priest in things pertaining to God, to make reconciliation for the sins of the people. For in that he himself hath suffered being tempted, he is able to succour them that are tempted." Heb. 2:17, 18.

These verses clearly indicate that the days of His earthly sojourn were days of preparation, "that he might be a merciful and faithful high priest." Heb. 2:17. In view of this we may safely assert that His life on earth was a preparation for His high priesthood, and that His ministry did not begin until His preparation had ended.

This effectively disposes of the contention that Christ officiated as priest before His incarnation. Two things made this impossible: first, He had not finished His preparation; second, He had not shed

His blood, and hence did not have it to offer. That He was the lamb slain from the foundation of the world, that He was mediator from eternity, is not denied but asserted. He was Saviour in the same sense that He was the slain lamb: in the purposed plan of God that stems from the days of eternity. But we are not to confuse this with His actual death in time, nor with His actual ministry in heaven based on His death on Calvary.

"If he were on earth, he should not be a priest." The rules of the Levitical priesthood were strictly enforced and if Christ were on earth, He would not be able to qualify. Only those of the tribe of Levi were eligible, and Christ belonged to the tribe of Judah. His was an independent priesthood and a heavenly one. The priests offered gifts and sacrifices "according to the law." Christ "through the eternal Spirit offered himself." Heb. 9:14. His priesthood was a spiritual one.

Confusion and disagreement in regard to the ministry of Christ can be avoided if the distinction between His official induction into office *in time* is distinguished from His work as mediator since sin began. Christ was appointed mediator in the counsels of eternity. Men were saved by His mediation in the Old Testament, the same as in the New. And as there is only one name by which we may be saved, Christ was a Saviour as verily a thousand years before His incarnation as a thousand years after. He was the "lamb slain from the foundation of the world." Rev. 13:8. There has never been any other Saviour.

When Christ was born in Bethlehem, a Saviour was born. He had always been a Saviour, but now He was revealed *in time.* And from this viewpoint it could truly be said, "Call his name Jesus; for he *shall save* his people from their sins." Matt. 1:21. In view of the incarnation salvation could be spoken of as future.

We therefore hold that Christ was mediator from eternity, but that the actual and official induction into His high priestly office took place in time, and that He could not *officiate* as priest until His installation consequent upon His ascension. He had given His life on Calvary; the victim had died, and the blood had been shed. Now He had something to offer, and God introduces and acknowledges Him as high priest after the order of Melchisedec. His birth was real; His death was real; the blood was real; its ministration is real. Christ's eternal mediation should not be confused with the visible manifestation of it in time. To hold that the blood shed on Calvary is real, but that its ministration is not real; to believe that Christ's earthly life was a preparation and fitting that "He might be a merciful and faithful high priest," and yet reject and deny the actual ministry for which He made the preparation, seems inconsistent. If there is not a real ministry in heaven then consistency would demand that those who deny such ministry should also deny the literality of the death and of the blood poured out, and join those critics who deny the reality of both the blood and the atonement.

Verse 5. "Example and shadow." There are vital differences between the ministration on earth and the one in heaven, yet the earthly was an example and shadow of the heavenly. A shadow at times is longer than the object, at other times shorter; details are lacking, and it is hazardous to draw too many inferences from a shadow. Yet the general outline is discernible, and a fairly clear idea may ordinarily be had of that which casts the shadow.

"Example" is a little more definite than shadow. Although "shadow" has specific reference to the general outlines of the sanctuary and its two apartments, "example" would more easily fit the services of the sanctuary. These examples would not be exhaustive, but they would be representative; and again it may be supposed that they would give a fairly correct idea of the general ministration and ritual.

Those who reject the idea that there is any vital likeness between the service on earth and the service in heaven fail to understand the message of the book of Hebrews, and thus must fail to co-operate with Christ in the important work now going on above.

On the other hand those who attempt to make every little detail, every board and nail in the tabernacle, have some special significance, and rein others up who refuse to accept their interpretations, are equally at fault. "Example" and "shadow" are God's terms to describe the earthly sanctuary. We will do well to hold to this.

Hebrews 8:6–13. "But now hath he obtained a more excellent ministry, by how much also he is the mediator of a better covenant, which was established upon better promises. For if that first covenant had been faultless, then should no place have been sought for the second. For finding fault with them, he saith, Behold, the days come, saith the Lord, when I will make a new covenant with the house of Israel and with the house of Judah: not according to the covenant that I made with their fathers in the day when I took them by the hand to lead them out of the land of Egypt; because they continued not in my covenant, and I regarded them not, saith the Lord. For this is the covenant that I will make with the house of Israel after those days, saith the Lord; I will put my laws into their mind, and write them in their hearts: and I will be to them a God, and they shall be to me a people: and they shall not teach every man his neighbour, and every man his brother, saying, Know the Lord: for all shall know me, from the least to the greatest. For I will be merciful to their unrighteousness, and their sins and their iniquities will I remember no more. In that he saith, A new covenant, he hath made the first old. Now that which decayeth and waxeth old is ready to vanish away."

In this section the author enters upon a discussion of the covenants. The Greek word for "covenant" occurs in the New Testament thirty-three times, and is translated "covenant" twenty-one times and "testament" twelve, though the original word in all cases is the same. As this word may mean both "covenant" and "testament," the context must determine which translation is most appropriate for the occasion.

Christ's ministry is more excellent than the earthly ministry of the Aaronic priests, as He is mediator of a better covenant. There was no fault to be found with the old covenant as such, for God Himself had prescribed the terms. It was the people who were at fault. *They* continued not in the covenant. This statement places the stress where it should be placed. Had the people continued in the covenant, it would have been a good covenant and there would have been found no place for a second. When the people failed, God was compelled to recognize their failure and establish a new covenant. The law which they had broken He now writes in the heart, and provision is made to restore them by forgiveness should they come short.

Verse 6. "A more excellent ministry." As the reality is more perfect than the shadow, so is Christ's ministry, "more excellent" than its type. The ground for the more excellent ministry is found in the fact that He is the mediator of a better covenant established upon better promises.

Mediator in the New Testament is the same as "daysman" in the Old. (Job 9:33.) A daysman was so called because he appointed a day upon which he would hear and decide upon the case appealed to him, and attempt to bring the parties at variance to an agreement. The American Revised Version has "umpire," which is defined as "a person to whose sole decision a controversy or question between the parties is referred." Job hoped that such a daysman "might lay his hand upon us both," drawing both together and establishing justice and peace.

A mediator must understand both parties to the controversy, the rights and claims of each, and must have their confidence if he is to be successful in his work. He must be fair to both sides, impartial, without bias.

Of the six times the word "mediator" occurs in the New Testament, four times it refers to Christ. He is the daysman between God and man, and can lay His hands on both. As God, He understands God and can speak for Him. As man He understands man and can transact for man with God. Only the God-man can be daysman. He only understands both.

"A better covenant," "better promises." Christ is the mediator of the better covenant. The word "better" suggests that the first covenant was not as good as the second, that it was faulty and needed replacement.

The question immediately arises, In what respect is the new covenant better than the old? The answer is suggested by the fact that the new was established on better promises. But again the question occurs:

Better promises by whom? by God? by man? or both? This needs to be determined.

Verse 7. "That first covenant" was not faultless. Had it been, there would have been no need for a second. This brings up some other questions. How did it happen that God made a covenant with Israel which He knew was faulty and had to be replaced? Would it not have been better to omit the first and establish only the better covenant?

The word "covenant" occurs nearly three hundred times in the Old Testament. The Hebrew word is *berith*. Its derivation is uncertain, probably from "to cut," referring to the ancient custom of cutting a victim to pieces, as in Genesis 15:17 and Jeremiah 34:18, 19.

Davidson makes the following comment:

At any rate the word *bond* would approximate more nearly towards expressing the various usages of *berith* than any other word, for the term is used not only where two parties reciprocally bind themselves, but where one party imposes a bond upon the other, or where a party assumes a bond upon himself." —*A Dictionary of the Bible*, James Hastings, editor, vol. 1, pp. 509, 510, art. "Covenant."

The definition that a covenant is an agreement between two or more persons is correct as far as it applies to equals, where the covenant is mutually imposed and mutually binding. Where God and man are concerned, it may be better to state that a covenant consists of promises made by the Creator, suspended upon conditions to be fulfilled by the creature, and an appropriate penalty for failure to fulfill the conditions. God is always the one who proposes the covenant and determines the conditions.

The Bible recognizes only two conditions upon which life and happiness may be obtained: perfect obedience, or faith. The covenant of life, existing from eternity, rested upon perfect obedience. It was this covenant that was offered Adam and Eve in the Garden of Eden. In Adam the world had its probation. When he failed, the world failed. As its federal head, mankind was represented in him.

Christ, as the second Adam, assumed the place and obligation of the first Adam, and fulfilled the unsatisfied covenant. In virtue of this He became the new head of humanity, and God now deals with Him as man's representative. Thus in Christ mankind is restored. It now becomes the duty of Christ to bring men into satisfactory relation to God. By His demonstration that mankind—He Himself in His humiliation—can keep the law, He wins a second trial for man. It is His work to bring man back to the point where he can keep the law. This will take much of the grace of God, much patience, but Christ has contracted to make man more precious than the gold of Ophir, and He perseveres till His work is done and He can present a people who keep the commandments of God.

In order to accomplish this work, there must needs be forgiveness, for man has a bent to sinning, and it is necessary that he be forgiven again and again. This forgiveness constitutes the covenant of grace, and is based upon the promise of the Father that He will be merciful to man.

This covenant of grace in its manward aspect is between Christ and the sinner. Christ continues to work with the sinner until he is fully restored. When this is accomplished, Christ presents man as fulfilling the original covenant offered Adam in the garden, the same covenant through which Christ won the right to become man's representative. For a further study of the covenants, see notes on "The Covenants," at the end of this chapter.

Verses 8, 9. We are here told that the weakness of the first covenant was not in the covenant itself, nor did the fault lie in God. It was the people who were faulty. "They continued not in my covenant," God says. They started out well, they promised to do, but they soon forgot and did not continue in the covenant. For this reason God "regarded them not." Yet He did not cut them off entirely. He was willing to make a new covenant with them, a covenant established upon better promises. As the fault lay with the people, as they were the ones who did not continue in the covenant, though they had promised to do so, they needed to make some new and better promises, which they would keep.

But how could their new promises, however well meant, have any more validity than their first promises? They might promise once more, but there was no surety that they would not again break their promise. They needed someone to come to their rescue and promise for them, or become surety for the fulfillment of their promise. Only thus could a covenant be made, established upon better promises. When God, therefore, says that the new covenant will be established upon better promises, He means that the promises must be better than those which the people made and broke. This was done by Christ assuming man's place, and promising for him.

We raised the question as to why God made a covenant with Israel when He knew they would break it. God did this because it was the only thing He could do. Had He refused to grant them the privilege of a trial, they would ever have contended that God did not give them an opportunity to show what they *could* do; that they were abundantly able to do just what they said they would do; but that God had refused to let them try. So God had no choice. He must give them the opportunity of trying. There was no other way to satisfy them.

That God knew they would not and could not keep their promise in any strength of their own is evident from the fact that while He had made an agreement with them which did not include any provision for forgiveness, God immediately called Moses into the mount and gave him instruction about the sanctuary, the whole service of which revolved about forgiveness. The people had not asked for a clause about forgiveness to be inserted in the covenant. They had, in effect, rejected it as unnecessary; they felt perfectly able to do all that God had commanded; but God made elaborate preparations in the sacrificial system for forgiveness before the people ever transgressed by dancing about the golden calf. At the end of the forty days Moses had complete instructions in regard to the sanctuary. These instructions, recorded in chapters twenty-five to thirty-one of Exodus, were given before God took official notice of the covenant-breaking idol worship of the people.

God had called the attention of the people to the fact that the covenant they were about to enter contained no provision for failure. "Behold, I send an Angel before thee, to keep thee in the way, and to bring thee into the place which I have prepared. Beware of him, and obey his voice, provoke him not; for he will not pardon your transgressions: for my name is in him," Ex. 23:20, 21. But this warning did not make any impression on them. They felt able to do their part. (Ex. 19:8; 24:3, 7.) But God knew better, and He was working out a plan by which forgiveness might be had.

These considerations justify the belief that while the old covenant did not contain a provision for forgiveness of sin as did the new, it was not God's fault. He was willing to insert it, but as the people did not feel any need of it, there was nothing that God could do but give them a trial that they might show what they could do. This was necessary to demonstrate to them their inability to do what they had promised, and to make them realize their need of help from on high.

ADDITIONAL NOTES

The Covenants

Adam, upon his creation, was promised life on condition of obedience. This was communicated to him by God Himself. "And the Lord God commanded the man, saying, Of every tree of the garden thou mayest freely eat: but of the tree of the knowledge of good and evil, thou shalt not eat of it: for in the day that thou eatest thereof thou shalt surely die." Gen. 2:16, 17. This is merely another way of saying, "Obey and live; disobey and perish."

Nature, as God created it, was harmonious. Every creature, every bird, every animal and fish, every plant, every flower and shrub, everything living, could and did have life only as it conformed to the rules of life governing its existence. The fishes were given water as the element in which they might enjoy life. Should they change their natural habitat, and attempt to continue life on land, they would perish. The plants were rooted to the ground, and the rules of life demanded that they so remain. Animals were made to roam the fields, and any attempt to live like a fish or fly like a bird would end disastrously.

When Adam was created he found an ordered world where each creature had its allotted place, where law governed, and where all had life on condition of conforming to the rules of life. Over such a world he was set as ruler.

To him, as to all creation, life was given on condition of obedience to the law of life. The laws of nature applied to him as to all that God had created. He was given his food as other creatures were given theirs, and his field of activity and place in the general scheme of creation appointed him. He was to be fruitful and multiply; he was to subdue the earth; he was to have dominion over every living thing. He was to rule over all. (Gen. 1:28.)

There was an important difference, however, between Adam and the creatures of the field which God had created. Adam was created in the image of God, endowed with intellect and freedom of choice. This put his obedience on a higher level than that of the rest of the creatures.

Animals obeyed God and nature's laws, not by any voluntary act, but from instinct. There was no moral value attached to their obedience. Adam, on the contrary, could refuse to obey; he could defy God should he so choose; always, of course, as a responsible being abiding by the consequences.

This made it necessary for God to devise a test that would reveal Adam's intention to obey, or to go his own way. It would not be wise for God to give him independent authority or endow him with unconditional life, until he had been tested to see whether he would abide by the rules of life laid down by God as the condition of continued existence. All nature was under law, and every creature obeyed law. Would man voluntarily submit himself? This must be shown.

The command not to eat of the tree of the knowledge of good and evil was not the only command Adam was to obey. It was merely a test to determine his willingness to obey God in other things. Of this Charles Hodge, in his *Systematic Theology*, says:

"It was given simply to be the outward and visible test to determine whether he was willing to obey God in all things. Created holy, with all his affections pure, there was the more reason that the test of his obedience should be an outward and positive command; something wrong simply because it was forbidden, and not evil in its own nature. It would thus be seen that Adam obeyed for the sake of obeying. His obedience was more directly to God, and not to his own reason."
—Volume 2, p. 119.

A. A. Hodge has this to say:

"The command to abstain from eating the forbidden fruit was only made a special and decisive test of that general obedience. As the matter forbidden was morally indifferent in itself, the command was admirably adapted to be a clear and naked test of submission to God's absolute will as such." —*Outlines of Theology*, pp. 230, 231.

The command not to eat of the forbidden fruit was a positive command, given for the purpose of test. It is called positive because its sole. ground is a "Thus saith the Lord." A positive command concerns that which is not wrong in itself but wrong because it is forbidden, and not evil in its own nature. God had created the tree of the knowledge of good and evil as well as the other trees. The evil did not inhere in the tree as such, but in disobedience to God's command. Had God chosen any other tree and forbidden man to eat of it, the test would have been the same. In any case it would have been a positive command, grounded solely in God's will. In obeying such a command, man lays aside his own reasoning and accepts God's, and in doing this, he recognizes a mind and an authority higher than his own.

THE COVENANT OF LIFE

Adam and Eve at their creation had a knowledge of the law of God. As. in the new covenant God writes His law on the tables of the heart, so God wrote His law in the hearts of our first parents. All their emotions, thoughts, words, and acts were in harmony with, and in perfect conformity to, the will of God.

That they accepted God's will as the rule of life, and acknowledged His right to command obedience, is shown by Eve's reply to the serpent, in which she accepted God's definition of what they might or might not do. "The woman said unto the serpent, We may eat of the fruit of the trees of the garden: but of the fruit of the tree which is in the midst of the garden, God hath said, Ye shall not eat of it, neither shall ye touch it, lest ye die." Gen. 3:2, 3.

This answer reveals that she understood that the eating of the fruit of the tree of the knowledge of good and evil was forbidden; that transgressing the command meant death; and her slight hesitancy in accepting Satan's invitation to eat of the fruit shows that she felt under obligation to obey God.

The conditions laid down by God whereby our first parents were promised life on condition of obedience, contain in themselves the elements of a covenant, and have been variously called a covenant of nature, a legal covenant, a covenant of works, and a covenant of life. They were simply the rules of life, conformity to which would bring happiness and life everlasting, and the transgression of which would mean death. Hosea refers to this covenant when he says, "They like Adam [margin] have transgressed the covenant" (Hosea 6:7), which such men as Hitzig, Pusey, Keil, and Wunsche consider the right reading, and which is noted in the margin of the Authorized Version and in the text of the Revised.

The test given our first parents was the lightest conceivable. It was so light that there could be no possible excuse for transgression. There were many trees in the garden, and by no flight of the imagination can it be thought that the prohibition to eat of *one* tree could cause any hardship. Indeed, had the prohibition concerned *all* the trees except one, there could still have been no hardship. As it was, their transgression was without excuse. Their sin was deliberate.

After Adam's fall God could have let Adam and Eve die, and started again with a new pair. But that would be to confess failure. Would it not be better to give Adam and Eve another opportunity? Perhaps they had learned their lesson, and would not disobey again. God could simply forgive them, and give them another trial. But that involved other considerations. If given another probation, and if they again should fail, would not still another trial have to be given them, and another and another, without end? And if that were done would they ever learn the lesson that death lurks in the least deviation from God's will? Unless they learned this, safety could never be attained in this world or in the universe. God could indeed forgive, but the matter was not so simple as that. Man had sinned, and it was necessary that he learn what the wages of sin are, and that God does not arbitrarily decree death because of transgression, but that death is wrapped up in the sin itself.

However, God did not wait until Adam sinned to plan for his restoration. From eternity a plan was laid which now was brought into execution, and which would save man from his lost estate, teach him the nature of sin, and restore him to the place where God could again enter into covenant with him. Before discussing this, let us consider what a covenant is, and how it operates as between God and man.

COVENANT DEFINITIONS

A covenant between equals is an agreement between two or more persons in which the conditions are mutually agreed upon, mutually imposed, and mutually binding. A covenant between unequals, as between a government and its subjects, or between God and man, called a sovereign covenant, or a commanded covenant, is of a different nature, and may better be conceived of as a law or a promise, both of which in their nature fulfill the conditions of a covenant as between God and man. Webster defines a covenant in the theological sense as "the promise of God to man, usually carrying with it a condition to be fulfilled by man."

Thus a covenant imposed by the Creator may well be expressed as follows:

1. Promises on the part of the Creator.
2. These promises conditioned on obedience to specific rules.
3. A penalty attached for the violation of the rules.

In a covenant between equals, which partakes of the nature of a contract, the persons involved talk the matter over and agree on the terms upon which the covenant is to be based. In a commanded covenant, on the contrary, there is no bargaining. The superior simply announces the conditions, and it is assumed that the inferior accepts and obeys.

This may be illustrated in the case of a person who wishes to become a citizen of a country. It is necessary for him to declare his willingness to respect and honor the constitution of the country of which he wishes to become a citizen, and to solemnly affirm that he will obey the laws of the land. In return, he will have the protection of the government as its part of the covenant. In this case there is no bargaining. The government imposes the rules, and the man subscribes to them.

The person who is born a citizen does not formally subscribe to the constitution and the laws, but is under as solemn covenant to keep these as though he had sworn to do so. And he is under obligation to observe not only the laws in existence at the time he was born but all laws enacted thereafter. He may be living in a monarchy; he may have nothing whatever to do with the enactment of these laws, but he is under solemn obligation to keep them. His birth places him under the covenant rules, and in times of stress, as during war or rebellion, he may be asked to re-affirm his allegiance. But he was under obligation of obedience before he made the pledge as well as after. His continued residence in a country is in itself a covenant pledge.

God made a covenant with His people when He took them out of Egypt. Said Moses, "The Lord spake unto you out of the midst of the fire: ye heard the voice of the words, but saw no similitude; only ye heard a voice. And he declared unto you his *covenant, which he commanded* you to perform, even ten commandments; and he wrote them upon two tables of stone." Deut. 4:12, 13.

The Ten Commandments are here called a covenant that God commanded, or a commanded covenant. Another such covenant God made with Israel in the land of Moab. (Deut. 29:1.) This was also a commanded covenant, and contained this provision: "Neither with you only do I make this covenant and this oath; but with him that standeth here with us this day before the Lord our God, and *also with him that is not here with us this day.*" Verses 14, 15.

This covenant was made with Israel, and also "with him that standeth here with us this day," that is, the stranger who perhaps had no intention of entering into a covenant. And not only with those who were present was the covenant made, but "also with him that is not here with us this day.,,

A commanded covenant, in this sense, is merely an announcement of a law that imposes a universal duty of observance upon all, those who are present and those who arc absent. In this sense the Ten Commandments are a commanded covenant of universal obligation. In another and more limited sense the commandments are the basis of the specific covenant made with Israel. Thus the law of God *is* the covenant, and is also the *basis* of the covenant.

Even a promise is a covenant, according to Webster's definition quoted above, that in a theological sense a covenant is "the promise of God to man, usually carrying with it a condition to be fulfilled by man." Conditions are attached to all God's promises. When God promises His people certain blessings and attaches to them certain conditions, the elements of a covenant are present.

Thus God's promise to Adam, of life on condition of obedience, was in itself a covenant. The conditions laid down by God, decided upon in the councils of eternity, were "Obey and live; disobey and perish." These conditions could not be changed any more than God Himself could be changed, for they were the basis of life, and not arbitrary commandments. As man cannot live submerged in water, as a fish cannot live out of water, so man cannot violate the laws of his being and live. The laws of nature, the laws of life, forbid it, not as arbitrary rules, but as inviolable conditions of existence.

GOD'S PLAN

God being infinite, eternal, immutable, and omniscient, must from eternity have formed a plan that would provide for all foreseen emergencies. Knowing of the apostasy of Lucifer and the fall of man, with all the resulting consequences, He created the world with a view to redemption. It is utterly unlike God, as well as unworthy of Him, to embark upon such an important enterprise as creation, fraught as it is with eternal consequences both to His creatures and to Himself, without having a plan which would provide a solution to all the problems that would arise, and would meet all challenges of His adversaries. Furthermore, in the outworking of this plan, it would conform with God's nature so to conduct His work that the eventual outcome will not only reveal His wisdom, love, and justice, but also meet with the approval of His creatures, even of such as should not care to take advantage of the life offered them. This would justify God in creating.

As has been intimated, God's decision to create intelligent, thinking beings with freedom of will, involved serious consequences to His creatures, but even more to God Himself. In the decision to create lay imbedded the incarnation, suffering, and death of the Son of God. The deep reasons for creation may ever remain a mystery, but we believe them to be grounded in God's love, and in His desire to share with others the life that is His. "Because I live," said Christ, "ye shall live also." John 14:19.

God must have known—God did know—that creation would cost Him His Son. Under these conditions it is inconceivable that the decision to create was not the result of a council of the members of the Godhead, specifically between the Father and the Son.

It is doubtless to such a council the prophet refers when he speaks of the "Branch" who shall "build the temple of the Lord; and he shall bear the glory, and shall sit and rule upon his throne; and he shall be priest upon his throne: and *the counsel of peace shall be between them both.*" Zech. 6:12, 13. While some see in this only a local fulfillment in the crowning of Joshua, it cannot be contended that this local fulfillment exhausts the prophecy. He that is here spoken of is king and priest; he rules upon his throne and is a priest upon the throne; he "shall bear the glory," and "the counsel of peace shall be between them both." This can find its complete fulfillment only in the council of eternity, where the plan was laid that eventuated in Christ's becoming a priest on His throne, and in the building of the temple of God reared without hands.

THE ETERNAL COVENANT

That a covenant has existed from eternity between the Father and the Son is evident both from Scripture and from reason. We present the following considerations:

Christ considered His life and work on earth as the fulfillment of an agreed and prearranged plan. In Psalms 40:7 the pre-incarnate Christ announced His coming in response to the call of God: "Lo, I come: in the volume of the book it is written of me, I delight to do thy will, O my God: yea, thy law is within my heart." This coming was in perfect conformity to His own desires, as expressed in the words: "I delight to do thy will; O my God," and in the still stronger statement, "My meat is to do the will of him that sent me." Ps. 40:7; John 4:34.

Christ was sent of God. To this He repeatedly refers: "The Father which sent me." John 12:49. (John 6:44.) "That they may believe that thou hast sent me." John

11:42. "They know not him that sent me." John 15:21. "Jesus Christ, whom thou hast sent." John 17:3. The time of His coming was also predetermined: "When the fulness of the time was come, God sent forth his Son." Gal. 4:4.

Christ was aware of the fact that in coming to this earth He was fulfilling a divine mission, and faithfully followed the instructions given Him. From the earliest moment of conscious appreciation of His divinity, He knew that He must be about His Father's business. (Luke 2:49.) He could of a true heart say, "I do always those things that please him." John 8:29.

The work that Christ did on earth was according to a divine commission, and the Father not only communicated to Him the plan and gave Him a work to finish, but helped Him in the execution of the plan. "As the Father gave me commandment, even so I do." John 14:31. "1 must work the works of him that sent me." John 9:4. "The works which the Father hath given me to finish." John 5:36. "The Father that dwelleth in me, he doeth the works." John 14:10.

Christ did not speak His own words, but only those given Him of the Father. "For I have not spoken of myself; but the Father which sent me, he gave me a commandment what I should say, and what I should speak." John 12:49. "The word which ye hear is not mine, but the Father's which sent me." John 14:24. "As my Father hath taught me, I speak these things." "I speak to the world those things which I have heard of him." John 8:28, 26. Even in regard to the doctrine which Christ taught, He could say, "My doctrine is not mine, but his that sent me." John 7:16.

When Christ was about to leave this earth He declared, "I have finished the work which thou gavest me to do." John 17:4. The vital part of this work is that mentioned by John when he says that God "sent his Son to be the propitiation for our sins." 1 John 4:10. This included the suffering and death of the Son of God, and this also was according to God's plan. "This commandment have I received of my Father." John 10:18.

Toward the close of His work Christ gave utterance to a most unique request. "Father," He said, "I will that they also, whom thou hast given me, be with me where I am." John 17:24. This is not an ordinary prayer. In fact, it is a demand more than a prayer. Christ prayed, and taught others to pray, "Thy will be done." But now He does not say, "Thy will be done," but simply announces, "I will." He is not asking a favor; He is claiming a victor's reward.

In His high priestly prayer Christ repeatedly refers to those who have been given Him of God. (John 17:6, 9, 11, 12, 24.) It is these He claims. "They have kept thy word," He says. Having fulfilled the conditions of making them more precious than fine gold; even a man than the golden wedge of Ophir," He demands that they be given Him and be with Him. Isa. 13:12.

The foregoing texts suggest an agreement whereby Christ was to do a certain work, and in return be given those who should meet the conditions set. As the salvation of men was the object of His coming to this earth; as He announced that He had finished the work given Him to do; and as He claims as a reward those who have been given Him by the Father, we find the elements of a covenant present: the very thing we have been led to believe from other scriptures.

A covenant between the Father and the Son must in its very nature be eternal, as of necessity it must have been made before creation took place. For God to bring men and angels into existence—knowing that sin would result—without making provision for their restoration, and giving them the opportunity of a second trial should they wish to retrace their steps; for God to create beings, some of whom would reject the proffered mercy, without making provision for the eventual eradication of sin from the universe, would show either shortsightedness on the part of God, or a lack of consideration commensurate with His power. Either of these would be unworthy of God, and would call in question His right to the claim of being a kind and merciful Father.

Such considerations as these make it clear that creation must have included every provision for the safety of God and man, and that the whole plan must have been completed before God ever began to create.

The plan of salvation, as revealed in the Scriptures, is best understood in the light of a covenant in which the contracting parties are the Father and Christ; the Father reprelenting the Godhead in their unity, the Son representing those who should elect Him as their substitute and surety. On their behalf Christ promised and guaranteed the fulfillment of the conditions laid down for eternal life, and the Father promised to give the Son all those who should meet the requirements and for whom Christ should stand sponsor. The administration of the covenant as regards men was left in Christ's hands, He becoming surety for the faithful performance of all conditions. When He had finished His work in and with the believers, and could certify that "they have kept thy word," He would present them for acceptance, "faultless before the presence of his glory with exceeding joy." John 17:6; Jude 22.

The working out of the covenant would be on this wise: The moment Adam failed to live up to the requirement of God, thus forfeiting his right to life, Christ would take man's place and become his surety, thereby saving him from immediate death and ensuring him another trial. As the second Adam, Christ would become the head of a new humanity, and God would deal with Him as man's representative. This could be done, however, only on condition that Christ became truly man, and took man's place in every way, even to the point where He would take upon Himself the punishment justly due to man's sin. As the second Adam He would have to stand test and trial as did the first Adam, and by strict obedience demonstrate that it is possible for man to obey God, and thus redeem Adam's disgraceful failure. In His obedience He would justify God, and disprove Satan's claim that God was requiring of man that which could not be done; and He would also encourage man to believe that by the help of God he could reach the standard set by God for man.

The covenant between the Father and the Son in regard to the salvation of man may rightly be called the covenant of redemption, for its provisions made possible man's salvation. It was the substitution of the second Adam for the first, and the taking over by Christ of all the obligations incurred by man. On God's part, it was the acceptance by Him of Christ's assurance to bring man back to obedience, and present him at last before the throne of God, without spot or blemish, a fit candidate for immortality. God promised to forbear awhile the execution of the penalty due to sin, give man time to recover himself; that is, grant him probationary time, not reckon unto him his trespasses, and turn the entire administration of the provisions of the covenant over to Christ, delegating to Him all powers in heaven and in earth. As Christ is man's representative, God deals only with Him; and as man deals only with Christ, He becomes the go-between, the daysman, the mediator between God and man. Any request we may have is addressed to the Father through Christ; any communication from the Father comes to us through Christ. He is our mediator and surety.

THE COVENANT OF GRACE

The covenant of grace is by some considered the same as the covenant of redemption, but though they are closely related, for the sake of clarity it may be best to consider them separately. The covenant of grace is in reality Christ's administration of the covenant of redemption as related to man. In the covenant of redemption between the Father and the Son, Christ undertook to make man "more precious than fine gold; even a man than the golden wedge of Ophir." Isa. 13:12. The covenant of grace concerns itself with preparing man for his high destiny and getting him ready to stand the inspection of God. It is merely an arrangement for bringing man back to the place where he can keep the commandments of God, where he can stand the test to which God will put him, and be worthy of the reward of the overcomer.

This work embraces two distinct phases: the forgiveness of sin, with the consequent and complete blotting out of the evil past; and the impartation of strength for the doing of the will of God. If man could have all his sins blotted out; if by some means he could be born again, have his mind and whole attitude changed, and become an entirely new creation; if the old man could die and be buried, and a new man arise, with new hopes and aspirations; if all the old things should pass away, and all things become new; in other words, if he could simply die and be raised again, he could start life over without any handicap of past sins. This is the first of the two steps, and is provided for in conversion and regeneration, through which man has all the experiences here mentioned. This undoes all that the first birth brought him, and he stands where Adam stood, without a single sin charged to him.

The second step is the acquisition of power adequate for the work that is required of the new man. He will need more power than Adam did; for even though he is a new creature, he is far below Adam in strength, and will need a special enduement of power from on high. Not only is he weaker than Adam, but the temptations are stronger. Of this condition God will have to take account. He will need to remember that "this man was born there," and so arrange matters that "where sin abounded, grace did much more abound." (Ps. 87:4, 6; Rom. 5:20.) If this is done, every man will have the same opportunity Adam had. No more can be asked.

Strict justice demands that the one who breaks the rules of life shall perish. But fairness also demands that one who is born in sin, for which he is in no way responsible, shall have his disabilities removed, be placed on vantage ground, and be given the same chance which the first man had. This is not a matter of mercy but of justice. It is to this question of justice John refers when he says that God "is faithful and just [literally "righteous"] to forgive us our sins." 1 John 1:9. Whereas it is merciful of God to forgive us our trespasses, it is also true that there is justice in God's removing the sins for which we are not responsible—inherited weaknesses and sins—and not imputing them to us. Paul agrees with this when he states that it is God's righteousness, not merely His mercy, that is shown in the remission of sins. (Rom. 3:25, 26; Heb. 6:10.)

God does not deviate one hair's breadth from justice in dealing with men, either good or bad, nor is His mercy confined to the righteous. "He maketh his sun to rise on the evil and on the good, and sendeth rain on the just and on the unjust." Matt. 5:45. Only when men, despite His pleadings, deliberately turn from Him to evil, does He reluctantly permit them to reap the fruit of their ill-doing.

When man sinned, God did not change the sentence of death that He had pronounced upon the transgressor, but in view of Christ's mediation He delayed its execution. This delay granted Adam—and all men—is what we call probationary time. This is a time of grace, granted in mercy to all alike, to give men opportunity to think things through. Unless, by repentance and a definite turning to God, man shows that he repudiates sin, the death sentence will at last be carried out. But even in the case of the righteous, God's mercy does not conflict with His justice. Whether man be good or bad, he at last faces death; but in the case of the righteous there is a resurrection unto life. For such, death becomes a sleep from which he is raised again to life everlasting.

Probation is therefore God's solution to the problem of giving men continued existence though they have violated the law of life. It is a day of grace granted all, during which time God does not impute to them their sins but does all that love can contrive to win them back to obedience. It is a time of suspended sentence, a time of parole, but it is so only in a legal sense. It is a time of intense activity on the part of God to woo men to repentance, to show His love to them, to give them a glimpse of the joy that awaits the faithful, and also to warn them of the loss that will be theirs should they reject God's invitation.

Christ's work, under the covenant of grace, is to take sinners and make them into saints. With unfailing kindness He will help those who are weak, forgive them their sins, seventy times seven if need be, forgive as long as there is any hope that man will at last turn to God, take hold of His strength, and walk in newness of life. He will suit the test to each man's strength, and not permit any to be tempted above that which he is able to bear. As soon as a man has passed one test, and gained a little strength as well as confidence, He will give him another test, carefully gauged to his peculiar need, until he gradually grows in strength and grace, and finally comes to the point where he will die rather than sin. When he has reached this decision, the work is done; he has completed his training; he is sanctified, ready for the kingdom. Christ will then present him before the Presence with exceeding joy. Satan is defeated, and God stands vindicated. A soul is saved.

It should be emphasized beyond any possibility of misunderstanding, that the aim of the covenant of grace is not merely the forgiveness of sin, but it is to bring men back to the place where they can, by the grace of God, keep the commandments and live. What God required of Adam in the garden, He requires of every man. God has not changed His requirements and cannot change them without laying Himself open to the charge of inconsistency and of being a respecter of persons. For His own sake He must not change; for man's sake He must not change. To require less now than He did of Adam would be disastrous. It was perfect obedience then. It is perfect obedience now.

A SUMMARY

The Covenant of Life. By this is meant the general rules of life, or the law of life, under which all things created have their being. Thus all forms of life—plants, flowers, trees, creeping things, animals, birds, or fish—must conform to their peculiar conditions of life, or perish. So, likewise, men and angels, and whatever other kinds of intellectual life God has created, must conform to the rules of life governing their existence. From the very nature of these rules they are inviolable, and continued existence depends upon strict adherence to them. "Obey and live; disobey and perish," is written upon every rule. The consequences of disobedience are not penal in their nature; they are a *result* of trangression, the *wages* of sin rather than a punishment for sin. The man who drinks poison violates the rules of life and suffers the consequences. The punishment is inherent in the act itself.

This law of life is variously called a covenant of nature, or a natural covenant, a legal covenant, a covenant of works. As stated above, it is merely the rules of life by which all things consist, and with which all must comply. It is not a covenant entered into formally. All nature is subject to it, animate and inanimate. Thus God made a covenant with day and night, and also with fowl, cattle, and every beast, and set the rainbow in the heavens as a token of "the everlasting covenant between God and every living creature." (Jer. 33:20, 25; Gen. 9:9–17.)

We prefer to call this the covenant of life, as it is the general all-inclusive covenant embracing the whole creation, and by which life is promised on condition of obedience.

The covenant of redemption is that part of the everlasting covenant in which the Father and the Son enter into a solemn compact that they will save man at any cost to themselves. This covenant involves the incarnation, suffering, and death of the Son of God. Christ will take man's place, and as the second Adam fulfill all man's obligations; and God promises that He will accept not only this Son of *man* but also all those whom Christ can restore, and for whom He will become surety. Christ guarantees that He will make a man more precious than fine gold, restore the image of God in the soul, build him up to a holy temple of God, and at last present him faultless before the throne of God.

In this covenant Christ represents man, and the covenant is thus between God and man—the man Christ Jesus—a covenant established upon promises that cannot be broken. The administration of this covenant as regards man devolves upon Christ.

The Covenant of Grace. This covenant concerns the administration of the covenant of redemption, by which Christ is to redeem men and restore them to the favor of God. It is a covenant between Christ and fallen man, wherein, upon condition of turning *from sin* and turning *to Him,* Christ will forgive men their shortcomings, and help them become strong in their desire to do right. His work for man includes two distinct, yet closely connected, parts: forgiveness of sin and sanctification.

When Christ's work in the human heart is done, He will present His work before the Father. Each man must stand the test for himself. Those who stand the test—and they include all for whom Christ, is mediator and surety—will be saved.

This covenant of grace was first made with man in the Garden of Eden after he fell. It is the covenant under which every redeemed man will be saved. There is no other way. It is the same covenant which God made with Abraham and all the saints of old. It is the covenant of salvation.

It is to be noted that this covenant is not an end in itself but merely the administration of the covenant, of redemption—God's way of preparing men to stand the test that will come to every man. It brings man back to the place where Adam stood before the fall, and now he must stand the test of obedience before he can be admitted to the benefits of the covenant of life and be accepted by the Father. This is the final test, and for this the covenant of grace prepares him.

The old covenant was formed between God and Israel at Sinai. Men have never ceased to believe that they are able to establish their own righteousness. When Jesus asked the two disciples who desired a high place, if they were able to pay the price that such position would cost, they promptly answered, "We are able." Matt. 20:22. There was not the slightest doubt in their minds as to their ability to do what was required. When Christ asked the young man to keep the commandments, he immediately replied, "All these things have I kept from my youth up: what lack I yet?" Matt. 19:20. There was no question in his mind that he not only kept the commandments but had always done so. That he took for granted. "What lack I yet?" is a most revealing statement. When God at Sinai asked Israel to keep the law as a condition of His favor, they unhesitatingly answered, "All that the Lord hath spoken we will do." Ex. 19:8.

When Israel thus answered, God had little choice as to what to do. He had miraculously delivered Israel at the Red Sea, when they were utterly helpless against the army of Pharaoh. He hoped they had learned their lesson of dependence upon Him. But they had not. He was still ready to help them, and hoped they might realize their utter helplessness and their need of divine aid. But they felt no such need. They felt fully able to keep the law.

To make very sure that the people knew the contents of the covenant they were entering into, God publicly proclaimed to them the law, the Ten Commandments. To make doubly sure that there would be no misunderstanding as to the extent of their obligation, He made a detailed application of the principles of the Ten Commandments to their situation, so that they would know exactly what was demanded of them. (Ex. 20–22 to 23–33.) In the course of these explanatory judgments and statutes, He warned them of what they were facing. "Behold," said God, "I send an Angel before thee....Beware of him, and obey his voice, provoke him not; for *he will not pardon your transgressions*: for my name is in him." Ex. 23:20, 21.

These significant words should have made them pause. Did they still feel that there was no cause for alarm? Did they still feel that they were able to keep the law? They did. They had learned nothing. They felt no need of pardon. They did not ask for any. They were willing to enter into covenant with God.

God, of course, knew that they would fall. But He had no choice. Had He refused them the opportunity of trying, had He said that it was no use, and that He would not even give them the privilege of showing what they could do, Israel could justly have claimed that they had not had a fair chance, that they *could* have kept the law, but that God would not give them a chance to prove it. God had no choice but to let them try it. The result was failure, as God foreknew.

God, however, did not intend to leave Israel to their own devices and to discouragement at their failure. Even while they were dancing around the golden calf, God was instructing Moses to build Him a tabernacle that He might dwell among them and teach them His ways more perfectly. They needed to understand the heinousness of sin, and that even the least transgression meant death, They needed to know more of the holiness of God and the need of forgiveness. They needed to have a more vivid conception of the need of a heavenly mediator, prefigured in the earthly priesthood. They needed to know that without an intercessor there was no way for them to approach God. All this God meant to teach them in the sanctuary service.

When God told Moses in the mount that the people were worshiping a golden calf, he could scarcely believe it. But when he saw with his own eyes what the people had done, his "anger waxed hot." The two tables of stone upon which were written the Ten Commandments, he threw to the ground and broke to pieces. The golden calf he ground to powder and strewed on the water, and made Israel drink it. He then made a call for consecration, and those who had transgressed and did not respond, and who stubbornly refused to yield, were killed. He then "returned unto the Lord, and said, Oh, this people have sinned a great sin, and have made them gods of gold. Yet now, if thou wilt forgive their sin—; and if not, blot me, I pray thee, out of thy book which thou hast written." Ex. 32:31, 32.

Israel had broken the covenant which they had solemnly made with God. "They continued not in my covenant," said God, "and I regarded them not." Heb. 8:9. God proposed to Moses that He reject the people, and make of Moses a great nation. But Moses interceded for the people, asking God to spare them, and he was successful. (Ex. 32:11–14) But when he asked the Lord to forgive their sin, God rather curtly responded, "Whosoever hath sinned against me, him will I blot out of my book." Verse 33.

God then commanded Moses to lead the people to the place which He had chosen, stating that He would not go with them Himself, but would send His angel instead. Then He repeated His warning of punishment to come: "Nevertheless in the day when I visit I will visit their sin upon them." Verse 34.

As a sign of God's displeasure, the tabernacle was pitched "without the camp, afar off from the camp." Ex. 33:7. As a result of this "every one which sought the Lord went out unto the tabernacle of the congregation, which was without the camp." Verse 7.

Moses then appeared as the mediator of his people. God had rejected Israel; they had broken the covenant, and He regarded them not. They were no longer His people. He did not own them as His, but spoke of them to Moses as "thy people, which thou broughtest out of the land of Egypt." Ex. 32:7. Moses, however, came back with the rejoinder that they were God's people, not his. "Lord," he said, "why doth thy wrath wax hot against thy people, which thou hast brought forth out of the land of Egypt?" Verse 11.

Moses was not satisfied with having an angel go with them on the journey. He wanted the Lord Himself to go up with them. He had found favor with God, and made the most of it. "If I have found grace in thy sight," he said, "shew me now thy way, that I may know thee,...consider that this nation is *thy* people." Ex. 33:13. God relented and said, "My presence shall go with thee." Verse 14. Moses felt encouraged by this, but was not yet satisfied. He boldly asked not only that God's presence go with them, but "that *thou* goest with us." Verse 16. God graciously answered, "I will do this thing also that thou hast spoken." Verse 17.

But Moses was not yet satisfied. He pressed the point: "Shew me now thy way, that I may know thee." He urged, "Shew me thy glory." Verse 18. God's glory is His character.

Justice is part of God's glory, but so is mercy. Thus far God had shown mostly the justice side of His character, but Moses now asked to be shown God's *ways*, that he might know *Him.* He well knew that if he could get God to reveal Himself, such a revelation would stress God's mercy and loving kindness, and that this would give him an opportunity to call upon God to be gracious to His people.

And Moses was not mistaken. He was given a revelation of "The Lord, The Lord God, merciful and gracious, longsuffering, and abundant in goodness and truth, keeping mercy for thousands, forgiving iniquity and transgression and sin, and that will by no means clear the guilty; visiting the iniquity of the fathers upon the children, and upon the children's children, unto the third and to the fourth generation." Ex. 34:6, 7.

The Lord having revealed Himself as a merciful and gracious God, Moses made his final request. God had already promised that instead of sending an angel, He Himself would go with the people. Moses asked two things. First: "O Lord, let the Lord, I pray thee, go in the *midst* of us." Verse 9, R.V. God had been dwelling without the camp, "afar off." Ex. 33:7. Moses now asked that He go up "in the midst of us." This request had been once denied when God said, "I will not go up in the midst of thee." Verse 3. The other request was this: "Pardon our iniquity and our sin, and take us for thine inheritance." Ex. 34:9.

To both of these requests God answered, "Behold, I make a covenant." Verse 10. This was as much as to say, "My dwelling in your midst and forgiving your sins depends upon your attitude. I make a covenant. Upon the faithful adherence to this covenant will hang My decision."

When Moses was called up into the mount at this time, he was told to appear there alone. Six weeks before, Aaron, Nadab, Abihu, and seventy of the elders were also called up. (Ex. 24:9.) There "they saw the God of Israel....They saw God, and did eat and drink." Verses 10, 11.

But not so this time. Now Moses only appeared. It is with him God speaks. It is with him, primarily, that the covenant was made. The usual formula, "Speak unto the children of Israel and say unto them," did not appear. Moses represented Israel. When the covenant was finally made, God said, "I have made a covenant with *thee* and with Israel." Ex. 34:27. No representative of the people was called up into the mount; they were not called upon to ratify or agree to the covenant; Moses was the only one with whom God dealt. Israel indeed had a part in it, for the covenant was made with them as well as with Moses, though in a secondary sense. "I have made a covenant with thee *and* with Israel."

This covenant is different from the one recorded in Exodus, chapters 19–24. There it was said of the angel, "Take ye heed before him, and hearken unto his voice; provoke him not; for *he will not pardon your transgression:* for my name is in him." Ex. 23:21, A.R.V. *Here* God reveals Himself as the merciful and gracious God, who forgives iniquity, transgression, and sin. In the first covenant there was no mediator. In the covenant of Exodus 34, Moses pleads for the people, and at last gains God's good will and forgiveness, based upon obedience to the commandments. In this covenant mercy is the outstanding feature. God reveals Himself in a special manifestation as the merciful God who forgives, and He graciously accepts Moses as the mediator for the people. This covenant has all the marks of the new covenant, established under Old Testament conditions. God moves back into the midst of the camp; the sanctuary service is established, all the ceremonies of which point to forgiveness; a mediator—in the person of the high priest—is established, and in him Israel appears before the Lord and obtains forgiveness for all their uncleanness, transgression, and sins. True, it is all in type, but it is prophetic of that better covenant of which Christ Himself is the mediator, and through whose merits sins are in verity forgiven and blotted out.

Extracts From the Writings of Mrs. E. G. White on the Covenants

Father, Son, and Holy Spirit. —"The salvation of human beings is a vast enterprise, that calls into action every attribute of the divine nature. The Father, the Son, and the Holy Spirit have pledged themselves to make God's children more than conquerors through Him that has loved them. The Lord is gracious and long-suffering, not willing that any should perish. He has provided power to enable us to become overcomers." —*Review and Herald*, Jan. 27, 1903, p. 8.

Covenant of Mercy. —"The salvation of the human race has ever been the object of the councils of heaven. The covenant of mercy was made before the foundation of the world. It has existed from all eternity, and is called the everlasting covenant. So surely as there never was a time when God was not, so surely there never was a moment when it was not the delight of the eternal mind to manifest His grace to humanity." —*Signs of the Times*, June 12, 1901, p. 371.

The Covenant of Grace. —"As the Bible presents two laws, one changeless and eternal, the other provisional and temporary, so there are two covenants. The covenant of grace was first made with man in Eden, when after the fall, there was given a divine promise that the seed of the woman should bruise the serpent's head. To all men this covenant offered pardon, and the assisting grace of God for future obedience through faith in Christ. It also promised them eternal life on condition of fidelity to God's law. Thus the patriarchs received the hope of salvation." —*Patriarchs and Prophets*, p. 370.

Clasped Hands. —"Before the foundations of the earth were laid, the Father and the Son had united in a covenant to redeem man if he should be overcome by Satan. They had clasped their hands in a solemn pledge that Christ should become the surety for the human race. This pledge Christ has fulfilled. When upon the cross He cried out, 'It is finished,' He addressed the Father. The compact had been fully carried out. Now He declares, Father, it is finished. I have done Thy will, O My God. I have completed the work of redemption. If Thy justice is satisfied, 'I will that they also, whom Thou hast given Me, be with Me where I am.' John 19:30; 17:24." —*The Desire of Ages*, p. 834.

Not an Afterthought. —"The plan for our redemption was not an afterthought, a plan formulated after the fall of Adam. It was a revelation of 'the mystery which hath been kept in silence through times eternal.' Rom. 16:25, R.V. It was an unfolding of the principles that from eternal ages have been the foundation of God's throne. From the beginning, God and Christ knew of the apostasy of Satan, and of the fall of man through the deceptive power of the apostate. God did not ordain that sin should exist, but He foresaw its existence, and made provision to meet the terrible emergency. So great was His love for the world, that He covenanted to give His only-begotten Son, 'that whosoever believeth in Him should not perish, but have everlasting life.'" —*Ibid.*, p. 22.

"Before the foundations of the earth were laid, the covenant was made that all who were obedient, all who should through the abundant grace provided, become holy in character, and without blame before God, by appropriating that grace, should be children of God. This covenant, made from eternity, was given to Abraham hundreds of years before Christ came. With what interest and what intensity did Christ in humanity study the human race to see if they would avail themselves of the provision offered. " —*Fundamentals of Christian Education*, p. 403.

Father Forbears Execution of Death.—"The Son of God pities fallen man. He knows that the law of His Father is as unchanging as Himself. He can only see one way of escape for the transgressor. He offers Himself to His Father as a sacrifice for man, to take their guilt and punishment upon Himself, and redeem them from death by dying in their place, and thus pay the ransom. The Father consents to give His dearly beloved Son to save the fallen race; and through His merits and intercession promises to receive man again into His favor, and to restore holiness to as many as should be willing to accept the atonement, thus mercifully offered and obey His law. For the sake of His dear Son the Father forbears awhile the execution of death, and to Christ He commits the fallen race." —*Spiritual Gifts*, vol. 3, pp. 46, 47.

Christ Invites the Father. —"Under the mighty impulse of His love, He took our place in the universe, and invited the Ruler of all things to treat Him as a representative of the human family. He identified Himself with our interests, bared His breast for the stroke of death, took man's guilt and its penalty, and offered in man's behalf a complete sacrifice to God. By virtue of this atonement, He has power, to offer to man perfect righteousness and full salvation. Whosoever shall believe on Him as a personal Saviour shall not perish, but have everlasting life." —*Review and Herald*, April 18, 1893, pp. 241, 242.

Christ to Complete His Work. —"Jesus refused to receive the homage of His people until He had the assurance that His sacrifice was accepted by the Father. He ascended to the heavenly courts, and from God Himself heard the assurance that His atonement for the sins of men had been ample, that through His blood all might gain eternal life. The Father ratified the covenant made with Christ, that He would receive repentant and obedient men, and would love them even as He loves His Son. Christ was to complete His work, and fulfill His pledge to 'make a man more precious than fine gold; even a man than the golden wedge of Ophir.' Isa. 13:12. All power in heaven and on earth was given to the Prince of life, and He returned to His followers in a world of sin, that He might impart to them of His power and glory."—*The Desire of Ages*, p. 790.

Christ Claimed. —"In the intercessory prayer of Jesus with His Father, He claimed that He had fulfilled the conditions which make it obligatory upon the Father to fulfill His part of the contract made in heaven with regard to fallen man." —*Redemption—Resurrection*, pp. 77, 78.

Relation Clearly Defined. —"He also had a request to prefer concerning His chosen ones upon earth. He wished to have the relation clearly defined that His redeemed should hereafter sustain to Heaven, and to His Father. His church must be justified and accepted before He could accept heavenly honor. He declared it to be His will that where He was, there His church should be; if He was to have glory, His people must share it with Him. They who suffer with Him on earth must finally reign with Him in His kingdom. In the most explicit manner Christ pleaded for His church, identifying His interest with theirs, and advocating, with a love and constancy stronger than death, their rights and titles gained through Him." —*Spirit of Prophecy*, vol. 3, pp. 202, 203.

According to the Covenant Promise. —"To have them with Him is according to the covenant promise and agreement with His Father." —*Review and Herald*, Oct. 17, 1893, p. 645.

Infinite Truths. —"That which in the councils of heaven the Father and the Son deemed essential for the salvation of man, was defined from eternity by infinite truths which finite beings cannot fail to comprehend." —*Fundamentals of Christian Education*, p. 408.

Simply an Arrangement. —"Though this covenant was made with Adam and renewed to Abraham, it could not be ratified until the death of Christ. It had existed by the promise of God since the first intimation of redemption had been given; it had been accepted by faith; yet when ratified by Christ, it is called a new covenant. The law of God was the basis of this covenant, which was simply an arrangement for bringing men again into harmony with the divine will, placing them where they could obey God's law." —*Patriarchs and Prophets*, pp. 370, 371.

Adam and Eve Instructed by Angels. —"Our first parents were not left without a warning of the danger that threatened them. Heavenly messengers opened to them the history of Satan's fall, and his plots for their destruction, unfolding more fully the nature of the divine government, which the prince of evil was trying to overthrow. It was by disobedience to the just commands of God that Satan and his host had fallen. How important, then, that Adam and Eve should honor that law by which alone it was possible for order and equity to be maintained." —*Ibid.*, p. 52.

Free Moral Agents. —"God instructed our first parents in regard to the tree of knowledge, and they were fully informed relative to the fall of Satan, and the danger of listening to his suggestions, He did not deprive them of the power of eating the forbidden fruit. He left them as free moral agents to believe His word, obey His commandments and live, or believe the tempter, disobey and perish." —*Spirit of Prophecy*, vol. 1, p. 40.

Adam and Eve Assured the Angels. —"The angels graciously and lovingly gave them the information they desired. They also gave them the sad history of Satan's rebellion and fall. They then distinctly informed them that the tree of knowledge was placed in the garden to be a pledge of their obedience and love to God; that the high and happy estate of the holy angels was to be retained upon. condition of obedience; that they were similarly situated; that they could obey the law of God and be inexpressibly happy, or disobey, and lose their high estate, and be plunged into hopeless despair....Adam and Eve assured the angels that they should never transgress the express command of God; for it was their highest pleasure to do His will." —*Ibid.*, pp. 33–35.

Through Christ Alone. —"The Father had given the world into the hands of His Son for Him to redeem from the curse and the disgrace of Adam's failure and fall. Through Christ alone can man now find access to God. And through Christ alone will the Lord hold communication with man." —*Redemption—Temptation*, p. 17.

Another Trial.—When Christ died "God bowed His head satisfied. Now justice and mercy could blend. Now He could be just, and yet the Justifier of all who should believe on Christ. He looked upon the victim expiring on the cross, and said, 'It is finished. The human race shall have another trial.'" —*The Youth's Instructor*, June 21, 1900, p. 195.

The Book of Hebrews

"That the transgressor might have another trial...the eternal Son of God interposed Himself to bear the punishment of transgression." —*Review and Herald,* Feb. 8, 1898, p. 85.

"Infinite wisdom is revealed in Christ. He suffered in our stead, that men could have another test and trial." —*Special Instruction Relating to Review and Herald Office,* p. 28.

Christ "proposed the only means that would be acceptable with God, that would give them another trial, and place them again on probation." —*Redemption—Temptation,* p. 14.

"The very test that God brought upon Adam in Eden, will be brought upon every member of the human family. Obedience to God was required of Adam, and we stand in the same position that he did to have a second trial, to see whether we will listen to the voice of Satan and disobey God, or to the word of God and obey." —*Review and Herald,* June 10, 1890, p. 354.

God's Requirement. —"God requires at this moment just what He required of Adam in paradise before he fell perfect obedience to His law. The requirement that God makes in grace is just the requirement He made in paradise. We want to understand the claims of God upon us that we may reach the hearts of men, and teach them what God's Word requires of them in order that they may have eternal life. We must live by every word that proceedeth out of the mouth of God." —*Ibid.,* July 15, 1890, p. 433.

Law Can Be Kept.—"He [Christ] was a representative before men and before angels, of the character of the God of heaven. He demonstrated the fact that when humanity depends wholly upon God, men may keep God's commandments and live, and His law be as the apple of the eye." —*Special Testimonies to Ministers,* no. 3, p. 59.

Christ Gives Strength. —"In his own strength the sinner can not meet the demands of God. He must go for help to the One who paid the ransom for him. It is

258

impossible for him of himself to keep the law. But Christ can give him strength to do this. The Saviour came to this world and in human flesh lived a life of perfect obedience, that the sinner might stand before God justified and accepted." —*Signs of the Times*, July 31, 1901, p. 482.

At Cross Purposes With God. —"The temptations to which Christ was subjected were a terrible reality. As a free agent, He was placed on probation, with liberty to yield to Satan's temptations and work at cross-purposes with God. If this were not so, if it had not been possible for Him to fall, He could not have been tempted in all points as the human family is tempted." —*The Youth's Instructor*, Oct. 1899, p. 519.

Adam's Disgraceful Failure. —"Christ consented to leave His honor, His kingly authority, His glory with the Father, and humble Himself to humanity, and engage in contest with the mighty prince of darkness, in order to redeem man. Through His humiliation and poverty Christ would identify Himself with the weaknesses of the fallen race, and by firm obedience show that man might redeem Adam's failure, and by humble obedience regain lost Eden." —*Redemption-Temptation*, p. 14.

Plead to Die. —"When. Adam and Eve realized how exalted and sacred was the law of God, the transgression of which made so costly a sacrifice necessary to save them and their posterity from utter ruin, they plead to die themselves, or to let them and their posterity endure the penalty of their transgression, rather, than that the beloved Son of God should make this great sacrifice." —*Spirit of Prophecy*, vol. 1, p. 50.

Endured the Penalty. —"All who, before the universe of heaven, are adjudged to have, in Christ, endured the penalty of the law, and in Him fulfilled its righteousness, will have eternal life. They will be one in character with Christ." —*Special Instruction Relating to Review and Herald Office*, p. 29.

Victor on Own Account. —"Will man take hold of divine power, and with determination and perseverance resist Satan, as Christ has given him example in His conflict with the foe in the wilderness of temptation? God cannot save man against his will from the power of Satan's artifices. Man must work with his human power, aided by the divine power of Christ, to resist and to conquer at any cost to himself. In short, man must overcome as Christ overcame. And then, through the victory that it is his privilege to gain by the all-powerful name of Jesus, he may become an heir of God, and joint-heir with Jesus Christ. This could not be the case if Christ alone did all the overcoming. Man must do his part; he must be victor on his own account, through the strength and grace that Christ gives him. Man must be a co-worker with Christ in the labor of overcoming, and then he will be partaker with Christ of his glory." —*Testimonies*, vol. 4, pp. 32, 33.

Overcame in Human Nature. —"When Christ bowed His head and died, He bore the pillars of Satan's kingdom with him to the earth. He vanquished Satan in the same nature over which in Eden Satan obtained the victory. The enemy was overcome by Christ in His human nature. The power of the Saviour's Godhead was hidden. He overcame in human nature, relying upon God for power. This is the privilege of all. In proportion to our faith will be our victory." —*The Youth's Instructor*, April 25, 1901, p. 130.

"The Saviour overcame to show man how he may overcome. All the temptations of Satan, Christ met with the Word of God. By trusting in God's promises, He received power to obey God's commandments, and the tempter could gain no advantage." —*Ministry of Healing*, p. 181.

Principles of Law. —"The Sabbath of the fourth commandment was instituted in Eden. After God had made the world, and created man upon the earth, He made the Sabbath for man. After Adam's sin and fall nothing was taken from the law of God. The principles of the ten commandments existed before the fall, and were of a character suited to the condition of a holy order of beings. After the fall, the principles of those precepts were not changed, but additional precepts were given to meet man in his fallen state." —*Spiritual Gifts*, vol. 3, p. 295; or *Facts of Faith*, vol. 1, p. 295.

Law Was Adapted. —"The law of God existed before man was created. It was adapted to the condition of holy beings; even angels were governed by it. After the fall, the principles 'of righteousness' were unchanged. Nothing was taken from the law; not one of its holy precepts could be improved. And as it has existed from the beginning, so will it continue to exist throughout the ceaseless ages of eternity. 'Concerning Thy testimonies,' says the psalmist, 'I have known of old that Thou hast founded them forever.'" —*Signs of the Times*, April 15, 1886, p. 226.

Arranged and Expressed. —"The law of God existed before the creation of man or else Adam could not have sinned. After the transgression of Adam the principles of the law were not changed, but were definitely arranged and expressed to meet man in his fallen condition. Christ, in counsel with His Father, instituted the system of sacrificial offerings; that death, instead of being immediately visited upon the transgressor, should be transferred to a victim which should prefigure the great and perfect offering of the Son of God." —*Ibid.*, March 14, 1878, p. 81.

More Explicitly Stated. —"The law of Jehovah, dating back to creation, was comprised in the two great principles, 'Thou shalt love the Lord thy God with all thy heart, and with all thy soul, and with all thy mind, and with all thy strength. This is the first commandment. And the second is like, namely this: Thou shalt love thy neighbor as thy self. There is none other commandment greater than these.' These two great principles embrace the first four commandments, showing the duty of man to God, and the last six, showing the duty of man to his fellow-man. The principles were more explicitly stated to man after the fall, and worded to meet the case of fallen intelligences. This was necessary in consequence of the minds of men being blinded by transgression." —*Ibid.*, April 15, 1875, p. 181.

Religious Precepts. —"In consequence of continual transgression, the moral law was repeated in awful grandeur from Sinai. Christ gave to Moses religious precepts which were to govern the every-day life. These statutes were explicitly given to guard the ten commandments. They were not shadowy types to pass away with the death of Christ. They were to be binding upon men in every age as long as time should last. These commands were enforced by the power of the moral law, and they clearly and definitely explained that law." —*Ibid.*

Garment of Human Flesh. —"Christ mourned for the transgression of every human being. He bore even the guiltiness of Caiaphas, knowing the hypocrisy that dwelt in his soul, while for pretense he rent his robe. Christ did not rend His robe, but His soul was rent. His garment of human flesh was rent as He hung on the cross, the sin-bearer of the race. By His suffering and death a new and living way was opened." —*Review and Herald*, June 12, 1900, p. 370.

According to Covenant Promise. —"Listen to the prayer of our Representative in heaven: 'Father, I will that they also, whom Thou hast given Me, be with Me where I am; that they may behold My glory.' O, how the divine Head longed to have His church with Him! They had fellowship with Him in His suffering and humiliation, and it is His highest joy to have them with Him to be partakers of His glory. Christ claims the privilege of having His church with Him. 'I will that they also, whom Thou hast given Me, be with Me where I am.' To have them with Him is according to covenant promise and agreement with His Father. He reverently presents at the mercy-seat His finished redemption for His people. The bow of promise encircles our Substitute and Surety as He pours out His petition of love, 'Father, I will that they also whom Thou hast given Me, be with Me where I am; that they may behold My glory.' We shall behold the King in His beauty, and the church will be glorified." —*Ibid.*, Oct. 17, 1893, p. 645.

No Miracles. —"But it was part of the covenant made in heaven, that Christ, having taken humanity, was not to work miracles in His own behalf, but was to stand as a man among men." —*Southern Watchman*, March 1, 1904, p. 142.

Covenant Book. —"Moses had written—not the ten commandments, but the judgments which God would have them observe, and the promises, on conditions that they would obey Him. He read this to the people, and they pledged themselves to obey all the words which the Lord had said. Moses then wrote their solemn pledge in a book, and offered sacrifice unto God for the people. 'And he took the book of the covenant, and read in the audience of the people, and they said, All that the Lord hath said will we do, and be obedient. And Moses took the blood, and sprinkled it on the people, and said, Behold the blood of the covenant, which the Lord hath made with you concerning all these words.' The people repeated their solemn pledge to the Lord to obey all that He had said, and to be obedient."—*Spiritual Gifts*, vol. 3, pp. 270, 271.

CHAPTER 9

OF THE BOOK OF HEBREWS

Our High Priest in Heaven

SYNOPSIS OF CHAPTER

IN ANY evaluation of the book of Hebrews the ninth chapter must stand high. In it the author is approaching the climax in his argument concerning Christ as high priest.

After giving a brief survey of the tabernacle built by Moses, the building, the furniture, and the service, the apostle informs us in verse 8 that the Holy Spirit signifies by this that "the way into the holiest of all was not made manifest, while as the first tabernacle was yet standing."

He then proceeds to contrast the earthly tabernacle with the heavenly, showing that the earthly was only a figure for the time then present. (Verses 9, 10.) Through the greater and more perfect tabernacle Christ has entered into the holy places with His own blood and obtained eternal redemption for us. (Verses 11–14.)

Christ is mediator of the new covenant which became effective at His death. In like manner death took place at the dedication of the first covenant, though it was only the death of calves and goats, the blood of which was sprinkled upon the book of the covenant, the people, the tabernacle, and the vessels. (Verses 15–21.)

According to the law almost all things are cleansed or purged with blood. It was therefore necessary that the pattern of the things in heaven be cleansed with the blood of calves and goats, but the heavenly things with better sacrifices, even the blood of Jesus. (Verses 22, 23.) Christ has entered the holy places in heaven now to appear before the face of God for us. When He comes the second time He shall appear without sin unto salvation to them that look for Him. (Verses 24–28.)

Hebrews 9:1–10. "Then verily the first covenant had also ordinances of divine service, and a worldly sanctuary. For there was a tabernacle made; the first, wherein was the candlestick, and the table, and the shewbread; which is called the sanctuary. And after the second veil, the tabernacle which is called the Holiest of all; which had the golden censer, and the ark of the covenant overlaid round about with gold, wherein was the golden pot that had manna, and Aaron's rod that budded, and the tables of the covenant; and over it the cherubims of glory shadowing the mercy seat; of which we cannot now speak particularly. Now when these things were thus ordained, the priests went always into the first tabernacle, accomplishing the service of God. But into the second went the high priest alone once every year, not without blood, which he offered for himself, and for the errors of the people: the Holy Ghost this signifying, that the way into the holiest of all was not yet made manifest, while as the first tabernacle was yet standing: which was a figure for the time then present, in which were offered both gifts and sacrifices, that could not make him that did the service perfect, as pertaining to the conscience; which stood only in meats and drinks, and divers washings, and carnal ordinances, imposed on them until the time of reformation."

The author assumes that his readers are well acquainted with the tabernacle which he describes, and remarks that he cannot now speak particularly about that which is so well known. However, he deems it advisable to recount the more important phases of the service in the earthly tabernacle, before he gives his whole attention to the heavenly. As there are many parallels between the two sanctuaries, he reasons that it will help his readers if they have clearly in mind both the arrangement and the service in the earthly.

The Mosaic tabernacle becomes of special importance when we learn that the Holy Spirit asserts that there is a significance in it beyond what is seen. It was a figure for the time then present, until the time of reformation.

Verse 1. "The first covenant had also ordinances." The fact that the first covenant also had ordinances takes for granted that the new covenant has them. As the author is about to compare the earthly and the heavenly tabernacle, it is interesting to note that he takes the ordinances in the heavenly sanctuary for granted.

"A worldly sanctuary;" better, "a sanctuary of this world."

Verse 2. "A tabernacle...the first." The first apartment of the sanctuary is here called the first tabernacle, and is considered an entity in itself as regards the daily service. This apartment was used every day during the year. The second apartment, also called the most holy, was open only a short time on the Day of Atonement. The first apartment is therefore considered an institution in itself and is called the first tabernacle.

"The candlestick." The writer is describing the tabernacle built by Moses, in which there was only one candlestick. In Solomon's temple there were twelve. The candlestick was the sole means of illumination in the tabernacle, as there were no windows in the building. Even though there were seven lamps on the candlestick, at best the light must have been rather dim, especially as all the lamps would not ordinarily be burning at the same time. The candlestick was of gold and of intricate workmanship. (Ex. 37:17–24.)

"The table." This was used for the shewbread and the drink offering, as well as for the utensils used in the sanctuary. It was made of shittim wood overlaid with gold. (Ex. 37:10–16.) Each Sabbath twelve fresh loaves were placed on it, one for each tribe. (Ex. 25:30; Lev. 24:5–9.)

"The shewbread"—literally, the bread of the Presence, so called because it was to be "before the Lord continually." Lev. 24:8.

"Called the sanctuary," "called the Holy place." (R.V.)

Verse 3. "After the second veil." Here only we have the second veil mentioned as such.

"Holiest of all," or most holy. This was half the size of the first apartment, and constituted a cube, being of equal length, width, and height.

Verse 4. "Had the golden censer." The reading here is unique. The American Revised Version reads, "a golden altar of incense," instead of "golden censer." The original word might be translated either "altar" or "censer." We believe "altar" is here intended, for if we translate "censer," then the altar of incense is not mentioned in these verses, which seems improbable.

The altar of incense was the most important article in the holy place, and it is unlikely that in such a carefully written treatise as Hebrews the author would omit mentioning it, especially as he is enumerating the articles of furniture.

But even if we translate "altar of incense" instead of "censer," we are still confronted with the fact that it is mentioned as being in the most holy place, instead of in the holy place, where it undoubtedly stood. (Ex. 30:6.) On this altar incense was offered daily, and as the priests who offered the incense were not permitted to enter the most holy place under pain of death, it is clear that the altar must have been in the first apartment. Why, then, does the author here place it in the second apartment?

It is to be noted that the author does not state that the altar stood in the second apartment; but only that the most holy "had" it. This reading is both peculiar and significant.

A possible solution may be found in 1 Kings 6:22. In this chapter we are told that Solomon prepared an oracle in the house within "to set there the ark of the covenant of the Lord." Verse 19. This oracle is the most holy place. (Verses 23–25.)

"And the whole house he overlaid with gold, until all the house was finished: also the whole altar that belonged to the oracle he overlaid with gold." Verse 22, A.R.V. The altar here mentioned is the altar of incense, and it is said to have "belonged to the oracle," or the most holy. As stated above, there is no assertion that the altar *stood* in the most holy, but merely that it *belonged* to it, or as Hebrews says, "had" it.

The incense offered daily on the altar was directed toward the mercy seat. There God dwelt between the cherubim; and as the incense ascended with the prayers, it filled the most holy as well as the holy place. The veil that separated the two apartments did not extend to the ceiling but reached only part way. The incense could thus be offered in the first apartment—the only place where the priests might enter—and yet reach the second apartment, toward which place it was directed. Thus the altar stood in the holy place and yet "belonged" to the most holy.

"And the ark of the covenant." This was so called because it contained the two tables of stone on which God had written the Ten Commandments, which was the covenant and also formed the basis of the covenant made with Israel. This ark was the central object in the sanctuary; for it was with reference to the law it contained that atonement was made.

"The golden pot." The golden pot and Aaron's rod that budded were in the ark of the original tabernacle. They were doubtless later removed, for we are specifically told that at the time of the dedication of Solomon's temple "there was nothing in the ark save the two tables of stone, which Moses put there at Horeb, when the Lord made a covenant with the children of Israel, when they came out of the land of Egypt." 1 Kings 8:9.

"The tables of the covenant." In Exodus these tables are called "the two tables of testimony," and the words written on them "the words of the covenant, the ten commandments." Ex. 34:28, 29. In Deuteronomy the Ten Commandments are called the "covenant, which he commanded you to perform, even ten commandments; and he wrote them upon two tables of stone." Deut. 4:13.

Verse 5. "The cherubims of glory." On top of the ark were two cherubims made of solid gold and of one piece with the mercy seat. (Ex. 37:6–9.)

"Of which we cannot now speak particularly." The apostle takes for granted that his readers are acquainted with the general appearance of the sanctuary, and that he need not dwell on that which is so well known. He might say a great deal about the cherubims of glory, as well as of other things in the tabernacle, but as that is not his present object, he passes it by. What he is interested in is the service of the sanctuary and the work of the priests. To this he now turns his attention.

Verse 6. "The priests went always into the first tabernacle." Part of the daily service was performed in the tabernacle and required that the priests should go morning and evening into the first apartment and offer incense. In early times the high priest himself did this. (Ex. 30:7, 8.) This ordinance being performed daily, the incense came to be called "perpetual incense." (Verse 8.)

Verse 7. "But into the second went the high priest alone once every year." Only the high priest could enter the most holy place, and he only once a year, on the Day of Atonement.

"Not without blood." On that day a special atonement was made, and only the high priest could officiate. The blood of the bullock, which he carried into the sanctuary, was for himself and for the errors of the people. The blood of the Lord's goat cleansed the sanctuary, and with that the people.

The Jews, to whom Paul wrote, were familiar with the details of the sanctuary service; but not all Christian readers have as clear a conception of this ritual as the Jews had. For this reason we present a brief study of the sanctuary service in the notes, to which we refer the interested reader. (See pages 311–353.)

Verses 8–10. "The Holy Ghost this signifying." Some Christians see little of value either in the sanctuary or in its services. The Holy Spirit here announces that there is value and spiritual import in the Hebrew ritual. This pronouncement by the Spirit raises the sanctuary and its services from the level of mere history to the high plane of an inspired account of a prophetic institution of symbolic significance.

"The way into the holiest of all." The sanctuary and its services were intended to show the way to God. This they did, but in doing this they also revealed their own temporariness and imperfections. God was said to dwell between the cherubims in the most holy place of the sanctuary, but access to Him could be had by only one person. The heathen could approach only as far as the first court, the court of Gentiles. Women could come no nearer than the second court, the court of women. The third court, that of the men, was the prescribed limit for the Jews. The priests had their own court and also the privilege of going into the first apartment of the sanctuary, the holy place, but only when appointed to do so and for a specific purpose. Even then there was a veil separating them from the Shekinah in the most holy place, and through this veil they could never pass. The high priest alone, and he but one day in the year, could enter the presence of God. He only had the right to draw aside the veil; and even then he must be covered with a cloud of incense, that he die not." (Lev. 16:2.) After he had gained access he could remain but a short time; then another year must elapse before he could appear before God again.

From this it is clear that whereas the sanctuary ritual showed that man *could* have access to God, the arrangement was far from satisfactory. There was no free approach to Him such as the gospel contemplates, or as our first parents had in the Garden of Eden. There *was* access, but only for *one* person once a year.

There are three expressions that need definition before we shall be able to determine what is meant by "the Holy Ghost this signifying." They are "holiest of all" (one word in Greek), "tabernacle," and "standing."

"Holiest of all." The Greek term for this phrase occurs eight times in the book of Hebrews, and is translated as follows: chapter 8:2, "sanctuary"; chapter 9:2, "sanctuary"; verse 8, "holiest of all"; verse 12, "holy place"; verse 24, "holy places"; verse 25, "holy place"; chapter 10:19, "holiest"; chapter 13:11, "sanctuary." Thus the one Greek word is translated five different ways in the eight texts—"sanctuary" thrice; "holy place" twice; "holy places," "holiest," and "holiest of all," once each.

The American Revised Version is more consistent, as it translates the Greek word "holy place" seven times, and "sanctuary" once. (Heb. 8:2.)

As noted, the original Greek is the same in all eight places, and in each case is in the plural. This the Authorized recognizes in one place, Hebrews 9:24, where it has "holy *places.*" Thus the Authorized Version is correct in one case of the eight, and the American Revised, though more consistent, incorrect in all eight.

It might, however, be noted that "sanctuary," meaning the two apartments, is an acceptable translation if the *whole* sanctuary is meant, and not one apartment only; but as "holy places"—or better still, "holies"—is an extact translation, and properly emphasizes the two apartments of the structure, it is better to use this.

Placing the two versions side by side, we have this picture:

	Authorized	*American Revised*
Heb. 8:2	sanctuary	sanctuary
9:2	sanctuary	holy place
9:8	holiest of all	holy place
9:12	holy place	holy place
9:24	holy places	holy place
9:25	holy place	holy place
10:19	holiest	holy place
13:11	sanctuary	holy place

Besides these eight places, the word occurs in the singular (only place in the New Testament) in Hebrews 9:1, where both versions translate "sanctuary"; and in a compound form in chapter 9, verse 3, where the Authorized has "holiest of all," and the American Revised, "Holy of holies."

It is clear that where one word is translated five different ways in eight occurrences, personal judgment must have influenced the translators. And as this word is vital to an understanding of the subject under consideration, it is unfortunate that such discrepancies should creep in. Although the American Revised Version helps in that it is more consistent in its translation, it is unfortunate that it should use the singular in every case, whereas the original uses the plural.

Let it therefore be understood and emphasized that the original is plural in every case; that it can never mean the "holy place" only, or the "most holy" only; but that in each of the eight cases it is in the plural and means "holies," or "holy places," and includes both the holy and the most holy apartment. Consistency therefore demands that in each of the eight instances we translate "holies," though as noted above, "sanctuary" might be admissible, if it is definitely understood to include *both* apartments and not one only.

"Tabernacle," the second word to be defined, refers, as used in Hebrews, both to the true tabernacle in heaven made without hands and to the tabernacle built by Moses in the wilderness. (Heb. 8:2; 9:11, 21.) The distinction between these is clear, and there need be no misunderstanding as to which is meant.

In Hebrews 9:2, 3, 6 the word is used in a special sense, not found elsewhere. There the "first tabernacle" means the first apartment in the tabernacle on earth; and the tabernacle "after the second veil" means the most holy place. That is, "tabernacle" is here used in the sense of apartment.

The "first tabernacle" is also mentioned in Hebrews 9:8, where its meaning depends upon the interpretation given to "holiest of all" in the same verse. If "holiest of all" here means the second apartment, then "the first tabernacle" may well mean the first apartment. But if, as we have shown, "holiest of all" is a mistranslation and should be "holies," then "the first tabernacle" here has the ordinary meaning of the Mosaic structure as contrasted with the "true holies" in heaven. Robertson, in his *Word Pictures*, on Hebrews 8:2 says:

" 'Of the holy places' (*ta hagia*), without any distinction (like 9:8 f; 10:19; 13:11) between the holy place and the most holy place as in 9:2 f." —Volume 5, p. 389.

That is, in the text before us, Hebrews 9:8, the correct rendering is holy *places*, without any distinction between the holy and the most holy place, such as is found in verse 2 and on.

Knowing that the translation "holiest of all" is incorrect; knowing that it is plural and means "holies," embracing both apartments and not one apartment only, we have no hesitation in stating that the comparison in verse 8 is between the first, or Mosaic, tabernacle and the true sanctuary in heaven.

"Standing." This is the third word requiring definition. This word, as connected with "tabernacle," does not denote the standing of the *building* as such, but has reference to its *use*, and rather means "retaining its standing, place, position"; "filling its appointed place"; "retaining its divinely appointed status," in the same way as we speak of the standing of a person, institution, or society. Verse 8 means that the way into the true holies was not manifested so long as the service in the Mosaic tabernacle was still meeting the mind of God.

With these orientating remarks we are now ready to evaluate the meaning of the statement that the way into the holiest of all—or as we have learned—into the holies, was not made manifest while the first tabernacle was still filling its appointed place.

Of this passage there are two leading interpretations. The first is based on the mistranslation, "holiest of all," and the text is thus made to say that the way into the most holy was not open as long as service was carried on in the first apartment. Though this statement is true in itself, it cannot be the meaning here. It was, indeed, necessary that the service in the holy place should end before the service in the most holy could begin. (Lev. 16:17.) But this the author has just told his readers in the preceding verses, and this every Jew knew.

"The Holy Ghost this signifying." What is it the Holy Ghost signifies? It cannot be the fact that the service in the first apartment must cease before the service in the second can begin, for this is the very thing which He says *signifies* something, and a thing cannot signify itself. That would be tautology and worse: it would be meaningless. And such we cannot attribute to the Holy Spirit. It would merely be reasoning in a circle, and would make an important announcement of the Holy Spirit an empty phrase. It would be equivalent—on a lower level—to a mathematician's stating the obvious fact that seven times seven are forty-nine. All would admit the truth of this. Then in solemn tones he would add, "There is a great significance in this." "And what is the significance?" "The great significance is this, that seven times seven are forty-nine!" He has said exactly nothing. He has insulted the intelligence of his hearers. We do not attribute a similar pronouncement to the Holy Spirit.

We can think of no reason for the author's giving a detailed description of the work done in the two apartments of the sanctuary, showing that the service in the first apartment was finished before the high priest went into the second, and making a solemn announcement that the Holy Spirit signifies something by this, and then bringing the matter to an anticlimax by stating that what the Holy Spirit signifies by this is the fact itself. Such reduces the utterance of the Holy Spirit to an absurdity.

This view becomes still more untenable when we learn that verse 8 says nothing whatever of either the first or the second *apartment,* but merely mentions the Mosaic, or first, tabernacle, and contrasts this with the heavenly holies, or sanctuary.

The second view holds that the author in this verse makes the transition in his argument from the earthly to the heavenly sanctuary, and is here beginning to contrast the Mosaic tabernacle with the heavenly sanctuary, the true "holies." That he makes such a transition is clear, for the remainder of the chapter is given to a comparison and contrast of the two. The only question is *where* the transition is made. We believe it to be in verses 8–10.

This second view makes the Holy Spirit place its stamp of approval on the ordinances of the old sanctuary as having spiritual significance, and it also makes a divine pronouncement that the way to the heavenly sanctuary would be open when the earthly sanctuary had fulfilled its appointed mission. This view gives consistency to the whole passage, makes the saying of the Holy Spirit of vital interest and significance, and prepares the way for a discussion of the true tabernacle of which Christ is minister. (Heb. 8:2; 9:11.)

Verse 9. "Which was a figure." "Which" refers to the whole Levitical system, and not to any particular part, as seems evident from the verses that follow. It may be presumed, however, that the writer had particularly in mind the arrangement of the tabernacle just mentioned, and the services culminating in the Day of Atonement ritual.

Whereas "figure" in some instances means "type," as in Romans 5:14, here it is better to translate "parable." The use of this word is significant. There is danger that we may place too great stress on the word "type" and attempt to make every little detail in the tabernacle find its heavenly counterpart. Of this we are warned in chapter 10, verse 1, where we are told that the old tabernacle had "a shadow" and "not the very image of the things," and here that it is a parable. We get from this the impression that the general outlines of the two sanctuaries and services are the same, but we are warned not to attempt to make the parable go on all fours," that is, not to attempt to make every little thing have its counterpart.

"Could not make him...perfect." The difficulty which the author points out is the fact that the gifts and sacrifices offered "could not make him that did the service perfect, as pertaining to the conscience." This was a vital fault, which we have discussed elsewhere as the chief objection to the Levitical system.

God requires perfection of His people. In His opening sermon on the mount Christ declared, "Be ye therefore perfect, even as your Father which is in heaven is perfect." Matt. 5:48. Paul's hope for the church was "that ye may stand perfect and complete in all the will of God," so that "we may present every man perfect in Christ Jesus." Col. 4:12; 1:28. That this matter of perfection is a fundamental necessity in religion is clear from the statement that if "perfection were [possible] by the Levitical priesthood...what further need was there that another priest should rise after the order of Melchisedec?" Heb. 7:11. "The law made nothing perfect" and "can never with those sacrifices which they offered year by year continually make the comers thereunto perfect." Heb.7:19; 10:1.

Perfection is God's goal for His people, and this could not be reached by offering gifts and sacrifices. They "could not make him that did the service perfect."

This fault was inherent in the service itself. Surely, no one can believe that the blood of an animal can atone for the sin of the soul. The forgiveness men obtained did not permanently make them any better. Day by day the people brought their sacrifices, and day by day the priest ministered the blood, and the sinner went away with the assurance of sins forgiven. But next day the service was repeated, and so throughout the year; and year after year, an endless round.

Forgiveness does not lead to perfection. A man may be forgiven a thousand times and yet keep on sinning. An Israelite might bring sacrifices to the sanctuary every day of his life, and yet never reach perfection. Even "thousands of rams" could not do this. And as perfection was the goal, something more than forgiveness must be obtained if perfection was to become possible.

There was a hint of perfection in the services of the Day of Atonement. "On that day shall the priest make an atonement for you, to cleanse you, that ye may be clean from all your sins before the Lord." Lev. 16:30. Here cleansing is brought to view. Forgiveness the people had obtained during the year through the services in the first apartment. But now a new day had come, and with that new day the promise "that ye may be clean from all your sins before the Lord." This was more than forgiveness: it was cleansing, cleansing from *all* sins.

But even this service was not satisfactory. As soon as the Day of Atonement was over, the veil again barred the way to the most holy place, and not for another year could anyone enter. Israel was given a glimpse of the possibilities before them, and then the door was closed. This showed that the way was not open, and that perfection could not be obtained by this service. Something better must be provided to reach the goal.

This something better was foreshadowed in the Old Testament. A man might inadvertently have become defiled, or perhaps have spoken unadvisedly with his lips. He confesses his sin and error, offers the appropriate sacrifice, and is forgiven. He is happy; yet he can but feel that there are other and more serious sins that need forgiveness, but which do not and can not come under the heading of unintentional sins. Led astray by his heathen neighbors, he has attended one of their festivals and participated in their Baal worship; he has profaned the Sabbath and not guarded its edges; he has coveted his neighbor's wife; he has taken God's name in vain.

These sins come to his mind and weigh him down. What can he do? Bring an offering? No; the law of sin offerings provided only for unintentional sins—with a few exceptions—and he himself feels that his sin is too great to be atoned for by an animal. Then he remembers David's sin and repentance, and that God does not want animal sacrifices or burnt offerings for such sins. He hears David say, "The sacrifices of God are a broken spirit: a broken and a contrite heart, O God, thou wilt not despise." Ps. 51:17. He bows his heart before God, confesses his sin, and is forgiven. He brings to God a broken and a contrite heart, and God hears his prayer.

David's experience shows conclusively that men in the Old Testament understood the limited value of sacrifices. How else could David say after his great sin, "Thou desirest not sacrifice; else would I give it: thou delightest not in burnt offering." Ps. 51:16. He knew that a broken heart and a contrite spirit counted with God, and not the blood of animals.

While Israel, therefore, in the sacrificial system was taught that even small errors counted, and that without shedding of blood there could be no forgiveness of sin, they also understood that the sacrifices could never make perfect them that brought them. Real forgiveness could be obtained only through confession and humbling of soul, as they with a broken heart and contrite spirit came before God.

Verse 10. "Meats and drinks." The author contrasts the ceremonial offerings with the great offering of Christ which he is about to consider. He makes it clear that these ceremonies were of little avail when it came to purifying the conscience or bringing perfection into the life.

"Divers washings." There were many acts of ceremonial washing that the Jews had to perform. Some of these were instituted by God, and had value in teaching sanitation and personal cleanliness aside from the spiritual implications they might have. To these ordinances the leaders in Israel had added many others which God had never commanded, but which they nevertheless enforced.

"Carnal ordinances." This does not mean either sinful or worthless ordinances, but such as pertained to the flesh and were of benefit to the flesh only.

Hebrews 9:11, 12. "But Christ being come an high priest of good things to come, by a greater and more perfect tabernacle, not made with hands, that is to say, not of this building; neither by the blood of goats and calves, but by his own blood he entered in once into the holy place, having obtained eternal redemption for us."

The apostle now begins a consideration of the work that Christ came to do, contrasting it with that of the high priest of old. Having refreshed the minds of his readers in regard to ceremonies with which most of them were familiar, he now turns to the higher service above.

Verse 11. "But Christ." The "but" places what follows in contrast to what has gone before. Previously the writer had contrasted Christ with some of the great personages in the Old Testament; he now contrasts Christ's *service* in heaven with that which was done on earth.

"Being come," that is, having at last come, after a wait of four thousand years from the first promise of a Redeemer in the Garden of Eden.

"An high priest of good things to come." The old ceremonies have been enumerated in the preceding verses. The good things to come are the promises of the gospel: forgiveness, sanctification, victory over sin, everlasting righteousness, holiness; not merely in figure, but in reality.

"By a greater and more perfect tabernacle." Commentators are divided on the meaning of this phrase, some contending that the greater and more perfect tabernacle is the tabernacle in heaven, and others that it is Christ's glorified body, in the sense in which Christ speaks of His body as the temple; again others that it is the church of God.

The preposition *by* is used three times. "By a...tabernacle"; "by the blood of goats"; "by his own blood." In the original the same word is used in each case. The Revised Version has "through" instead of "by."

"Holy place" in the Greek is in the plural, as noted before, and may be translated "holy places" or "sanctuary," if by sanctuary we mean the *whole* sanctuary, consisting of two apartments. "Tabernacle" is not defined as being either the first or the second tabernacle, as in verses 2 and 6, but simply "tabernacle" without further definition, though it should be noted that it is called *the* tabernacle in the original, not *a* tabernacle.

With this in mind we may therefore translate: "Christ, by [means of] the greater and more perfect tabernacle, not by [means of] the blood of goats and calves, but by [means of] His own blood entered into the holy places." With the Revised Version we may substitute "through" for "by," leaving the other reading the same.

We now inquire what the "greater and more perfect tabernacle" is, by or through which Christ entered the "holy places" in heaven. We have already mentioned that different views are held by commentators. We shall now consider the two main ones.

The first view is that which considers the greater and more perfect tabernacle the lower heavens through which Christ passed into heaven itself. By the lower heavens is meant the abode of the angels as distinguished from the inner heaven where God's throne is. The lower heavens and the real heaven according to this view correspond to the first and the second apartments in the sanctuary, the holy and the most holy.

This interpretation necessitates the changing of "by" for "through," in the verse before us, as it could not be said that Christ "by means of" the lower heaven passed into heaven itself. The proponents of this view therefore translate that Christ "through the

283

lower heavens passed into heaven itself." It should be noted, however, that even with this change it is necessary in this one place to give "by" another meaning than is given to the same word in the other two places where it is used in this verse, in which other cases the word of necessity must mean "by" or "in virtue of."

To this interpretation we offer the following objections:

Although this view correctly presupposes two apartments in the heavenly sanctuary, it makes the holy place, the lower heavens, merely a passageway through which Christ passed into the most holy, whereas the first apartment in the sanctuary on earth was an entity in itself, wherein services were daily conducted. It was a separate institution and not merely an entrance to another apartment. If the lower heaven were the first apartment, why mention it at all, thus recognizing its existence while denying it any liturgical or other spiritual value? Why should the first part of chapter nine give a detailed description of the first apartment, mention the table, the shewbread, the incense, call the whole arrangement a "figure" for the time then present, and then tell us that Christ ignored it all and counted it only a passageway? Why should the two apartments be specifically mentioned in verses 2 to 7, and in verse 24 be called "figures of the true," and then this arrangement be ignored in verse 1? In verse 6 the priests go "continually" (R.V.) into the first apartment "accomplishing the service of God." In verse 11, according to this interpretation, Christ accomplishes nothing there. The fact that the priests continually go into the first apartment is one of the points mentioned by the Holy Spirit as having significance. How, then, could Christ completely ignore any mention of the service in the first apartment in heaven, when this service was in fulfillment of the type on earth?

On these grounds we must reject the interpretation that the "greater and more perfect tabernacle" here designates the holy place. It would be passing strange that such a glorious title as "greater and more perfect tabernacle" should be given to a passageway, and yet have no standing or service that would entitle it to such a distinguished name. Evidently the title is meant to convey some exalted place. The interpretation given to it in the view here presented does the exact opposite.

But there is another and most potent reason why we must reject this interpretation. This reason is inherent in the reading itself, which forbids any such conclusion that the "greater and more perfect tabernacle" is the first apartment.

The insurmountable obstacle to this interpretation is that there is nothing said in this verse of either the first or the second apartment. The two expressions are the "greater and more perfect tabernacle" and the "holy places." There is no ground or reason for calling the greater and more perfect tabernacle the first apartment, nor for restricting the "holy places," plural, to the second apartment. There would be as good reason to confine "holy places" to the first apartment only. But it does not mean the first apartment or the second. It means, and must mean, both apartments—the sanctuary as a whole.

Note, therefore, what the text does *not* say: It does *not* say that Christ passed through the earthly tabernacle into the heavenly; it does *not* say that He passed through the earthly tabernacle into the most holy in heaven; it does *not* say that He went through the greater and more perfect tabernacle into the most holy. It does *not* mention the first tabernacle or first apartment; it does *not* mention the most holy. What the text *does* say is that Christ by virtue of, by means of, or through, the greater and more perfect tabernacle entered once into the holy *places*. We must therefore reject all interpretations which are based on readings not supported by the text itself.

The second view to which we would call attention is that which appears to us to be the correct view, based on the wording of the text before us. The reading is that "Christ...by a greater and more perfect tabernacle...entered in once into the holy place" (places). The two things mentioned are the tabernacle, and the holy places, or the sanctuary. This at once raises the question of whether there is a tabernacle in heaven as well as a sanctuary, for Christ goes by, or through, the one into the other. We have shown that the "greater and more perfect tabernacle" cannot mean or be made to mean the first apartment, nor can "holy places," or "sanctuary," be confined to the second apartment. What, therefore, is the meaning of these expressions?

We would again call attention to the preposition "by," which is used three times: "by a...tabernacle"; "by the blood of goats"; "by his own blood." The last two uses of "by" are clearly that of the instrumental case, by virtue of, by means of, in virtue of. If we give the first "by" the same meaning as in the other two cases, we would have the statement that Christ by virtue of, or by means of, or in virtue of, the greater and more perfect tabernacle entered into the sanctuary in heaven. Interpreting the "greater and more perfect tabernacle" to be the first apartment, we would have this reading: "Christ, by virtue of the first apartment entered into the sanctuary in heaven."

But this would not make sense. We must either change "by," and give it a meaning different from that in the other two cases, or else we must give to "tabernacle" a meaning different from that of first apartment. As we have already shown that there is no ground or proof for considering the "greater and more perfect tabernacle" the first apartment; and in view of the fact that consistency would suggest that we give to "by" the same meaning in all three cases in which it occurs in our text, we feel under obligation to give attention to the true meaning of "tabernacle" as it is here used.

Let us first of all declare our belief in the existence of a sanctuary in heaven. We believe that as truly as there was a sanctuary on earth, so there is a sanctuary in heaven. If we are asked whether we believe this to be a building of wood or stone, we admit that we have no certain knowledge. We do not know the nature of heavenly things, but the whole description of the sanctuary in heaven is couched in language definitely conveying the idea that it is real. The "things" are real to the point where cleansing of them is stated to be necessary. (Heb. 9:23.) We have difficulty in believing that the real blood shed on Calvary is ministered in a nonexistent, spiritual sanctuary. True, there are other things of which we cannot conceive, but consistency demands that a real sanctuary must exist if there was real blood shed. This sanctuary in heaven is called temple as well as tabernacle. (Rev. 11:19; 15:5.)

The New Testament writers make a unique use of the word "temple," to which we call attention. The following scriptures are of interest in this connection: Christ spoke of His body as the temple. "Jesus answered and said unto them, Destroy this temple, and in three days I will raise it up. Then said the

Jews, Forty and six years was this temple in building, and wilt thou rear it up in three days? But he spake of the temple of his body." John 2:19–21. (See also Matt. 26:61; 27:40; Mark 15:29.) The false witnesses testified, "We heard him say, I will destroy this temple that is made with hands, and within three days I will build another made without hands." Mark 14:58. Although these were false witnesses, and stated that Christ had said that He would destroy the temple made with hands—which He had never said—they were stating a truth when they said that in three days He would "build another made without hands." In these places, as in all texts in the New Testament, the Greek word for "temple" may rightly be translated "sanctuary" as well as "temple," as is noted in the margin of the Revised Version.

In the New Testament the church of Christ is said to be the temple, or sanctuary, of God.

"Now therefore ye are no more strangers and foreigners, but fellowcitizens with the saints, and of the household of God; and are built upon the foundation of the apostles and prophets, Jesus Christ himself being the chief corner stone; in whom all the building fitly framed together groweth unto an holy temple in the Lord: in whom ye also are builded together for an habitation of God through the Spirit." Eph. 2:19–22.

"Know ye not that ye are the temple of God, and that the Spirit of God dwelleth in you? If any man defile the temple of God, him shall God destroy; for the temple of God is holy, which temple ye are." 1 Cor. 3:16, 17.

"And what agreement hath the temple of God with idols? for ye are the temple of the living God; as God hath said, I will dwell in them, and walk in them; and

I will be their God, and they shall be my people." 2 Cor. 6:16.

"To whom coming, as unto a living stone, disallowed indeed of men, but chosen of God, and precious, ye also, as lively stones, are built up a spiritual house, an holy priesthood, to offer up spiritual sacrifices, acceptable to God by Jesus Christ." 1 Peter 2:4, 5.

The same picture is presented in Hebrews, where the church is spoken of as God's house:

"And Moses verily was faithful in all his house, as a servant, for a testimony of those things which were to be spoken after; but Christ as a son over his own house; whose house are we, if we hold fast the confidence and the rejoicing of the hope firm unto the end." Heb. 3:5,6.

Peter uses the illustration of a tabernacle when he says, "As long as I am in this tabernacle," and again, "I must put off this my tabernacle." 2 Peter 1:13, 14.

Paul agrees with this when he says that "if our earthly house of this tabernacle were dissolved, we have a building of God, an house not made with hands, eternal in the heavens." 2 Cor. 5:1.

If we sum up the contents of these texts we get the following picture: We are Christ's house. (Heb. 3:6.) This spiritual house is built of lively stones: "Ye also, as lively stones, are built up a spiritual house." 1 Peter 2:5. It is erected on a solid foundation, being "built upon the foundation of the apostles and prophets, Jesus Christ himself being the chief corner stone." Eph. 2:20. Consisting of lively stones, "all the building fitly framed together groweth unto an holy temple [or "sanctuary," Revised Version, margin] in the Lord." Eph. 2:21. In this temple God will dwell:

"Ye are the temple of the living God; as God hath said, I will dwell in them, and walk in them." 2 Cor. 6:16. (See also Eph. 2:22.) This temple or sanctuary of God is holy and must not be defiled: "If any man defile the temple of God, him shall God destroy; for the temple of God is holy, which temple ye are." 1 Cor. 3:17. In the sanctuary of old God dwelt among His people. "Make me a sanctuary; that I may dwell *among* them." Ex. 25:8. In this sanctuary God dwells *in* His people. "I will dwell in them." "Christ in you, the hope of glory." "That Christ may dwell in your hearts by faith." 2 Cor. 6:16; Col. 1:27; Eph. 3:17. In this temple not only are we living stones, but Christ Himself is "a living stone, disallowed indeed of men, but chosen of God, and precious." 1 Peter 2:4. In this spiritual house the saints are priests, and offer spiritual sacrifices: They "are built up a spiritual house, an holy priesthood, to offer up spiritual sacrifices acceptable to God by Jesus Christ." They are "a royal priesthood." 1 Peter 2:5, 9. As we are both living stones in the temple and also priests, so Christ is a living stone, the chief cornerstone, and high priest. (1 Peter 2:5; Heb. 5:5; 8:1.)

These texts, taken from various parts of the New Testament, present a consistent picture of the church as the temple, or sanctuary, of God. The Jewish tabernacle was in reality a type of the Christian church. We fall short of God's intent when we study the ceremonies and the ritual of the sanctuary, and forget that they are vitally connected with the living church of God on earth.

Not only is the church in its composite capacity the temple of the Most High God, but each individual member is also a temple. "Know ye not that ye are the temple of God?" 1 Cor. 3:16. This temple we are not to defile, lest we be destroyed. (Verse 17.) As priests of the Most High God we are to offer up spiritual sacrifices *acceptable* to God by Jesus Christ. To these verses we may add Peter's statement of the body as a tabernacle, and Paul's that if this earthly tabernacle is dissolved we have a building of God in heaven, a house not made with hands. (2 Peter 1:13, 14; 2 Cor. 5:1.)

When we therefore are told that Christ by or through the greater and more perfect tabernacle entered into the heavenly holy places, we understand it to mean that by virtue of His perfect life, having made His body a fit and clean temple for the indwelling of the Spirit of God, He appeared before God, not bringing the blood of goats and calves but His own blood, and that this gained Him entrance into the sanctuary above. As the priests gained entrance into the sanctuary by means of blood, so Christ through the greater and more perfect tabernacle, His body temple, gained entrance into the heavenly sanctuary by His own blood, His life.

In Christ, God's ideal found perfect expression. God does not dwell in temples made with hands. He does not want to dwell *among* His people merely. He wants to make *them* temples and dwell *in* them, and walk *in* them. This He did in Christ. In Him God found the ideal temple in which to dwell.

The temple in Jerusalem was a wonderful structure, perfect in all its parts. But few of the Jews understood its significance. They did not realize that God had placed it in their midst to teach them the way to God, that they might become fit temples for His holy presence. They did not understand fully that it was their sin that defiled the holy places, and that God wanted them to finish transgression and make an end of sin. They had no conception of the body temple, and when Christ used what should be to them a familiar figure of the body as the temple of God, they completely misunderstood Him, and did not know that "he spake of the temple of his body." John 2:21. The very thing Christ had come to demonstrate to them—that the body could be made a dwelling place for God—they used as the means to accuse Him and cause His death. (Matt. 26:61; 27:40.)

The view that by "the greater and more perfect tabernacle" is meant Christ's divine-human nature, was held by the early church. They based their view on John 2:18–21, where Christ speaks of His body as the temple; also on the statement attributed to Him by His enemies that "within three days I will build another made without hands"; as well as on Paul's statement that if our earthly tabernacle is dissolved, we have a building of God in heaven, "an house not made with hands." (Mark 14:58; 2 Cor. 5:1.) This they connected with the "greater and more perfect tabernacle, not made with hands, that is to say, not of this building." Heb. 9:11. In further support they quoted John 1:14: "The Word was made flesh, and dwelt [Greek: tabernacled] among us."

This view gives due emphasis to the various parts of the work of Christ. It is consistent in its use of the preposition *by,* which in each case means "by virtue of." It gives emphasis to the work Christ did in His human body, making it a fit dwelling place for God, recognized by the statement, "greater and more perfect tabernacle," or, as the original has it, "*the* greater." It emphasizes the fact that Christ gained entrance by virtue of His blood, His life, and that the perfect body which He presented for inspection to the Father met the standard set, and admitted Him to God's presence. This interpretation I believe to be the correct one. For authoritative statements supporting the view here presented, the reader is referred to the notes following this chapter. (Pages 353–357.)

Verse 12. "Having obtained eternal redemption for us." "Having obtained," or "thereby obtaining," either being admissible. If we consider Christ's conquest of death as being the redemption spoken of, we may translate "having obtained." If we consider redemption as including final victory over sin both in the individual and in the world, then we must translate, "thereby obtaining." As usual, when God chooses a word or phrase that can rightly mean two things, there is generally truth in both meanings. We so consider it here. Christ did a definite work on the cross. But He is also doing a definite work now, and "obtaining" for us redemption that will at last issue in accomplished salvation and glorification for all who accept and obey Him. The particular form of this verb is found only here in the New Testament, and has the force of "obtaining by one's own labor and effort, to find for oneself, to win, to gain." It may rightly be rendered "obtained by or for oneself," this translation thus emphasizing the fact that Christ by His life obtained eternal redemption for or by Himself, and that this redemption is imputed to us.

Eternal redemption is in contrast with the redemption and temporary atonement that the high priest of old obtained for the people. The atonement as well as the forgiveness provided in the sanctuary service was provisional and temporary, and needed to be repeated. Christ's atonement and redemption are everlasting, as is His righteousness. These are the "good things" that Christ came to bring.

Hebrews 9:13, 14. "For if the blood of bulls and of goats, and the ashes of an heifer sprinkling the unclean, sanctifieth to the purifying of the flesh: how much more shall the blood of Christ, who through the eternal Spirit offered himself without spot to God, purge your conscience from dead works to serve the living God?"

Bulls and goats were used in the expiatory services on the Day of Atonement, but we have no record of the use of ashes on that day. Although the author principally has the Day of Atonement in mind, he includes more in his survey than the specific services on that day.

Verse 13. "Blood...and ashes." The water in which the ashes of the red heifer were put, is called the "water of separation," and was used as a purification of sin or sin offering. (Num. 19:9, A.R.V.) Of Christ it is said that He came "not by water only, but by water and blood." 1 John 5:6. When He died, there flowed out blood and water. (John 19:33, 34.) The apostle, in his recital of the redemption obtained in Christ, includes the water in which ashes were put as a purification of sin, and places the water alongside the blood. This is highly suggestive, and the interested student will be amply rewarded in his exploration of this field.

Verse 14. "How much more." Paul is approaching the high point in his argument. If the blood of animals and the ashes of a heifer can sanctify to the cleanness of the flesh, how "much more" shall the blood of Jesus purge the conscience from dead works.

"The blood of Christ." Peter calls it the "precious blood of Christ, as of a lamb without blemish and without spot." 1 Peter 1:19. Paul calls it the blood of God. (Acts 20:28.)

Christ "offered himself." This statement is the basis of the oft-used expression that Christ was both priest and victim. He was not an unwilling sacrifice.

He offered Himself. God gave His Son, but it is equally true that the Son gave Himself. (John 3:16; Gal. 1:4.)

"Through the eternal Spirit." "Through" is the same word that is translated "by" in verses 11 and 12, and has the meaning of "by means of," "in virtue of." Which Spirit is this? Is it the Holy Spirit, or is it Christ's Spirit? The absence of the article "the" in the original points to the reading, "his spirit," as in the margin of the Revised Version. This also fits in with the general argument. Christ offered Himself by virtue of His divine nature. To ask the Holy Spirit to offer Christ, in His blood, seems both unnecessary and incongruous in view of the fact that Christ and not the Holy Spirit is High Priest. Christ died and shed His blood on Calvary, and now He enters the sanctuary with His own blood. (Heb. 9:12.) Why should He let anyone else do His work? The Holy Spirit is not high priest, nor is He called an eternal Spirit. As noted, the article is lacking, which would be most unusual if the Holy Spirit is meant; for that would make Him *an* eternal Spirit, instead of *the* eternal Spirit.

The Old Testament states that "it is the blood that maketh an atonement for the soul," or as the Revised Version puts it, "It is the blood that maketh atonement *by reason of the life*." Lev. 17:11, A.R.V. This is preceded by the statement that "the life of the flesh is in the blood." The Hebrew word for "life" is "soul." When Christ gave Himself for us He gave His whole self, He made "his soul an offering for sin." Isa. 53:10. That included His divine-human nature, His own eternal Spirit, His divine personality. When He made His soul an offering for sin, He gave His all and withheld nothing; He gave His very self in supreme devotion, a voluntary sacrifice in contrast with the Levitical sacrifices which—on the part of the victim—were neither voluntary nor in obedience to God's command, and had no moral value. Christ, by that which was highest in Him, His eternal Spirit, offered Himself by a purposed, self-determined act in fulfillment of the provisions of an eternal covenant involving man's destiny. He had power to lay down His life, and He had power to take up that life again. (John 10:18.) "By Himself" He purged us from our sins. (Heb. 1:3.) In like manner it was through His eternal Spirit that He offered Himself in a planned, predetermined, voluntary act of the highest moral value; and in that same Spirit He continues His work in the sanctuary above.

"Purge your conscience." Christ's work is here viewed not as a past act but as a present reality. Christ did a definite work on the cross in obtaining redemption for us, but that work and that redemption need to be applied to the individual soul. Our consciences must be purged from dead works to serve the living God; and this is a present, constant work needful in every generation. Those who claim that Christ's work was finished on the cross fail to take into consideration the continued, daily application of the blood necessary to man's salvation. No more than God created the world and set it in motion and then left it to run by itself, does Christ by one act on Calvary set redemption in motion, and then leave it to work by itself. The slaying of the sacrificial lamb in the sanctuary was a definite act which provided the means of reconciliation, the blood. But the blood had to be ministered to be efficacious, and the ministration was equally vital with the death. The blood shed on Calvary is mighty to the cleansing and purifying of the conscience from dead works, not as a past act merely, but as a living, present reality.

"To serve." God's work in the soul has a definite end in view. Our lives, our consciences, are purged that we may serve. To have our sins forgiven that we may have a clear conscience is not an end in itself, wonderful though that is. We are saved to serve, purged to serve.

Hebrews 9:15–17. "And for this cause he is the mediator of the new testament, that by means of death, for the redemption of the transgressions that were under the first testament, they which are called might receive the promise of eternal inheritance. For where a testament is, there must also of necessity be the death of the testator. For a testament is of force after men are dead: otherwise it is of no strength at all while the testator liveth."

These verses are by many considered difficult, as they apparently introduce two different aspects of the covenant, and commentators are not agreed as to when the Greek word *diatheke*, should be translated "covenant," and when "testament." We believe that the context is a safe guide and will lead to a correct understanding.

Verse 15. "For this cause;" that is, because the blood of Christ is efficacious and can thoroughly cleanse the conscience.

"Mediator of the new testament." As noted before, the Greek word for testament may be translated both "testament" and "covenant," and the context is necessary to a determination of the right meaning. In the present case "covenant" seems preferable, as only a covenant requires a mediator. A testament is a document executed by one person, and no mediator is needed. A covenant is executed between two or more persons who agree to do or to abstain from doing certain things. Here a mediator is needed. A testament comes in force only at death. A covenant ceases to be in force at death. A testament needs an executor; a covenant, a mediator.

"New covenant." (R.V.) This is the covenant of which Jeremiah speaks in his book, chapter 31:31–34. Moses was mediator of the old covenant. (Ex. 20:19; 32:30–32; Gal. 3:19.) Christ is mediator of the new.

"By means of death." We have mentioned before that in the ceremonial law of the old dispensation there was no provision for willful transgression. Thus many sins were committed "from which ye could not be justified by the law of Moses." Acts 13:39. Let not this be misunderstood. There was forgiveness in the Old Testament the same as in the New. But there was no provision *in the law of Moses* for such forgiveness. This verse holds out the hope that all "might receive the promise of eternal inheritance" through the death of Christ. This was the joyful news Paul preached when he told the Jews "that through this man is preached unto you the forgiveness of sins: and by him all that believe are justified from all things, from which ye could not be justified by the law of Moses." Acts 13:38, 39.

A paraphrase and interpretation of Hebrews 9:15 might read thus: "Because Christ is able to purge the conscience from dead works—which the sacrifices under the old covenant could not do—He has become mediator of the new covenant. His death provides real redemption and atonement for all the transgressions for which no offering could be made under the provisions of the Mosaic law, thus making it possible for those which are called—whether under the new or old covenant—to receive the promise of eternal inheritance."

It is interesting to note "*eternal* redemption" in verse 12; "*eternal* Spirit" in verse 14; and "*eternal* inheritance" in verse 15.

Verse 16. The Greek word which the author has thus far used in the sense of covenant, he now associates with that of testament. The "eternal inheritance" mentioned in verse 15. suggests the idea of a will or testament. The phrase, "a death having taken place" (A.R.V.), reminds him of the fact that as Christ died leaving us an inheritance, so in the first covenant a death also took place, and this death became the ratification of the covenant. (Ex. 24:5–8.) The Greek word means both covenant and testament—as noted above—therefore the author is justified in using it in whatever sense may best serve his purpose. He has used it in the sense of covenant. He now calls attention to the fact that it is also a testament.

A testament does not become effective until after death has taken place. It is therefore "of necessity" that there be the "death of the testator." In the Old Testament the ratification by blood was the official declaration that the covenant was in force and that its terms had become effective. So also in the New.

Hebrews 9:18–22. "Whereupon neither the first testament was dedicated without blood. For when Moses had spoken every precept to all the people according to the law, he took the blood of calves and of goats, with water, and scarlet wool, and hyssop, and sprinkled both the book, and all the people, Saying, This is the blood of the testament which God hath enjoined unto you. Moreover he sprinkled with blood both the tabernacle, and all the vessels of the ministry. And almost all things are by the law purged with blood; and without shedding of blood is no remission."

Verses 18, 19. The first covenant was ratified by the blood of calves and goats." Moses took "water, and scarlet wool, and hyssop, and sprinkled both the book, and all the people." The record in Exodus 24:5–8 does not mention the sprinkling of the book, nor the use of goats as sacrifice. It is supposed that the writer of Hebrews had access to sources not now available to us.

The sprinkling of the tabernacle and the, vessels with blood has caused some perplexity among commentators, for the tabernacle was not in existence at the time of the ratification of the covenant, and not until about nine months later was it ready for dedication. We accept the view that the writer considers the tabernacle, its ministry and vessels, as a vital part of the covenant, and hence includes their dedication and God's acceptance of the sanctuary as part of the ratification ceremonies. The sanctuary contained "the ark of the covenant." In the side of this ark the book of the law was kept, and inside the ark were the tables of the covenant. (Deut. 31:26; 9:9; 10:5.) In a certain sense it may therefore be said that when God accepted the sanctuary as His dwelling place and a depository for His holy law, and caused fire to come down from heaven, He confirmed His part of the covenant.

There is an undoubted reference to the Day of Atonement in the verses before us. The Old Testament states that the tabernacle was anointed with oil, but we have no record that blood was used in its dedication such as is stated in these verses in Hebrews. Not only was the tabernacle anointed with oil, but also the altar and its vessels. (Lev. 8:10–12.) The altar was sprinkled with blood as well as anointed with oil, and Aaron, his sons, and their garments were anointed with oil as well as sprinkled with blood. (Verses 24, 30.) But nothing is said of the tabernacle's being sprinkled with blood at the time of dedication. However, in the sixteenth chapter of Leviticus, which records the services of the Day of Atonement, the sanctuary, both the holy and the most holy, the mercy seat and the altar—all were sprinkled with blood. (Lev. 16:14–19.) As the writer of Hebrews, in recording the ratification of the covenant, not only tells what was done at the time of ratification but includes the dedication of the sanctuary, and then refers to the sprinkling of the sanctuary with blood, it seems evident that he had not only the dedication ceremonies in mind but also the Day of Atonement service. This would be all the more natural, for the service of dedication was much like the services on the Day of Atonement. Both effected dedication and cleansing.

Verse 22. "Almost all things." Not all, but almost all, things were cleansed with blood. "Almost" belongs to and qualifies both clauses of the verse. Some things were cleansed with fire or water without any use of blood. (Num. 31:23, 24.) Under certain conditions sins could be atoned for by flour instead of blood. (Lev. 5:11–13.) The ashes of the red heifer were used as a sin offering without any immediate use of blood. (Numbers 19.) Though ordinarily blood was used in cleansing, there were exceptions, as noted. But they were only exceptions. The rule was blood.

Hebrews 9:23–28. "It was therefore necessary that the patterns of things in the heavens should be purified with these; but the heavenly things themselves with better sacrifices than these. For Christ is not entered into the holy places made with hands, which are the figures of the true; but into heaven itself, now to appear in the presence of God for us: nor yet that he should offer himself often, as the high priest entereth into the holy place every year with blood of others; for then must he often have suffered since the foundation of the world: but now once in the end of the world hath he appeared to put away sin by the sacrifice of himself. And as it is appointed unto men once to die, but after this the judgment: so Christ was once offered to bear the sins of many; and unto them that look for him shall he appear the second time without sin unto salvation."

At first sight it may appear strange that there should be anything in heaven that needs cleansing. Yet we know that Satan was once an angel, and that he sinned in heaven. We also understand that the record of men's sins are there inscribed as well as their good deeds, and that when the time comes that sin and sinners shall be no more, there will be a cleansing of all that has ever come in contact with sin. When at last the very record of sin is destroyed, there will be nothing left to call sin to mind. Such a cleansing of heavenly things would fitly correspond to the cleansing of the sanctuary on earth. The statement is definite that as the things on earth were cleansed, so it was necessary that the things in the heavens also be cleansed.

Verse 23. "It was therefore necessary." In the very nature of things it was necessary that the earthly tabernacle and its vessels of ministry be cleansed. This was done before the sanctuary was put into use as a matter of dedication and consecration, and it was done yearly thereafter as long as the sanctuary services continued. When that which is the result of human workmanship is to be used for the service of God, it is not only eminently fitting but necessary that it be consecrated to set apart for holy use. As the services in the sanctuary mostly concerned sin, there was a continual defilement both of the holy places and things "because of the uncleanness of the children of Israel, and because of their transgressions in all their sins." Lev. 16:16. And so once a year on the Day of Atonement a cleansing took place that included both the most holy, the holy, and the altar. (Verses 16–20.) This cleansing, the writer says, was necessary.

"The patterns of things in the heavens." The earthly tabernacle in all its appointments was a pattern, a copy, a representation of the "things in the heavens." The word "patterns" is translated "example" in Hebrews 8:5, where the service on earth is said to be an "example and shadow of heavenly things." "Delineation" or "representation" is perhaps the best translation here.

"The heavenly things themselves." There is no word for "things" in the original, and the reading is therefore, "The heavenlies themselves." Some supply "things," others "places," both being admissible. In view of the fact that in the cleansing of the earthly sanctuary on the Day of Atonement both, the holy places and the "things" were cleansed, we are inclined to the belief that "the heavenlies themselves" is correct, including both the sanctuary and the "things."

"Better sacrifices." The plural "sacrifices" expresses the general idea of sacrifice, the many forms used in the Levitical service being included in Christ's one great sacrifice.

The question that most concerns us is the statement that there is something in heaven that needs cleansing. On this Westcott makes this significant remark: "The whole structure of the sentence requires that 'cleansed' should be supplied in the second clause from the first, and not any more general term as 'inaugurated.'" —*The Epistle to the Hebrews*, p. 271.

The point Westcott makes is this, that as it was necessary for the earthly sanctuary to be *cleansed*, so likewise it is necessary for the heavenly to be *cleansed*, not merely dedicated or inaugurated. That is, the heavenly sanctuary must of necessity be cleansed in a manner parallel to the cleansing of the earthly sanctuary. Delitzsch says that such as "would substitute in the second clause the more general notion of *dedication* or *consecration*...merely...evade the difficulty: a dedication by means of sacrificial blood would still involve the notion of *cleansing* or *atonement*." —*Commentary on the Epistle to the Hebrews*, vol. 2, p. 124.

After quoting and rejecting the opinions of several scholars, Delitzsch continues:

"Stier's interpretation comes very near the truth, when he says: 'In consequence of the presence of sin in us the holy of holies in the heavenly world could not be re-opened for our approach until it had been first itself anointed with the blood of atonement.' He is wrong, however, in restricting the ἐπουράνα here to a celestial holy of holies: the 'heavenly things' here spoken of include, as we have seen, celestial antitypes of the earthly tabernacle as well as of its inner sanctuary; and so the question still remains: In what sense could these heavenly things be said to be cleansed, not in figure only, but in truth, by the atoning death and blood of Jesus? Unless I be mistaken in my view of it, the sacred writer's meaning is fundamentally this: The supramundane holy of holies, called in ver. 24 αὐτὸς ὁ οὐρανός, *ipsum cœlum*, i.e. the eternal uncreated heaven of God Himself, though in itself untroubled blessedness and light, yet needed cleansing (χαὖαρίζεσὖαι), in so far as its light of love had been lost or transmuted for mankind, through the presence of sin, or rather had been overclouded and bedarkened by a fire of wrath; and in like manner, the heavenly tabernacle, the place of God's loving self-manifestations to angels and to men, needed also a cleansing, in so far as mankind through sin had rendered unapproachable to themselves this their spirit's natural and eternal home, until by a gracious renewal of God's forfeited mercy it should have been once more transformed into a place for the manifestation of His love and favour. In reference, therefore, to the entire τ ἐπουράνια, i.e. both the τ ἀγια, or eternal sanctuary, and the σχηνή, or heavenly tabernacle, there was required a removal of the consequences of human sin as affecting them, and a removal of the counter-workings against sin, *i.e.* of divine wrath, or rather (which comes to the same thing) a change of that wrath into renewed love." —*Ibid.*, p. 125.

Lest some reader fail to get the full force of this quotation, an attempt will be made to simplify it.

Delitzsch approves of Stier's interpretation that the "holy of holies" in heaven is to be "anointed with the blood of atonement," but he does not agree with him that it is only the holy of holies that is to be so anointed. He believes that the "heavenly things here spoken of include, as we have seen, celestial antitypes of the earthly tabernacle as well as of its inner sanctuary"; that is, the cleansing includes the first apartment as well as the most holy, which he calls "the eternal sanctuary." Both apartments of the heavenly sanctuary are to be cleansed, and not the most holy only. In summing up he concludes that in reference to both the most holy and the holy in heaven "there was required a removal of the consequences of human sin as affecting them, and a removal of the counterworkings against sin, *i.e.* of divine wrath." We agree with this as far as the removal of the consequences of human sin is concerned. We believe further that the cleansing of the heavenly sanctuary involves not only or merely the *consequences* of sin but the removal of sin itself, and that this includes "the destroying by death him that had the power of death, that is, the devil," which Delitzsch quotes approvingly. (—*Ibid.*, pp. 124, 125.)

I believe this fairly represents the meaning of the verse we are studying. As the sanctuary on earth was cleansed, so the heavenly sanctuary must be cleansed. This "is necessary," as the cleansing of the sanctuary on earth was necessary. This cleansing of the sanctuary in heaven was not a dedication or consecration only. The word "cleansing" is too definite to be limited to that interpretation. True, there was a dedication of the heavenly sanctuary; there was an anointing of the "heavenly things." But that does not exhaust the meaning of "cleansing," which definitely points to the antitypical day of atonement and is satisfied in none other. If we extend the analogy between the earthly and the heavenly sanctuary—and we are justified in doing this by the fact that the earthly sanctuary is "an example and shadow of heavenly things"—we might expect that as there was a dedication of the earthly sanctuary before the service proper began, so there was a dedication of the heavenly sanctuary before the service was officially inaugurated. We might likewise expect that as after the yearly round of services in the earthly sanctuary a day of reckoning came when all sins were brought in review before God—called the Day of Atonement, the day when the sanctuary was cleansed of all accumulated sins—so there will be a parallel work at the close of Christ's ministration in heaven. And this is just what our text leads us to expect, and what it says. For a fuller explanation of the Day of Atonement the reader is referred to the discussion at the end of this chapter.

Verse 24. As noted before, the Greek word for "holy places" is in the plural and is here correctly rendered in the plural, as it should be also in verse 12, where it is incorrectly translated in the singular.

"Figures of the true." The ellipsis here compels the reading "true *holy places*." These true holy places are here said to be "heaven itself." As the sanctuary in heaven is God's dwelling place, the designation of the holy places as heaven itself is significant. We speak of the blue atmosphere as heaven; we also think of the starry heaven, of the place where angels dwell; but God's abode is heaven itself. And that is where Christ has gone, and where He now appears in the presence of God for us.

"In the presence of God," is literally "before the face of God." The high priest appeared before God with a cloud covering him, "lest he die." In contrast Christ appears openly before God.

The significance of this should not escape us. The meaning is not that Christ appears before and sees God, but that God sees Him. Christ appears openly before God, for us, *for inspection.* This appearance took place as He returned from the earth, having finished the work given Him to do. He presented Himself before God to hear the words of approval and to be assured that the sacrifice was acceptable. His work must stand the test of close inspection. As the second Adam He underwent a trial on earth infinitely more severe than the first Adam, and now He appears officially before God, representing man. On God's acceptance of Him hangs the fate of mankind. If He is accepted, man is accepted.

But more than this. Christ appears *continually* before the face of God for us, in our stead. We are the ones who should be inspected. Can we stand the test? Can we stand to have God throw the full light on us? We can if Christ appears for us, and in no other way.

And herein lies the glory of the "now" in our text. This is the eternal now, not merely a point in time, but a continuous appearance for us. He appears "now," and He appears continually for us.

Delitzsch answers the objection that the Greek construction of "appear" cannot be used of a continuous action, but must mean just one appearance and no more. He admits the construction "does not in itself express the continuousness of the self -presentation here; but that lies in and is inferred from the νῦν [now] which undoubtedly refers to the continuous present of the new dispensation (commencing with Christ's entrance into the heavenly places), the contrast with the typical and shadowy past. This νῦν, therefore, is no isolated point of time, but the commencement of a long-linked series: Christ's activity on our behalf before the Father, consisting in a perpetual presentation of Himself as of Him who died for our sins and is risen again for our justification." —*Commentary on the Epistle to the Hebrews* vol. 2, pp. 127, 128.

Christ's appearing before the Father is therefore not an "isolated point of time, but the commencement of a long-linked series...a perpetual presentation of Himself as of Him who died for our sins and is risen again for our justification." Delitzsch ends the consideration of this verse by saying:

"The final object of His entrance as high priest and sacriifice into the eternal heaven is there to appear before God *for* us, presenting on our behalf no exhausted sacrifice, nor one of transient efficacy or needing repetition, but Himself in His own person, as an ever-present, ever-living victim and atonement. And this object is attained at once, and attained for ever." —*Ibid.*, p. 129.

Verses 25, 26. The priests entered the first apartment daily, the high priest once every year when he went into the most holy with the blood of the bullock and the goat. But Christ was not thus to offer Himself often. This information is given in view of the previous verse where the statement is made that Christ appears before the Father not once merely, but, as Delitzsch remarks, in "a long-linked series" of appearances. Christ, though He appears continually, died only once, His one death being of perpetual validity and duration. Bearing in His body the blood of the atonement, He presents His body "a living sacrifice, holy, acceptable unto God." Rom. 12:1.

"Now, once, in the end of the world," rather, "at the consummation of the ages." There is a general unanimity of opinion that this expression has reference to Christ's manifestation in the flesh, His incarnation, His coming to the world as a babe in the manger. It is somewhat different from "these last days" in Hebrews 1:2, which simply means the last period of the present age, while the expression here means the consummation or termination of a series of ages that at last comes to a climax. All the ages that had gone before were preparations for the coming Saviour; all pointed to that event, and had significance only as they marked the way to the consummation. Now it had come; Christ had appeared, and a new age was at hand. This appearing of Christ to put away sin by the sacrifice of Himself is in contrast to His appearing "the second time without sin," as mentioned in verse 28.

Verses 27, 28. Men die, and after this comes the judgment. So Christ was once offered to bear the sins of many, but He shall appear the second time without sin unto salvation.

The parallel which the writer here draws concerns itself with the judgment. As men die once, so Christ also died once. After death comes the judgment—not an immediate judgment, but the day of judgment. So likewise in Christ's case. He died. Next He will come in judgment, not immediately, but when He shall "appear the second time." To them that look for Him He shall then appear "unto salvation."

This is doubtless in harmony with the appearance of the high priest who, after finishing the work of expiation on the Day of Atonement, came forth. (Lev. 16:24.) When Christ comes the second time He comes to bring salvation to them that look for Him. To the others He comes in judgment—another parallel to the Day of Atonement when those who did not on that day afflict their souls were cut off. (Matt. 25:31 ff; Lev. 23:29.)

"Christ was once offered." This is by some considered a unique statement. We are told that Christ gave Himself, but here we are told that He was offered. Immediately we ask, By whom was He offered? Can Christ offer Himself and at the same time be offered?

We take this to be a statement parallel to that in which we are told that Christ gave Himself, and that God gave His Son. (Gal. 1:4; John 3:16.) The one is not inconsistent with the other. Isaac may willingly permit himself to be bound to the altar and thus offer himself, and it may as truly be said that Abraham offered Isaac. We find no contradiction in this.

Christ was offered "to bear the sins of many." This expression is taken from Isaiah 53:12, and presents Christ as vicariously bearing sin. Peter says that He bore "our sins in His own body on the tree," or as it might better be translated, "carried up our sins in His own body to the tree." 1 Peter 2:24. When Christ comes the second time, He will not bear sin. He will appear apart from sin, having made full atonement.

ADDITIONAL NOTES

The Sanctuary

(Condensed and Adapted From *The Sanctuary Service*)

It was not long after the giving of the law at Mount Sinai that the Lord told Moses to "speak unto the children of Israel, that they bring me an offering: of every man that giveth it willingly with his heart ye shall take my offering." Ex. 25:2. This offering was to consist of "gold, and silver, and brass, and blue, and purple, and scarlet, and fine linen, and goats' hair, and rams' skins dyed red, and badgers' skins, and shittim wood, oil for the light, spices for anointing oil, and for sweet incense, onyx stones, and stones to be set in the ephod, and in the breastplate." Verses 3–7. It was to be used mostly in the construction of the sanctuary and in the services generally. (Verse 8.)

The sanctuary here mentioned is usually called the tabernacle. It was really a tent with wooden walls, the roof consisting of four layers of material, the inner being of fine twined linen, the outer of "rams' skins dyed red, and a covering above of badgers' skins." Ex. 26:14. The building itself was not very large, about fifteen by forty-five feet, with an outer enclosure called the court, about seventy-five feet wide by one hundred and fifty feet long.

The tabernacle was so made that it could be taken apart and easily moved. At the time it was erected the Israelites were journeying through the wilderness. Wherever they went they took the tabernacle with them. The boards of the building were not nailed together as in an ordinary structure, but were separate, each set upright in a silver socket. (Ex. 36:20–34.) The curtains surrounding the court were suspended from pillars set in brazen sockets. The whole construction, though beautiful, and even gorgeous in design, showed its temporary nature. It was intended to serve only until such time as Israel should settle in the Promised Land and a more permanent building could be erected.

The building itself was divided into two apartments, the first and larger one called the holy, and the second apartment, the most holy. A rich curtain, or veil, divided these apartments. As there were no windows in the building, both apartments, especially the inner one, had they been dependent upon daylight, must have been dark. In the first apartment, however, the candles in the seven-branched candlestick gave sufficient light for the priests to perform the daily service which the ritual demanded.

There were three articles of furniture in the first apartment, namely, the table of shewbread, the seven-branched candlestick, and the altar of incense. Entering the apartment, from the front of the building, which faced the east, one would see near the end of the room the altar of incense. To the right would be the table of shewbread, and to the left the candlestick. On the table would be arranged in two piles the twelve cakes of the shewbread, together with the incense and the flagons for the drink offering. On it would also be the dishes, spoons, and bowls used in the daily service. (Ex. 37:16.)

The candlestick was made of pure gold. "His shaft, and his branch, his bowls, his knops, and his flowers, were of the same." Verse 17. It had six branches, three branches on each side of the center one. The bowls containing the oil were made after the fashion of almonds. (Verse 19.) Not only the candlestick was made of gold, but also the snuffers and the snuff dishes. (Verse 23.)

The most important article of furniture in this apartment was the altar of incense. It was about thirty-six inches in height and eighteen inches square. This altar was overlaid with pure gold, and around its top was a crown of gold. It was on this altar that the priest in the daily service placed the coals of fire taken from the altar of burnt offering, and the incense. As he put the incense on the coals on the altar, the smoke would ascend, and as the veil between the holy and the most holy did not extend to the top of the building, the incense soon filled not only the holy place but also the most holy. In this way the altar of incense, although located in the first apartment, served the second apartment also. For this reason it was put "before the vail that is by the ark of the testimony, before the mercy seat that is over the testimony, where I will meet with thee." Ex. 30:6.

In the second apartment, the most holy, there was only one piece of furniture, the ark. This ark was made in the form of a chest, about forty-five inches long and twenty-seven wide. The cover of this chest was called the mercy seat. Around the top of the mercy seat was a crown of gold, the same as on the altar of incense. In this chest Moses placed the Ten Commandments written on two tables of stone with God's own finger. For a time, at least, the ark also contained the golden pot that had the manna, and Aaron's rod that budded. (Heb. 9:4.)

On the mercy seat were two cherubim of gold, of beaten work, one cherub on one end and the other cherub on the other. (Ex. 25:19.) Of these cherubim it is said that they shall "stretch forth their wings on high, covering the mercy seat with their wings, and their faces shall look one to another; toward the mercy seat shall the faces of the cherubims be." Ex. 25:20.

Here God would commune with His people. To Moses He said, "There I will meet with thee, and I will commune with thee from above the mercy seat, from between the two cherubims which are upon the ark of the testimony, of all

313

things which I will give thee in commandment unto the children of Israel." Ex. 25:22.

Outside in the court, immediately in front of the door of the tabernacle, was a laver, a large basin containing water. This laver was made of brass from the mirrors which the women had contributed for this purpose At this laver the priests were to bathe their hands and feet before entering the tabernacle or beginning their service. (Ex. 30:17–21; 38:8.)

In the court was also the altar of burnt offering, which had a most important part to serve in all sacrificial offerings. This altar was about five feet high, and the top was eight feet square; it was hollow inside and overlaid with brass. (Ex. 27:1.) On this altar the animals were placed when offered as burnt sacrifice. Here also the fat was consumed and the required part of the meat offering placed. At the four corners of the altar were hornlike projections. In certain of the sacrificial offerings the blood was placed on these horns or sprinkled on the altar. At the base of the altar the rest of the blood not used in sprinkling was poured out.

When Solomon began to reign, the old tabernacle must have been in a dilapidated condition. It was several hundred years old and had been exposed to wind and weather for that long time. David had purposed to build the Lord a house, but had been told that because he was a man of blood he would not be permitted to do so. His son Solomon was to do the building. This temple "was built of stone made ready before it was brought thither: so that there was neither hammer nor axe nor any tool of iron heard in the house, while it was in building." 1 Kings 6:7.

Solomon's temple, as it came to be called, was a permanent structure, in every way more magnificent than the temporary tabernacle used during Israel's wilderness wanderings. It retained the old division of the building into two apartments, the holy and the most holy, and the principal furniture—the altar of incense in the first apartment and the ark in the second—was the same. Otherwise, doubtless because of the increased size of the building, certain other enlargements and embellishments were made. In the old tabernacle there were two cherubim. (Ex. 25:18–20.) In Solomon's temple two other cherubim made of "olive tree" covered with gold were placed in the most holy (1 Kings 6:23–28). These were placed on the floor, their wings reaching from wall to wall, while the original cherubim remained on the mercy seat on the ark.

In the first apartment of the temple some other changes were made. Instead of one candlestick there were now ten, five placed on one side and five on the other. These candlesticks were of pure gold, as were also the bowls, the snuffers, the basins, the spoons, and the censers. (1 Kings 7:49, 50.) Instead of one table containing the shewbread, there were ten, "five on the right side, and five on the left." 2 Chron. 4:8.

The altar of burnt offering, or the brazen altar, as it is called, was considerably enlarged in Solomon's temple. The old tabernacle altar was about seven and one-half feet square. Solomon's altar was considerably larger, about thirty feet square, and about fifteen feet high. The pots, shovels, fleshbooks, and basins used for the service of the altar were all of brass. (2 Chron. 4:11, 16.)

The original tabernacle had a laver for bathing purposes. In the temple a much larger one was placed in the court. It was a large basin of bronze, fifteen feet in diameter, seven and one-half feet high, having a capacity of nearly twenty thousand gallons of water, and was called the molten sea, doubtless because of its size. (1 Kings 7:23–26.) Beside this large sea there were ten smaller lavers placed upon wheels, each containing about four hundred gallons of water. (1 Kings 7:27–37.) These could be moved from place to place as they were needed.

Although such changes were made from the original pattern given Moses in the mount, the essential characteristics of two apartments—the altars of incense and burnt offering, and the ark in the most holy place—were retained. And as the pattern given Solomon by David, from which the temple was built, was "had by the Spirit," we may believe that Solomon's temple was merely an enlargement of the old sanctuary with such changes as were made necessary by its increased size.

Solomon's temple was destroyed in the invasions of Nebuchadnezzar in the sixth century before Christ. When it was rebuilt by Zerubbabel, the poverty of the people made impossible another temple to rival in splendor the one built by Solomon. So inferior was it that "many of the priests and Levites and chief of the fathers, who were ancient men, that had seen the first house, when the foundation of this house was laid before their eyes, wept with a loud voice; and many shouted aloud for joy: so that the people could not discern the noise of the shout of joy from the noise of the weeping of the people: for the people shouted with a loud shout, and the noise was heard afar off." Ezra 3:12, 13.

There was one important omission in this temple: there was no ark in the most holy place. During the troublous times of the captivity it had disappeared, and a stone served as a substitute for the ark.

Zerubbabel's temple served until the time of Christ, when it was rebuilt by Herod the Great, who became king in 37 B.C. About 20 B.C. he began building, tearing down the old structure little by little as he was ready to build the new. The services were thus never discontinued, and the one structure gradually replaced the other. John 2:20 states that the temple in the time of Christ had been forty and six years in building, and it was not until A.D. 66, just before the destruction of Jerusalem by the Romans, that Herod's temple was finished. This temple was patterned after Solomon's temple, and rivaled it in magnificence and glory. It retained—as had the other structures—the two apartments, the holy and the most holy; it had the altar of burnt offering, the laver, the candlesticks, the shewbread tables, and the altar of incense; but the most holy place had no ark.

THE DAILY SERVICES

The altar of burnt offering, which stood in the court outside the tabernacle, was always in use; that is, there was always a sacrifice on the altar. Each morning a lamb was offered for the nation, and this lamb, after being prepared by the priests, was placed on the altar, where it was slowly consumed by the fire. It was not permitted to burn quickly, for it was to last till evening, when another lamb was offered, which was to burn till the morning offering was ready.

Thus there was always a sacrifice on the altar, day and night, a symbol of the perpetual atonement provided in Christ. There was no time when Israel was not covered by a propitiatory sacrifice. At whatever time they sinned they knew that a lamb was on the altar and that forgiveness was theirs upon repentance. The *Jewish Encyclopedia*, volume 2, page 277, says, "The morning sacrifice atoned for the sins committed during the previous night, the afternoon sacrifice for the sins committed in the daytime."

This morning and evening oblation was offered every day of the year and was never to be omitted. Even though there might be special occasions that called for more elaborate sacrifices, the morning and evening burnt sacrifice for the nation was always offered. On the Sabbath day this offering was doubled: two lambs were offered in the morning and two in the evening. Even on the Day of Atonement this ritual was carried out. Sixteen times in chapters 28 and 29 of Numbers does God emphasize that no other offering is to take the place of the continual burnt offerings. Each time another sacrifice is mentioned, it is stated that this is besides the "continual burnt offering." From its perpetual nature it was called the continual, or daily, sacrifice.

The priests who officiated in the sanctuary were divided into twenty-four courses, or divisions, each of which served twice a year, one week at a time. The Levites were similarly divided, as were also the people. The lambs for the evening and morning sacrifices were provided by the people; and the section of the people which provided the lambs for any particular week would send its representatives to Jerusalem for that week to assist in the services, while the rest of the people conducted a special week of devotion.

The lamb offered in the daily service was a burnt offering. Though it was offered for the nation as a whole, it nevertheless served a definite purpose for the individual. When an Israelite had sinned he was to bring an appropriate offering to the temple and there confess his sin. It was not always possible, however, to do this. An offender might live a day's journey, or even a week's, distant from Jerusalem. It was impossible for him to come to the temple every time he sinned. For such cases the morning and evening sacrifice constituted a substitutionary and temporary atonement. It signified both consecration and acceptance by substitution. Of the *individual* burnt offering it is said, "It shall be accepted for him." Lev. 1:4. In like manner the national offering was accepted for the nation.

It hardly needs to be emphasized that the temporary provision made for sin in the daily sacrifice for the nation became efficacious only as the offender made personal confession of sin and brought his individual sacrifice for sin, just as a sinner is now saved by Christ's sacrifice on Calvary only if he personally accepts Christ. The death of the Lamb of God on Golgotha was for all men, but only those who accept the sacrifice and make personal application of it will be saved. In the light of these considerations the statement in 1 Timothy 4:10 becomes luminous: Christ "is the Saviour of all men, specially of those that believe." From day to day the lives of sinners have been spared; they have been saved temporarily and provisionally. But this extended grace will not avail them unless they repent and turn to God.

In the general provisional atonement provided by the morning and evening sacrifice, the blood of the lamb both registered the sins committed and provided a covering for them until the individual offender brought a sin offering, or until the Day of Atonement in the case of the unrepentant.

It is readily understood that some of the sins thus covered were never confessed. The record of such sins simply remained on the altar without being marked forgiven. These sins as well as others defile the tabernacle of the Lord. (Num. 19:13, 20.) The period of grace for impenitents and apostates expired on the Day of Atonement, when whoever did not afflict his soul was "cut off from among his people" (Lev. 23:29), that is, he was put outside the pale of the church—excommunicated. Since on that day the altar was cleansed "from the uncleanness of the children of Israel" (Lev. 16:19), the record of unconfessed sins was disposed of in the final ceremonies of that solemn occasion.

Spiritually viewed, the national burnt offering signified two things: first, Christ sacrificing Himself for man, providing atonement for all; second, the people dedicating themselves to God by putting all on the altar. It is to this latter that Paul referred when he admonished Christians, "Present your bodies a living sacrifice, holy, acceptable unto God, which is your reasonable service." Rom. 12:1.

GENERAL BURNT OFFERINGS

In contrast to the mandatory sin offerings, burnt offerings were voluntary, and sweet-savor offerings. Sin offerings were neither. Burnt offerings were *always* burned on the altar . Sin offerings were *never* burned on the altar, though the fat was. In burnt sacrifices the offerer could choose the kind of animal or bird he would use. In sin offerings God prescribed the kind of animal He wanted, and man had no choice. There were also other differences, chiefly in the ministration of the blood, which will later be discussed.

The burnt offerings were the most universal and characteristic of all offerings. They contained in themselves the essential qualities and elements of the other sacrifices. Although they were voluntary, dedicatory offerings, and as such not directly associated with sin, yet atonement was effected through them. (Lev. 1:4.) Job offered burnt offerings for his children, for "it may be that my sons have sinned, and cursed God in their hearts." Job 1:5. They are singled out as "ordained in Mount Sinai for a sweet savour, a sacrifice made by fire unto the Lord." Num. 28:6.

For a burnt offering, the offerer could bring any clean animal ordinarily used for sacrifice. It was required, however, that the animal be a male without blemish. The person was to offer "of his own voluntary will at the door of the tabernacle of the congregation before the Lord." Lev. 1:3. When he had selected the animal he brought it into the court for acceptance. The priest examined it to see whether it complied with the regulations for sacrifices. After it had been examined and accepted, the offerer would put his hand upon the head of the animal. He would then kill the animal, flay it, and cut it into pieces. (Verses 4–6.) As the animal was killed, the priest caught the blood, and sprinkled it round about upon the altar. (Verse 5, 11.) After the animal had been cut into pieces, the inwards and legs were washed in water, that all filth might be removed. After this the priest took the pieces and put them in their proper order upon the altar of burnt offering, there to be consumed by the fire. (Verse 9.) The sacrifice thus placed on the altar included all the parts of the animal—the head, the feet, the legs, and the body itself, but did not include the skin. This was given to the officiating priest. (Lev. 1:8; 7:8.)

In case turtledoves or young pigeons were used, the priest did the killing by wringing off the head, and sprinkling or wringing out the blood on the side of the altar. After this the body of the bird was placed on the altar and was there consumed as the ordinary burnt offering, the feathers and the crop being first removed. (Lev. 1:15, 16.)

Burnt offerings were used on many occasions, such as the cleansing of lepers (Lev. 14:19, 20), the cleansing of women after childbirth (Lev. 12:6–8), and also for ceremonial defilement (Lev. 15:15, 30). In these cases a sin offering was used as well as a burnt offering. The first atoned for sin: the second showed the offerer's attitude toward God in wholehearted consecration. The offerer thus placed himself symbolically on the altar, his life wholly devoted to God.

The burnt offering was prominent in the consecration of Aaron and his sons (Ex. 29:15–25; Lev. 8:18), as well as in their induction into the ministry (Lev. 9:12–14). It was also used in connection with the Nazarite vow. (Num. 6:14.) In all these instances it stood for complete consecration of the individual to God.

MEAL AND PEACE OFFERINGS

The name given to meal offerings in the Authorized Version is "meat offerings." However, as there was no flesh used in these offerings, and as they were chiefly vegetable offerings, it may be better to use the term "meal offerings" as being more correct. They consisted of such products as flour, corn (or grain), oil, wine, salt, and frankincense. When they were offered to the Lord, only a small part was placed upon the altar; the rest belonged to the priest. "It is a thing most holy of the offerings of Jehovah made by fire." Lev. 2:3, A.R.V. As the burnt offering signified consecration and dedication, so the meal offering signified submission and dependence. The burnt offerings stood for entire surrender of a life; the meal offerings were an acknowledgment of sovereignty and stewardship, of dependence upon a superior. They were an act of homage to God and a pledge of loyalty.

Meal offerings were generally used in connection with burnt and peace offerings. When the meal offering consisted of fine flour, it was mingled with oil, and frankincense was placed upon it. (Lev. 2:1.) A handful of this flour with oil and frankincense was burned as a memorial upon the altar of burnt offerings. It was "an offering made by fire, of a sweet savour unto the Lord." Lev. 2:2. Whatever was left after the handful had been placed upon the altar, belonged to Aaron and his sons. It was "a thing most holy of the offerings of the Lord." Verse 3.

When the offering consisted of unleavened cakes or wafers, it was to be made of fine flour mingled with oil, cut in pieces and oil poured on it. (Verses 4–6.) At times it was baked in a frying pan. (Verse 7.) When it was thus presented, the priest took a part and burned it upon the altar for a memorial. (Verses 8, 9.) What was left of the wafers belonged to the priests and was counted most holy. (Verse 10.)

It seems evident that the offering of flour and unleavened wafers anointed with oil was meant to teach Israel that God is the sustainer of all life, that they were dependent on Him for daily food, and that before partaking of the bounties of life they were to acknowledge Him as the giver of all. This acknowledgment of God as the provider of temporal blessings would naturally lead their minds to the source of all spiritual blessings. The New Testament reveals this source as the Bread sent down from heaven, which gives life to the world. (John 6:33.)

Peace offerings were offered as a kind of thank offering to God for His mercy, and on all occasions that called for joy and happiness. They were not occasions for *making* peace, but rather a celebration in view of the fact that peace had been established. Two might have been at variance. They became reconciled, and in their joy offered a peace offering to God. Or one had been saved from great danger and was thankful or wished to make a vow. All these occasions called for a peace offering.

In selecting a peace offering, the offerer was not limited in his choice. He could use a bullock, a sheep, a lamb, or a goat—male or female. In most offerings a sacrifice had to be "perfect to be accepted." Lev. 22:21. However, when a peace offering was presented as a free-will offering, it need not be perfect. It would be used even if it had "anything superfluous or lacking in his parts." Lev. 22:23. As in the case of the burnt offering, the offerer must lay his hand upon the head of the sacrifice and kill it at the door of the tabernacle. The blood was then sprinkled upon the altar round about by the priest. (Lev. 3:2.) After this the fat was burned: "It is the food of the offering made by fire unto the Lord." Verse 11. "All the fat is the Lord's. It shall be a perpetual statute for your generations throughout all your dwellings, that ye eat neither fat nor blood." Verses 16, 17.

Burnt offerings stood for dedication and consecration on the part of the offerer. Meal offerings recognized the offerer's dependence upon God for all temporal needs and his acceptance of the responsibility of stewardship. Peace offerings were a praise offering for mercies received, a thank offering for blessings enjoyed; a voluntary offering from an overflowing heart. They asked for no favors as such; they ascribed praise to God for what He had done, and magnified His name for His goodness and mercy to the children of men.

Burnt offerings were wholly burnt on the altar; sin offerings were either burned outside the camp or eaten by the priest; but peace offerings were divided not merely between God and the priest, but a part—the greater part—was given to the offerer and his family. God's part was burned on the altar. (Lev. 3:14–17.) The priest received the wave breast and the heave shoulder. (Lev. 7:33, 34.) The rest belonged to the offerer, who could invite any clean person to partake with him. It must be eaten the same day, or in some cases the second day, but not later. (Verses 16–21.)

SIN OFFERINGS

When an Israelite sinned "through ignorance against any of the commandments of the Lord his God concerning things which should not be done, and" was guilty, and when that "wherein he hath sinned, come to his knowledge," then he was to bring a sin offering according to specific directions given by God. (Lev. 4:22, 23.) The kind of offering to be brought varied with the standing and rank of the sinner. If a priest, he must bring "a young bullock without blemish." Verse 3. If a ruler, he was to bring "a kid of the goats, a male." Verse 23. If one of the common people, he must present a "kid of the goats, a female." Verse 28. For certain other sins he was to bring "a female from the flock, a lamb or a kid of the goats." Lev. 5:6. "If he be not able to bring a lamb, then he shall bring for his trespass, which he hath committed, two turtledoves, or two young pigeons." Verse 7. If he was not able to bring these, "then he that sinned shall bring for his offering the tenth part of an ephah of fine flour for a sin offering." Verse 11,

It is to be noted that these offerings were all for sins done through ignorance. (Lev. 4:2, 13, 22, 27.) A person might commit a sin and not know it. It may be "hid from him," as noted in chapter 5, verses 2, 3, 4, and also in chapter 4, verse 13. However, when he discovers his sin, "when he knoweth of it, then he shall be guilty." Lev. 5:3, 4. In such cases a man was required to bring an offering for his sin. But this could not be done where the sin was done knowingly or persistently. The law concerning conscious or presumptuous sins, sometimes called "sins done with a high hand," reads: "But the soul that doeth ought presumptuously, whether he be born in the land, or a stranger, the same reproacheth the Lord; and that soul shall be cut off from among his people. Because he hath despised the word of the Lord, and hath broken his commandment, that soul shall utterly be cut off; his iniquity shall be upon him." Num. 15:30, 31.

This point should be remembered. When Israel sinned deliberately in worshiping the golden calf, and defiantly refused God's call to repentance, "there fell of the people that day about three thousand men." Ex. 32:28. When a man was found gathering sticks on the Sabbath day in willful violation of God's command, he was not counseled to bring an offering for his sin. The command went forth, "The man shall be surely put to death." Num. 15:35. When two commit adultery, "then they shall both of them die." Deut. 22:22. If one curse his father or his mother, he "shall surely be put to death." Ex. 21:17 This rule holds good in all willful transgressions. It would cheapen man's conception of the holiness of God if he were permitted to bring an ox or a lamb for a deliberate transgression of the law.

This, however, does not mean that a man could not have such sins forgiven. Sins, however dark, could be and were forgiven, as they are now, by repentance and restitution. A man could be forgiven for adultery—as was David—but not by making an offering. David fully understood that a lamb or a he-goat, or a thousand of them, could never pay for his transgression. He truly said, "Thou desirest not sacrifice; else would I give it: thou delightest not in burnt offering. The sacrifices of God are a broken spirit: a broken and a contrite heart, O God, thou wilt not despise." Ps. 51:16, 17.

This is in full harmony with the prophetic message throughout the Bible. "Wherewith shall I come before the Lord, and bow myself before the high God? shall I come before him with burnt offerings, with calves of a year old? will the Lord be pleased with thousands of rams, or with ten thousands of rivers of oil? shall I give my first-born for my transgression, the fruit of my body for the sin of my soul? He hath shewed thee, O man, what is good; and what doth the Lord require of thee, but to do justly, and to love mercy, and to walk humbly with thy God?" Micah 6:6–8. (Isa. 1:11; 1 Sam. 15:21, 22.)

When a man in Old Testament times had sinned ignorantly, doing "somewhat against any of the commandments of the Lord concerning things which ought not to be done, and be guilty" (Lev, 4:27), he was to bring a sacrifice, the precise kind depending upon his rank in the nation and also his financial ability. But whatever the animal he brought, the preliminary steps were the same for all.

First of all, "it shall be, when he shall be guilty in one of these things, that he shall confess that he hath sinned in that thing." Lev. 5:5. This is an important step. Confession and acknowledgment of sin is a first requisite for forgiveness. This is not a general confession. He is to "confess that he hath sinned in that thing." It is "that thing" that counts. A general confession will not suffice.

Having acknowledged his sin, he is to "lay his hand upon the head of the sin offering, and slay the sin offering." Lev. 4:29.

There has been much discussion among theologians as to the significance of placing the hand upon the sin offering. Those who do not believe in vicarious suffering, who do not believe it possible for one to suffer for another, stoutly deny that there is any specific significance in this laying on of the hand beyond that of a certain fellowship or identification of one with the other. Another group—and we are among them—see in this laying on of the hand a most vital step in God's plan of atonement: the transfer of sin from the sinner to the blameless victim. In this view the laying on of the hand has deep significance; but in the other it loses all meaning.

This brings us directly to a consideration of the possibility of transfer of sin. So vital is this that it may be said that if there is no transfer of sin possible, then Christ cannot and does not bear our sin. On the other hand, if such transfer is possible, the placing of the sinner's hand on the innocent sacrifice is a most fitting illustration of this.

It seems superfluous to attempt to prove that the Bible teaches vicarious sin bearing. Though critics may deny the essential Messianic nature of the fifty-third chapter of Isaiah, the simple Christian has no doubt of it. When he reads of one who "hath borne our griefs, and carried our sorrows," who was "wounded for our transgressions" and "bruised for our iniquities," he refuses to apply it to anyone but Christ. To avoid the issue by saying that it refers to some unknown personage or to Israel personified or to offer any one of a number of other suggestions, seems too much like trying to construct a theory to avoid the possibility of vicarious suffering and death. In the light of the clear statement of John 1:29, "Behold the Lamb of God, which taketh away [margin, 'beareth'] the sin of the world," we feel justified in applying Isaiah's statements to Christ, upon whom is laid "the iniquity of us all." Isa. 53:6. Of none but Christ can it be said, "He shall bear their iniquities." Verse 11. Only He can make "intercession for the transgressors," because "he bare the sin of many," and "for the transgression of my people was the stroke upon him." Verses 12, 8, margin.

These texts fairly represent the Biblical teaching of Christ's substitutionary work for us. He took our sins upon Him and bore the penalty. By His stripes we are healed, He "bare our sins in his own body on the tree." 1 Peter 2:24. "The wages of sin is death." Rom. 6:23. "The soul that sinneth, it shall die." Eze. 18:4. Only on the theory that Christ took our sins upon Himself and became responsible for our misdeeds, can His death be understood. And this is the very thing the Bible affirms.

Under these conditions why should it be thought a strange thing if in the typical teaching of the atonement this fact should be revealed? That sin can be transferred is plainly affirmed in Leviticus 16. Note this statement: "And Aaron shall lay both his hands upon the head of the live goat, and confess over him all the iniquities of the children of Israel, and all their transgressions in all their sins, *putting them upon the head of the goat,* and shall send him away by the hand of a fit man into the wilderness." Verse 21.

Here Aaron is said to confess "all the iniquities of the children of Israel, and all their transgressions in all their sins, putting them upon the head of the goat." This supposes a double transfer of sin; first, Aaron bears all the sins of Israel. This means that in some way they have been transferred to him from Israel. Second, Aaron places these sins on the scapegoat, which is then said to "bear upon him all their iniquities unto a land not inhabited." Verse 22. It is clear that here is a definite transfer of sins recorded. Aaron places the sins upon the goat, and the goat bears the sins. The transfer is from the people, to Aaron, to the goat.

A transfer is similarly effected in the case of the sin offering. The man has sinned. He confesses his sins, places his hand on the head of the animal, then kills it. The animal carries the sin, and sin means death. So the animal is killed, and the man is free.

This is effectively taught in the ceremonies connected with the cleansing of leprosy—a significant symbol of sin. "This shall be the law of the leper in the day of his cleansing: he shall be brought unto the priest: and the priest shall go forth out of the camp; and the priest shall look, and, behold, if the plague of leprosy be healed in the leper, then shall the priest command to take for him that is to be cleansed two birds alive and clean, and cedarwood, and scarlet, and hyssop; and the priest shall command that one of the birds be killed in an earthen vessel over running water: as for the living bird, he shall take it, and the cedar wood, and the scarlet, and the hyssop, and shall dip them and the living bird in the blood of the bird that was killed over the running water: and he shall sprinkle upon him that is to be cleansed from the leprosy seven times, and shall pronounce him clean, and shall let the living bird loose into the open field." Lev. 14:2–7.

Two birds are taken, and one is killed. Then the living bird is dipped in the blood of the killed bird, after which it is let "loose into the open field." One dies, and the other is let go, free. Who can fail to see the beautiful symbolism in this?

In case the anointed priest or the whole congregation sinned, a young bullock without blemish was presented as an offering. After the bullock had been killed, the priest was to "dip his finger in the blood, and sprinkle of the blood seven times before the Lord, before the vail of the sanctuary." Lev. 4:6, 17. The priest was also to put "some of the blood upon the horns of the altar of sweet incense before the Lord, which is in the tabernacle of the congregation; and shall pour all the blood of the bullock at the bottom of the altar of the burnt offering, which is at the door of the tabernacle of the congregation." Verse 7.

When a ruler or one of the common people sinned, the blood was not carried into the sanctuary, as in the case where a priest or the whole congregation sinned, nor was it sprinkled before the veil or put on the horns of the altar of incense. It was not carried into the sanctuary at all. In such cases "the priest shall take of the blood of the sin offering with his finger, and put it upon the horns of the altar of burnt offering, and shall pour out his blood at the bottom of the altar of burnt offering." Verse 25. (See also verses 30, 34.)

The question might now justly be raised: If it is true that sins were transferred to the sanctuary by means of blood, how could that be accomplished when in these cases the blood was not carried into the sanctuary at all?

To this the answer might be given that in such cases the blood was placed on the horns of the altar of burnt offering, and that this altar was a part, and a vital part, of the sanctuary. But there is also an additional answer.

In cases where the blood was not carried into the sanctuary, not sprinkled before the veil, and not put on the horns of the altar of incense, the law provided that the priest should eat a part of the flesh of the sin offering. "The law of the sin offering," recorded in the sixth chapter of Leviticus, provides: "Speak unto Aaron and to his sons, saying, This is the law of the sin offering: In the place where the burnt offering is killed shall the sin offering be killed before the Lord: it is most holy. The priest that offereth it for sin shall eat it: in the holy place shall it be eaten, in the court of the tabernacle of the congregation." Lev. 6:25, 26.

This statement is illuminating. The priest that offered the sin offering was to eat it, though he was to share it with the other priests. "All the males among the priests shall eat thereof: it is most holy." Verse 29. There is an exception, however, noted in verse 30: "No sin offering, whereof any of the blood is brought into the tabernacle of the congregation to reconcile withal in the holy place, shall be eaten: it shall be burnt in the fire." This verse simply means that when the blood was carried into the sanctuary, as when the anointed priest or the whole congregation sinned, the flesh was not to be eaten. Only in the cases where a ruler or one of the common people sinned and the blood was not carried into the sanctuary, was the flesh to be eaten. Why was this?

An interesting, informative incident occurred early in the history of the sanctuary. "Moses diligently sought the goat of the sin offering, and, behold, it was burnt: and he was angry with Eleazar and Ithamar, the sons of Aaron which were left alive, saying, Wherefore have ye not eaten the sin offering in the holy place, seeing it is most holy, and God hath given it you to bear the iniquity of the congregation, to make atonement for them before the Lord? Behold, the blood of it was not brought in within the holy place: ye should indeed have eaten it in the holy place, as I commanded." Lev. 10:16–18.

Moses was angry because Eleazar and Ithamar, the priests, had burned the sin offering, and he demanded to know why they had "not eaten the sin offering in the holy place." The reason Moses gave was that "the blood of it was not brought in within the holy place," and seeing this was not done, he said, "Ye should indeed have eaten it in the holy place, as I commanded." A further and most important reason was given: "God hath given it you *to bear the iniquity of the congregation.*" That is, in eating of the flesh they took upon themselves the iniquity of the people and bore their sins, that they might "make atonement for them before the Lord."

These verses make a vital contribution to our knowledge of the atonement as revealed to Israel of old. This plan included the making of an atonement for the people by the priest, who, in order to do so, had to eat of the flesh of the sin offering, thus taking upon himself, or into himself, sinful flesh—carrying sin. As the priests ate of the flesh they would "bear the iniquity of the congregation," and symbolically being representatives of Christ, they could "make atonement for them before the Lord."

It is interesting in the particular case before us to note that Aaron, defending his sons, says, "Behold, this day have they offered their sin offering and their burnt offering before the Lord; and such things have befallen me: and if I had eaten the sin offering to day, should it have been accepted in the sight of the Lord?" Verse 19.

Two of Aaron's other sons had been killed that day as they. ministered before the Lord. (Lev. 10:1, 2) From the context it is clear that they were intoxicated and offered strange fire, for which reason the warning concerning strong drink is given in verses 8–11. Aaron, as might be expected, was greatly upset because of this, and neither he nor his two remaining sons were entirely reconciled to what had taken place. When the sons were rebuked by Moses for not eating the flesh of the sin offering, Aaron came to their rescue by reminding Moses of what had happened, saying in effect that under these conditions they did not feel they could carry the people's sins. It was enough for them to carry their own. "And when Moses heard that, he was content." Verse 20.

We now review this situation. When the priest or the whole congregation sinned, the blood was taken directly into the sanctuary. When a ruler or a common man sinned, the priest put some of the blood on the horns of the altar of burnt offering outside in the court but did not carry the blood into the sanctuary. Instead he ate some of the flesh of the sin offering. Jewish tradition says that he had to eat a piece at least the size of an olive. By eating this flesh he took sin upon himself. However, when the blood was carried into the sanctuary in the two cases first mentioned, the flesh must not be eaten. It was burned without the camp, according to the rule laid down in Leviticus 6:30: "No sin offering, whereof any of the blood is brought into the tabernacle of the congregation to reconcile withal in the holy place, shall be eaten: it shall be burnt in the fire." The writer of Hebrews acknowledges this same rule when he says, "The bodies of those beasts, whose blood is brought into the sanctuary by the high priest for sin, are burned without the camp." Heb. 13:11.

It seems clear that when the priests took the sins of the congregation upon themselves by eating the flesh of the sin offering, they could do so only because previously the sins had been placed upon the animal by confession and the laying on of the hand. The goat had not sinned; yet it bore "the iniquity of the congregation," and when the priests ate the flesh, *they* bore the iniquity, and God had arranged that they should take it upon them by the eating of the flesh. This is the meaning of the statement which says that "God hath given it you to bear the iniquity." Lev. 10:17.

As Christ came in the likeness of sinful flesh, so the priests ate the sin-laden flesh of the goat upon which the sinner had confessed his sins and placed his hand. Thus the sin was transferred from the sinner to the priest. The man was free; he was forgiven; but the sin now rested upon the priest, or perhaps more correctly, the priesthood. Thus all confessed sins were in figure transferred to the priesthood, who in the person of the high priest dealt directly with God.

When the officiating priest took sin upon himself by eating the flesh of the sin offering, he became a sinner. He might officiate for ten people or a hundred during his week of service at the tabernacle. He would thus carry the sins of that many people, but they were now *his* sins, not theirs. The people had been forgiven and gone away happy. What had in reality been accomplished was the transfer of the sin to the priest. A *record* of the confessed sin had been placed upon the horns of the altar of burnt offering. Jeremiah puts it: "The sin of Judah is written with a pen of iron, and with the point of a diamond: it is graven upon the table of their heart, and upon the horns of your altars." Jer. 17:1. But the sin itself was borne by the priest, and he was now a sinner.

Not being able to atone for his own sin, he must now bring an offering for all the sins he bears. This he does; he places all the sins he has taken upon himself upon the innocent beast, and as the blood was carried *into* the sanctuary when a priest sinned, so now the blood is brought into the holy place and there put upon the horns of the altar of incense and sprinkled before the veil, behind which is the transgressed law.

Thus, in figure, the sins were brought into the sanctuary in the blood sprinkled and put on the horns of the altar in the holy place—some sins, those of the priests and the whole congregation, directly; those of the rulers and the common people, indirectly by the priest's eating the flesh of the sin offering and then bringing a sin offering for the sins he carried, the blood of which also was brought in before the veil. Thus all sins, whether of priest or people, eventually found their way into the sanctuary.

It is ever to be borne in mind that the service which the priests performed they did as assistants and deputies of the high priest, as it was impossible for him to attend to all the work himself. In the beginning Aaron performed all the work of the sanctuary. He offered the daily sacrifice; he trimmed the lamps; he arranged the shewbread; he sprinkled the blood. As the work grew, definite tasks were assigned others, but the priests merely substituted for the high priest. It was reckoned as if the high priest did it. Of this *The International Standard Bible Encyclopedia*, volume 4, page 2439, says:

"The high priest was to act for men in things pertaining to God, 'to make propitiation for the sins of the people' (Heb. 2:17). He was the mediator who ministered for the guilty. 'The high priest represented the whole people. All Israelites were reckoned as being in him. The prerogative held by him belonged to the whole of them (Ex. 19:6)...' (Vitringa). That the high priest did represent the whole congregation appears, first, from his bearing the tribal names on his shoulders in the onyx stones, and, second, in the tribal names engraved in the twelve gems of the breastplate. The divine explanation of this double representation of Israel in the dress of the high priest is, he 'shall bear their names before Jeh [Jehovah] upon his two shoulders for a memorial' (Ex. 28:12, 29). Moreover, his committing heinous sin involved the people in his guilt: 'If the anointed priest shall sin so as to bring guilt on the people' (Lev. 4:3). The LXX reads, 'If the anointed priest shall sin so as to make the people sin.' The anointed priest, of course, is the high priest. When he sinned, the people sinned. His official action was reckoned as their action. The whole nation shared in the trespass of their representative. The converse appears to be just as true. What he did in his official capacity, as prescribed by the Lord, was reckoned as done by the whole congregation: 'Every high priest...is appointed for men' (Heb. 5:1)."

Note these statements: "The high priest represented the whole people. All Israelites were reckoned as being in him....When he sinned, the people sinned. His official action was reckoned as their action. The whole nation shared in the trespass of their representative. The converse appears to be just as true."

The high priest in his official capacity was not simply a man. He was an institution; he was a symbol. Not only did he represent Israel, but he was the embodiment of Israel. He bore the names of Israel in the two onyx stones "upon his two shoulders for a memorial." Ex. 28:12. In the twelve precious stones in the breastplate he bore "the judgment of the children of Israel upon his heart before the Lord continually." Ex. 28:30. He thus carried Israel on his shoulders and on his heart. On his shoulders he carried the burden of Israel; in the breastplate, signifying the seat of affection and love, he carried Israel on his heart. In the golden crown upon the miter, inscribed with "Holiness to the Lord," he bore the "iniquity of the holy things, which the children of Israel shall hallow in all their holy gifts," and this that "they may be accepted before the Lord." Verses 36–38.

Adam was the representative man. When he sinned, the world sinned, and death passed upon all men. (Rom. 5:12.) "By one man's offence death reigned; …by one man's disobedience many were made sinners." Verses 17–19.

So likewise, Christ, being the second man and the last Adam, was the representative man. "It is written, The first man Adam was made a living soul; the last Adam was made a quickening spirit…. The first man is of the earth, earthy: the second man is the Lord from heaven." 1 Cor. 15:45–47. "As by the offence of one judgment came upon all men to condemnation; even so by the righteousness of one the free gift came upon all men unto justification of life." Rom. 5:18. "For as by one man's disobedience many were made sinners, so by the obedience of one shall many be made righteous." Verse 19. "For as in Adam all die, even so in Christ shall all be made alive." 1 Cor. 15:22.

The high priest, being in a special sense a figure of Christ, was also the representative man. He stood for all Israel. He carried their burdens and sins. He bore the iniquity of all the holy things. He bore their judgment. When he sinned, Israel sinned. When he made atonement for himself, Israel was accepted.

We call particular attention to the statement previously quoted in regard to the golden plate which the high priest wore on his miter. The record of this is found in Exodus 28:36–39 and reads thus: "Thou shalt make a plate of pure gold, and grave upon it, like the engravings of a signet, HOLINESS TO THE LORD. And thou shalt put it on a blue lace, that it may be upon the miter; upon the forefront of the miter it shall be. And it shall be upon Aaron's forehead, that Aaron may bear the iniquity of the holy things, which the children of Israel shall hallow in all their holy gifts; and it shall be always upon his forehead, that they may be accepted before the Lord."

"Holiness to the Lord," was inscribed on the golden plate, but in sharp contrast to this is the statement that he was to wear it, "*that Aaron may bear the iniquity* of the holy things,"…"that they Israel *may be accepted* before, the Lord." Aaron, as a representative of God, is considered holy, and holiness is inscribed on the plate. But he wears it, *that he may bear the iniquity of the holy things* and make atonement. Note the statement, "the iniquity *of the holy things.*" Inanimate things, of course, are incapable of moral action; a dead thing is not evil, nor can it commit sin. Yet the statement is made that the high priest bore the iniquity of the holy *things.* The holy things of the sanctuary were defiled, but this was "because of the uncleanness of the children of Israel, and because of their transgressions in all their sins." Lev. 16:16.

As blood was sprinkled or put on the horns of the altar, as it was sprinkled toward the veil, as it was carried into the most holy in a vessel and there sprinkled, these apartments and these things became defiled and needed cleansing. This was done on the Day of Atonement. But the significant thing about the statement before us is this: though the holy *things* were defiled by sins and transgressions of Israel, it was the high priest who bore *the iniquity* of these things. The horns of the altar bore the record of sins committed; the high priest bore the sins themselves. Note again that when a man had sinned, the priest dipped his finger in the blood and made a mark on the horns of the altar. (Lev. 4:25, 30, 34.)

As we now make a fingerprint, so the priest put his bloody finger on the horns, and this fingerprint constituted a record of sins committed and was also evidence that an offering had been brought for this sin. Read again Jeremiah 17:1: "The sin of Judah is written with a pen of iron, and with the point of a diamond: it is graven upon the table of their heart, and upon the horns of your altars."

As it is of course impossible for a *thing*, as such, to bear sin, we may confidently state that the defilement of the holy things of the sanctuary came about "because of the uncleanness of the children of Israel, and because of their transgressions in all their sins," symbolized by the sprinkling of the blood in the daily service. As the blood of the sin-laden animals was sprinkled from day to day in the sanctuary, the holy places were defiled and in time would need cleansing. But it should be had in mind that sin exists only as it is connected with personality, and that though the record of sin was written in blood in the sanctuary, in reality sin could be borne only by a person. It is with this in mind that the statement is made that the high priest was always to wear the golden plate in his forehead, that he "may bear the iniquity of the holy things," that the people "may be accepted before the Lord." Ex. 28:38.

Only he who is holy can bear sins for others. The high priest, wearing the inscription "Holiness to the Lord" on his forehead, was as perfect a symbol of Christ as humanity can present. And as such he bore the sins of the people. At the same time he also represented Israel. He thus represented Christ in His incarnate state.

We do not deny—we affirm—that sins were transferred by means of blood to the sanctuary, though it might be better to say that the *record* of sins was thus transferred, if by this statement it be understood that even the record of sin must be blotted out in order to do away effectively and finally with sin. This is in harmony with the statement found in *Patriarchs and Prophets*, page 358: "Thus the sanctuary will be freed, or cleansed, from the record of sin."

Though we hold that blood defiled the sanctuary, we do not hold that this was the only way it was defiled. Sin defiles, and any sin, wherever committed, whether the person presented his offering or not, defiled the holy places. This is distinctly stated in the nineteenth chapter of Numbers: "The man that shall be unclean, and shall not purify himself, that soul shall be cut off from among the congregation, because he hath defiled the sanctuary of the Lord: the water of separation hath not been sprinkled upon him; he is unclean." Verse 20. Here is a man who is unclean, and does not purify himself; he does not bring an offering for his sin; he makes no effort of cleansing. For this reason he is to be cut off—"*because he hath defiled the sanctuary.*" He did not come near the sanctuary; yet he defiled it. That is, sin in itself defiles, whether the man brings an offering or not. (See also verse 13.) This principle has a vital bearing on the disposition of sins committed but unrepented of.

These statements make it clear that it was the sins of Israel that defiled the sanctuary and the altar. This defilement took place throughout the year in the daily ministration. Each morning and evening a lamb was slain and its blood sprinkled upon the altar "round about." This defiled the altar. Offenders brought their sin and trespass offerings. In the case of a priest or the whole congregation, the victim's blood was sprinkled in the holy place. This defiled the sanctuary. In the case of a ruler or one of the common people, the blood was put upon the horns of the altar of burnt offering and the flesh eaten by the priests. This transferred the sins to the priesthood and also defiled the altar. Through these means the sanctuary and the altar were defiled and the priesthood was made to bear sins. The services of the Day of Atonement were to dispose of all these sins and to cleanse both sanctuary and priesthood as well as people.

THE DAY OF ATONEMENT

The daily sprinkling of the blood in the sanctuary made a periodic cleansing necessary. This would be true in a purely physical sense, but with this we shall not deal. We are particularly interested in the sprinkling of the blood as a symbolic act, transferring sin and its record to the holy places. This transfer we have already discussed, and we shall now consider the yearly cleansing, which is recorded specifically in the sixteenth chapter of Leviticus.

In the thirty-third verse we are informed that atonement should be made for the holy sanctuary, the tabernacle of the congregation, and the altar, and also for the priests, and for the people.

This divides the atonement into two parts: atonement for the sanctuary, that is, for the holy things; and atonement for persons, that is, for priests and people. The purpose of the atonement for the people is said to be "to cleanse you, that ye may be clean from all your sins before the Lord." Verse 30. As for the sanctuary, the statement is made, "He shall make an atonement for the holy place, because of the uncleanness of the children of Israel, and because of their transgressions in all their sins: and so shall he do for the tabernacle of the congregation, that remaineth among them in the midst of their uncleanness." Verse 16. Concerning the altar it is stated, "He shall sprinkle of the blood upon it with his finger seven times, and cleanse it, and hallow it from the uncleanness of the children of Israel." Verse 19.

It will be noted that the holy places were cleansed not because of any inherent sin or evil in the sanctuary as such, but "because of the uncleanness of the children of Israel, and because of their transgressions in all their sins." The same is true of the altar. The priest is to "cleanse it, and hallow it from the uncleanness of the children of Israel." Verse 19.

The question may well be raised, Why was any cleansing needed by the people? Had they not brought their sacrifices from time to time throughout the year, confessed their sins, and gone away forgiven? Why would they need to be forgiven twice? Why should "a remembrance" be "made of sins every year"? Should not "the worshippers once purged" "have had no more conscience of sins"? Heb. 10:3, 2. These questions demand an answer.

It may be pertinent to remark that salvation is always conditioned upon repentance and perseverance. God forgives, but the forgiveness is not unconditional and independent of the sinner's future course. Note how Ezekiel puts it: "When the righteous turneth away from his righteousness, and committeth iniquity, and doeth according to all the abominations that the wicked man doeth, shall he live? All his righteousness that he hath done shall not be mentioned: in his trespass that he hath trespassed, and in his sin that he hath sinned, in them shall he die." Eze. 18:24.

This text states that when a man turns away from the right, all his good deeds "shall not be mentioned." The converse is also true. If a man has been wicked, but turns from his evil way, "all his transgressions that he hath committed, they shall not be mentioned unto him: in his righteousness that he hath done he shall live." Verse 22.

God keeps an account with each man. Whenever a prayer for forgiveness ascends to God from a true heart, God forgives. But sometimes men change their minds. They repudiate their repentance. They show by their lives that their repentance is not permanent. And so God, instead of forgiving absolutely and finally, marks forgiveness against men's names and waits with the final blotting out of sins until they have had time to think the matter through. If at the end of their lives they are still of the same mind, God counts them faithful, and in the day of judgment their record is finally cleared.

So with Israel of old. When the Day of Atonement rolled round, each offender had a chance to show that he was still of the same mind and wanted forgiveness. If he was, the sin was blotted out, and he was completely cleansed.

Day by day during the year the transgressors had appeared at the temple and received forgiveness. On the Day of Atonement these sins came in review before God, or, as Hebrews puts it, there was "a remembrance again made of sins." Heb. 10:3. On that day every true Israelite renewed his consecration to God and confirmed his repentance. As a result, he was not only forgiven but cleansed. "On that day shall the priest make an atonement for you, to cleanse you, that ye may be clean from all your sins before the Lord." Lev. 16:30.

It must have been with happiness in their hearts that Israel went home in the evening of that day "clean from all your sins." Wonderful assurance! The same promise is given in the New Testament: "If we confess our sins, he is faithful and just to forgive us our sins, and to cleanse us from all unrighteousness." 1 John 1:9. Not only forgiven, but cleansed! Cleansed from "all unrighteousness," from "all your sins"!

> "Oh, the bliss of the glorious thought—
> My sin, not in part but the whole."

On the Day of Atonement the high priest officiated first in the daily morning sacrifice, which was conducted on this day as on other days. (Num. 29:11.) After this service was over, the special services began. The record in the sixteenth chapter of Leviticus yields the following information:

The high priest was first to bathe and put on the holy white garments. Throughout the year he had been wearing the high priestly insignia, the beautiful robe and ephod with the precious stones and breastplate. On this day, however, before going into the most holy, he put off these garments and put on the white garments of the priest, the difference between his attire and that of the priest being that the girdle was white, and that he wore the linen miter of the high priest instead of the bonnet of the priest. (Lev. 16:4; Ex. 28:39, 40; 39:28.)

As he began the service, the high priest received from the congregation two goats and a ram, which, together with his own sin offering, a bullock, were presented before the Lord. He killed the bullock, which was for himself, and a priest caught some of the blood in a bowl, stirring it so that it would not coagulate, while the high priest performed another part of the service.

After the bullock was killed, the high priest took coals from the altar of burnt offering and put them in a censer. He also took his hands full of sweet incense, and, carrying both the coals and the incense, he went into the tabernacle and entered the most holy. There he placed the censer on the mercy seat, "that the cloud of the incense may cover the mercy seat that is upon the testimony, that he die not." Lev. 16:13.

Having finished this part of the ceremony, he went outside and received from the priest the blood of the bullock, which he carried into the most holy. There he sprinkled the blood with his finger upon the mercy seat eastward. "And before the mercy seat shall he sprinkle of the blood with his finger seven times." Verse 14. By this act he made "atonement for himself, and for his house." Verse 6.

Before the bullock was killed, another ceremony had taken place. Lots had been cast upon the two goats, one lot for the Lord and the other for the scapegoat. (Verse 8.) The goat upon which the lot fell for the Lord was to be offered as a sin offering. (Verse 9.) The other, the scapegoat, was to be presented alive before the Lord, "to make an atonement with him, and to let him go for a scapegoat into the wilderness." Verse 10.

After the high priest came out from the most holy, having performed the ritual with the blood of the bullock, he killed the goat of the sin offering that was for the people. He again entered the most holy and sprinkled the blood of the goat as he had sprinkled the blood of the bullock upon the mercy seat and before the mercy seat. (Verse 15.) This made atonement for the most holy, "because of the uncleanness of the children of Israel, and because of their transgressions in all their sins." Verse 16. He then did the same thing for the tabernacle of the congregation, that is, the holy place. Having made atonement for the sanctuary, he went out to the altar and made atonement for it, putting upon the horns of the altar both of the blood of the bullock and of the blood of the goat. He sprinkled it with his finger seven times, to "cleanse it, and hallow it from the uncleanness of the children of Israel." Verse 19.

Having thus "made an end of reconciling the holy place, and the tabernacle of the congregation, and the altar, he shall bring the live goat: and Aaron shall lay both his hands upon the head of the live goat, and confess over him all the iniquities of the children of Israel, and all their transgressions in all their sins, putting them upon the head of the goat, and shall send him away by the hand of a fit man into the wilderness: and the goat shall bear upon him all their iniquities unto a land not inhabited: and he shall let go the goat in the wilderness." Lev. 16:20–22.

This part of the service being finished, Aaron put off the linen garments, washed himself in water, and put on his regular high priestly garments. (Verses 23, 24.) He then came out and offered a burnt offering for himself and one for the people. (Verse 24.) The fat of the sin offering was then burned on the altar. The man who led the scapegoat into the wilderness was to bathe himself and wash his clothes before he could come back into the camp. The man who disposed of the bullock whose blood was brought into the sanctuary and whose body was burned without the camp, had also to wash his clothes and bathe himself in water before he could return. (Verses 26–28.) The special offering mentioned in Numbers 29:7–11, consisting of a bullock, a ram, and seven lambs for a burnt offering, and "one kid of the goats for a sin offering; beside the sin offering of atonement," was then offered before the regular evening sacrifice.

Of the work done on that day the record states, "On that day shall the priest make an atonement for you, to cleanse you, that ye may be clean from all your sins before the Lord." Lev. 16:30. A summary is given in verse 33: "He shall make an atonement for the holy sanctuary, and he shall make an atonement for the tabernacle of the congregation, and for the altar, and he shall make an atonement for the priests, and for all the people of the congregation."

It now becomes our duty to inquire just how the atonement was brought about and how the symbolism answers to the reality. How could the sanctuary be cleansed with blood when by that very means it was defiled? Would not more blood defile the sanctuary still further rather than cleanse it?

We call attention to the statement found in Numbers 35:33: "So ye shall not pollute the land wherein ye are: for blood it defileth the land: and the land cannot be cleansed of the blood that is shed therein, but by the blood of him that shed it."

This text embodies a principle which by analogy is applicable to the cleansing of the sanctuary. "Blood it defileth the land." This is clear. "The land cannot be cleansed...but by the blood of him that shed it." According to this, blood defiles and blood cleanses. This is the situation in the sanctuary.

It is to be had in mind that no type is an exact counterpart of that which it is intended to portray. The real work of the atonement in heaven involves so many factors that it is not possible to find an exact earthly parallel. Christ lived, died, and rose again. How can a fitting type be found to illustrate this? A lamb may represent Christ and be slain as He was. But how can the resurrection be shown? Another live animal may be used, but the type is not perfect.

The high priest typified Christ. But Christ was sinless, and the high priest was not. Any offering which the high priest offered because of his own sins, could therefore not be true to type. For these reasons many ceremonies were necessary to illustrate the complete work of Christ; and yet they failed to illustrate fully. The priest typified certain aspects of Christ's ministry. So did the high priest, the veil, the shewbread, the incense, the lamb, the goat, the meal offering, and many other items in the sanctuary service.

The holy apartment had its signification; so had the most holy, the court, the altar, the laver, the mercy seat. Almost everything was symbolical, from the priests' dress to the ashes used in sprinkling the unclean. Yet all of it put together did not constitute a complete type, and much of it did but imperfectly mirror its original.

We have noted before that Aaron not only represented the people but was practically identified with them. What he did they did. What they did he did. Let us stress this again.

The high priest "represented the whole people. All Israelites were reckoned as being in him." In him "everything belonging to the priesthood gathered itself up and reached its culmination." "When he sinned, the people sinned."

Adam was the representative man. By him "sin entered into the world." By his "disobedience many were made sinners." And so "by one man's offence death reigned by one," and "through the offence of one many be dead." Rom. 5:12, 19, 17, 15.

Christ also was the representative man. He was the second man and the last Adam. "The first man is of the earth, earthy: the second man is the Lord from heaven." 1 Cor. 15:47. This second man, "the Lord from heaven," undid all that the first man had done by his transgression. By the disobedience of the first man "many were made sinners." By the obedience of the second man "shall many be made righteous." Rom. 5:19. By the offence of the first man, "judgment came upon all men to condemnation." By the righteousness of the second man, "the free gift came upon all men unto justification of life." Verse 18. And so, "as in Adam all die, even so in Christ shall all be made alive." 1 Cor. 15:22.

The high priest was a type of Christ and a representative of the nation. As a representative of the nation he was identified with their sins and was worthy of death. As a type of Christ he was their mediator and savior. In either case he transacted with God for the people. In this sense he *was* the people. If God rejected him He rejected the people in him. For this reason the people were anxious to hear the sound of the bells on the Day of Atonement. When at last the atonement had been effected and the reconciliation was complete, the sound of the bells as the high priest resumed his high-priestly garments was the sign that God had accepted the substitute. As he stepped outside and the sound was clearly heard by all, their joy and thankfulness were profound. God had once more accepted them in the person of the high priest.

When the high priest went into the most holy on the Day of Atonement, he went in as the representative of the people. In him Israel appeared before the Lord to give account of the sins of the year. The record of these sins appeared in blood on the altar of burnt offering and in the holy place. With the Day of Atonement the day of reckoning had come, the day of judgment, when all sins were to come in review before God. The high priest appeared in God's presence, though the veil of incense shielded him. For the first time that year sin was brought before God in the most holy. The high priest sprinkled the blood of the bullock "upon the mercy seat eastward; and before the mercy seat shall he sprinkle of the blood with his finger seven times," and received "atonement for himself, and for his house." Lev. 16:14, 11. He was clean. Whatever sins he was identified with, whatever sins he was responsible for, had in figure been transferred to the sanctuary. He was clean; but the sanctuary was not.

In our consideration of sacrifices for sin, stress has been laid on the placing of the hand upon the victim's head, whereby sin is transferred to the victim. In each case the victim dies with guilt on its head, dies for sin. Thus Christ took our sins upon Himself and was made sin. Being made sin, He must die, for the wages of sin is death.

Christ, however, died not only for sin but for sinners. When He died for sin He died because He identified Himself with us and took our sins upon Himself. He died for sins because our sins were laid upon Him, and He must bear the penalty. Dying thus for sinners, He satisfied the claims of the law.

Christ died not only as a substitute for the sinner but also as the Sinless One. Taking our sins upon Himself—we say it reverently—He ought to die, the law demanded it. But personally Christ had not sinned. He was sinless; yet He died. And the death of the Sinless One is a definite part of the plan of God. His death as a sinner satisfies the claims of the law. His death as the Sinless One provides the ransom and frees the sinner from death.

After the high priest had offered the bullock and sprinkled its blood upon the mercy seat and before the mercy seat, he was told to "kill the goat of the sin offering, that is for the people, and bring his blood within the vail, and do with that blood as he did with the blood of the bullock, and sprinkle it upon the mercy seat, and before the mercy seat: and he shall make an atonement for the holy place, because of the uncleanness of the children of Israel, and because of their transgressions in all their sins: and so shall he do for the tabernacle of the congregation, that remaineth among them in the midst of their uncleanness." Lev. 16:15, 16.

It has before been noted, but should here be emphasized, that the blood of the bullock and that of the goat accomplish two different things. The first makes atonement for Aaron and his house. The second makes atonement for the people and the sanctuary. (Verses 11, 15, 16.) Nothing is said of the blood of the bullock's making atonement for or cleansing the sanctuary, but this is definitely stated of the blood of the goat. (Verses 15, 16.) This may be accounted for on the following grounds:

In all cases where atonement is made for a person, with one minor exception, the atonement is accomplished by means of blood, and indicates transfer of sins to the sanctuary. The sinner transfers his sins to the victim, which is slain, and the blood is sprinkled on the altar of burnt offering or in the holy place in the sanctuary. The blood which—because of sins' having been confessed on the victim—might be called sin-laden blood, typically and ceremonially defiles the place where it is sprinkled. Thus the sanctuary is made unclean.

When the high priest on the Day of Atonement came out after sprinkling the blood of the bullock, he was cleansed. Whatever sins he carried, for which he was responsible, had been confessed and transferred to the sanctuary. When he stepped out of the most holy he was cleansed, free, holy, a type of Christ, the Sinless One. He had confessed his sins, they had been forgiven him, and he had no further confession to make. The Lord's goat, whose blood he was about to sprinkle, also typified the Sinless One. In all the offerings during the year the death of Christ as the sin bearer was portrayed. He was made sin who knew no sin. In the goat on the Day of Atonement He was typified as the chosen of God, harmless, undefiled, sinless.

To repeat: In the goat offered on the Day of Atonement we have symbolic reference to the death of the sinless Christ, "who is holy, harmless, undefiled, separate from sinners, and made higher than the heavens." Heb. 7:26. The blood of this goat has cleansing efficacy. It makes possible the cleansing of the sanctuary.

The earthly tabernacle service was typical of the work carried on in the sanctuary above, where a complete record is kept of sins committed and of sins confessed. When the Day of Atonement came, all Israel were supposed to have that confession recorded in blood in the sanctuary. To complete the work, it was necessary to have the record removed, to have the sins blotted out, to cleanse the sanctuary of its blood defilement. Before this specific cleansing was done, the high priest went into the most holy with the blood of the bullock and made atonement for himself and for his house. This having been done, the work of cleansing began. The most holy was cleansed with the blood of the goat, and then the holy. Thus the record of sin was blotted out. After this the altar was cleansed. "He shall sprinkle of the blood upon it with his finger seven times, and cleanse it, and hallow it from the uncleanness of the children of Israel." Lev. 16:19.

Thus he makes "an end of reconciling the holy place, and the tabernacle of the congregation, and the altar." Verse 20. After the ceremonies of this day were carried out, all was then cleansed, reconciled, and atoned for.

THE SCAPEGOAT

When lots were cast upon the two goats taken from the congregation, one lot was for the Lord and the other for the scapegoat. (Lev. 16:8.) Some believe both goats to be symbolic of Christ, representing two phases of His atoning work. Others believe that they represent two opposing forces, and that as one is "for the Lord," and the other "for Azazel," the latter must mean "for Satan." Some scholars, probably the majority, hold that Azazel is a personal, wicked, superhuman spirit; others contend that it means "one who removes," especially "by a series of acts." It seems most reasonable to believe that as the one goat is for the Lord, a personal being, so the other also is for a personal being. Moreover, as the two goats are evidently antithetical, the most consistent view would be that which holds that Azazel must be opposed to the Lord. He could then be no other than Satan.

While we believe the weight of evidence to be in favor of considering Azazel a personal, wicked spirit, there are certain difficulties in this view which should have consideration. Chief among these is the statement that the scapegoat "shall be presented alive before the Lord, to make an atonement with him, and let him go for a scapegoat into the wilderness." Lev. 16:10. If Azazel represents Satan, how can it be possible to "make an atonement with him"?

We believe that a consideration of the office of the scapegoat furnishes a solution to this problem.

The scapegoat was brought into prominence on the Day of Atonement only after the work of reconciliation was completed. After Aaron "hath made an end of reconciling the holy place, and the tabernacle of the congregation, and the altar, he shall bring the live goat: and Aaron shall lay both his hands upon the head of the live goat, and confess over him all the iniquities of the children of Israel, and all their transgressions in all their sins, putting them upon the head of the goat, and shall send him away by the hand of a fit man into the wilderness: and the goat shall bear upon him all their iniquities unto a land not inhabited: and he shall let go the goat in the wilderness." Lev. 16:20–22.

The priest had made *an end* of reconciling; the sanctuary and the altar *had been* cleansed; atonement *had been* made; *an end* had been made of cleansing; then, and not until then, did the scapegoat appear in its special role. Thus the scapegoat had no part in the atonement which had already been accomplished with the blood of the Lord's goat. That work was completed.

The objection is made that as the iniquity of the children of Israel was put upon the head of the scapegoat, our argument cannot be sound. The text in question reads that Aaron shall "confess over him all the iniquities of the children of Israel, and all their transgressions in all their sins, putting them upon the head of the goat, and shall send him away by the hand of a fit man into the wilderness." Lev. 16:21.

Let us consider this.

Most sins admit of shared responsibility. The person committing the sin is often most to blame, though this is not always the case. Some are more sinned against than sinning. The man who educates a child to steal cannot escape responsibility by saying that he himself does not steal. The parents who fail to instill right principles into their children must someday give an account. This is as it should be. Except in the case of Satan, responsibility for sin is not traceable to one person only.

This brings us to a consideration of the sins which Satan bears, the sins which men bear, the sins which Christ bears. It is to be borne in mind, however, that only Christ bears sins in substitutionary atonement. Men and Satan bear sins by way of desert and punishment.

That Satan should suffer for his personal sins is axiomatic. He is a murderer from the beginning and the originator of sin. If sin is to be punished at all, Satan cannot escape. His responsibility reaches beyond that of his personal sins to the sins which he has caused others to commit. This embraces all sin, by whomsoever committed. He is responsible for the sins of the angels which fell, and he is responsible for the sins of men. There is no sin committed anywhere, in heaven or on earth, for which he is not primarily responsible. Whether the sin is committed by saint or sinner, Satan is the instigator of it. This does not mean that the angels who sinned will not have to suffer for what they did; nor does it mean that men are without responsibility. It is only fair and just that each sinner bear the punishment of his sins to the extent to which he is guilty. Satan does not bear *their* sin as such. They must bear their own sin. The sin for which he will be held responsible is his evil work in tempting them to sin, urging them on, luring them to their ruin.

The principle of joint responsibility is illustrated in the sin of our first parents, Satan tempted them, and they fell. Because of Satan's part in the sin, the serpent was cursed; because of Adam and Eve's sin, they were banished from Eden. God did not hold Adam and Eve solely responsible, neither did He excuse them. Satan was guilty; so was man. There were no extenuating circumstances. All were guilty, and all were punished, each according to his deserts. This principle of joint responsibility, illustrated in God's treatment of the first sin, still holds good. It is God ordained, and its justice finds response in man's own sense of right.

As Satan is primarily responsible for the sins of all men, these sins must finally be placed on him, and he must bear the punishment due him. This punishment is not expiatory; nor is it substitutionary; neither is it atoning, except in the sense that a criminal atones for his sins by being hanged on the gallows. He simply suffers for his own sins and for his influence in causing others to sin.

The principle of joint responsibility is true of all sin except the personal sins of Satan. "When he speaketh a lie, he speaketh of his own: for he is a liar, and the father of it." John 8:44. We can conceive of a man fallen so low that he needs little prompting by Satan to go deeper. But even in such cases Satan bears his part of the responsibility, for he started the man in his downward path. He is accountable in the case of the worst of sinners as well as in the case of "respectable" sinners.

Satan's guilt is particularly heinous in the case of professed Christians. No Christian wishes to sin. He abhors it. But Satan tempts him. A thousand times the man resists, and a thousand times Satan comes back. At last the man yields; he sins. But he soon repents; he asks forgiveness. The sin has been recorded in heaven. Now forgiveness is placed against it. The man is happy. He is forgiven. He has placed his sins upon Christ, the great sin bearer, who willingly takes them upon Himself, pays the penalty, and suffers the punishment due the sinner.

Then comes the final judgment. The sin is blotted out. The man's record is clear. But what about Satan's part in causing him to fall? Has that been atoned for? It has not. Satan must suffer for it himself.

Some have mistakenly concluded that if the sins of Israel are finally placed on Satan, he must have some part in the atonement. This is a great error. Satan has no part whatever in the vicarious atonement; the saints are in no way indebted to him; his bearing of sin is in no way related to salvation; his work is evil and only evil.

As the Lamb of God, Christ bore the sin of the world. (John 3:16.) All the accumulated sins of men were placed upon Him. He is "the Saviour of all men, specially of those that believe." 1 Tim. 4:10. While Christ died for all, He died efficaciously only for those who should accept His sacrifice. Those who do not accept Him as their Saviour must finally bear their own sins.

But even those who finally reject the offer of salvation have been the beneficiaries of Christ's atonement. No sinner has any inherent right to life, and his continued existence and opportunity of accepting salvation is provided for him only by the sacrifice on Calvary. Probationary time is granted him in which to make his decision, and this time is blood bought.

When at last he finally and irrevocably decides that he will not accept life on the conditions on which it is offered, the die is cast, and he must bear the consequences. God can do no more for him. Salvation has been offered him again and again, and he has spurned it. The Holy Spirit leaves him. He has settled his own case.

In the sanctuary service the simple principles of salvation were clearly taught. A repentant sinner brought his lamb, laid his hand on its head, confessed his sin, and then killed the lamb. The priest then ministered the blood and ate of the flesh, while the man went away forgiven. By eating the flesh the priest took the sin on himself, thus becoming a type of Him who became sin for us. On the Day of Atonement the high priest, bearing the accumulated sins of the year, made atonement for all confessed sins with the blood of the Lord's goat, thus blotting them out with not even the record remaining. Repentant Israel that day not merely had their sins forgiven, but had them blotted out, and they existed no more. Those who had not confessed their sins and had not received forgiveness were cut off, excommunicated, a type of their final cutting off from the favor of God and the land of the living.

This is the simple lesson of salvation as taught in the sanctuary. In the daily burnt-offering Israel saw Christ as the Saviour of all men, a continual sacrifice available to all, providing temporarily and provisionally for all sin, confessed and unconfessed. In the sin offering they saw men accepting by faith the proffered salvation and receiving forgiveness. On the Day of Atonement they saw the high priest making atonement, and providing complete cleansing for those who already had their sins forgiven and were still penitent, humbly bowing before God's dwelling place. With this the atonement was complete, and nothing needed to be or could be added. The sins were that day blotted out, and even the record was nonexistent. In the scapegoat they saw God's final judgment upon Satan and sin, and the assurance of a clean universe.

As the goat was led away, not in triumphant march headed by the high priest, but in a mournful procession led by a man appointed thereto, they saw in figure the fate of all who turned away from God. As a criminal is led to the gallows, so the goat with a rope around its neck was led to destruction. As the criminal thus atones for his transgression, so the goat likewise atoned—not atonement unto salvation, but punitive atonement unto death.

The day of final judgment includes not only the blotting out of the sins of the righteous but also the eradication of sin from the universe. It includes placing upon the head of Satan all sin for which he is responsible, and the "cutting off" of all who have not afflicted their souls. So likewise in the sanctuary service the sins were placed on the head of the scapegoat after the cleansing of the sanctuary had been completed. Then those who had not repented were "cut off." (Lev. 16:20–22; 23:29.)

The leading away of the scapegoat must have been a solemn moment for all Israel. In him each man had a vivid illustration of what would happen to him as he failed in his duty toward God. Driven out of the camp, out into the wilderness, alone and forsaken, the prey of hunger and thirst, of heat and cold by night, surrounded by wild animals and other dangers of the night, laden with sin and with the curse of God resting upon him—this was the fate of the scapegoat, and this would be the fate of such as departed from God. The lesson must have been vivid and powerful, and one not easily forgotten.

Extracts From the Writings of Mrs. E. G. White on the Temple

"From eternal ages it was God's purpose that every created being, from the bright and holy seraph to man, should be a temple for the indwelling of the Creator. Because of sin, humanity ceased to be a temple for God. Darkened and defiled by evil, the heart of man no longer revealed the glory of the divine One. But by the incarnation of the Son of God, the purpose of Heaven is fulfilled. God dwells in humanity, and through saving grace the heart of man becomes again His temple. God designed that the temple at Jerusalem should be a continual witness to the high destiny open to every soul." —*The Desire of Ages*, p. 161.

"In the cleansing of the temple, Jesus was announcing His mission as the Messiah, and entering upon His work....In cleansing the temple from the world's buyers and sellers, Jesus announced His mission to cleanse the heart from the defilement of sin,—from the earthly desires, the selfish lusts, the evil habits, that corrupt the soul." —*Ibid.*

"Jesus did not design that the skeptical Jews should discover the hidden meaning of His words, nor even His disciples at that time. After His resurrection they called to mind these words He had uttered, and they then understood them correctly. They remembered that He had also said that He had power to lay down His life and to take it again. Jesus was acquainted with the path His feet had entered upon, even unto the end. His words possessed a double meaning, referring to the temple at Jerusalem as well as His own material body." —*Redemption—First Advent*, p. 81.

"God commanded Moses for Israel, 'Let them make Me a sanctuary, that I may dwell among them,' and He abode in the sanctuary, in the midst of His people. Through all their weary wandering in the desert, the symbol of His presence was with them. So Christ set up His tabernacle in the midst of our human encampment. He pitched His tent by the side of the tents of men, that He might dwell among us, and make us familiar with His divine character and life. 'The Word became flesh, and tabernacled among us (and we beheld His glory, glory as of the only begotten from the Father) full of grace and truth.'" —*The Desire of Ages*, p. 23.

"The Jewish tabernacle was a type of the Christian church....

"The church on earth, composed of those who are faithful and loyal to God, is the 'true tabernacle,' whereof the Redeemer is the minister. God, and not man, pitched this tabernacle on a high, elevated platform. This tabernacle is Christ's body, and from north, south, east, and west, He gathers those who shall help to compose it....

"A holy tabernacle is built up of those who receive Christ as their personal Saviour....

"Christ is the Minister of the true tabernacle, the High Priest of all who believe in Him as a personal Saviour."—*Signs of the Times*, Feb. 14, 1900, p. 98.

"Through Christ the true believers are represented as being built together for an habitation of God through the Spirit. Paul writes: 'God who is rich in mercy, for His great love wherewith He loved us, even when we were dead in sins, hath quickened us together with Christ...and hath raised us up together, and made us sit together in heavenly places in Christ Jesus; that in the ages to come He might show the exceeding riches of His grace in His kindness toward us through Christ Jesus. For by grace are ye saved through faith; and that not of yourselves; it is the gift of God; not of works, lest any man should boast. For we are His workmanship, created in Christ Jesus unto good works, which God hath before ordained that we should walk in them....Ye are no more strangers and foreigners, but fellow-citizens with the saints, and of the household of God; and are built upon the foundation of the apostles and prophets, Jesus Christ Himself being the chief corner-stone; in whom all the building fitly framed together groweth unto a holy temple in the Lord; in whom we also are builded together for a habitation of God through the Spirit.' Eph. 2:4–22." —*Ibid.*

"The revelation at Sinai could only impress them with their need and helplessness. Another lesson the tabernacle, through its service of sacrifice, was to teach,—the lesson of pardon of sin, and power through the Saviour for obedience unto life.

"Through Christ was to be fulfilled the purpose of which the tabernacle was a symbol,—that glorious building, its walls of glistening gold reflecting in rainbow hues the curtains inwrought with cherubim, the fragrance of ever-burning incense pervading all, the priests robed in spotless white, and in the deep mystery of the inner place, above the mercy-seat, between the figures of the bowed, worshiping angels, the glory of the Holiest. In all, God desired His people to read His purpose for the human soul. It was the same purpose long afterward set forth by the apostle Paul, speaking by the Holy Spirit:—

"'Know ye not that ye are the temple of God, and that the Spirit of God dwelleth in you? If any man defile the temple of God, him shall God destroy; for the temple of God is holy, which temple ye are.'"—Education, p. 36.

"To every man is given his work,—not merely work in his fields of corn and wheat, but earnest, persevering work for the salvation of souls. Every stone in God's temple must be a living stone, a stone that shines, reflecting light to the world. Let the laymen do all that they can; and as they use the talents they already have, God will give them more grace and increased ability."—Testimonies, vol. 8, p. 246.

"The sacrificial service that had pointed to Christ passed away; but the eyes of men were turned to the true sacrifice for the sins of the world. The earthly priesthood ceased; but we look to Jesus, the minister of the new covenant, and to the blood of sprinkling, that speaketh better things than that of Abel.' 'The way into the holiest of all was not yet made manifest, while as the first tabernacle was yet standing; ...but Christ being come an high priest of good things to come, by a greater and more perfect tabernacle, not made with hands,...by His own blood He entered in once into the holy place, having obtained eternal redemption for us.

"'Wherefore He is able also to save them to the uttermost that come unto God by Him, seeing He ever liveth to make intercession for thern.' Though the ministration was to be removed from the earthly to the heavenly temple; though the sanctuary and our great high priest would be invisible to human sight, yet the disciples were to suffer no loss thereby. They would realize no break in their communion, and no diminution of power because of the Saviour's absence. While Jesus ministers in the sanctuary above, He is still by His Spirit the minister of the church on earth. He is withdrawn from the eye of sense, but His parting promise is fulfilled, 'Lo, I am with you alway, even unto the end of the world.' While He delegates His power to inferior ministers, His energizing presence is still with His church."—*The Desire of Ages*, p. 166.

"We are. in the day of atonement, and we are to work in harmony with Christ's work of cleansing the sanctuary from the sins of the people. Let no man who desires to be found with the wedding garment on, resist our Lord in His office work. As He is, so will His followers be in this world. We must now set before the people the work which by faith we see our great High Priest accomplishing in the heavenly sanctuary. Those who do not sympathize with Jesus in His work in the heavenly courts, who do not cleanse the soul temple of every defilement, but who engage in some enterprise not in harmony with this work, are joining with the enemy of God and man in leading minds away from the truth and work for this time.

"The Spirit of truth has a refining, elevating, heavenly influence upon mind and character. We are to study the mind of Christ, and to receive the truth as it is in Jesus. We are to watch and pray, to consult the living oracles of God. When any lust takes possession of the mind in any way or to any degree, and there is a yielding to fleshly desires, we lose the image of Christ in spirit and character. The work in the heavenly sanctuary becomes obscure to the minds of those who are controlled by the temptations of the evil one, and they engage in side issues to gratify their own selfish purposes, and their true moral standing is determined by their works."—*Review and Herald*, January 21, 1890.

CHAPTER 10

OF THE BOOK OF HEBREWS

Complete Sanctification

SYNOPSIS OF CHAPTER

CHAPTER 10 continues the discussion of the ineffectiveness of the ceremonial law in making men perfect. The chief proof which the author puts forward in this chapter is the evident fact that if the law really made the comers perfect, sin offerings would cease. As men would have no more consciousness of sin, they would not bring any sin offering. (Verses 1–4.)

Having proved this point, the writer goes on to show that Christ, through the offering of His body once for all, has perfected forever them that are sanctified. The first demonstration of this He made in the body in which He came to do God's will. The second demonstration He makes in those whose sins and iniquities are remitted. For such there is no more offering for sin. (Verses 5–18.)

Where there is remission of sins and no more consciousness of them, there can be boldness before God; for them it is possible with Christ as their forerunner to enter into the holies by virtue of His blood. (Verses 19–22)

The rest of the chapter is given to exhortation to hold fast the faith without wavering, to encourage one another in view of the fact that the great day of God is approaching. In a little while He that shall come will come and will not tarry. (Verses 23–39.)

Hebrews 10:1–4. "For the law having a shadow of good things to come, and not the very image of the things, can never with those sacrifices which they offered year by year continually make the comers thereunto perfect. For then would they not have ceased to be offered? because that the worshippers once purged should have had no more conscience of sins. But in those sacrifices there is a remembrance again made of sins every year. For it is not possible that the blood of bulls and of goats should take away sins."

Christ nowhere decreed the abolition of the sacrificial law. Paul, on the other hand, is very emphatic that the ceremonial law is abrogated. It therefore becomes incumbent on the apostle to give weighty reasons for his position. If he can show that Christ brought in perfection, which the Levitical law could not and did not do, he has scored a decisive point; for cessation of sin would not only make sin offering unnecessary, but also the law which demanded them. The vital point is to show that Christ came to do away with sin. If Paul can do this, he needs no more proof of the annulment of the law that required sin offerings. There would be no need of such a law.

Admittedly the work in the first apartment of the earthly sanctuary was unsatisfactory, because it had to be repeated day by day. The apostle shows that the work in the second apartment was equally inadequate, in that while it did temporarily and provisionally blot out sin, the service had to be repeated year after year, showing that it was not a permanent work.

Verse 1. "A shadow of good things to come." By the law, of course, is meant the Levitical law. It is significant that the statement is made that it had a shadow, "and not the very image of the things," which is equivalent to saying that it had only a shadow; and hence that too close similarity between the shadow and the object casting it is not to be expected. An image, a photograph, a statue, give considerably more detail than does a shadow, yet even these but imperfectly mirror the original. From this we may expect the law to show only the outlines of the reality. Consequently, it is not safe to draw too close parallels.

Verse 2. "Would they not have ceased to be offered?" The chief weakness of the sanctuary service, as has been noted before, was that it did not and could not "make the comers thereunto perfect." This was evident in the very plan itself, which provided for a yearly recurring service. If the sacrifices had accomplished their intended purpose, "would they not have ceased to be offered? because that the worshippers once purged should have had no more conscience of sins." But as soon as the yearly round of services ended, another round began that culminated in another Day of Atonement. No sooner were the expiatory services on the Day of Atonement concluded than the evening sacrifice began again, the lamb was killed, and the blood sprinkled—all showing that even the great atonement which had been made that day had not accomplished its purpose; it had not made the worshipers perfect. They still needed atonement, and a year from that day they would repeat the entire service, thereby admitting its inefficiency to accomplish perfection or sanctification.

"Would they not have ceased to be offered?" is an interesting and far-reaching question, and the writer so puts it as to demand an affirmative answer: they *would have* ceased to be offered because the worshipers once purged would have had no more conscience of sin.

Verses 3, 4. It would be unjust to blame the service for what it did not do; and this for the simple reason that it *could not* do that which needed to be done: it was "not possible that the blood of bulls and of goats should take away sins"; it would "never...make the comers thereunto perfect."

"A remembrance...every year." On the Day of Atonement "shall the priest make an atonement for you to cleanse you, that ye may be clean from all your sins before the Lord." Lev. 16:30. Throughout the year forgiveness was had by confession and the offering of the prescribed sacrifice. On the Day of Atonement all these sins were again brought to remembrance. On that day the high priest personally performed all the services: he offered the incense; he killed the bullock and the goat; he sprinkled the blood on the ark, the holy place, and the altar. The people had no part to act in this service: they brought no lamb; they did not place their hand on the sacrifice; they did not kill the victim; it was all done for them, in contrast to the daily service. It is to this service on the Day of Atonement the writer has reference when he, says that those "sacrifices which they offered year by year" could never make the worshipers perfect. He then draws the conclusion that if the sacrifices had made them perfect they would have had no more conscience of sin, and sin offerings would have ceased.

Some erroneously think that Christ by an official pronouncement declared the Levitical law abrogated. Christ made no such announcement. He did no sin

Himself; so in His case there was no need for any sin offering. And it would be the same in the case of anyone else who stopped sinning. And if all stopped sinning, sin offerings would simply cease. This would be the ideal way to abrogate the ceremonial law.

Hebrews 10:5–10. "Wherefore when he cometh into the world, he saith, Sacrifice and offering thou wouldest not, but a body hast thou prepared me? In burnt offerings and sacrifices for sin thou hast had no pleasure. Then said I, Lo, I come (in the volume of the book it is written of me,) to do thy will, O God. Above when he said, Sacrifice and offering and burnt offerings and offering for sin thou wouldest not, neither hadst pleasure therein; which are offered by the law; then said he, Lo, I come to do thy will, O God. He taketh away the first, that he may establish the second. By the which will we are sanctified through the offering of the body of Jesus Christ once for all."

Did Christ in reality do what the law could not do? It is necessary to show this; for if Christ did not make perfection attainable, then He failed in the very point where the sacrificial law failed, and then we would be no better off than before. The apostle therefore shows that Christ in the body given Him worked out God's will in every particular, and showed how perfection might be attained. Having given a demonstration that the attainment of perfection is possible, He offers to sanctify those who will come to Him.

Verse 5. "Sacrifice and offering." The blood of bulls and of goats cannot take away sin. Because of this, when Christ came into the world, He said, "Sacrifice and offering thou wouldest not, but a body hast thou prepared me."

This quotation is taken from the Septuagint Version of the fortieth psalm, which is assigned to

David. The psalm is entitled "To the chief Musician, A Psalm of David." The first five verses refer to David's experience when persecuted by Saul, but verses six to eight are so evidently Messianic that no proof of this is necessary. Christ is both the subject and the speaker.

"A body hast thou prepared me." A reference to the Authorized Version of the fortieth psalm will show that the reading there is, "Mine ears hast thou opened." As is known, a translation of the Hebrew Scriptures into Greek, called the Septuagint Version, was made some time before Christ for the use of the Jews who did not know the Hebrew language. This version was in general use in the time of Christ, and both He and the disciples quoted from it. The quotations from the Old Testament in the book of Hebrews are mostly from this translation. The Hebrew reads, "Mine ears hast thou opened." The Septuagint translation reads, "A body hast thou prepared me." Various attempts have been made to reconcile these statements, but we have not enough facts to guide us. Under these conditions let us study both statements. We will first consider the Septuagint translation as in Hebrews 10:5: "A body hast thou prepared me."

The Jews brought animal sacrifices to their altars as an offering to God, though they knew, or should have known, that in and of themselves these offerings could never cleanse the soul. God meant them to be object lessons to teach men that the wages of sin is death, and that even the least sin merits punishment. Instead of this, Israel came to believe that the offerings constituted a kind of payment for sin, and that when they brought the prescribed sacrifice, their sin was canceled.

But, as noted, they should have known better. No brute beast compares in value to a human soul. To offer God a bullock or a goat in atonement for a human being would be an insult, and would place man on a level with the beast, and make a farce of the atonement. No beast, of course, could consent to die as a substitute—its death must be forced and unwilling—and to believe that such a death could make atonement, would be unworthy of a thinking being. All this is summed up in the statement that the blood of bulls and goats cannot possibly take away sin. They might be symbolic of something higher, but in themselves they could have no atoning value.

When Christ came, a body was prepared for Him. He who was God became man, and mysteriously combined the two natures in one, becoming the God-man. The body prepared for Him was subject to death. It was a human body of flesh and blood, so prepared as to be capable of suffering to the utmost; otherwise He could never have survived either the temptation in the wilderness or the agony of Gethsemane, the suffering of which would ordinarily cause death. When He had endured as much as human nature could stand, and fell dying to the ground, an angel was sent, not to remove the cup, but to strengthen Him to drink it. In Gethsemane Christ was strengthened *for the purpose of* suffering. There He *tasted death*; on the cross He died.

Christ's body was a human body, prepared of God for the specific purpose of atonement and redemption. In that body Jesus worked out the plan of salvation and redeemed Adam's disgraceful failure. To that body came every temptation to which man is subject, and in that body every temptation was met and conquered.

Men react differently to specific temptations. To some, certain temptations constitute no problem, and are easily resisted. To others the same temptations are most severe, and a terrific struggle ensues, and often men are overcome.

To Christ every temptation must come at least in equal strength to that of the most tempted on earth. If in any sin one is tempted harder than Christ was tempted, then God would have to excuse that man for yielding; for he could justly say that Christ never was tempted so severely as he, and that the reason Christ was not so tempted was because He could not endure it and come off victorious.

But that has never been, nor can be. No one will ever be able to say that Christ was not tempted so severely as he. A man might withstand temptation to the utmost, and die. resisting unto blood. Who can do more? Yet even to such a one Christ can say, "Dear one, I was tempted on the same point, and resisted unto blood as you did. But I went a little further. You died, and that was the end of your suffering. I was not permitted to die as you were. In Gethsemane I drained the cup."

Let no one believe that a Christian would ever say or think such, or that Christ would answer as above. No one will have any desire to compare sufferings or to boast of his temptations. We have presented it merely to make more vivid what Christ's sufferings and temptations meant.

Every temptation that has ever come to any man came to Christ, and each temptation came to Him in greater force than it ever came to any other man. However hard we are pressed, we may know that Jesus understands. He has gone the way before us.

It can readily be seen that if the temptations of the world are to be gathered up in one body and felt to the full, such a body must be possessed of physical and spiritual qualities that will make suffering and temptations possible without a break of the life line, which would end suffering.

We have no disposition to enlarge upon this, but would impress upon all that Christ's temptations were real, and that the statement "A body hast thou prepared me" has a deeper significance than that of merely conveying the information that Christ had a body. This we already know. What God tells us here is that Christ had a *prepared* body, not a brute body like those used in burnt and sin offerings, but a human body; that He was made in the image of God, a worthy representative of the race; and that His offering upon the cross as the God-man fulfilled the demands of the law and actually accomplished that which the Levitical sacrifices dimly foreshadowed in promise. "Those sacrifices which they offered year by year continually" could never "make the comers thereunto perfect," "but a body hast thou prepared me," and in that body was fulfilled God's complete intent, and to the possessor of that body came the heavenly approbation, "This is my beloved Son, in whom I am well pleased." Matt. 3:17.

If we therefore accept the Septuagint translation as it is found in Hebrews 10:5, "A body hast thou prepared me," we see in these words a significant reference to the work Christ did in that body. God did not want sacrifices and offerings. They were indicative of sin. Every offering brought to the temple testified to the fact that someone had sinned. God wanted men to stop sinning. Could men stop sinning? To demonstrate this, God prepared a body for Christ; and in that body Christ showed that men need not sin, however much they are tempted. He resisted unto blood; He resisted unto death, and even beyond the point of death, as it were. In all things He was victorious. The demonstration was complete. Man need not sin. This Christ showed in the body given Him.

With these considerations in mind we are ready to defend and accept the Septuagint translation, which says, "A body hast thou prepared me."

Let us now consider the translation as found in the fortieth psalm, which according to the Hebrew translation reads, "Mine ears hast thou opened." Ps. 40:6. For "opened" the margin has "digged, bored, or pierced." Many hold that this expression is taken from Exodus 21, and the similarity between Christ and the Hebrew servant there portrayed justifies the reference.

The account in Exodus reads: "Now these are the judgments which thou shalt set before them. If thou buy an Hebrew servant, six years he shall serve: and in the seventh he shall go out free for nothing. If he came in by himself, he shall go out by himself: if he were married, then his wife shall go out with him. If his master have given him a wife, and she have born him sons or daughters; the wife and her children shall be her master's, and he shall go out by himself. And if the servant shall plainly say, I love my master, my wife, and my children; I will not go out free: then his master shall bring him unto the judges; he shall also bring him to the door, or unto the door post; and his master shall bore his ear through with an aul; and he shall serve him for ever." Ex. 21:1–6.

The parallel account in Deuteronomy reads: "And it shall be, if he say unto thee, I will not go away from thee; because he loveth thee and thine house, because he is well with thee; then thou shalt take an aul, and thrust it through his ear unto the door, and he shall be thy servant for ever. And also unto thy maidservant thou shalt do likewise." Deut. 15:16, 17.

This custom was common in Israel. A man might hire himself out as a servant or slave, but the period must not exceed six years. At the end of that time he was to be set free and his master was to load him down with all kinds of good things, remembering that "he hath been worth a double hired servant to thee." Deut. 15:18.

There were certain conditions, however, inherent in this arrangement. If the man was unmarried when he began his servitude, he would go out free, but alone, at the end of six years. If he was married when he arrived, both he and his family were to go out free. But if he came as a single man, and married during the six years, he could go out free alone if he so chose, but his wife and children belonged to the master, and must remain.

If a man loved his wife and his children, it may be presumed that he would not accept freedom for himself upon such conditions. If he could take his family with him, he would be happy to be free. But if he could not, he would likely decide to stay with his master. In such a case the master was to take him to the door and the doorpost, bore his ear through with an aul, and then he was to serve forever. The opening in his ear was a sign of servitude, but also a sign of love. He so loved his own that he was willing to serve forever rather than be separated from them.

As noted above, in Psalms 40:6 Christ is spoken of as having His ears opened or digged. The words used for piercing the ear in Exodus 21:6, Deuteronomy 15:17, and Psalms 40:6, while not identical, all convey the same meaning, that of thrusting through, digging, piercing.

It is instructive to note the parallel between the Hebrew servant and Christ. Christ came to this world to serve, not "to be ministered unto, but to minister." He came alone, and of the people there were none with Him. When the years of His service were ended, He could have gone out alone, according to the law. But He did not want to go out alone. "I will," He said, "that they also whom thou hast given me, be with me where I am; that they may behold my glory, which thou hast given me: for thou lovedst me before the foundation of the world." John 17:24.

While here on earth, Christ had fallen in love with humanity. He had come alone, but He did not want to go out alone. In the words of the servant in Exodus, "I love my master, my wife, and my children; I will not go out free." Under these conditions the master was to take the servant and bring him to the door and the doorpost and "bore his ear through with an aul; and he shall serve him for ever." Ex. 21:6. And so Christ, according to the fortieth psalm, had His ears bored through with an aul, and now He was to serve forever.

Christ's ears, of course, were not bored through literally, but His hands, His feet, and His side were pierced. As the opening in the ears was a sign not only of servitude but also of love, so Christ bears the marks of His love, and ever will. He could have gone out alone; He could have escaped the cross and the suffering. But He chose to stay, and bound Himself to humanity with bands that will never be severed.

This, then, is the story of the fortieth psalm, according to the Hebrew rendering. In the Septuagint rendering it is the story of Christ's body as an all-sufficient sacrifice which accomplished for man that which the blood of animals could not do. Both renderings indicate obedience, suffering, love, a willingness to bear and to do. In the absence of any authoritative voice telling us which translation to use, and in view of the fact that both renderings convey significant meanings, we accept both as teaching essential truth.

Verses 7–9. "Lo, I come." Christ knew full well what it meant to come to this world. The whole. path lay clear before Him. He knew the suffering and agony that would be His. But He hesitated not. "Lo I come," is His answer to the challenge. And so He came, according to what was written and promised in "the volume of the book."

"He taketh away the first, that He may establish the second." What is the first which He takes away? And what is the second which He establishes?

"Above when he said, Sacrifice and offering and burnt offerings and offering for sin thou wouldest not, neither hadst pleasure therein; which are offered by the law." This is the first.

"Then said he, Lo, I come to do thy will, O God." This is the second.

The first, then, is "sacrifice and offering and burnt offerings and offering for sin." This is the ceremonial law. This He takes away.

"Lo I come to do Thy will," is the second. This is the law of God. This He establishes.

Throughout the Old Testament, God's complaint against the people was that they substituted offerings for obedience. They brought thousands of rams and ten thousands of rivers of oil, but they did not heed the voice of the prophets who called them to repentance. God tried to teach them that "to obey is better than sacrifice"; through the prophets He called on them to cease to do evil and learn to do well. (1 Sam. 15:22; Isa. 1:16.) But to no avail. It was apparent that Israel would not learn the lesson of the sacrifices. They perverted their entire intent.

And so Christ came. He came, not to sacrifice, but to do God's will. "Lo, I come," He says, or rather, "Lo, I *am* come, to do thy will, O God." He takes away the first, the sacrifices with all their ceremonies, and establishes the second, the will of God; as the psalmist puts it, "I delight to do thy will, O my God; yea thy law is within my heart." Ps. 40:8.

Christ came to do God's will, to render obedience to His commands; not to offer sacrifices for having broken them. Israel had transgressed throughout the years, and then sacrificed. Christ came, not primarily to do away with sacrifices, but to substitute obedience for sacrifice, to teach the people that "to obey is better than sacrifice," or in His words to the sinful woman, "Go, and sin no more." John 8: 11. Doing away with sin would automatically cause sacrifice and oblation to cease, To believe and teach that Christ merely abolished the law of ceremonies does not adequately describe His work. He came to do away with sin, to substitute obedience for sacrifice. Doing away with sin canceled the law of offerings.

"I delight to do thy will." For Christ, obedience was no hard, unpleasant task: God's law was in His heart. He took away the first—all transgression, with the accompanying sacrifices and offerings in which God had no pleasure. He established the second, voluntary, cheerful obedience, culminating in the one great sacrifice on Calvary that forever abolished all lesser sacrifices. "I am come to do thy will, O God."

Verse 10. "By the which will we are sanctified." In Thessalonians, Paul says, "This is the will of God, even your sanctification." 1 Thess. 4:3. The sacrifices that Israel offered year by year could never make the worshipers perfect. They could and did bring sins to "remembrance" every year. As the sacrifices could not "take away sins," to bring them to remembrance only served to emphasize the inefficacy of multiplied offerings.

But now Christ has come. He shows the way. He delights to do God's will, and "through the offering of the body of Jesus Christ once for all" He sanctifies all that come to Him.

"Offering of the body of Jesus Christ." "A body hast thou prepared me." The contrast is between the sacrifices that were offered continually year by year and that could never take away sin or make the comers perfect, and "the offering" of the body of Jesus Christ "once for all" which can take away sin and make us perfect.

Hebrews 10:11–18. "And every priest standeth daily ministering and offering oftentimes the same sacrifices, which can never take away sins: but this man, after he had offered one sacrifice for sins for ever, sat down on the right hand of God; from henceforth expecting till his enemies be made his footstool. For by one offering he hath perfected for ever them that are sanctified. Whereof the Holy Ghost also is a witness to us: for after that he had said before, This is the covenant that I will make with them after those days, saith the Lord, I will put my laws into their hearts, and in their minds will I write them; and their sins and iniquities will 1 remember no more. Now where remission of these is, there is no more offering for sin."

In the preceding section the author showed that Christ in the body given Him perfected God's will. In this section he shows that He by one offering "perfected for ever them that are sanctified." This is accomplished by having the law written in the heart, in the same way that Christ had the law in His heart. (Ps. 40:8.) Thus the apostle's argument is complete. Christ had the law written in the heart, and He fully met God's standard of perfection. In the new covenant God writes the law in the hearts of the believers, and Christ perfects forever them that are sanctified. Thus they also will meet the standard set.

Verse 11. "Every priest standeth." The author, for the sake of emphasis, goes over the ground again. The priests offer the same sacrifices daily, going through a continual round of service. Despite this they accomplish nothing permanent, for these sacrifices "can never take away sins."

Verses 12, 13. "But this man...sat down." Christ offered one sacrifice for sins, after which He "sat down on the right hand of God." This "sat down" is the same word used in Hebrews 1:3 and 8:1, and denotes the formal and official seating of our royal High Priest at the Father's right hand, where He will remain until the final downfall of all opposition to God, referred to in 1 Corinthians 15:23–26.

The question may be raised as to whether this sitting of Christ at the right hand of God is not in contradiction to the teaching of other parts of the epistle which present Christ as the minister of the sanctuary in heaven who constantly appears for us in the courts above, and who by Stephen is seen *standing* and not sitting. (Acts 7:55.)

Commentators see this difficulty and discuss it. Delitzsch refers to chapter 8: 1, where Christ is spoken of as being active, a minister of the sanctuary, and says: "Those statements are not contradicted here, but explained to mean that the heavenly priesthood of Christ, consisting solely in the presentation of Himself as the high-priestly sacrifice, involves no changes of ministerial activity, and imposes no further burden of atonement-making work; He is now and henceforth the High Priest upon His throne—none other, in fact, than the Eternal King, seated in unapproachable and everlasting rest."—*Commentary on the Epistle to the Hebrews*, vol. 2, p. 162.

Again he asks whether the author's statement is not inconsistent with Paul's statement in 1 Corinthians 15:23–26, which presents Christ's work as consisting in putting down all rule and authority and power, and abolishing death. To this he answers: "A reference to ii.14 and ix.28 is sufficient to show that our author himself could have meant no otherwise. The antithesis on which he is here dwelling is simply between the labour and passion of His earthly life, and the unchanging blessedness of its perfection above. Christ no more descends to fight; His strivings are over: He takes part as to His whole being in the omnipotent dominion of the heavenly Father, and awaits the final manifestation of His power."—*Ibid.*

Lange's *Commentary* says: "The *waiting* of the Royal Priest, who is enthroned at the right hand of God, for the complete subjection of all His enemies, does not involve the idea of His personal inactivity until the time of His second coming, but expresses, in contrast with that *activity of the earthly priests which never attains to its end,* the exalted repose of the Mediator, who, *in every relation, has reached the goal of perfection;* who, after bringing to actual realization the ideal of propitiation which was typically announced in the Aaronic high-priesthood, now receives forever the position typically predicted in the royal priesthood of Melchisedek, a position exempted from future sacrifices, and fraught with unlimited homage, honor, and capacity for the bestowment of blessings."—*Hebrews.*, p. 172, par. 6.

When Christ therefore is said to be henceforth expecting—or waiting—till His enemies are made His footstool, He is not waiting in idle expectancy, but as Westcott says: "Christ Himself in His royal majesty 'waits' as the husbandman for the processes of nature (James v,7) and the patriarchs for the divine promise (chap. xi,10)."—*The Epistle to the Hebrews*, p. 34. Neither the husbandman nor the patriarch sat with folded hands waiting for something to happen. They waited in the same sense in which God's people are waiting now for the Lord to come, not in idle dreaming, but busily engaged in the work at hand. And so Christ is waiting; waiting for sin to be over; waiting for the reign of Satan to end; waiting for the resurrection, when all the saints will be raised from death. The waiting here meant is that of the soul's longing for the promised rest, for sin to end, and the kingdoms of this world to become the kingdoms of Christ.

Verse 14. "By one offering he hath perfected for ever them that are sanctified." Here Christ is said to do that which sacrifices and offering could never do. These could never "make the comers thereunto perfect" nor take away sin. (Heb. 10:1.) Though the priests "offered year by year continually," their work was ineffective and imperfect. Now Christ by one offering has done what they could never do.

"Perfected for ever." This is said to be accomplished "by one offering," which points to the cross where the offering was made.

"Them that are sanctified," or more literally, "them that are being sanctified," or as Bleek and also Lunemarm translate, "all that receive sanctification now and in the future." As this text is used by those who reject Christ's ministry in the sanctuary above, it may be well to consider this further.

Christ by one offering "hath perfected for ever them that are being sanctified." They are not yet completely sanctified, but are in the process of being so. Christ is now carrying on a work of sanctification in the hearts of men, and this work will not be completed until He presents every man perfect in Christ Jesus. Paul declares himself, not as one having "already attained, either were already perfect." Phil. 3:12. He expresses the hope and is confident, "that he who began a good work in you will perfect it until the day of Jesus Christ." Phil. 1:6. "Finish it," the Authorized Version has in the margin.

It would seem needless to point out that Christ's work in the human heart is not finished. In many hearts the work has just begun; in many others it has not even started. As the Father works hitherto, so the Son and the Spirit are working, and this work will not be finished till Christ comes. When, therefore, the statement is made that Christ by one offering hath perfected forever them that are being sanctified, it can be true only provisionally and potentially. Many of the saints then living were not as yet perfected—Paul one of them. Many who were later to be saved had not as yet accepted Christianity. Millions who were as yet unborn would in time accept the gospel. And from the work of perfecting these souls we must not exclude Christ. He did His work on the cross; He died there, and will never die again. That work is finished and will never need to be repeated. From that He rests. But Christ's work in the human heart is not finished. That is still going on. But we have the promise that He who began it will also finish it.

We therefore hold that Christ finished His work on the cross, as far as it could be finished. It was finished in the same sense that the work was finished at the altar when a sin offering was slain in the sanctuary service. The work at the altar was indeed finished and the blood shed, but the man was not atoned for until the priest ministered the blood.

So the work was finished on the cross, and the blood, the means of atonement, provided. Christ will never die again. But we are not to think that there is no atoning efficacy in Christ's ministering His blood in the heavenly sanctuary, there to appear before the face of God for us. It seems destructive of sound doctrines to confine the totality of the atonement to the cross. The cross is vital, the cross is central. Christ finished His earthly work there. But then He ascended to heaven to continue His work of redemption in the sanctuary above. This work is now going on and will continue until the end. Whoever limits Christ's work to the cross limits the atonement.

When our text states that Christ by one offering hath perfected forever them that are being sanctified, we accept the statement as it reads. Christ's one offering has perpetual validity, and never needs to be repeated. Whatever perfection is to be attained by the saints at any time in history must be in view of Christ's work on the cross; for there is salvation in no other. The outworking of the efficacy of the cross is still being extended to such as are being sanctified. The totality of the atonement extends to the end of time. This is the work that Christ is now doing as He represents us before the Father.

Verses 15–17. This is the same quotation from Jeremiah that occurs in Hebrews 8:10–12, with six clauses left out after verse 16, as can be seen by a comparison of the passages.

The Holy Ghost bears witness to what has been said about perfecting them that are sanctified, as well as of Christ's work and His session at the right hand of God; "for after that he had said before, This is the covenant that I will make with them after those days, saith the Lord."

The covenant is here mentioned, in connection with the forgiveness of sins. The writer has been affirming that although sacrifices and offerings can never take away sin or make the worshipers perfect, Christ's offering can do this. This, He says, is according to the covenant promise, the Spirit also witnessing to it.

And how is this work of perfecting the saints to be accomplished? God will put His laws into the heart and write them in the mind. When the law is thus written on the heart and in the mind, not merely on tables of stone; when keeping the law becomes not a matter of legal requirement but of the heart; when obedience is based on love and not merely on duty, then sin has ceased to attract, then Christ will enter the heart, and with Him we will say, "I delight to do thy will, O my God: yea, thy law is within my heart." Ps. 40:8.

The law in the heart, or the law on tables of stone, this is the important difference between the new and the old covenant, The law is the same in both cases.

But in one case it is a legal enactment written in stone; in the other it is the law of love written in the heart. God be thanked that whereas once we were the servants of sin, now we obey "from the heart that form of doctrine which was delivered you," and this is "obedience unto righteousness." Rom. 6:17, 16.

The new covenant promises are two: first, God will write His law in the heart; second, He will remember our sins and iniquities no more. These two are closely related, and one is dependent on the other. Only as the law is in the heart as it was in that of Christ's, can and will God fulfill the second promise.

It would be well to examine ourselves to see whether we are in covenant relation with God. All that are under the new covenant will cherish and love the law. Those who hate the law and neglect it, and who scoff at those who love it, have no part in the new covenant, nor can they claim the promise that God will not remember their sins and iniquities. That promise is only for those who love God and keep His commandments. The lawless ones, those who neglect or despise the law, have no lot or part with God's people.

Before verse 17 many translators put, "Then he saith." This seems to be required to fill out the sense. It would then read, "After that he had said before...then he saith." As this is the reading in some manuscripts, the insertion is acceptable.

Verse 18. "There is no more offering for sin." This is the same idea as advanced in verse 2 that when sin ceases, sin offerings cease also.

Hebrews 10:19–25. "Having therefore, brethren, boldness to enter into the holiest by the blood of Jesus, by a new and living way, which he hath consecrated for us,

379

through the veil, that is to say, his flesh; and having an high priest over the house of God; let us draw near with a true heart in full assurance of faith, having our hearts sprinkled from an evil conscience, and our bodies washed with pure water. Let us hold fast the profession of our faith without wavering; (for he is faithful that promised;) and let us consider one another to provoke unto love and to good works: not forsaking the assembling of ourselves together, as the manner of some is; but exhorting one another: and so much the more, as ye see the day approaching."

The apostle has presented Christ as fulfilling all God's requirements. Christ took man's place, and on his behalf redeemed Adam's disgraceful failure and showed the possibility of man when linked up with God. Because of being both God and man, Christ became man's surety and mediator, and through the provisions of the new covenant restored man to his first estate. Christ desires to present us perfect before the throne of God; He wants us to follow Him into the heavenly holy places by the new and living way which He has consecrated for us; He wants us to be accepted by the Father as He was accepted.

It is this high point that is reached in these verses. As Christ gained entrance to God's dwelling place by virtue of His life, His blood, so He wants us to gain entrance by the new way which He has consecrated. Through the veil, that is to say His flesh, we are to enter. As the high priest's garments were sprinkled with blood; as he was to wash his body with pure water before he dared enter before God; so we are to have hearts sprinkled and our bodies washed: we must be spiritually and physically clean to see God.

Verse 19. "Boldness." This is the third time this word appears in the epistle. It appears previously in chapter 3:6, where the Authorized Version has "confidence," and in chapter 4:16. The high priest on earth never entered the sanctuary with boldness, but with trembling and fear. As children we are to approach God with boldness. In fact, we are counted members of the household of God only as "we hold fast our boldness and the glorying of our hope firm unto the end." Heb. 3:6, R.V.

"The holiest," rather the holies, or holy places, the original being in the plural. Christ has opened the way and dedicated it for us. This includes the whole sanctuary, not just one apartment.

"By the blood of Jesus," rather, in the blood, in virtue of the blood.

Verse 20. "A new...way." Physically speaking, there was only one way to enter either the holy or the most holy place on earth, and this was through the veil that hung before each apartment. There was no other way.

When, therefore, Christ opened for us a new way, this must be spiritually applied. A possible interpretation may be found in the means of entrance, in that which admitted the priests to the divine presence. What gave the priests the right of entrance? Blood. Without this no man could enter. The high priest could enter the most holy once every year, but "not without blood." (Heb. 9:7.) Whenever he did enter, it was always "with blood of others." (Verse 25.) This was the condition of admission.

The blood, in virtue of which the priests entered, was the blood of dead animals, blood that had no atoning value as such. Yet by faith in God the priests were permitted to enter, though the stay was short, and the entrance immediately barred for another year. The blood of animals opened the way, but also demonstrated its own inefficacy; for the door did not remain open. All that Israel received through the service was a brief interview with Deity, and then they were shut out again. It must have been clear to them that the way was not yet open.

Christ's way was a new way. He was admitted to the Father's presence not for a fleeting moment only. Christ went in, and remained there. The blood He carried was not the blood of a dead animal but the blood of a living personality which had the power of an endless life. The new way was a living way. In virtue of the power of a dedicated life He went in, presenting Himself as a living sacrifice, holy and acceptable to God.

This was indeed a new way of gaining admittance to the throne room of Deity. Compare the high priest who comes tremblingly carrying the blood of a dead bullock or goat, with the Prince of life who presents His blood—His life—as a living reality before God; He who through death has destroyed him who has the power of death; who has gained complete victory over all temptation and sin, and now presents His body—the body God prepared for Him—as a fit dwelling for God.

This entrance that Christ thus gained for us was "through the veil, that is to say, his flesh." It was through the body in which Christ had wrought out righteousness that He gained entrance to the Father. God had given Him the body, and that same body Christ now presents for inspection. "Christ is not entered into the holy places made with hands, which are the figures of the true; but into heaven itself, now to appear in the presence of God for us." Heb. 9:24. See comments on this verse.

God never wanted the blood of animals; He wanted obedience. He wanted men to do His will, not to bring sacrifices for transgression. Christ answered the call of God and came to this earth, and "when he cometh into the world, he saith, Sacrifice and offering thou wouldest not, but a body hast thou prepared me: in burnt offerings and sacrifices for sin thou hast had no pleasure. Then said I, Lo, I come (in the volume of the book it is written of me,) to do thy will, O God." Heb. 10:5–7. And when His work was done, He presented Himself before God for acceptance. The body given Him of God; the body in which He conquered temptation and gained complete victory; the body in which He suffered and died; the body that could not be holden of death; the body in which He rose triumphantly; the body cleansed and purified from every defilement; the temple body which He would raise up in three days; the body in which was fulfilled all that the services for more than a thousand years had prefigured; the cleansed, holy, sanctified, consecrated body in which God's ideal for man was at last realized—this body Christ presents before the Father, and the Father accepts it, and through it He gains entrance. The Father stands justified, the law is honored, justice and mercy have kissed each other, and heaven rings with praises. Christ has gained access to God by a new and living way: He has gained access "through...his flesh."

This "new and living way" is the way of obedience, as contrasted with the way of sacrifices and offerings. Christ abolished these, and established the will of God. "Lo, I come," He says, "to do thy will, O God." Verse 9. And God's will He does, and does it so perfectly that His life restores free access to God. Now no mere blood of dead animals was to be used. Life, the perfect life of Christ, takes its place.

This new way is a living way, the way of life, the way of perfect obedience. This way Christ consecrated for us, and we may enter in with Him, in the power of that life, in His blood and by virtue of it, always remembering that the blood is the life, and entering in virtue of His blood is entering in virtue of His life. *He* entered through—by means of—the flesh, the body which had been given Him and in which He worked out salvation for us, and presented Himself before God holy and spotless. *We* enter in virtue of His blood. He has shown us the way; He has walked the way and consecrated it for us to follow.

Consecrated, Delitzsch says, "in Hellenistic Greek is the term for dedicating or setting apart for future use."—*Commentary on Epistle to the Hebrews,* vol. 2, p. 170. So Christ has consecrated a new way for us. We are not to come before God with the evidences of transgression in our hands—the body of a dead beast. We are to come in virtue of the life, the blood, of Christ. And so coming, we can come with boldness. Let us repeat, this new and living way is the way of obedience as contrasted with the way of sacrifices and offerings. It is the way of the new covenant in which the law is written in the heart.

Verses 21, 22. High priest; literally, great priest.

"Let us draw near." This is strictly a priestly term, for priests were such as "drew near" to God. God's people are considered priests, and in view of what Christ has done for them in opening the new and living way, they are encouraged to draw near.

"True heart," "full assurance," "hearts sprinkled," "bodies washed." These are the four qualifications for those who "draw near."

A "true heart" is an honest heart without hypocrisy or deceit of any kind. Isaiah speaks of a "perfect heart," one in which no good thing is lacking. (Isa.

38:3.) Loyalty, sincerity, singleness of purpose, characterize such a heart.

"Full assurance of faith." Doubt, disbelief, unbelief, diffidence, have no place in the Christian's experience. He must be confident of what he believes, trusting, and firm. He that would please God must believe that He is, and that He is a rewarder of them that diligently seek Him. (Heb. 11:6.)

"Hearts sprinkled." At Sinai the blood of the covenant was sprinkled on the book and on the people. (Heb. 9:19.) At the dedication of the sanctuary the priests were anointed with blood. This was symbolic of dedication to a task. So God's people are to have their hearts sprinkled, the inmost being dedicated to God and His service.

"Bodies washed." At the dedication of the sanctuary the priests were washed by Moses. (Lev. 8:6.) Also before they began their daily ministration and each time they entered the sanctuary, they were to wash themselves. On the Day of Atonement the high priest washed many times.

Verse 23. "Let. us hold fast." This is another of the many exhortations in the book. It is an encouragement to steadfastness.

"Our faith." The original has "hope," and this is the correct translation. Verse 22 speaks of faith, verse 23 of hope, verse 24 of love.

In Hebrews 3:6 the saints are told they must "hold fast the confidence and the rejoicing of the *hope* firm unto the end." In chapter 6, verse 11, the apostle voices the "desire that every one of you do shew the same diligence to the full assurance of hope unto the end." In verses 18 and 19 of the same chapter we are told that "we might have a strong consolation, who have fled for refuge to lay hold upon the hope set before us: which *hope* we have as an anchor of the soul, both sure and stedfast, and which entereth into that within the veil." In chapter 7, verse 19, the statement is made that "the law made nothing perfect, but the bringing in of a better *hope* did; by the which we draw nigh unto God."

In view of the nearness of the Roman armies when this was written, we can better understand the need of hope and courage. The apostle does not promise prosperity here on earth. Rather, he wants all to lay hold of the hope which is an anchor of the soul. Indeed, to instill hope in the believers is one of the chief purposes of the epistle. The writer knew that in the days to come they would need an anchor. He aims to show them how they might obtain this hope.

The saints are to hold on without wavering. Trying days were ahead, and they might be tempted to waver. Let them, and let all, remember that He who promised is faithful. He will not fail, though at times we may be sorely tried.

Verse 24. "Let us consider one another." Too many Christians pay little heed to this admonition. Being intent upon their own work, they fail to give due consideration to the needs and well-being of others.

In Christian fellowship there must be no unlawful striving for supremacy. The interests of one are bound up with the prosperity of all. In a boat race each man in the crew must pull his own oar to the measure of his ability; nevertheless, victory is possible only as all pull together.

"Bear ye one another's burdens, and so fulfil the law of Christ," Paul counsels in Galatians 6:2. Again he says, in Romans 12:10, "Be kindly affectioned one to another with brotherly love; in honour preferring one another." True Christian courtesy is one of the Christian graces too often neglected. The principle of courtesy is acknowledged by the world and outwardly practiced by cultivated people. In true inward courtesy Christians should be the leaders.

Courtesy, however, is not all that is meant by the admonition to consider one another. A deep, heartfelt concern for a struggling soul; a vital interest in the financial difficulties of the poor; an understanding attitude toward the spiritual problems of those young in the faith; a sympathetic solicitude for the children and young people of the flock, the aged, the sick, the infirm, the shut-ins, the lonely, the newcomers—all this is included in the counsel given us.

"Provoke unto love and to good works." It is not enough that we ourselves are considerate to others: we are to provoke them to follow our example and have them join us in the good work. This will cause each member of the church to work for the good of his brother, and. selfishness and strife for personal honor and glory will cease. Such a church, such a community, would indeed be a miracle.

"Good works," rather, noble works. In the. Greek there are two words used for "good." One of them has the added meaning of beautiful, noble. This is the word here used. The works unto which we are to provoke one another not only are good in themselves but are possessed of moral beauty. (For examples of this word that indicates beauty as well as goodness, see Matthew 5:16; 26:10; Mark 14:6; 4:8, 20; 1 Peter 2:12.

For the other word that means good, essentially good, but not necessarily connected with beauty, see Romans 2:4; 13:3; 2 Corinthians 9:8; Ephesians 2:10; Colossians 1:10; 2 Thessalonians 2:17;

1 Timothy 2:10; 5:10; 2 Timothy 2:21; 3:17; Titus 1:16; 3:1; Hebrews 13:21.)

Verse 25. "Not forsaking the assembling." Although this counsel is of general application, it had a special meaning for the Christian at the time it was written. In many places it was only with difficulty that the Christians could meet for corporate worship. Persecution both by pagans and Jews was the rule. In some places edicts forbade assemblies, and even in Jerusalem there were many hindrances. Wars and rumors of war caused fears and uneasy feeling. In A.D. 66, Cestius began besieging Jerusalem, and when Hebrews was written, the war cloud was threatening. It was a time of general uneasiness and perplexity, and the assembling of themselves together presented problems. But it was at just such a time that they needed mutual encouragement. They needed their faith strengthened and their courage bolstered. This of all times was not the time to forgo the privileges of church assembly. Some were absenting themselves to their own harm, and the apostle admonishes them to do so no longer. This admonition holds good for the church today. We cannot afford to remain away from the hour of worship.

"Exhorting one another." This means more than preaching. It applies specifically to personal relationship among the members, encouraging one another, exchanging experiences, praying for and with one another.

"As ye see the day approaching." Thirty and more years had elapsed since Christ had ascended to heaven. He had told them of the destruction of Jerusalem and the temple, which He said would come in their generation. Now they saw the day approaching. There could be no doubt that the prophecy was about to be fulfilled. This was no time to stand apart. It was a time to draw together.

Jerusalem's destruction was a symbol of the destruction to take place at the end of the world. This is evident in the prophecy of Matthew 24. The disciples asked, "When shall these things be? and what shall be the sign of thy coming, and of the end of the world?" Matt. 24:3. In His answer Christ refers to the destruction of Jerusalem and also to the end of the world. We are therefore justified in applying the statement "so much the more, as ye see the day approaching" not only to that age, but to this time when we see the great day of God approaching and hastening on apace.

Hebrews 10:26–31. "For if we sin wilfully after that we have received the knowledge of the truth, there remaineth no more sacrifice for sins, but a certain fearful looking for of judgment and fiery indignation, which shall devour the adversaries. He that despised Moses' law died without mercy under two or three witnesses: of how much sorer punishment, suppose ye, shall he be thought worthy, who hath trodden under foot the Son of God, and hath counted the blood of the covenant, wherewith he was sanctified, an unholy thing, and hath done despite unto the Spirit of grace? For we know him that hath said, Vengeance belongeth unto me, I will recompense, saith the Lord. And again, The Lord shall judge his people. It is a fearful thing to fall into the hands of the living God."

Verse 26. "Sin wilfully." Some have been greatly distressed by these verses dealing with willful sin. They have taken them to mean that any sin which they might have done knowingly or with partial knowledge is the unpardonable sin. But this is not the case. Sin against the Holy Ghost is deliberate, persistent, defiant sin. It is total and final apostasy from which there is no turning back. It refers to those who turn from good to evil, despise the proffered mercy, resist the Spirit, and remain in obdurate rebellion. For such there is no hope.

"Received the knowledge of the truth." From this statement it is evident that those here contemplated are such as have once been Christians. If such fall away, there remain no more offerings for sin.

Verse 27. "A certain fearful expectation of judgment." (R. V.) Some magnify God's justice to the point of injustice, but there are others who minimize both punishment and the evil results of sin to the vanishing point. The writer does not minimize transgression, nor its results. He refers to the fact that those who set at nought the law of Moses died without compassion, and from this draws the conclusion that those who tread underfoot the Son of God, count the blood of the covenant an unholy thing, and do despite to the Spirit of God will be worthy of much sorer punishment. The Lord will recompense, the Lord will judge, and it will be no light punishment. "It is a fearful thing to fall into the hands of the living God," he concludes.

These are strong and even hard words. It is not often that God so speaks. When He does, it is because the matter is of supreme importance. We might confidently draw the conclusion that God considers a knowledge of the truth a most solemn responsibility, and that those who give up their faith in God and the truth are worthy of most severe punishment. It is not they themselves who alone are affected. A man who has talents and a knowledge of the truth, and then departs from the truth, not only loses his own soul , but also powerfully affects others. His own loss is perhaps the smallest loss. The thousands of others who are affected by his example, and the other thousands whom his apostasy deprives of his labor, are the greater part of the loss. In the final accounting it may not be the things we have done that will weigh the most; it is the influence we have exerted, the example we have given, the effect our lives have had on others.

Verse 28. "Two or three witnesses." In case of a serious crime, such as murder, two or three witnesses were required before a person could be held guilty. (Deut. 17:6.) This was both a merciful and a wise provision. It safeguarded justice and tended to discourage false accusations. The same principle holds good today.

Verse 29. "Trodden under foot the Son of God." The contrast is between those who transgressed the law of Moses, and those who transgress in the light of much greater knowledge today. All should know that to reject the offer of salvation is counted as treading underfoot the Son of God.

"The blood of the covenant...an unholy thing." A covenant sealed with blood is a most holy and fearsome thing. To count that which is holy and most sacred an unholy thing is the height of sacrilege. When at Sinai, God spoke in majesty from heaven, and the people fled in terror, men were given a demonstration of the holiness and the terror of God. For men today to count the blood of the covenant an unholy thing, the very blood that means sanctification to those who accept, will surely demand retribution.

"Despite unto the Spirit of grace." This is nothing but sin against the Holy Spirit, a settled condition of resistance, a way of life. For such there is no hope.

Verse 30. "The Lord shall judge." It is well for us not to judge or take matters into our own hands. God has a way of handling things in His own way; and when the time comes, He will act.

Vengeance belongs to God. He is not indifferent to wrong. He knows every slur, every unjust charge, every iniquitous act. It is not always easy for us to wait, but we may rest assured that in His own good time God will recompense.

Verse 31. "The hands of the living God." Words such as these may seem foreign to those who think of God only in terms of meekness and goodness. All know that God is kindness and love; but many forget that there is another side also to God's character, and that He will by no means clear the guilty. (Ex. 34:7.) Men do evil and are not punished in this life; they believe they have escaped the consequences of their transgressions. Let all remember that whatsoever a man soweth, that shall he also reap. It is a fearful thing to fall into the hands of the living God.

Hebrews 10:32–39. "But call to remembrance the former days, in which, after ye were illuminated, ye endured a great fight of afflictions; partly, whilst ye were made a gazingstock both by reproaches and afflictions; and partly, whilst ye became companions of them that were so used. For ye had compassion of me in my bonds, and took joyfully the spoiling of your goods, knowing in yourselves that ye have in heaven a better and an enduring substance. Cast not away therefore your confidence, which hath great recompence of reward. For ye have need of patience, that, after ye have done the will of God, ye might receive the promise. For yet a little while, and he that shall come will come, and will not tarry. Now the just shall live by faith: but if any man draw back, my soul shall have no pleasure in him. But we are not of them who draw back unto perdition; but of them that believe to the saving of the soul."

The apostle asks them to remember how in former days they had suffered, and how God had helped them to take it joyfully. He now asks them to be patient, for it will not be long before they will receive the promise. He encourages them to be faithful and not to draw back.

Verse 32. "The former days." According to 1 Thessalonians 2:14, the early churches in Judea, including Jerusalem, suffered persecution. After they had been "illuminated" they "endured" a "great fight of afflictions." "Fight" here means combat such as an athlete might engage in, whether of wrestling, sword, or endurance. Acts 4–9, 12 record some of the persecutions of the Jerusalem church.

Verse 33. "Gazingstock," or spectacle. The figure is taken from the custom of exhibiting criminals to. public gaze and ridicule in the stocks, and at times to punishment and death in an arena or theater. As it only mentions reproaches and afflictions, it is likely that their trials were confined to these, though torture and death were not uncommon. The reproaches were probably the slanders against the church. The persecutions were not only against the offenders but against those who "were companions of them that were so used."

Verse 34. "Ye had compassion of me in my bonds." This would fit Paul's case, but we have no further details than are here revealed. The persecution and the spoiling of their goods they took joyfully, knowing that in heaven they would be more than repaid for their sorrow here.

Verse 35. "Confidence." Persecution and loss of worldly goods would naturally exert a depressing influence. For this reason they are counseled not to sink into despondency but to hold fast their confidence, or boldness, which has great reward.

Verse 36. "Need of patience," endurance. Patience is not necessarily a negative virtue. The real meaning of patience is endurance, capacity to suffer, the decision not to give up, but to continue to the end. It includes the ordinary meaning of being uncomplaining in tribulation, but its larger meaning is that of unfailing determination to continue despite weariness and obstacles, and not slacken the pace.

"The promise." As an athlete receives the prize after having successfully finished the course, so after having done the will of God the Christian will receive the promise. This promise is that of entering into His rest. (Heb. 4:1; 9:15; 11:13.)

Verse 37. "Yet a little while." There seems to be little doubt that the early church expected deliverance in a little while. As many of them associated the end of the world with the fall of Jerusalem, they expected deliverance, and hoped the Lord would come. Although Paul had a clearer view and wrote of certain things that must first come to pass (see 2 Thess. 2:1–5), there were evidently some things in his letters which they took to mean that he taught "that the day of Christ is at hand." (Verse 2.) This hope of the church is not to be wondered at. It is doubtful that even the strongest in faith would have received much encouragement from the knowledge that the coming of Christ would be delayed centuries and millenniums. "It is not for you to know the times or the seasons, which the Father hath put in his own power." Acts 1:7.

"Will not tarry." This is an undoubted reference to Habakkuk 2:3, where "wait" in the Septuagint is the same word as "endured" in Hebrews 10:32. The noun is translated "patience" in verse 36, but as noted the real meaning is "endurance" rather than the virtue of patience. It is the same word that Christ uses when He says, "He that shall endure unto the end, the same shall be saved." Matt. 24:13.

Verse 38. "The just shall live by faith." This clause is quoted from Habakkuk 2:4, and is used by Paul in Romans 1:17, and Galatians 3:11. It contains in itself the great and wonderful truth of justification by faith, and was the basis of the Protestant reformation.

"Draw back." This has been variously translated: If he draw in, sneak away, slink away and hide; if he flinch. It is a nautical term used when taking in the sails, hauling them down, in view of an approaching storm.

It is often a wise precaution to trim the sails lest the craft be capsized by a strong wind. But the apostle here uses it in the sense of being overcautious. He sensed that the storm was coming. At the time when he wrote there were clear indications that erelong the Roman armies would be at the city gates. This was according to Jesus' prophecy of the destruction of Jerusalem as recorded in the twenty-fourth chapter of Matthew. Doubtless the apostles, and the disciples in general, had pondered much about the coming events.

And now the prophecy was about to be fulfilled. It seems unthinkable that the disciples should remain silent and not use the occasion for calling attention to the truthfulness of Jesus' prediction. This was the opportune moment for them to proclaim the gospel of

Jesus, and they must have been highly remiss had they failed to do so.

It was under these circumstances that some were becoming fainthearted. The signs all showed that destruction was at hand, but instead of taking advantage of the apprehension of the people and the troublous times, they began to draw back, to trim their sails, to flinch. They were cautious, overcautious, and not fully. awake to their opportunity of using the unsettled conditions to impress their message upon the people.

And so Paul warns them. Caution is good; but it may be carried too far. Precious opportunities might be lost unless they stepped into the troubled waters. This was the very time for which they had waited more than thirty years; prophecy was fulfilling before their very eyes—and now some were becoming fainthearted. This was no time to draw back.

There are those who are too bold, and do harm. They rush in where angels fear to tread. But where there is one who is too bold, there are ten who are too timid; and timidity is no better than overboldness. At times it is better to go ahead, even though mistakes are made, than to hold back and do nothing. There are times when risks must be taken if there is to be progress.

Paul repeatedly urges to boldness. In fact, as previously mentioned, Paul counts boldness as one of the signs of sonship. He himself was bold and did not shrink from taking a risk. The result was progress all along the line, and God blessed him. If Paul had not been bold, he never could have done the work he did. To venture something for God, to take advantage of conditions, is one of the privileges of the Christian. Is not this one reason for God's permitting us to be placed in certain conditions and circumstances? What if Esther had not been bold at the right time? or Nathan, or Daniel, or the three young Hebrews, or David in meeting Goliath? God permits conditions to develop, then places us where we can take advantage of them, and leaves us to improve the opportunity He has provided.

Paul knew that there were troublous times just ahead—times that parallel ours. He called for courage, for boldness. That same call holds true today. *They* stood before the events to be fulfilled in the destruction of Jerusalem. *We* stand before the larger fulfillment of Jesus' prophecy in regard to the end of the world. This is no time to haul down the colors, no time to shrink back or be fearful, no time to be timid.

Verse 39. "Draw back unto perdition." The trials may be hard, but there must be no drawing back. We must take our stand with those who believe to the saving of the soul. "Them that believe" forms the transition and introduction to the next chapter, which deals with faith.

ADDITIONAL NOTES

Sanctification

Sanctification is one of the least understood doctrines of the Bible. All kinds of religious excesses have been committed in the name of sanctification, and, precious as the true Bible doctrine is, its perversion has done much injury to the cause of Christ in general, and in particular to those individuals who have become victims of unsound doctrine and religious fanaticism.

It should be had in mind that those who are led astray by the extravagant claims and false doctrine of sanctification are not the religiously careless and indifferent ones. It is often such as are fervent in spirit, and anxious to do God's will, but who have imbibed wrong notions and false ideas, and whose Christian experience tends to shallowness and outward demonstration, while they neglect the solid teaching of the Word of God. They are likely to depend more upon impressions and feelings than upon the revealed will of God in His Word. Only an unusual measure of the Spirit and power of God can ever retrieve them. Thinking they are led by the Spirit of God, they are in the snares of the evil one. The fact that they appear to be deeply religious makes their recovery the more difficult.

Many scoffers have been given occasion to blaspheme because of the religious excesses of fanatical holiness movements, but the greatest harm has been done to the devotees themselves. As has been noted, they may be honest though misguided souls who sincerely wish to serve. This only gives the more point to sound doctrine. In view of this we consider it a duty to present the true Bible doctrine on this important phase of Christianity.

The author of Hebrews considers sanctification as the goal and climax of Christian experience, and one which all should reach. In the tenth chapter he invites all to enter with boldness into the very presence of God through the veil that has been parted for us. (Heb. 10:19, 20.) Again and again throughout the book he presents to his readers the idea of perfection, which rites and ceremonies could never effect, but which has been made possible by the gospel. (Heb. 6:1; 7:19; 9:9; 10:1, 2; 12:10, 14; 13:21.) It may indeed be said that the intent of the writer of Hebrews is to produce holiness, sanctification, in his readers. He is much more intent on this than to write a theological thesis.

CONVERSION AND JUSTIFICATION

It is well to consider conversion and justification before entering upon a discussion of sanctification. The Christian pathway may be illustrated by the following diagram, beginning with conversion and ending with holiness.

$$\left.\begin{array}{l} \text{Conversion} \\ \text{Justification} \end{array}\right\} \text{ THE WAY OF SANCTIFICATION } \left\{\begin{array}{l} \text{Holiness} \\ \text{Perfection} \\ \text{Glorification} \end{array}\right.$$

At conversion a man turns from sin to righteousness, from evil to God. The things he once loved he now hates. He is a new creature. By one act of decision the whole direction of his life is changed, and he begins to follow and imitate the Master.

Conversion may take place in a moment, or it may cover a period of time. Paul's life was changed suddenly on his way to Damascus. He had been a hater of Christians and Christianity, but suddenly he turned and began preaching the very doctrine he had formerly hated.

Conversion, however, is not always accomplished in a moment. It often takes a longer time, as in the case of Nicodemus. One night Christ had a long talk with him and told him that he needed to be born again. (John 3:1–13.) Nicodemus did not understand Christ's language, and not until after the crucifixion does he appear as a converted man and a follower of Christ. (John 19:39.)

There are others who do not seem to pass through any distinct period of conversion. Among these are John the Baptist and Jeremiah, both of whom, we are told, were sanctified from birth. (Luke 1:15; Jer. 1:5.)

From these examples it is clear that no one need be discouraged if he is unable to tell the exact day and hour of his conversion. Whereas Paul was in no doubt as to the exact time of his conversion, Nicodemus would hesitate if he were asked when the change took place. He might name the time when Christ talked to him, but further reflection would indicate to him that conversion took place some time later. John the Baptist and Jeremiah might both hold that they never were converted: they always had been godly men.

We record this because of the fact that some who claim sanctification insist that all must know of a certainty the day and hour of conversion and sanctification, or they are not Christians. Such is not Bible teaching.

The Hebrew word for conversion means "return," "repentance," and is derived from another word which means "to turn back," "to turn again." The Greek word means a change of mind. Both indicate a radical change by which a man turns from his past sinful life, and starts for the kingdom.

We should be guarded, however, in defining conversion as merely a change of mind. Even though it is a change of mind, it is a change that affects the whole life, and is not merely a change of opinion or a change from one kind of theology to another; nor is it a transfer of church membership. Paul describes it thus: "Let this mind be in you, which was also in Christ Jesus." Phil. 2:5. The Christian no longer thinks or talks or acts as he did before. Upon conversion he faces in another direction; his tastes, habits, and pleasures are changed; he is a new creature in Christ Jesus. Old things are passed away; all things have become new.

True conversion means a complete turnabout. In its totality it includes conviction of sin; sorrow for sin; confession; an honest effort at restitution where there has been any misappropriation; acceptance by faith of the glorious promises of forgiveness; public acknowledgment of our new standing with God, including baptism and union with the believers in church fellowship; and last—but not least—a solemn decision by the grace of God to be done with sin forever and to follow Christ's counsel—"Go, and sin no more." John 8:11.

To many, conversion is merely an emotional decision to accept Christ, and does not mean or effect a thorough reformation of life. It would be well for such to study the seven steps presented, all of which are necessary to complete conversion, though the steps need not come in the exact order in which they are here placed. Let us emphasize them by way of repetition.

1. Conviction of sin. In order to abstain from sin, it is necessary to know what sin is. This does not mean that a person must know sin by experience in order to recognize it. But it does mean that it is necessary to know sin and its appearance, so as to be able to avoid it. Some things appear innocent and are likely to deceive the unwary, unless he has some unerring standard by which to recognize sin. This standard is found in the Bible and is exemplified in Christ's life. It is summed up in the Ten Commandments. John says, "Sin is the transgression of the law." 1 John 3:4. However, it is to be remembered that the law is spiritual, and that more is included in the law than appears by a first casual reading of it. It not only deals with outward acts but reaches the motives and intents of the heart.

2. Sorrow for sin. This means personal sorrow in the individual heart. One may be sorry for the sin that is in the world without feeling sorry for his own sins. The conviction must come home to each soul as it did to David when the prophet told him, "Thou art the man." 2 Sam. 12:7.

3. Confession. A sorrow for sin that does not lead to confession is not real sorrow. Confession should be made to God first, then to man. The nature of the confession measures the depth and sincerity of the confession. It must be heartfelt, spontaneous, unforced, free. Failing in any of these, it fails to measure up to God's standard.

4. Restitution. To some, this is the hardest part of conversion, as it means bringing to remembrance some things we would gladly forget. To confess to God the theft of money or other valaubles is a soul-searching experience; to return these stolen valuables to the persons concerned is in some cases very humiliating. Yet there is no other way. But though it may be humiliating, it is also a most blessed experience. It humbles the soul before man; it exalts it before God.

5. Faith in God. Without faith it is impossible to please God. (Heb. 11:6.) It is strange indeed that after God has forgiven a man his sin, he is often tempted to doubt God. Satan would like to have him believe that his sins are so

great that God has not forgiven and cannot forgive him fully. But God requires that we believe Him. However dark or red our sins are, God is able to forgive and cleanse. (Isa. 1:18; 1 John 1:9.) This God asks us to believe.

6. Public acknowledgment. To hide the fact of conversion, to attempt to keep it secret, is not God's plan. God has provided for the public acknowledgment of our changed attitude toward Him. "Go home to thy friends," Christ said to the man possessed with the devil, "and tell them how great things the Lord hath done for thee, and hath had compassion on thee." Mark 5:19. This was a personal testimony of a redeemed soul. The public acknowledgment includes baptism and union with the believers. (Acts 2:38, 41, 47.)

7. Sin no more. This involves faith that God who has begun the good work in us will also finish it.

To the converted sinner God says, as to the sinful woman, "Go, and sin no more." John 8:11. It is of little use to have one's sins forgiven unless we also accept the provision made for complete future triumph over every sin. God has provided this victory for each soul who wishes it. By faith he must claim the power of God not only to forgiveness but to holiness of life.

SANCTIFICATION

This brings us to the subject of sanctification, which is the culminating experience in the life of the Christian here on earth. God's power to salvation is not exhausted in the forgiveness of sins that are past. This is wonderful, but God has an even greater power in reserve, namely that of keeping us from falling.

The diagram on page 399 shows the way of sanctification reaching from conversion to holiness. This is the way each Christian must walk if he is to gain heaven.

Holiness is not obtained at a bound; it is a slow, laborious process, little by little and step after step attaining the height that at first may seem insurmountable. Perseverance and a bountiful supply of the grace of God will accomplish the task.

Sanctification is defined to be "the act or process of God's grace by which the affections of men are purified or alienated from sin and the world, and exalted to a surpreme love of God." Another definition is "the work of the Holy Spirit whereby the believer is freed from sin and exalted to holiness of life." Both definitions are essentially the same.

Sanctification and holiness are generally thought to be identical, and they are indeed used interchangeably. Yet there is a difference. Sanctification is "the act or process of God's grace by which the affections of men are purified or alienated from sin." Though sanctification is an act or process, it may also denote the finished product, and as such is equivalent to holiness. Holiness may be defined as the state resulting from sanctification. It is not so much a process as a result. It is perfected sanctification. Thus considered, conversion is the beginning of the Christian race; sanctification, the way or road the Christian must travel to reach the mark; and holiness, the goal or the end of the road, the equivalent of perfection. God is holy; God is perfect. He does not become so; He always has been. Man is asked to strive after these same virtues, but should be hesitant in claiming their possession.

A man at conversion finds himself happy and joyous at the thought that all his past wicked life is forgiven. He knows the many evils of which he has been guilty and rejoices at the wonderful goodness of God in pardoning him. His joy knows no bounds. He has been a slave to drink and other sinful habits, but now he is free.

Or is he? Some are, and never have another craving. But others are still tempted and have a daily battle to resist evil. They do not give in to the tempter, but the craving is still there, and at times it seems more than they can bear. But they are determined to gain the victory, determined to persevere, and though they battle to the death they do not yield; and at last they are free, and Satan leaves them. What a wonderful experience and what a wonderful day is this! Victory in Christ! No more temptations.

But let no one be deceived by Satan's tactics. He may leave, and stay away, but he may also return. He did this in the case of Christ. "When the devil had ended all the temptation, he departed from him *for a season.*" Luke 4:13. And so he may do with men. For this reason we are counseled, "Let him that thinketh he standeth, take heed left he fall." 1 Cor. 10:12. Many times those who have congratulated themselves on their accomplishment are at that very moment in the greatest danger of falling.

The man who resists unto blood, striving against sin, will receive due credit for his attainment. But God's plan includes a higher experience than this. It is possible to attain to such a degree of hatred for sin that it ceases to be a temptation. The man who has decided by the grace of God to gain the victory over intoxicants and tobacco may manfully resist every temptation and never once fall. He is credited with victory and will receive his reward. But someday the conviction will come to him that the same God who can keep him from falling can also remove the desire for evil and cause him to hate it. He has never prayed for hatred before; but now he begins to pray, not merely that God will take away the taste, but that He will give him a hatred for the evil. And in response to earnest pleading God gives the man his desire, and he has complete victory. The things he once loved he now hates. He is sanctified completely on that point.

One trouble with Christians who long for deliverance is that they expect God in some miraculous way to get them ready for the kingdom. They have asked God to forgive their sins and give them victory, and having done so, they consider their part done, and now it is for God to work. But God expects them to co-operate. The Bible counsel is to "work out your own salvation with fear and, trembling. For it is God which worketh in you both to will and to do of his good pleasure." Phil. 2:12, 13.

There may be those who can battle ten enemies at once, but most of us are unable to do this. The man who is attacked by the demon Drink has about all he can do to handle this one demon, and is unable to take on half a dozen others. He must concentrate on the case in hand. Only when he has successfully disposed of one enemy is he ready for another. God in mercy will generally give him a little breathing spell to regain his strength for the next encounter.

Christians are in danger of making the mistake of attempting to battle all the evil forces at once. Few, if any, can do this. Even David did not challenge the whole Philistine army at once. It might have been disastrous. He had enough to do in concentrating on Goliath. And God gave him a glorious victory.

In like manner Christians would do well to concentrate on some particular sin or weakness, instead of scattering their efforts. We may pray for the conversion of the world in general, but for our own personal task it is better to confine our work to a few souls on whom we bestow special efforts. As we win souls one by one, so let us attack evils one by one.

As we thus walk along the way of sanctification, meeting one problem after another as it comes to us, we are progressing in sanctification and nearing the goal of holiness. From the moment we start, God is imputing righteousness to us. We are indeed not perfected, but we are headed in the right direction, and should we die before we reach the goal, God will adjudge our motives and give us credit for what we would have done had we had the opportunity.

The fruit of a tree is not perfected in a day. It takes weeks and months from the time when the bud first appears before a tree produces a ripe apple. Yet each stage reveals perfection. The bud is perfect, so is the first incomplete fruit, and so is the perfected fruit. So it is also with a human being. The little babe may be perfect, so the child, so the developing youth, so the grown man. Perfect, but not complete.

The Bible uses the word "perfect" to denote two things—the incomplete though perfect stage, and the completed perfection. Note Paul's statement in Philippians

3:12: "Not as though I had already attained, either were already perfect."

Paul did not claim to have been "made perfect" (A.R.V.); but in verse 15 he states, "Let us therefore, as many as be perfect, be thus minded." In verse 12 he states that he is not perfect; in verse 15 he says he is. Young translates verse 12: "Or have been already perfected"; and verse 15 "As many, therefore, as are perfect." Robertson, in *Word Pictures*, says that "perfect" in verse 12 is the "perfect passive indicative (state of completion) of *teleioo*....Paul pointedly denies that he has reached a spiritual impasse of non-development. Certainly he knew nothing of so-called sudden absolute perfection by any single experience. Paul has made great progress in Christlikeness, but the goal is still before him, not behind him." On "perfect" in verse 15 he says, "Here the term *teleioi* means relative perfection, not the absolute perfection so pointedly denied in verse 12."—Volume 4, pp. 454, 455.

This explains Paul's statement. He does not claim absolute perfection, which is equivalent to holiness, but he does claim relative perfection. This is emphasized in verse 16: "Whereto we have already attained," or better, "To the place where we have come." Paul did not claim that all had proceeded equally far on the Christian highway, but "whereto we have come," wherever that place may be, we are to be relatively perfect.

Will any ever attain to the perfection to which Paul said he had not. attained? We should be disappointed if Paul had claimed absolute perfection; for no man who attains to this will ever claim it, or perhaps know it. God knows, but man himself will make no such claim.

But will any ever reach that stage? We believe so. Read the description of the 144,000 in Revelation 14:4, 5: "These are they which were not defiled with women; for they are virgins. These are they which follow the Lamb whithersoever he goeth. These were redeemed from among men, being the firstfruits unto God and to the Lamb. And in their mouth was found no guile: for they are without fault before the throne of God."

Note that these are "without fault before the throne of God." They will be among those of whom it is said, "He that is holy, let him be holy still." Rev. 22:11. This, as will be noted from verse 12, refers to those who are living before the Lord comes and who have attained to holiness. Had they not so attained, it could not truly be said, "Let him be holy still."

Anyone who claims to have attained to a state of holiness may confidently be said to be destitute of it. The nearer a sinful man comes to God, the more aware he is of his own shortcomings. Only when a man loses sight of God does he claim holiness.

This is not written to discourage anyone from attaining perfection, but from making claims to having reached it. There is, indeed, a definite call for men to give themselves wholly to the power of God for the attainment of holiness. Before the end comes God will have a people behind in no good thing. They will reflect the image of God fully.

THE 144,000

When Paul, in Hebrews 10:19, 20, speaks of entering into the holy places by (margin, "in") the blood of Jesus, he has particular reference to the 144,000, those who "follow the Lamb whithersoever He goeth." Rev. 14:4. Only the high priest was permitted to enter the most holy place. Ordinary priests could not do so. When the 144,000, therefore, are said to follow the Lamb wherever He goes, and when we know that He as high priest goes into the most holy, then we know that the 144,000 are high priests, if they are to go with Him into the holiest of all. As God's people are kings and priests, so this special company are kings and high priests, following Him wherever He leads.

The priests of old were commissioned to transact with God. They bore heavy responsibilities in offering for and representing the people. But their work, important as it was, did not begin to compare with that of the high priest. In him, Israel appeared before God; he bore the golden band with the inscription "Holiness to the Lord," and he only could enter the most holy on the Day of Atonement. His entrance on that day was accomplished only after the most thorough preparation. Seven days before the great day he left his home and spent day and night in confessing his sins and communing with God. When on the Day of Atonement he tremblingly approached God, removed his royal garments, put on the garments of humility, and lifted the veil that separated him from God's immediate presence, there was not a personal sin remaining in him, or he would have been blotted out of existence. Only he who is holy can bear sins; hence the high priest must be without spot or wrinkle. Only thus could he approach God.

This thorough preparation gives a view of what God expects of His chosen people in these days. They also must be without fault before the throne of God; not a sin must cleave to them.

It is in those 144,000 that God will stand justified. They are of the last generation, the weakest of the weak, bearing the results of the sins of past generations. In them God makes the demonstration of His power in humanity—what He can do in and with sinful man. Long enough has Satan taunted God, "Where are they that keep the commandments of God and the faith of Jesus?" With the 144,000 before Him, God can quietly answer, "Here are they that keep the commandments of God, and the faith of Jesus." Rev. 14:12.

When Christ entered the sanctuary in heaven, it was not with the blood of dead animals, but "by his own blood he entered once into the holy place, having. obtained eternal redemption for us." Heb. 9:12. When we "enter into the holiest by [in] the blood of Jesus" we enter by the new and living way which He has consecrated for us. (Heb. 10:20.)

There was nothing in Christ that needed any blood or incense to shield or cover Him in the presence of God. His life was pure and holy, not a spot or fault anywhere. He could enter with boldness, for He had done the Father's will and had not come short in anything. it was in and by virtue of His life that He entered; and it is by virtue of the same we enter. "It is the blood that maketh atonement *by reason of the life."* Lev. 17:11, A.R.V. It was the life Jesus had lived that as man gave Him access to the Father in our behalf. In His divinity He needed no enabling blood as means of entry. As the perfect man He entered with boldness in virtue of His blood, His life.

The 144,000 have the patience of the saints; they keep the commandments of God, and they also have the faith of Jesus. For them the doors of heaven will swing wide open. They enter as those who have a right to the tree of life, and with holy boldness they go with Jesus even into the presence of God. In this group God completes the demonstration of His power to save. The vilest sinners can be made fit companions for the saints in light. If these persons chosen from the last and weakest generation can endure the test given them, there is no excuse for the fall of Adam. He, in the fullness of strength, failed in the smallest test; these, in all the weakness of humanity, pass.a test infinitely greater. Hence, God cannot be accused of requiring more of Adam than he could do.

God is now looking for candidates for immortality. He is looking for men and women to make up the number required in the last demonstration. He wants converted, sanctified, dedicated people, such as will not boast of their attainments, but who in humility will follow in the Master's footsteps, exercise the faith He did, have the patience needed to finish the work, and at last enter with Him through the gates into the city.

CHAPTER 11

OF THE BOOK OF HEBREWS

Faith

SYNOPSIS OF CHAPTER

THE PREVIOUS chapters have presented a very high standard to which the Christian must attain. The standard indeed is so high that some may conclude that, it is impossible for them to reach it. How can a sinful man ever attain to holiness? How can he ever expect to enter the holy places by the new and living way that Christ has opened for us?

The eleventh chapter of Hebrews answers these questions. Here are portrayed men and women, common men and women, who "all died in the faith" and "obtained a good report." Some of them were good people, as men count goodness. Some were not so good. Some were bad, very bad. In that list are men who broke the commandments; women who lived in sin; men of little faith; one murderer; one whose very name declared his unfitness for the kingdom. Yet all died in faith. God did miracles for them.

As this chapter is read,, many will catch the point of view from which it was written. Of whatever sins anyone may be guilty, he will find in this list names that will cause him to say, "I have been wicked, and have done shameful things. But I do not believe I have done worse things than these. If these people can be saved, there is hope for me also."

It is for this purpose that God has placed this chapter where it is in the book of Hebrews.

Hebrews 11:1–3. "Now faith is the substance of things hoped for, the evidence of things not seen. For by it the elders obtained a good report. Through faith we understand that the worlds were framed by the word of God, so that things which are seen were not made of things which do appear."

Verse 1. "Faith is the substance of things hoped for." For "substance" see comment on chapter 1, verse 3, where "Person" is the same word in the original as "substance" here. This verse is not so much a definition of faith as a statement of what faith will do. It presents faith so strong and vital that the person not only feels himself in possession of that which he has not as yet received but is caused to experience the strength, the courage, and the confidence that ordinarily only actual possession would give. Faith thus enables a Christian not only to claim promised blessings but to *have* and enjoy them now. "The powers of the world to come," become a present possession; and the kingdom of heaven is not merely a future possibility; it is even now within. Faith gives the "good things to come" a real subsistence in the soul and mind. They are no longer dreams to be fulfilled in the future; they are living realities which the soul enjoys and appreciates. They cease to be far-off visions, and become substance. We see the invisible. The old Syriac Version of the Scriptures well translates: "Now faith is the persuasion of things that are in hope, as if they were in fact; and the manifestation of things not seen."

"The evidence of things not seen." "Evidence" here is not merely an abstract belief that evidence exists, but convincing proof already demonstrated, and the soul, persuaded of its truth, rests secure in that belief.

Verse 2. "The elders obtained a good report." There are those who doubt that all the persons mentioned in this chapter obtained a good report. But if we are correct in our belief that this chapter is inserted at this place in Hebrews to encourage us to believe that there is a possibility that even the weakest may attain, then the list would appropriately include names of men about whom we might naturally entertain some doubt. If only the mighty heroes of faith were listed here, it would be of little encouragement to the common man. But if others are included—men of like passion as we are—and if we find that these also obtained a good report, then this chapter serves the purpose for which it was intended.

Verse 3. "Through faith we understand." Men today are confronted with two accounts of creation: one, the scientific account provided by those who believe in the evolution theory; and the other, the Biblical account found in the first chapters of Genesis. These theories do not agree. They are diametrically opposed one to the other. Attempts to harmonize them have not met with success. If men accept one, they must reject the other. There is no middle ground.

It would be incorrect, however, to suppose that in this dilemma we are confronted on one hand by ascertained scientific conclusions based upon fact and research in which faith has no place, and on the other hand by a naïve Biblical account, to accept which we must reject the finding of science and repudiate all scientific evidence. It is not quite so simple as that.

For clarification it may be stated that no believer in special creation by divine fiat has any quarrel with facts as such. That would indeed be folly. The disagreement is not on the facts as such but on the deductions drawn from them. It is well known that from the same set of facts different conclusions may be reached. This is the case in regard to the theory of evolution. No one disputes ascertained and verified facts. But the deductions drawn from them by proponents of the evolution theory are subject to grave doubts.

Believers in evolution are far from agreement among themselves. Even though the original Darwinian theory is no longer held, there is no unanimous agreement on any other theory. Some minimize these differences, and say that all evolutionists are in substantial agreement, but the facts do not justify such optimism. Also, the differences appear to become more pronounced with the years. All are clear that there are missing steps in the evolution ladder, and to some it seems that the gaps are so great as to make ascent impossible. Scientists are searching for the missing rungs and are hopeful of finding them, but so far they have not been successful. To the layman this is all very confusing. Up to the present time the scientists have presented no convincing case.

Turning from this confused picture, let us consider the Biblical account. In thirty-four short verses in the first and the second chapters of Genesis the story is told. It is a simple, straightforward account of how God created. Later God Himself confirmed the story when with His own voice from heaven He proclaimed to mankind that "in six days the Lord made heaven and earth, the sea, and all that in them is, and rested the seventh day: wherefore the Lord blessed the Sabbath day, and hallowed it." Ex. 20:11.

These words God Himself spoke from Sinai. They are part of the Ten Commandments accepted by Christians as the fundamental law of conduct, and a summary of the whole duty of man. They are the basis of all human law and justice. They cannot be lightly set aside as "Jewish" or provincial. They still abide as vital pillars both of society and of state.

In the midst of this law God tells us how the world was made. We can conceive of no other reason for God's announcing this from heaven than the evident intention to tell men the truth of creation in view of the situation which He knew would develop in the world and even among Christians.

There are those who reject the Mosaic account of creation as recorded in Genesis as unworthy of credence. Moses simply wrote down current tradition, they say. However, there is more involved than this. It is not the first chapter of Genesis only that is at stake. It is the Ten Commandments; it is the content of the revelation that God made from heaven the only time in which He spoke audibly to mankind. If a man has any faith whatever in the Bible, he has faith in the Ten Commandments. But he cannot retain that faith and also accept the theory of evolution. God says, "In six days the Lord made heaven and earth." Evolution says: "God did nothing of the kind. The six days were not six days but long periods of time, hundreds of millions of years each. Also, neither the heavens nor the earth were ever 'made'; they evolved. And in the final analysis, *God* did not do what was done. Unconscious forces were at work;

gradually and eventually life appeared; this life kept on evolving until man appeared; we are still on the upgrade, and the end is not in sight."

It should be clearly understood that there is no common ground between the theory of evolution and belief in the Genesis account of creation. It is one or the other, not both, nor parts of both. The line of demarcation is clear. Acceptance of the theory of evolution means a definite rejection of God's statement publicly proclaimed that *He* made the world and the universe.

It must be admitted that it is most unusual that a statement as to the method of creation should be incorporated in the constitutional law of the universe. As noted before, it seems that God did this for the avowed purpose of having it declared on the highest authority that God is Creator, and that men's contrary opinions in this matter have no weight.

God refers to creation in a unique way in another place. Job and his friends had declaimed learnedly concerning things of which they had little knowledge. In answer, God demands of Job, "Where wast thou when I laid the foundations of the earth? declare, if thou hast understanding." Job 38:4. Then He adds these ironic words, "Knowest thou it, because thou wast then born? or because the number of thy days is great?" Verse 21.

Not often does God use sarcasm. But these words are sarcastic, biting. We cannot believe that the rebuke was for Job alone, but also for those to whom it so fittingly applies today. The rebuke is for whomever it fits.

We do not wish to impute human motives to God, yet we feel impelled to say that God must be weary of hearing men talk learnedly of that of which they have

415

no knowledge. Of them it may truly be said, "Ye have wearied the Lord with your words." Mal. 2:17. As we survey the subject of creation, it seems to us that God considers it the height of folly and impudence for man to dispute His word in regard to creation. *God* was there; *He* spoke the word; *He* made the worlds; and now comes puny man and challenges God's truthfulness, tells how creation came about, or rather, denies that there was any creation! *That* makes God weary. That arouses Him to sarcastic words, and—if the supposition is true that Job is the oldest book in the Bible, written before Sinai—incites Him to include in the commandments proclaimed from heaven the statement that He is the Creator of all things, and that in six days He did that which is recorded in the first chapter of Genesis.

On the one hand, therefore, we have the word of science; which, however, has never claimed for evolution more than that it is merely a theory, and not an established fact. But this is only seeming humility. For though it is said to be only a theory, in reality it is accepted as a fact. To hold that it is only a theory may serve as a convenient excuse in case science should change its opinion. In that case it would be heralded far and wide that it has always been held only as a theory. It would be well if scientists announced this fact as loudly now as they will then.

On the other hand we have God's statement that He was the one who created, and that in six days He made heaven and earth. This is a simple straight-forward pronouncement that accounts for all the facts. True, it rests upon faith—faith in God and in His Word. But this faith is certainly much more intelligent than the belief that blind and unconscious forces are adequate to the production of intelligent life, of moral creatures, of spiritual beings.

"Things which are seen." This includes the whole visible universe with all the things therein. Of these it is stated that they "were not made of things which do appear." This may seem an awkward way of stating their origin, but we may take for granted that the words were chosen with care, and correctly interpret what God had in mind. These words do not directly affirm that what we see was made out of nothing, but they do say that it was not made of things which do appear. It is clear that creation took place in time, and that matter therefore had a beginning. Unless it is self-existent, there was a time when it did not exist, when it was not. That which then came into being at God's command had no previous existence. God was not indebted to pre-existing matter in the creation of this earth or any other world. He simply called into existence that which we now see. As it had not existed before, it was "creation out of nothing," or "of things which do not appear," by an act of God. While we cannot understand this language, nor how God created out of nothing, we by faith accept it.

The theory of evolution does not attempt to account for the beginning of things; that is, for how things came into existence. Evolutionists need a God to create matter as much as creationists do, unless they prefer to believe in the eternity of matter. But that is no easier than to believe in an eternal God. In either case faith is needed. But faith in a God who can create is much more reasonable than belief in self-created matter which in some way leaped the gulf from dead, unconscious, and blind forces to living organisms that eventually arrive at the point where they challenge the Almighty God, as evolutionists do.

Hebrews 11:4. "By faith Abel offered unto God a more excellent sacrifice than Cain, by which he obtained witness that he was righteous, God testifying of his gifts: and by it he being dead yet speaketh."

"By faith Abel." Abel "brought of the firstlings of his flock." Gen. 4:4. He brought the best he had. This is not said of Cain. He simply "brought of the fruit of the ground," evidently what came to hand without any attempt to bring the best. Verse 3. Abel offered "a more excellent sacrifice than Cain," not merely because he brought a slain animal, but because he offered it "by faith." As the whole chapter in Hebrews deals with faith, it is only natural that the author should stress faith more than the nature of the offering. However, it is to be had in mind that Abel's faith was shown by his works. We cannot escape the conclusion that Abel by faith grasped the promises of God, by faith saw the Lamb of God dying for him, and by faith brought his own lamb. As Cain brought the fruit of the ground, so did Abel, as the word "also" suggests. But he did more. By faith "he also brought of the firstlings of his flock." Abel's faith and the nature of his offering constituted his "a more excellent sacrifice than" Cain's.

"He obtained witness that he was righteous." Christ mentions "righteous Abel," or more correctly, "Abel, the righteous," in Matthew 23:35. Abel obtained this witness by faith, as evidenced by his works. As we are not given any detail concerning his life, nor told of any great thing he did, except in regard to his sacrifice, we may conclude that God considers right forms of worship important. We have no reason to believe that Cain previously had become an object of God's wrath. But the form of his worship, the nature and kind of his offering, displeased God. Cain worshiped, but the essential faith was lacking. This was the real ground of Cain's failure.

"God testifying of his gifts." God is not swayed by the gift of any man. The cattle upon a thousand hills are His. We cannot believe that God considers a lamb of so much more value than the fruit of the fields that for this reason He is pleased with Abel and displeased with Cain. The distinction is not in the gift as such, except as the gift reveals the character and the thinking of the giver. The stress therefore is laid on faith. Abel had faith, and by faith he offered a lamb, symbolic of the lamb of God.

"He being dead yet speaketh." The lesson of Abel is that of faith, of worship, of sacrifice. He has been dead nearly six thousand years, but his influence has not ceased. He took of his best and gave to God; he mixed faith with his offering; his faith and his work were in harmony. God testified to his righteousness, and the result of his faithfulness is still continuing. He "yet speaketh."

Hebrews 11:5, 6. "By faith Enoch was translated that he should not see death; and was not found, because God had translated him: for before his translation he had this testimony, that he pleased God. But without faith it is impossible to please him: for he that cometh to God must believe that he is, and that he is a rewarder of them that diligently seek him."

Verse 5. "By faith Enoch." Enoch was translated by faith, or because of his faith. As Abel, so also Enoch pleased God, "for before his translation he had this testimony, that he pleased God."

Enoch is one of the two men in the Old Testament who did not die but were translated, the other being Elijah. We have no record of any in the New Testament being thus honored, though some believe that Paul's hesitancy in choosing what he should do—being in a straight betwixt two—was connected with a possible translation. (Phil. 1:23, 24.)

Enoch's case is a demonstration of what God can do with sinful humanity. The record of his life is short. It tells only that "Enoch lived sixty and five years, and begat Methuselah: and Enoch walked with God after he begat Methuselah three hundred years, and begat sons and daughters: and all the days of Enoch were three hundred sixty and five years: and Enoch walked with God: and he was not; for God took him." Gen. 5:21–24.

In the record of Enoch's translation as compared with the death of Adam we find a beautiful example of God's love and mercy.

Adam was 622 years old when Enoch was born. As Adam lived to be 930 years old, he and Enoch lived contemporaneously more than three hundred years. The statement that Enoch walked with God three hundred years after the birth of Methuselah suggests that the greater responsibility of fatherhood made him more conscious of his need of God.

There is no record in the Bible of anyone's dying before Adam, with the exception of Abel, who was killed. It is, of course, possible that some, perhaps many, of those who had apostatized from God died, without that fact's being recorded in the Bible.

Adam, the first man to live, was also the first of the godly line to die, with the exception of Abel mentioned above. At Adam's death all his descendants were still living, including Noah's father, Lamech, who at that time was fifty-six years old. Thus these all had had opportunity to talk personally with the man whom God had created, who had been in the Garden of Eden, and who had associated with angels and with God. Their knowledge of conditions before the fall was therefore derived directly from Adam, and it must have been a thrill for them to commune with the man who had communed with God. With what interest they must have listened as he told of that first Sabbath when God was with man, when heaven and earth were one, and God talked with man face to face. And what an impression it must have made upon all as Adam told of the fall and his exclusion from Eden. Those interviews Were never to be forgotten.

But now Adam was dead. He was the father of all living, and his funeral was likely the largest ever held. From all over the then-inhabited earth men came; for even though many had forsaken God, upon the death of the first man all must have wanted to be present. There were doubtless some of the godly seed who had hoped that in the case of Adam an exception would be made, and that he would not need to lay down the life that had been given him of God. But no exception was made. The wages of sin is death, and even Adam must pay the penalty.

The death of the first man must have deeply affected saint and sinner alike. Doubtless he had many times warned the wayward ones of the result of their wickedness. Now his voice was stilled; but his death was in itself a testimony to the faithfulness of God. Adam had warned them of the judgment of God upon sin, and now they saw that God was no respecter of persons. If God did not spare Adam, surely He would not spare them. For them Adam's death was a solemn occasion.

It was no less solemn for those who served God. A thousand questions they had asked of Adam, and now there were a thousand others they would like to ask. But it was too late. No more would they hear the recital of the glories of the paradise of God; no more would they hear of the tragedy of being driven out from the garden. All that was in the past.

Especially must Enoch have been sorrowfully interested. He was then walking with God as had Adam in paradise, and many must have been the precious seasons they spent together. At the time of Adam's death Enoch was about three hundred years old, and had thus walked with God a long while. He must have felt very near to God as he associated with Him from day to day, and Enoch's companionship was doubtless a great comfort to Adam in his declining years.

However, beyond the personal loss which the mourners might have felt, the fact of Adam's death must have cast a shadow over all the future. Was death the portion of all living, whether they served God or not? Did God make no distinction between those who served Him and those who did not? Adam had sinned, but he had repented and turned to God. But that did not seem to make any difference: death had come to him as it doubtless would to all. With no clear hope of a resurrection, the future must have seemed dark to them. It was with deep forebodings that they returned to their homes.

It was necessary that God should make no exception in the case of Adam. Had He done so, the lesson of death as a result of sin would have been lost. As it was, all were deeply impressed with the fact that the wages of sin is death.

But necessary as it was that Adam should die, it was just as necessary that God give assurance of something better, assurance of a resurrection, of a life hereafter. This He did in the case of Enoch.

Enoch had faithfully walked with God many years. As God had shown in the case of Adam that the wages of sin is death, would it not be appropriate to show that he who serves God with fullness of affection will receive a reward? Such a demonstration would be as powerful a testimony to the mercy and kindness of God, as the death of Adam had been to His justice. And it would give courage and hope to all.

"And Enoch walked with God: and he was not; for God took him." These thirteen words contain a complete story of a man's life, its successful conclusion, and his acceptance by God. He was so thoroughly one with God that he walked with Him here, and, without seeing death, entered into eternal bliss.

In the translation of Enoch, God showed the universe that though sin may separate man from his Maker, there is a way whereby this separation may be annulled, and man come back to God again. This must have given courage to the patriarchs of old as they looked toward the future. There was no escaping the fact that sin meant death; that they had seen demonstrated in the death of Adam. But the lesson of Enoch was just as clear: man may walk with God here, and at last be taken home to the celestial abodes.

Enoch is a type of those who will be translated from the last generation. He became a friend of God, walked with Him, and at last went home with Him. Let all therefore take courage. God will not exclude anyone by reason of birth or age. Whoever serves God with a full heart and walks with Him will have an abundant entrance into the paradise of God.

Verse 6. "Without faith it is impossible to please him." According to this verse two things are necessary to faith: belief that God exists, and belief that He has a standard of moral values, a divine government, and that by the rules of that government those who diligently seek Him will be rewarded.

There are those who believe that God is morally indifferent; that He has given man freedom of choice, and is not concerned about the kind of choice he makes. This verse informs us that this conception is not true. God *does* care what men do, and virtue will not go unrewarded. God will reward those who diligently seek Him. Men need to know that God's government is a moral government, and of this we are here assured.

Hebrews 11:7. "By faith Noah, being warned of God of things not seen as yet, moved with fear, prepared an ark to the saving of his house; by the which he condemned the world, and became heir of the righteousness which is by faith."

Verse 7. "By faith Noah...prepared an ark." The history of Noah is of special interest to this generation, as he is a type of those who will be living at the time of the second coming of Christ. (Matt. 24:37–39.)

Noah was the great-grandson of Enoch, who had walked with God and who at last had been translated. His father, Lamech, lived 113 years contemporaneously with Enoch, and must therefore have been well acquainted with him. Lamech was fifty-six years old when Adam died, and it is reasonable to suppose that many times he told to his son the stories that he himself had heard from the father of the race. In those days the family ties were closer than they are now, and often several generations found shelter under the same roof. Doubtless Adam was the revered father of the household—age in those days was reverenced by all—and numerous were the times when he was called upon to relate the stories of the time when he was in paradise and talked with God. These stories Noah thus received from his own father, who had heard them related by Adam. It may justly be thought that the men of old had much better perception of the vital issues involved in the fall than some have now. They heard the account from the men directly involved, who had been eyewitnesses, and thus knew firsthand of what they spoke.

We know very little about Noah. Nothing is recorded of the first five hundred years of his life except the statement by God, "Thee have I seen righteous before me in this generation." Gen. 7:1. For this reason God promised that He would establish His covenant with him. (Gen. 6:18.) We therefore conclude that Noah was a good man, but that he lived an ordinary life, and that no great event happened to him until the time of the Flood. That he was not completely perfect is evident from the statements by God that he "was a just man and perfect *in his generations,*" and "thee have I seen righteous before me *in this generation.*" Gen. 6:9; 7:1. Despite this, God could use him, and did. Doubtless the times of Noah were such that the wickedness prevailing affected even the saints.

The fact that God calls Noah righteous, even though he had not reached the perfect standard, should be a matter of comfort to all. There are those who may have been reared where the light of the gospel has never penetrated fully, but who are living up to all the light they have. They are not perfect by the absolute standard of holiness; but in view of their surroundings, in view of the light they have, they are perfect *in their generation,* perfect considering the privileges they have. It may even be true that some of these are far more perfect according to the light they have than others who have much greater opportunities. We must beware lest we judge.

That God did not account the righteousness of Noah as an inferior kind is evident from the way it is mentioned in other places. Says God in Ezekiel 14:14, "Though these three men, Noah, Daniel, and Job, were in it, they should deliver but their own souls by their righteousness, saith the Lord God." This is repeated in verse 18. God places Noah with such men as Daniel and Job, giving due credit to the genuineness of Noah's experience

Even though God thus gives recognition to relative perfection, this is not to be taken by anyone as a lowering of His requirements. They are the same as ever. God simply applies the principle enunciated in Psalms 87:4–6: "I will make mention of Rahab and Babylon to them that know me: behold Philistia, and Tyre, with Ethiopia; this man was born there. And of Zion it shall be said, This and that man was born in her: and the highest himself shall establish her. The Lord shall count, when he writeth up the people, that this man was born there."

We are therefore not to think that increased light brings greater reward. It is not the light we have that determines our future; it is how we use the light. We may pity those who we think are in darkness, and contrast their position with the glorious light God has given us, But it is better not to despise any. In the sight of God they may be counted of more worth than others who are blessed with far greater opportunities.

"As the days of Noe were, so shall also the coming of the Son of man be." Matt. 24:37.

"Things not seen as yet." We do not know the way in which God chose to warn Noah—whether by dream, vision, or direct revelation. In any event, the things of which he was warned were not seen as yet. Moved with fear, he prepared an ark for the saving of his house. The fear that moved him was not fear of the coming Flood. "Fear" here is closely connected with "godly fear" in Hebrews 12:28. Noah believed God, though the things revealed to him were yet in the future. His confidence in God caused him to act out his faith, and by that act he condemned the world. The things that were coming were not seen, but Noah's faith *could* be seen in what he did. The same faith that condemned the world made him heir of the righteousness which is by faith.

It should be a matter of genuine concern to the people of God living at this time, to make sure whether their faith is such that their works condemn the world, or whether their works meet the approbation of the world and the displeasure of God. If the world is to be warned of "the things not seen as yet," and if God's people now are to do as effective a work as did Noah, they need to look after their works.

Although this eleventh chapter of Hebrews deals primarily with faith, it does not omit works. It will be noted that the men not only believed God but showed their faith by their works. Abel sacrificed, Enoch walked with God, Noah built an ark. And so with the other men in this chapter. They all had faith, and they all did something.

Hebrews 11:8–12. "By faith Abraham, when he was called to go out into a place which he should after receive for an inheritance, obeyed; and he went out, not knowing whither he went. By faith he sojourned in the land of promise, as in a strange country, dwelling in tabernacles with Isaac and Jacob, the heirs with him of the same promise: for he looked for a city which hath foundations, whose builder and maker is God. Through faith also Sara herself received strength to conceive seed, and was delivered of a child when she was past age, because she judged him faithful who had promised. Therefore sprang there even of one, and him as good as dead, so many as the stars of the sky in multitude, and as the sand which is by the sea shore innumerable."

Verse 8. "By faith Abraham...went out." Terah, the father of Abraham, lived in Ur of the Chaldees, but decided to move from there into the land of Canaan. Accordingly, he gathered his family together, "to go into the land of Canaan." Gen. 11:31. However, they never reached there. Instead, "they came unto Haran, and dwelt there. And the days of Terah were two hundred and five years: and Terah died in Haran." Gen. 11:31, 32.

Haran is a long distance from Ur, almost halfway to the Promised Land. We do not know why Terah decided to go that far, and then stop. But he did. And he stayed in Haran not merely to rest; but many years passed, and at last he died there.

After the death of Terah the word of the Lord came to Abraham while he yet dwelt in Haran, "Get thee out of thy country, and from thy kindred, and from thy father's house, unto a land that I will shew thee." Gen. 12:1. Accordingly, "Abram took Sarai his wife, and Lot his brother's son, and all their substance that they had gathered, and the souls that they had gotten in Haran; and they went forth to go into the land of Canaan; and into the land of Canaan they came." Gen. 12:5.

Note the likeness and the contrast between the two statements. Terah went "forth with them from Ur of the Chaldees, to go into the land of Canaan; and they came unto Haran, and dwelt there." Gen. 11:31. Abraham and his family "went forth to go into the land of Canaan; and into the land of Canaan they came." Gen. 12:5. Terah and Abraham both started for the same goal. Terah reached the halfway mark; Abraham went all the way.

"Not knowing whither he went." Abraham's journey was purely a matter of faith. He did not know where he was going, he knew nothing of the country; and when he arrived in Canaan, it was far from being what he might have expected. There was famine in the land; the Canaanites were not friendly to the newcomers, and Abraham was compelled to go down into Egypt temporarily. It was purely a matter of faith with him. He had prospered in Haran; he had gotten much substance and many souls there; and there was no reason for his going elsewhere. But at God's command he left Haran and did not return.

Verses 9, 10. Abraham did not feel at home in his new environs, and "sojourned in the land of promise as in a strange country, dwelling in tabernacles." But it never occurred to him to yield to the temptation to go back to Haran. He had orders to get out of that country, and when famine came he went down into Egypt instead. He was obeying God unquestioningly, and God honored his faith.

It was during this time of wandering that Abraham's mind was definitely called to a better country. He had no abiding place here, no settled home, and so "he looked for a city which hath foundations, whose builder and maker is God." God was weaning him away from the things of earth, and causing his mind to dwell on that better country.

Verses 11, 12. "Sarah herself received strength." Sarah was ninety years old when Isaac was born. She was "past age," and laughed at God when she was told she should have a son. But nevertheless through faith Sarah "received strength to conceive seed." See comments under Hebrews 6:13, 14.

No one can read the story of the birth of Isaac and fail to be impressed with the lack of faith displayed by both Abraham and Sarah before the birth of their son. True, Abraham had faith at first, but as the years rolled on and no son was born, his faith began to dim. At Sarah's suggestion he took to himself another wife, and a son was born; but he was told by the Lord that this was not the promised heir. When God at last told him that within a year Sarah should have a son, he laughed outright at God, and later Sarah laughed also. (Gen. 17:17; 18:12.) Yet within the year a son was born, and we are told in the verses before us in the book of Hebrews that it was done "by faith." Let no one fail to get the full significance of this. For twenty-five years Abraham and Sarah doubted, and laughed at the suggestion that a son should be born to them. Then a miracle happened to their faith. Sarah "received strength to conceive seed, and was delivered of a child when she was past age, because *she judged him faithful* who had promised." Isaac was a miracle child; but the previous and greater miracle was that of the sudden turn in Sarah's faith that enabled her to conceive. Of that we are given no further information. A miracle happened in the case of both Abraham and Sarah. A few days before they had no faith, and both laughed at the idea that they should have a child. Then a miracle occurred in regard to their faith or lack of it, and another miracle occurred based upon the first miracle, and the son was born.

This is doubtless one of the things written for our admonition and learning: God does not always wait for full fruition of faith before He acts. Abraham had many years of preparation, but did not fully grasp the promises, and showed disbelief. But despite all this, the moment faith came, God acted. He did not wait a year or ten. Immediately He accepted Abraham's faith, and in due time the heir was born.

Peter sinned grievously, and denied his Lord with cursing and swearing. Jesus could have cast him aside, or at least have let a year or two elapse before taking him back, and then given him a humble place. But not so God. Despite his apostasy, when the Day of Pentecost came, Peter was the one chosen of God to deliver the address that caused the conversion of three thousand. When David sinned, when Moses made a mistake, when Elijah cowardly fled from Jezebel, God could have justly rejected them all. But He did not do this. He took them back, and honored them signally. Two of these were taken to heaven, and the third was made progenitor of the Messiah, who when He comes shall sit upon the throne of David, His father. (Luke 1:32.)

What we wish to stress here is the suddenness with which God acts as soon as men turn to Him. When later in this chapter Samson is mentioned, and we wonder how he came to be listed among those who at last gained the kingdom, it will stand us in good stead to remember that God did miracles for Abraham and Sarah the moment they turned to God in faith. Sarah was "past age," and Abraham "as good as dead." But a miracle of faith happened to them, and all the past was forgotten. Those who previously had as little faith as a grain of mustard seed became shining examples of faith, and Abraham became the father of the faithful. If God could do this for Abraham and Sarah, He could accept Samson's repentance even at the last moment of life.

Hebrews 11:13–16. "These all died in faith, not having received the promises, but having seen them afar off, and were persuaded of them, and embraced them, and confessed that they were strangers and pilgrims on the earth. For they that say such things declare plainly that they seek a country. And truly, if they had been mindful of that country from whence they came out, they might have had opportunity to have returned. But now they desire a better country, that is, an heavenly: wherefore God is not ashamed to be called their God: for he hath prepared for them a city."

Verse 13. "These all died in faith." Those so far mentioned are Abel, Enoch, Noah, Abraham, Isaac, Jacob, Sarah. Doubtless many others met with God's approval, but these are especially mentioned. They saw the promises afar off, "were persuaded of them, embraced them, and confessed that they were strangers and pilgrims on the earth."

These all died "not having received the promises," but they died believing them. Four things are mentioned of them: they *saw* the promises afar off; they were *persuaded* of them; they *embraced* them; and they *confessed* themselves to be strangers and pilgrims.

Verse 14. "They seek a country." It must have been trying for Abraham and his family to go up and down in the land as strangers, when they might have settled down as did Lot, and had a permanent home. To live in tents may be pleasant for a while; but we can readily understand how great the temptation must have been for them to end their wanderings and settle down. They "looked for a city which hath foundations." To us who live in houses this cannot have the meaning that it had for them. A tent has no foundation, and the fact that they looked for a city with *foundations* is expressive of their longings for a permanent home. They died in hope, not having received the promise. The foundations of the heavenly city will have much more meaning to them than to others. At last they will have found a home.

Verse 15. "They might...have returned." They had a good home, doubtless, in Haran. And they might have returned. It was no farther to go there than to journey to Egypt. In Haran they were known, and would immediately fit into their former positions. "They might have had opportunity," but we are not told that they ever had the least inclination to return. They had started for the land of Canaan, and were not going back. A worthy example for others to follow.

Verse 16. "A better country." It is well that each man love the country of his birth or adoption. But the Christian must never forget that he has a better country, and that this better land is his real home. There is danger that we become so enamored of things here, and so well satisfied, that we shall forget the better country. This does not mean that we are to make ourselves miserable here in order that we may someday enjoy something better—which seems to be the Christianity of some. But we are to be ever careful lest we pitch our tents too near Sodom, so that we lose sight of the heavenly home.

"God is not ashamed." The wording suggests that there may be some of whom God is ashamed. But He is not ashamed of them that seek a better country, that is, a heavenly. For them He has prepared a city.

Hebrews 11:17–19. "By faith Abraham, when he was tried, offered up Isaac; and he that had received the promises, offered up his only begotten son, of whom it was said, That in Isaac shall thy seed be called: accounting that

God was able to raise him up, even from the dead; from whence also he received him, in a figure."

"Abraham...offered up Isaac." See comments on Hebrews 6:15. It is not easy for us to measure the faith of Abraham as he prepared to follow the command of God to offer his only son. It was forty years or more since God had first promised him the son, and now he was commanded to offer him as a sacrifice. What could God mean by this? If he offered his son, how could God's promise of a seed as numerous as the sands of the seashore ever be fulfilled? There must be some mistake. But at last Abraham solved the problem. He concluded that *God was testing him, and would raise Isaac from the dead.*

Even this must have been a terrific test for Abraham no less than for his son. But Abraham by this time had learned the lesson of faith and implicit obedience. In this one test he made up for all his past lack of faith. He believed God implicitly, and was ready to go the whole length of God's requirements, even though he did not understand all.

"He received him in a figure." Isaac did not die, and yet to all intents and purposes he did die. Abraham had gone all the way when he stood with his hand raised ready to slay his son, and Isaac also could go no further. And so Abraham received his son back from the dead, in figure. He had stood the test. He had become the father of the faithful.

Hebrews 11:20–22. "By faith Isaac blessed Jacob and Esau concerning things to come. By faith Jacob, when he was a dying, blessed both the sons of Joseph; and worshipped, leaning upon the top of his staff. By faith Joseph, when he died, made mention of the departing of the children of Israel; and gave commandment concerning his bones."

Verse 20. "Isaac blessed Jacob and Esau." Isaac did not intend that Jacob should have the blessing of the first-born. Esau was the older of the twins, and to him rightly would come the paternal blessing. But God meant it otherwise. When Isaac found out that he had been deceived by his wife and son, and had given the blessing to Jacob, though he "trembled very exceedingly, and said, Who? where is he that hath taken the venison and brought it me, and I have eaten of all before thou camest, and have blessed him?" yet when he found out that it was according to God's will, he said of Jacob, "He shall be blessed." Gen. 27:33.

Verse 21. "Jacob...blessed both the sons of Joseph." This was unusual, for ordinarily only the older received the blessing. In blessing them, Jacob put his right hand upon Ephraim, who was the younger, thus giving him the greater blessing.

"And when Joseph saw that his father laid his right hand upon the head of Ephraim, it displeased him: and he held up his father's hand, to remove it from Ephraim's head unto Manasseh's head. And Joseph said unto his father, Not so, my father: for this is the firstborn; put thy right hand upon his head. And his father refused, and said, I know it, my son, I know it: he also shall become a people, and he also shall be great: but truly his younger brother shall be greater than he, and his seed shall become a multitude of nations." Gen. 48:17–19.

Jacob "worshipped, leaning upon the top of his staff." The word "leaning" being italicized in the King James Version indicates that it is supplied, and not found in the original. This has caused the Roman

Catholic Church to claim that Jacob *worshiped* the top of his staff, and not that he worshiped *leaning* on the top of his staff.

The reference is to Genesis 47:31, where the reading is, "Israel bowed himself upon the bed's head." Israel, or Jacob as was his former name, was on his deathbed. As he worshiped, he bowed himself on the bed's head and prayed. It is this incident which the Roman Church uses as an instance of image worship.

The original word might mean both staff and bed, hence the difference in translation. In any event, Jacob leaned upon the staff, or on the head of the bed, and prayed. It seems farfetched to change this into an argument for image worship. It indicates the length to which some will go in their attempt to have Bible support for their customs.

Verse 22. "Joseph...gave commandment." The writer might have said much more about Joseph, for he was a truly great man. But he selects this little incident to show that Joseph had faith in the Word of God. God had made promise to Abraham that his seed should possess the land, and Joseph showed his faith in the promise by directing that he be buried in the land which God had given them.

Hebrews 11:23–28. "By faith Moses, when he was born, was hid three months of his parents, because they saw he was a proper child; and they were not afraid of the king's commandment. By faith Moses, when he was come to years, refused to be called the son of Pharaoh's daughter; choosing rather to suffer affliction with the people of God, than to enjoy the pleasures of sin for a season; esteeming the reproach of Christ greater riches than the treasures in Egypt: for he had respect unto the recompence of the reward. By faith he forsook Egypt, not fearing the wrath of the king: for he endured, as seeing him who is invisible. Through faith he kept the Passover, and the sprinkling of blood, lest he that destroyed the firstborn should touch them."

Verse 23. "Moses...was hid three months." It took no little faith and courage for the parents of Moses thus to hide the child against the express command of the king. Had the parents not hid Moses, God would doubtless have found other ways of protecting him; but the parents, by cooperating with God, are included in the honor roll of those who through faith inherited the promises.

"Proper child." In Exodus 2:2 he is called a *goodly* child; in Acts 7:20, a *fair* child. The meaning is that he had no deformities, that he was a healthy, normal child.

Verses 24–26. The story of Moses is well known, and need not here be repeated. When he grew up he renounced his connection with the court, gave up such titles or offices as he had, and chose rather to suffer affliction with the people of God than to enjoy the pleasures of sin for a season.

These statements are all significant. There were doubtless many pleasures in the king's palace. Oriental courts have always been noted for their licentious pleasures as well as for corruption, and there is no reason to believe that this particular court was any exception. Moses gave up a life of ease and pleasure that he might be with his people, even if it meant affliction.

In doing this, Moses did not in reality give up much. God had something better in store for him. Moses knew that the pleasures of sin were only "for a season," and that the day of reckoning would soon come. He had "respect unto the recompence of the reward." To him the reproach of Christ was greater riches than the treasures of Egypt. These treasures, in the light of what men in later years have found in the pyramids of Egypt, were not inconsiderable, Even by today's standards they represent colossal sums aside from their artistic worth. But none of these things attracted Moses. He knew the value of the treasures of Egypt; but he also knew the greater treasures of Christ. And he chose to cast in his lot with the people of God. He chose well.

Verse 27. "He forsook Egypt." Egypt was his home, but he was compelled to flee for his life because of the events recorded in Exodus 2:11–15. Some commentators refer this flight to the time when Moses led Israel out of Egypt, but it seems clear that it primarily refers to his flight after having killed the Egyptian, as Stephen also seems to infer in Acts 7:23–29.

Verse 28. "He kept the passover." The record of this is found in Exodus 12:11–27. God promised that He would spare the first-born when the angel saw the blood sprinkled on the doorposts. This sprinkling was purely a matter of faith, for all knew that there was no virtue in the blood of a dead lamb. Such virtue as there was would lie in obedience and in what the lamb represented. The sprinkling of the blood was a matter of faith, and lifted it from a carnal ordinance to one of faith in the Lamb of God.

Hebrews 11:29–31. "By faith they passed through the Red sea as by dry land: which the Egyptians assaying to do were drowned. By faith the walls of Jericho fell down, after they were compassed about seven days. By faith the harlot Rahab perished not with them that believed not, when she had received the spies with peace."

Verse 29. "They passed through the Red sea." In the twenty words of this verse in the English version are compressed some of the greatest events in history. The meeting of Moses and the king of Egypt; the plagues, which at last wrung the unwilling consent out of Pharaoh to let Israel go; the angel of death passing over the land; the flight of the people; the pursuit of Pharaoh; the opening of the Red Sea to the Israelites; and the drowning of the pursuing army all are included in the deliverance of Israel out of bondage.

Verse 30. "The walls of Jericho." Again, how much is compressed in a few words! Israel had no military might to cast down the massive walls of Jericho. It was a matter of faith for them to believe that anything could be accomplished by the means which God commanded to use. From an ordinary viewpoint it was folly to think that such maneuvers could break down any wall, however feeble. Critics, in their efforts to avoid miracles, teach that the combined shout of all the people as they surrounded the walls, created such atmospheric pressure as to overturn the walls. But this seems harder to believe than the simple account that it was done by faith in God. In any event, it can hardly be contended that the Israelites had any scientific theory in mind, or that they were convinced that from natural causes such effects could be brought about. They simply did as they were told, and when that happened which they had been told would happen, they naïvely believed that God had done it for them. Some might call this ignorance. God calls it faith.

Verse 31. "The harlot Rahab." Had we written this account, we would have omitted this name, as we would have omitted some other names. We can see no reason why God should use as many words to tell us of Rahab as about Israel's crossing the Red Sea. We must believe that God knows best.

The spies here mentioned are not the spies sent out as recorded in Numbers 13, 14. They were two young men sent out by Joshua, and their story is recorded in Joshua 2:1–24; 6:22–25.

Attempts have been made to show that Rahab was not a harlot but an innkeeper. The evidence, however, gives little reason to doubt that she was or had been a woman of questionable character. Whereas men are likely to think of some sins as particularly evil and others not so bad, the truth is that all sin is evil, and no worse in women than in men. Rahab, whatever her past life might have been, could renounce her sins as others renounce theirs, turn to God with a full heart, and receive forgiveness. And if Rahab had been a disreputable woman, so much more glory to God in her conversion. If God could take a woman, a sinner, in the New Testament, and make her a monument of mercy, could not God do the same in the Old Testament? Does not God get even more glory when it is shown that He can change such a life? James tells us that Rahab was "justified," and. Hebrews places her among those "of whom the world was not worth." (James 2:25; Heb. 11:38.) Rahab was later married to Salmon, the father of Booz, the father of Obed, the father of Jesse, the father of David, the father of Christ. (Matt. 1:5; Luke 1:32.)

We are now ready to retract the statement made above that we would not include Rahab in this list of worthies. We know little or nothing about her, but are glad her name is there. It shows what God can do; that He is no respecter of persons; and that the least can attain to the highest.

Hebrews 11:32. "And what shall I more say? for the time would fail me to tell of Gedeon, and of Barak, and of Samson, and of Jephthae; of David also, and Samuel, and of the prophets."

"Time would fail me." There is a lesson and a sermon in each of these names.

Gedeon. We might almost call him the faithless one, the disbelieving one, the Thomas of the Old Testament. He asked as a sign that the fleece should be wet with the dew, and all the rest dry. And so it was. He wrung "the dew out of the fleece, a bowl full of water." Judges 6:38. Having been given this sign—besides other previous evidences of the Lord's leading—he now asked that the miracle be reversed, that this time the fleece be dry. This also was done. (Verses 39, 40.) He had less faith even than Thomas.

This emphasizes the point previously made that the Lord in this chapter has purposely chosen ordinary people as examples, such as naturally did not have much faith, that we might be encouraged by their example, and not easily give up. If the cases mentioned had been confined only to those of outstanding faith, we might be tempted to think that only that kind of men can be used of God. But when He chooses men of ordinary capacity, even some of little faith, and shows what He can do with them, then we may take courage and believe that there is hope for us also. And so we are glad that Gedeon is mentioned. He did not have much faith; but God used the little he had, and did great things with and through him.

Barak. The story of Barak is found in Judges, chapters 4 and 5. His name is inseparably connected with that of Deborah, the prophetess of the Lord, who was the mouthpiece of God, and whom Barak followed faithfully. As Gedeon was an example of the disinterestedness of faith in his refusal of the kingdom, so Barak is an example of the humility of faith in his willingness to do exploits where he received no honor for himself. (Judges 8:23; 4:9.)

Samson seems a strange name to place among the heroes of faith. We can find little for which to commend him. Had it not been for the fact that his name appears in this list, we would be doubtful of his eventual salvation.

The eleventh chapter of Hebrews is written that we may have a little better conception of what the final judgment will be like. In the kingdom there will be some concerning whom we now may have our doubts. But after reading this chapter we should not be surprised to see some names included that we would exclude. This should teach us not to judge.

> *"There's a wideness in God's mercy,*
> *Like the wideness of the sea;*
> *There's a kindness in His justice,*
> *Which is more than liberty.*
>
> .   .   .   .
>
> *"There's no place where earthly sorrows*
> *Are more felt than up in heaven.*
> *There's no place where earthly failings*
> *Have such kindly judgment given.*
>
> *"For the love of God is broader*
> *Than the measure of man's mind,*
> *And the heart of the Eternal*
> *Is most wonderfully kind."*

No doubt Samson at last found himself, for God includes him in His list. That decides the question.

Samson belongs there, or he would not be there. But if this is so, then we may have to revise our opinion of what God can do, and who will eventually be saved. It may be best not to pass judgment upon men and send them to damnation, when God has no such thing in mind. There may be some who we think should be and ought to be lost who will be saved. Under these conditions is it not best for us to reserve judgment, and leave the whole matter with God?

"Jephthae; of David also, and Samuel." Paul is right when he says that time would fail him to tell of all these. We look at the names, and we recognize them as men who have done great things for God. Despite their weaknesses they persevered, and at last conquered.

It is not the author's intention to give a complete list of all who might be included. He has given enough to show that all of them needed and had faith, at least before they ended their journey. It is written that we may take courage, follow their example of faith, be warned by their failure, and have our names, with theirs, inscribed in the Lamb's book of life.

Hebrews 11:33–37. "Who through faith subdued kingdoms, wrought righteousness, obtained promises, stopped the mouths of lions, quenched the violence of fire, escaped the edge of the sword, out of weakness were made strong, waxed valiant in fight, turned to flight the armies of the aliens. Women received their dead raised to life again: and others were tortured, not accepting deliverance; that they might obtain a better resurrection: and others had trial of cruel mockings and scourgings, yea, moreover of bonds and imprisonment: they were stoned, they were sawn asunder, were tempted, were slain with the sword: they wandered about in sheepskins and goatskins; being destitute, afflicted, tormented."

Verse 33. We may point out particular ones to whom these references apply, but we have no complete record of what they did, or their trials. David, Joshua, Barak, and Gedeon subdued kingdoms. Abraham, Elijah, and the prophets generally, wrought righteousness, And Daniel stopped lions' mouths.

Verse 34. The three young Hebrews quenched the violence of fire. (Dan. 3:1–30.) Moses escaped the edge of the sword. (Ex. 18:4.) So did Elijah and David. Hezekiah, out of physical weakness, was made strong. (Isaiah 38.) Jonathan and David waxed valiant in fight. (1 Sam. 14:4, 27; 2 Sam. 22:30.)

Verse 35. The widow of Sarepta and also the Shunammite woman both received their sons from the dead. (1 Kings 17:22; 2 Kings 4:31–37.) Of torture we have no record in the Old Testament, though there is no doubt that torture was used. If we go to the New Testament, we find an abundant example in the sufferings both of Christ and of His apostles.

Verse 36. Though we are not sure of the mockings and scourgings, these are generally attributed to the treatment meted out to such as Joseph, Samson, and Jeremiah.

Verse 37. Two examples of stoning are recorded in 1 Kings 21:1–14, of Naboth, and of Zechariah, the son of Jehoiada, the priest in 2 Chronicles 24:20–22. Jewish tradition says that Isaiah was sawn asunder, but of this there is no reliable record. "Tempted" doubtless has reference to the many temptations offered men to prove false to God. From time immemorial men have been slain with the sword, as were the eighty-five priests by Doeg, and, in fact, the whole city of Nob. (1 Sam. 22:18, 19.) We cannot give the names of the destitute, afflicted, and tormented souls who, poor and despised, were glad for a sheep-skin to cover them.

Hebrews 11:38. " (Of whom the world was not worthy:) they wandered in deserts, and in mountains, and in dens and caves of the earth."

How true are the words that of these the world was not worthy! Men gave their lives, their all, to be of help to their fellow men, and in return received stripes and ill treatment. Of such the world is not worthy. In deserts, in mountains, in dens and caves of the earth, they wandered. As did Christ, so these came to their own, and their own received them not. Thus it has always been.

Hebrews 11:39. "And these all, having obtained a good report through faith, received not the promise."

"These all." This stresses the point made before, that all of these obtained a good report before their work was done. It seems wonderful that God could take such as these, some weak and even feeble in faith, strengthen them, and make them victorious. They did not receive the promise, but they did receive a good report. And the fulfillment of the promise is assured them.

Hebrews 11:40. "God having provided some better thing for us, that they without us should not be made perfect."

"Some better thing." They did not receive the fulfill-ment of their hopes. That could be had only in Christ, and He could not appear until the fullness of the times had come. But they shall not lose. They may sleep, but they have a good report, and when the time shall come, they with us shall be made perfect.

In many respects this chapter is the most encouraging in the whole Bible. At the beginning of this chapter it was mentioned that the standards set before us in the Bible; as well as in Hebrews, are so high that they seem impossible of fulfillment, and that mortal man can never reach the goal set before him. We are invited to enter with Him through the veil, and appear before the throne of God. But we shrink back; we feel ourselves unworthy. We can never reach the goal set by God.

Then, when we are thoroughly convinced that we can never reach God's high standard, that we are undone and of unclean lips, we consider the men and women of the eleventh chapter of Hebrews. This changes all. Not that the standard is lowered. But we are given a view of what God has done for others, and we take courage. If Gedeon, with his little faith, obtained a good report, then there is hope for us. If Rahab prevailed, then God can forgive our sins also. If Samson at last made his peace with God , He will not turn us away. If David was forgiven, then we may have hope. If Jacob at last gained heaven, we need not despair.

And so we thank God for the eleventh chapter of Hebrews, the chapter that not only speaks of faith but instills hope in every breast..

CHAPTER 12

OF THE BOOK OF HEBREWS

Exhortations to Faith and Constancy

SYNOPSIS OF CHAPTER

THE FIRST part of the twelfth chapter is an exhortation to constancy in faith, using the illustration of a race. (Verses 1, 2.)

Then follows a discussion of the blessing of chastening, which for the present is not joyous, but afterward brings rich reward. We are not to think that this is something strange, or proof that the Lord does not love us. Quite the contrary: chastening is an evidence of sonship. (Verses 3–11.)

In view of this chastening we are to be of good courage, and not fail of the grace of God, as Esau did. For a morsel of meat he sold the birthright, and was rejected. (Verses 12–17.)

Verses 18 to 29 contain the story of the establishment and ratification of the first covenant, as contrasted with the inauguration of the second. At Sinai the mountain burned with fire, and there was blackness and darkness and tempest, and the sight was so terrible that even Moses trembled. The inauguration of the second covenant takes place at Mount Sion, the city of the living God, where we meet an innumerable company of angels and the general assembly of the first-born, with Jesus, the mediator of the new covenant. The contrast between the two occasions is marked and profound. God spoke once from heaven. He will speak once more. In view of this we are warned not to refuse Him that speaketh from heaven.

Hebrews 12:1, 2. "Wherefore seeing we also are compassed about with so great a cloud of witnesses, let us lay aside every weight, and the sin which doth so easily beset us, and let us run with patience the race that is set before us, looking unto Jesus the author and finisher of our faith; who for the joy that was set before him endured the cross, despising the shame, and is set down at the right hand of the throne of God."

The figure of a race was not new to the dwellers in Jerusalem, for at this time all the sports of Greece had been introduced among the Palestinians, and the foot race was a common spectacle. Doubtless all had seen the athletes prepare for the contest by previous abstinence from things harmful, and had watched them throw aside all but the most necessary garments, that they might not be hindered in running. The apostle here uses their knowledge of these races to point a lesson for the Christian race.

Verse 1. "A cloud of witnesses." The picture presented to us is that of a race wherein we are partakers. The cloud of witnesses are those mentioned in chapter 11, who despite handicaps and hindrances of all kinds joyfully finished their course, and thus bear witness to the fact that the race is not to the swift but to those that endure. (Eccles. 9:11.) To excel in this race, we are to lay aside every weight, or encumbrance, that we may run the easier. As an athlete, about to run, strips himself of every hindering garment, so we are to lay aside everything that may impede our progress.

"And the sin." Much thought has been given to the kind of sin here meant. We are inclined to believe that not all men are hindered by the same sin, or sins, and that therefore the sin here meant is the particular sin that most concerns and hinders each. With some, this may be evil thoughts; with others, impurity. Some may be troubled by a hasty temper; others, by appetite; still others, by pride, selfishness, or love of the world. Whatever the sin that easily besets us, we are to lay it aside, as a runner lays aside his flowing robes and girds himself for the race. It will take all to win the crown, and we must not let anything hinder us. Every weight, every sin—all that hinders—must be sacrificed.

"Run with patience." We have noted before that "patience" means endurance, and in this verse it is evident that this is its meaning here. It is of little use in a race to start out strong, and then not finish. At times the going may be hard, but only he who endures to the end will win. To quit the race at any point means defeat.

Verse 2. "Looking unto Jesus." There may be those in a race who are watching their competitors rather than keeping their eye on the goal. They congratulate themselves on being in the lead, and while they are doing this, someone is passing them.

A man running a race must not be concerned with anything else. Whatever distracts, even for a moment, may have serious consequences. Runners have lost races this way; gladiators have lost their lives in combat by having their attention diverted at a critical moment; all of us have lost out at times because we did not give our whole attention to the matter in hand. The Christian must ever look to Jesus for guidance, for strength, for courage, for help in time of need.

"The author and finisher," better, "the captain or leader," and "the perfecter of faith." "Author" is the same word that is rendered "prince" in Acts 3:15 and 5:31, and "captain" in Hebrews 2:10. It means a leader or founder. "Finisher" is one who completes or finishes something, puts on the finishing touches, perfects. Christ is the beginning and the end, the alpha and the omega, the all. (Rev. 1:8, 11.)

"For the joy that was set before him." This joy was the joy of seeing souls saved, the joy of doing the Father's will. (Isa. 53:11; John 4:34.) The work accomplished by redemption more than repaid Christ for His suffering. When Christ looks upon the souls who are saved because of His work, He will be more than satisfied. "For," might properly be translated "instead of." Instead of the joy that might rightly be His, He endured the cross. We must guard against the thought that Christ calmly weighed what He should do, coming to the conclusion that He would have more joy by suffering first and have increased joy later, and thus selfishly chose that which would give Him more pleasure in the end, but we must also guard against the conclusion that the increased joy which would be His was no incentive to Him in the dark hours ahead. To be with His own, to see the travail of His soul, to know the joy that should come to the redeemed as they enter into the joy of their Lord, all weighed with Christ. He knew that at God's "right hand there are pleasures for evermore" and "fulness of joy." (Ps. 16:11.) To share these with the redeemed would be heaven indeed.

"Endured the cross." Crucifixion was considered a shameful death, as is hanging to a soldier. Death was bad enough, but crucifixion was shameful. But Christ despised the shame. Knowing what was before Him, He courageously said, "I know that I shall not be ashamed." Isa. 50:7.

"Set down" is the same here as the other places where we have noted that it is not the act of sitting down, but that of being officially seated at the right hand of God, and invested with power. One day Christ is hanging on the cross, despised of men, scourged, bleeding, spat upon. And a little later that same Jesus is installed in the seat of honor in the universe, at the Father's right hand.

Hebrews 12:3–11. "For consider him that endured such contradiction of sinners against himself, lest ye be wearied and faint in your minds. Ye have not yet resisted unto blood, striving against sin. And ye have forgotten the exhortation which speaketh unto you as unto children, My son, despise not thou the chastening of the Lord, nor faint when thou art rebuked of him: for whom the Lord loveth he chasteneth, and scourgeth every son whom he receiveth. If ye endure chastening, God dealeth with you as with sons; for what son is he whom the father chasteneth not? But if ye be without chastisement, whereof all are partakers, then are ye bastards, and not sons. Furthermore we have had fathers of our flesh which corrected us, and we gave them reverence: shall we not much rather be in subjection unto the Father of spirits, and live? For they verily for a few days chastened us after their own pleasure; but he for our profit, that we might be partakers of his holiness. Now no chastening for the present seemeth to be joyous, but grievous: nevertheless afterward it yieldeth the peaceable fruit of righteousness unto them which are exercised thereby."

As the author is about to discuss the chastisement that comes to every son, he asks his readers to consider "him that endured." Their trials had been comparatively light, and they are not to faint at that which is coming. God may permit them to suffer; but it is done in love, and in the end they will thank Him for it. Paul draws upon their own experience when they received chastisement from their earthly fathers. At the time this was not joyous, but as they think of it in retrospect, they realize it was for their good.

Verse 3. "Consider him." We have before been invited to consider Christ as apostle and high priest. (Heb. 3:1.) We are now invited to consider "him that endured." The apostle asks us to compare or contrast our experience with that of Christ, lest we think that we are tried above that which we are able to bear, lest we grow faint or weary, or perhaps think that God has forgotten us, and that we are enduring more than our just share. "Consider" is a different word from that used in Hebrews 3:1, and here means to reckon, to count up, to sum up, to consider analytically, to add up a sum of numbers. It means to go over point by point, again and again, considering each item separately. This would doubtless be a profitable thing for all to do. To spend a thoughtful hour from time to time, considering the cost of our salvation in terms of suffering, would be much worth while. We would find that salvation is cheap at any price.

Verse 4. "Resisted unto blood." It is one thing gently to turn away from temptation, expressing our disapproval of certain conduct. It is another thing to resist unto blood, "striving against sin." Christ "suffered being tempted." Heb. 2:18. In Gethsemane and at the cross He strove against sin, and resisted to the blood. When we are tempted and in danger of yielding, it is well to think of Christ, and His resisting unto blood.

Verses 5, 6. "Ye have forgotten." In the midst of some temptation it is easy to forget that he whom the Lord loves He chastens. We are often conscious of having deserved the chastening, and may feel the justice of it. But it is not easy to believe that the Lord loves us as we are chastened. This may spring from the fact that we were not conscious that our fathers loved us when they chastened us. On the contrary, we were aware that they were angry because of our misdeeds or transgressions; and we consider God in the same light. Parents sometimes chasten their offspring without the children's being aware that they love them at that particular moment. In this parents need to reform. God can chasten and love. We should be able to do the same.

The next time we are chastened of the Lord, let us consider that God is attempting to teach us a lesson that we sorely need. He is not angry with us. He loves us. In patience and love let us submit to whatever God has for us, thank Him for it, and love Him more because of it.

Verses 7, 8. "Endure chastening." Do not whine, do not complain, when the chastening hand of God is upon you. This is the counsel of God. Endure; take it patiently; take it like a man. You have deserved it. You have asked God to make you what you ought to be; and He is in the process of doing it. Now be submissive. Father knows what is best.

Chastening is a sign of sonship. "What son is he whom the father chasteneth not?" True, if that question were asked today, many a father would answer that he does not chasten his son, that it is not modern to do so. It would be well for such to consider the verses we are studying. Indiscriminate punishment is not in God's order. But fatherly chastening is recommended by God. This is not the place to consider family discipline, but we believe that every believer would do well to consider his responsibility in the light of God's counsel.

Verse 9. "We gave them reverence." It is a good thing for a child to be taught reverence. Indeed, the child who is brought up in ignorance of reverence is much handicapped. Reverence for what? Reverence for law, authority, religion, womanhood, age, Reverence for parents, for superiors, for life, for God, for oneself. As long as there is reverence there is hope. When reverence is gone, almost everything else is gone. Lack of respect for one's word, for contractual obligations, for the marriage vow, for life, for death—all these lacks mean a handicap that is hard to overcome. Many are the lads who in more mature years have wished that their parents had taken them in hand when they were young. Thus they would have been spared much grief and sorrow. And sad, but perhaps just, is the sorrow that comes to the parents of irreverent children. They have sowed, and they are reaping. And it is a reaping of tears and regrets. But alas, too often it is too late.

The fact that through discipline some children must be taught reverence may seem a small gain. And yet it may be a gain. For sooner or later in life that lesson has to be learned. And happy is the child who learns it when young. He may not think that much good was accomplished by the chastening, but the inculcation of reverence is in itself a great gain. The world has been sowing the wind. It is reaping the whirlwind. Lawlessness, crime, and violence prevail. All this is grounded in lack of respect, lack of reverence.

Verse 10. "For our profit." It is often the case that parents punish their children "after their own pleasure." This is reprehensible. But even so, many children, as they look back, are thankful for the restraining hand that saved them from greater difficulties. Should not also we, as we look back, and see how God has saved us from ourselves, be thankful? Surely He did it "for our profit, that we might be partakers of his holiness."

Verse 11. "Peaceable fruit." The author is stating an admitted truth that no chastening is joyous at the time. But afterward it yields the peaceable fruit of righteousness for them that learn the lesson. In retrospect we see what we did not appreciate at the time.

Hebrews 12:12-17. "Wherefore lift up the hands which hang down, and the feeble knees; and make straight paths for your feet, lest that which is lame be turned out of the way: but let it rather be healed. Follow peace with all men, and holiness, without which no man shall see the Lord! looking diligently lest any man fail of the grace of God, lest any root of bitterness springing up trouble you, and thereby many be defiled; lest there be any fornicator or profane person, as Esau, who for one morsel of meat sold his birthright. For ye know how that afterward, when he would have inherited the blessing, he was rejected: for he found no place of repentance, though he sought it carefully with tears."

We are not to become weak-kneed or discouraged because of chastening. We are rather to take heed to our path that the weak be not turned out of the way. We are to watch our influence lest others be led astray, and fail of the grace of God. No root of bitterness is to be permitted to spring up, for it may bear evil fruit as in the case of Esau, who at last sold his birthright for one morsel of meat. He attempted to repent but had gone too far, and found no place for repentance.

Verse 12. "Feeble knees." Too many Christians have feeble knees and hands that hang down. God does not encourage spiritual feebleness or invalidism. Too many neglect meeting with those of like faith, and then complain that no one visits them. Had they not encouraged spiritual and physical slothfulness, they would be able to visit others in their affliction rather than stay at home and complain. We are admonished to bear one another's burden, but we are also admonished to bear our own. (Gal. 6:2, 5.) The man who casts his burden on the Lord will not complain of the load.

We are convinced that too many have feeble knees, spiritually speaking. They are waiting for someone to carry them, and if this is not done, they question the Christianity of others. Such are a burden to themselves, their brethren, and God.

"Lift up the hands which hang down." To sit with folded hands while others work may indicate patience and resignation. But it may also indicate slothfulness and spiritual indolence.

Let not the sick, the aged, or the feeble think that this is said to rebuke them. God forbid. God loves these, and has placed them in our midst that we may help and encourage them. They are dear to God; and they should be dear to the church, and should be cared for tenderly. We are to be tender, kind, compassionate, and helpful to all such. It is not of these we speak, but of such as love to be feeble, who could be well and strong physically and spiritually if they would only lift up the hands that hang down, and use their feeble knees.

Verse 13. "Make straight paths." This instruction is for all. We should make straight paths for ourselves, and we should make straight paths for the sake of those who may follow us, and who look to us for example.

No man lives for himself. Each of us has others whom he influences for good or ill. Let no one think he has no influence, and that it does not matter what he does. Far more than we think we are followers of others, and are followed by others. A prizefighter, an athlete, a soldier, a common man, a minister—all have followers of which they know not. We cannot escape the responsibility of life, however much we may wish to. Let not the young girl or the mature woman think that she has no followers. Copyists are on every hand, and there is no way of escaping them. We ought therefore to make straight paths for our feet, lest the lame be turned out of the way.

"Let it rather be healed." There are those who are out of the way today because of our lack of understanding. We may have thought that small things do not matter. But we are watched when we are not aware of it. Every little thing matters. Let us do all we can to heal the wounds that have been inflicted by carelessness or wrong example.

Verse 14. "Follow peace." Of this Paul says in Romans, "If it be possible, as much as lieth in you, live peaceably with all men." Rom. 12:18.

"And holiness." The word here rendered "holiness" occurs ten times in the New Testament, and is several times translated "sanctification." It means inward purity, moral rectitude. Without this no man shall see the Lord.

Verse 15. "Looking diligently." We are to be careful lest we be found destitute of the grace of God. This indicates that there is danger that some may fail of the grace of God without their being aware of. it. This is doubtless closely connected with the next statement, that roots of bitterness may spring up and cause trouble and defilement.

The apostle has just mentioned holiness, without which no man shall see the Lord. He is now pointing out how easily one may fall from grace and be defiled. It may be caused by some root of bitterness that remains in the soul and not only troubles but defiles.

Bitterness may seem a small matter to cause the loss of the grace of God, but it is one way that the enemy of souls has found successful. Bitterness may not manifest itself in any outward act of sin or transgression. It may be kept repressed, and still the root remain and cause trouble. We are ill at ease. We do not love the brethren as we should. Discontent is added to bitterness, and the whole Christian experience becomes affected. A little root of bitterness too often results in loss of the sweet love and grace of God. We are to look diligently that this does not happen.

Verse 16. "Profane person." The apostle here brings in a specific illustration of what he has in mind. Esau put little value on his birthright, and sold it "for one morsel of meat." The birthright was his. He could have kept it, but he did not appreciate it. His experience is a fearful commentary on the danger of rejecting the blessings of God, or undervaluating them.

"He would have inherited the blessing." He was not shut out. He would have inherited it, but he rejected it, and the rejection was final. "Esau despised his birthright." Gen. 25:34. The birthright included not only property values but especially the right of the first-born to be the priest of the household and to inherit the blessing of the promise made to Abraham and his seed. When later in life Esau began to understand the great loss he had sustained, and craved the blessing, it was too late. He had not changed his way of life; he was a "profane person," unfit to exercise the right of the first-born.

"He found no place of repentance." There is some doubt as to what is meant by the statement that he "sought it carefully with tears." What does "it" stand for? Is it repentance he sought with tears? is it the inheritance? is it the blessing? We do not know, and good men are disagreed in regard to the matter. The preponderance of opinion seems to be in favor of the blessing. This also is in harmony with Esau's "great and exceeding bitter cry," when he asked his father, "Bless me, even me also, O my father." Gen. 27:34. Again, later, he said to the father, "Hast thou but one blessing, my father? bless me, even me also, O my father. And Esau lifted up his voice, and wept." Verse 38.

We have therefore this situation. Esau wanted the blessing, but he found no place for repentance. He wept, but he was unable to make the necessary changes in his life. He had gone too far for repentance.

The parable of the ten virgins in Matthew 25:1–13 holds a similar lesson. The five foolish virgins did not reject the invitation to the wedding. They accepted it, but they did not have sufficient oil in their lamps.

God does not shut the door against any who wish to enter, and who will put on the wedding garment. But the mere wish is not sufficient in itself unless men are willing to make the needed preparation that will admit them. They want to come in as they are; they want to come in on their own conditions; but this cannot be done. Some go so far in their own way that they are blinded to their own need. They may with cries and bitter tears seek entrance. But they are not ready, and they find no way of repentance. This is the lesson of Esau. And it is written for our admonition.

It is of interest to note that the American Revised Version translates: "When he afterward desired to inherit the blessing, he was rejected; for he found no place for a change of mind in his father, though he sought it diligently with tears."

Hebrews 12:18–29. "For ye are not come unto the mount that might be touched, and that burned with fire, nor unto blackness, and darkness, and tempest, and the sound of a trumpet, and the voice of words; which voice they that heard. intreated that the word should not be spoken to them any more: (For they could not endure that which was commanded, And if so much as a beast touch the mountain, it shall be stoned, or thrust through with a dart: and so terrible was the sight, that Moses said, I exceedingly fear and quake:) but ye are come unto mount Sion, and unto the city of the living God, the heavenly Jerusalem, and to an innumerable company of angels, to the general assembly and church of the firstborn, which are written in heaven, and to God the judge of all, and to the spirits of just men made perfect, and to Jesus the mediator of the new covenant, and to the blood of sprinkling, that speaketh better things than that of Abel. See that ye refuse not him that speaketh. For if they escaped not who refused him that spake on earth, much more shall not we escape, if we turn away from him that speaketh from heaven: whose voice then shook the earth: but now he hath promised, saying, Yet once more I shake not the earth only, but also heaven. And this word, Yet once more, signifieth the removing of those things that are shaken, as of things that are made, that those things which cannot be shaken may remain. Wherefore we receiving a kingdom which cannot be moved, let us have grace, whereby we may serve God acceptably with reverence and godly fear: for our God is a consuming fire."

The account of the experiences of Israel at Mount Sinai is a most impressive one. God gave them an exhibition of His majesty and might, an experience which they sadly needed. They had no just conception of the God who had led them out of Egypt. They had been so long among idolaters that they conceived of God in terms of the gods of Egypt. But when the earth shook and the mountain trembled, when the lightning flashed and the thunder rolled, when blackness and darkness and tempest enclosed them, and the voice of God shook the very earth on which they were standing, they all entreated that God speak no more to them; and even Moses was afraid.

In contrast to this is given a picture of the ratification of the new covenant in which all is glory and light. However, the warning is given that once more will God shake not the earth only but also the heavens. We are therefore warned not to refuse "him that speaketh from heaven."

Sinai

Verses 18–21. The day when Moses "brought forth the people out of the camp to meet with God" (Ex. 19:17), was a day of "blackness, and darkness, and tempest." "Mount Sinai was altogether on a smoke, because the Lord descended upon it in fire: and the smoke thereof ascended as the smoke of a furnace, and the whole mount quaked greatly." Ex. 19:18. "There were thunders and lightnings, and a thick cloud upon the mount, and the voice of the trumpet exceeding loud; so that all the people that was in the camp trembled." Verse 16. Bounds had been placed all about the mount, and the people were told that whoever touched the mount would be killed. (Verse 12.) "There shall not an hand touch it, but he shall surely be stoned, or shot through; whether it be beast or man, it shall not live: when the trumpet soundeth long, they shall come up to the mount." Verse 13.

In pitch darkness the people surged forward, groping for the fence, lest they go too far, and be killed. The lightnings flashed about them only to leave them in still greater darkness. The thunders rolled, the people trembled, and even "Moses said, I exceedingly fear and quake." Heb. 12:21.

Suddenly the mountain lights up. It is completely on fire. God is about to reveal Himself, "and the voice of the trumpet, exceeding loud," is heard. Ex. 19:16. It "sounded long, and waxed louder and louder, Moses spake, and God answered him by a voice." Verse 19. "I stood between the Lord and you at that time," said Moses, "to show you the word of the Lord: for ye were afraid by reason of the fire." Deut. 5:5.

As "the whole mount quaked greatly" (Ex. 19:18), tremblingly the people heard the words of the law, the Ten Commandments, proclaimed by God. "So terrible was the sight" that Moses himself trembled. "And all the people saw the thunderings, and the lightnings, and the noise of the trumpet, and the mountain smoking: and when the people saw it, they removed, and stood afar off. And they said unto Moses, Speak thou with us, and we will hear: but let not God speak with us, lest we die." Ex. 20:18, 19.

Reassuringly Moses said, "Fear not: for God is come to prove you, and that his fear may be before your faces, that ye sin not." Verse 20. While "the people stood afar off," "Moses drew near unto the thick darkness where God was," and God communicated further with him. (Verse 21.)

This is the setting of the giving of the law to which Paul refers in Hebrews. God gives an exhibition of His power and holiness "to prove you, and that his fear may be before your faces, *that ye sin not*" Verse 20. Truly, no greater exhibition of glory and majesty has ever been given.

The people stood face to face with the Lawgiver and judge of all the earth. They appeared before the judgment seat of God, and knew now "the terror of the Lord." 2 Cor. 5:11. Nevermore could they think lightly of sin. They had experienced the terror of the judgment.

In giving the law, God accomplished more than merely intimidating the people, and making them afraid. He showed them His mighty power of protection. With such a God on their side, what reason could there ever be for the people to fear, however many and strong were their enemies! God was abundantly able to protect them.

Sion

Verses 22–24. Having given a view of the inauguration of the old covenant, the writer now turns to the new. He has presented a powerful picture of what took place at Sinai, which should cause all to heed the admonition "that ye sin not." (Ex. 20:20.)

The giving of the law at Sinai was attended with a most wonderful exhibition of the power of God. Never before nor since has the world witnessed anything like it. It surpassed in grandeur and magnificence anything else since the creation of the world. It is the only time that God in audible voice spoke to the assembled multitudes of mankind.

No scene comparable to this took place when Christ on earth instituted the new covenant. Yet it would seem fitting that the inauguration of the new covenant should be attended with no less glory than the institution of the old. How do we account for this?

We believe that such an event *did* take place; however, this time it was not on earth but in heaven. The giving of the law on Sinai and the subsequent institution of the covenant with the ceremonial observances, was directly concerned with this earth. The new covenant has an even wider application, and the joyous celebration of this event, with the ratification of the new convenant, was transferred to heaven. In the verses before us we are invited to come to the "city of the living God," and there view the company assembled to celebrate the momentous event.

The place to which we are to come is Mount Sion, as contrasted with Mount Sinai. Mount Sion is the heavenly Jerusalem, the city of the living God. Christ is there, and is called Jesus the Mediator. He is mediator of the new covenant, and as such sprinkles the blood that speaks better things than that of Abel.

The occasion is called a "general assembly," or rather a "festival assembly." There is an innumerable company of angels, literally "myriads," tens of thousands, the same word as used in Daniel 7:10. With them is the church of the first-born, written, or registered, in heaven, and "the spirits of just men made perfect."

It may be well to place the contents of the two sections side by side for greater clarity.

The Meeting at Sinai	The Meeting at Sion
1. Sinai, an earthly mountain, enveloped in blackness, darkness, tempest.	1. Sion, a heavenly mountain, whose very name signifies sunny, and is the city of the living God.
2. Angels. Gal. 3:19; Acts 7:53; Deut. 23:2	2. Innumerable angels in festive assembly.
3. Israel surrounded by darkness; afraid, and ready to flee.	3. The church of the first-born registered in heaven, spirits of just men made perfect.
4. The Lord as lawgiver, thundering His commandments, shrouded in darkness.	4. The Lord as judge, sitting on Mount Sion, the hill of light.
5. Moses as mediator, himself trembling.	5. Jesus as mediator of the new covenant.
6. The blood of dead animals sprinkled on the book and the people, which never could take away sin.	6. The blood of a living Saviour, by which men might find cleansing from all the sins which could not be atoned for by the law of Moses.
7. The sound of the trumpet, and the voice of words inspiring fear.	7. The voice that speaks better things than the blood of Abel.

In the nature of things we would expect a solemn and joyful ratification of the new covenant, corresponding to, and exceeding in glory, the ratification of the old covenant on earth. At such an occasion God must be present as judge, and Christ must be there to give an account of the work He has done on earth. He must present Himself before the Father for examination, as it were, before His work can be approved. He must also present a first fruit of those who are to be saved, a sample of His work, and these He must present perfect before His glory. For them He is to appear in the the role of Mediator, as only through His mediation can they be accepted. While Abel's blood called for vengeance, the blood of Jesus speaks of better things—of reconciliation and salvation.

This is the joyful and solemn scene presented before us. The contrast is, striking; but there are also some striking similarities that call us back to the solemn scenes of Sinai. In both covenants God is the same, and His requirements are the same. The law, which was the basis of the covenant at Sinai, is also the basis of the new covenant, but with this difference: in the new covenant the law is written in the heart, not merely on tables of stone.

Verse 25. "Him that speaketh." God is the one who spoke at Sinai, and He is the one who now speaks. Farrar states: "Perhaps the writer regarded Christ as the speaker alike from Sinai as from Heaven, for even the Jews represented the Voice at Sinai as being the Voice of Michael, who was sometimes identified with 'the Shekinah' or the 'Angel of the Presence.'" —*The Epistle of Paul the Apostle to the Hebrews*, p. 161.

Verse 26. "Yet once more." Christ spoke from heaven once, and the earth shook, and "the whole mount quaked greatly." Ex. 19:18. Now He has promised that yet once more will He shake not the earth only but the heavens also. The expression "yet once more" means that God will again speak. And when He speaks, the very heavens will shake.

Verse 27. "And this word." The quotation is from the prophet Haggai, chapter 2:6, 7. "For thus saith the Lord of hosts; Yet once, it is a little while, and I will shake the heavens, and the earth, and the sea, and the dry land; and I will shake all nations, and the desire of all nations shall come: and I will fill this house with glory, saith the Lord of hosts."

There is good reason to believe that the shaking that is to come will be the result of God's voice. He once shook the earth, and He will do it again. Once more He will speak from heaven, and when He speaks, it will be final. He will speak no more. When that is done, all that can be shaken will be shaken. There are some things that cannot be shaken; these will remain.

We are not told *what*God will speak. But we are not far afield in believing that what He will say will not be out of harmony with what He spoke from Sinai. We do not know of any words that need to be repeated more than those God spoke of old. Men have made light of the commandments; they have ignored, broken, and ridiculed them. It is time for God to act, "for they have made void thy law." Ps. 119:126. When God speaks again, every question in regard to the law will be settled. And God will speak "yet once more."

Verse 28. "Let us have grace." One of the things that cannot be moved is the kingdom. This God has reserved for His children. "Thankfulness" is a better word than "grace." "Let us be thankful" is the wording. It is in view of the fact that we are to receive the kingdom that we are to be thankful.

"Reverence and godly fear." We have previously noted these virtues. They are most important virtues of which all are in need.

Verse 29. "A consuming fire." This brings our minds back to Sinai, where God revealed Himself in fire, and where those who came too near and were not prepared were consumed. It was not an arbitrary punishment that God inflicted on all indiscriminately. Moses came near and was not consumed. He touched the mount and went up in it. He talked with God face to face. God forbade Israel to touch the mount or come near it simply because they were still sinful and could not stand His presence. It was in mercy that God warned them not to come near. The apostle now warns that God is the same. He is still a consuming fire.

CHAPTER 13

OF THE BOOK OF HEBREWS

Parting Counsel

SYNOPSIS OF CHAPTER

THE APOSTLE has finished his work. He has presented Christ as Saviour and high priest and has instructed the people in regard to the work He is doing in the sanctuary above. It is now for them to follow Christ, going with Him without the gate, suffering His reproach. This they would experience in a very real way, for they soon would have to flee from Jerusalem and be scattered to all parts of the world. But whatever happened, they must not forget their Christianity, but must ever imitate their Master.

The parting salutation is a most significant and beautiful one, where the apostle once more calls their attention to the everlasting covenant:

Hebrews 13:1–4. "Let brotherly love continue. Be not forgetful to entertain strangers: for thereby some have entertained angels unawares. Remember them that are in bonds, as bound with them; and them which suffer adversity, as being yourselves also in the body. Marriage is honourable in all, and the bed undefiled: but whoremongers and adulterers God will judge."

The last chapter of the book contains much practical instruction. The writer has finished his main theme, ending with a comparison between Mount Sinai and Mount Sion. He now adds a few words of counsel.

Verse 1. "Let brotherly love continue." Brotherly love was not common among the Gentiles in those days, but appears to have been a special virtue among the Christians. The apostle does not here exhort the believers to love the brethren—this they were already doing—but to continue to do so.

Persecution had been and would be the lot of many, and it was needful that each should stand ready to help his brother. Christ had warned that when the time came to flee, there would be no opportunity to take anything along. (Matt. 24:16–18.) That time was nearing. Now was the time for all to be considerate and helpful.

Verse 2. "Entertain strangers." Inns were not common, and strangers were often considered with suspicion. Because of changed conditions, hospitality may not seem as necessary now as then. Though this may be true, the spirit of hospitality is as needful as ever.

Angels were entertained by Abraham, Lot, Manoah, and Gideon. (Gen. 18:2–22, 19:1, 2; Judges 13:2–14; 6:11–20.) In the judgment the entertainment of strangers will come into consideration. (Matt. 25:35.)

Verse 3. "Them which suffer adversity." The verse suggests that some of the believers at that time were in bonds. Paul himself had often been in prison, and had not forgotten those who ministered to him. He now asks that those who are in bonds be remembered.

Adversity may at times be well deserved because of lack of forethought, but it also strikes at times without apparent cause. In such cases we are not to judge but remember the afflicted, and let brotherly love continue. This exhortation to remember others in adversity is based on the consideration that we are still in the body and that like calamities may come to us.

Verse 4. "Marriage is honourable." The admonition is to chastity and against false notions that marriage is not honorable. It also strikes against celibacy. There were some at that time who were "forbidding to marry," as there are some now who believe that a higher state of Christianity can be reached in celibacy. (1 Tim. 4:1–3.) Such reasoning does not have the approval of God.

God frowns upon every species of unchastity. All lawless passions are condemned, within or without the marriage bond, and matrimony is to be held honorable. "God will judge." Men may cover up sin, but God will judge. He knows, and all things will someday be revealed.

Hebrews 13:5–8. "Let your conversation be without covetousness; and be content with such things as ye have: for he hath said, I will never leave thee, nor forsake thee. So that we may boldly say, The Lord is my helper, and I will not fear what man shall do unto me. Remember them which have the rule over you, who have spoken unto you the word of God: whose faith follow, considering the end of their conversation. Jesus Christ the same yesterday, and to day, and for ever."

Verse 5. The construction, "Let your conversation be without covetousness," is literally, "Let your turn of mind be without covetousness." "Conversation," as used in the Authorized Version, signifies life, daily life, manner of conduct. But here it has reference more to the "turn of mind" than to mere conduct. There are those who are covetous in mind even if not in deed. The injunction here goes back of the act to the state of mind. The reading is literally "be un-money-loving."

It is noticeable that those who have no money may be money lovers as well as those who are rich. There are covetous persons among the poor and rich alike. Let no one apply these admonitions to others merely. They are written for all, and all can profit by them.

"Content." The virtue of contentment is one of the most precious gifts of God. We are not to be content with what we are, but we are to be content with what we have. Too often we turn this about, and are comfortably content with ourselves, and our achievements, but discontented with what we have. Nothing is more disagreeable than a discontented person.

"I will never leave thee." The quotation is probably taken from Joshua 1:5, though like promises abound throughout the Bible. (Gen. 28:15; Isa. 41:17; 1 Chron. 28:20.)

Verse 6. "The Lord is my helper." This is taken from the Greek version of Psalms 118:6. The quotation breathes confidence. When the Lord is on our side, and we are on the Lord's side, we need not fear.

Verse 7. "Them which have the rule over you." God's church is a church of order and organization. Though there is to be no "lording it," there is respect due those who are leaders. The wording seems especially to refer to those who formerly were leaders, and who now were resting, but the principle applies to all time.

"Whose faith follow," or "whose faith imitate." As we earnestly contemplate the issue, or result, of their life, we are to imitate their faith.

Verse 8. "The same." One of the greatest blessings of Christianity is the fact that God is not changeable—in one mood today and in another tomorrow. The order of the words in the original is, "yesterday and today the same, and to the ages." This is practically the same statement as in chapter 1:12, "Thou art the same."

Hebrews 13:9–16. "Be not carried about with divers and strange doctrines. For it is a good thing that the heart be established with grace; not with meats, which have not profited them that have been occupied therein. We have an altar, whereof they have no right to eat which serve the tabernacle. For the bodies of those beasts, whose blood is brought into the sanctuary by the high priest for sin, are burned without the camp. Wherefore Jesus also, that he might sanctify the people with his own blood, suffered without the gate. Let us go forth therefore unto him without the camp, bearing his reproach. For here have we no continuing city, but we seek one to come. By him therefore let us offer the sacrifice of praise to God continually, that is, the fruit of our lips giving thanks to his name. But to do good and to communicate forget not: for with such sacrifices God is well pleased."

Verse 9. "Be not carried about." We are here exhorted to steadfastness. To hold steady, not to be easily shaken, is one of the marks of the mature Christian. Christ is the same ever, and so should we be.

"Divers and strange doctrines." Too many are easily affected by new and strange teachings. They have a flare for and love of innovations. The apostle alludes to those who are occupied with meats "which have not profited them." The stress is to be upon the fundamentals, upon grace, and not upon the minor things. This principle is as true today as then.

Verses 10–12. "We have an altar." The writer is here referring to the rule in the Levitical law, that when the blood of the sin offering was carried into the sanctuary, as in the case of the anointed priest or the whole congregation, the priest was not to eat of the flesh, but must burn it without the camp. (Lev. 6:30.)

This, however, was not true of all sin offerings. When a ruler or a common man sinned, the priest was not only permitted, but required, to eat the sin offering. "The priest that offereth it for sin shall eat it: in the holy place shall it be eaten, in the court of the tabernacle of the congregation." Lev. 6:26. The guiding principle was contained in these words: "And no sin offering, whereof any of the blood is brought into the tabernacle of the congregation to reconcile withal in the holy place, shall be eaten: it shall be burnt in the fire." Lev. 6:30.

It is to this application of the law that the writer of Hebrews has reference when he states that "the bodies of those beasts whose blood is brought into the sanctuary by the high priest for sin, are burned without the camp." Heb. 13:11.

The priests could not eat of the flesh when the blood of the sin offering was carried into the sanctuary. But "we have an altar, whereof they have no right to eat which serve the tabernacle." The author calls attention to a difference in the procedure between the old and, the new dispensation. *We* have an altar whereof *they* cannot eat. And the reason they could not eat was that the blood was brought into the sanctuary.

In harmony with this, Jesus "suffered without the gate." His blood was ministered by Himself in the heavenly sanctuary; He Himself carrying it in. (Heb. 9:12.) Therefore, according to the law just quoted, the flesh could not be eaten; it must be burnt. Yet in the institution of the Lord's supper, Christ took the bread and said, "Take, eat; this is my body, which is broken for you." 1 Cor. 11:24.

This was contrary to the Levitical law to which the apostle refers. Those who served at the altar had no right to eat of the flesh when the blood was brought into the sanctuary. But in the New Testament we have that right. "This cup is the new testament in my blood," said Christ. 1 Cor. 11:25. In the new covenant we become partakers of Christ, symbolized by the broken bread, which as we eat it, in a very real way becomes identified with the communicant. The priests of old ate the flesh, and thus carried sin. (Lev. 10:17.) The exact opposite is true in the New Testament, in which it is said that we become partakers of Him, symbolized by the ordinances of the Lord's house. We have an altar whereof they have no right to eat who serve the tabernacle. It is the blessed communion table.

Verse 13. "Let us go forth." This is an admonition drawn from the sanctuary service. As Christ went without the gate, so we are to follow Him, not shunning the reproach that He bore.

Verse 14. "Here have we no continuing city." The admonition to go without the camp is here based on the fact that we have no continuing city here. The earth is not our home. We are only pilgrims and strangers. But we seek, like the patriarchs of old, a city that has foundations, whose builder and maker is God.

Verse 16. "God is well pleased." Our sacrifices are not all to be with our lips. We are to do good and communicate or share with others. With such sacrifices God is well pleased. Our Christianity is not to consist in words only but in deeds. God is pleased with a practical Christianity.

Hebrews 13:17–19. "Obey them that have the rule over you, and submit yourselves: for they watch for your souls, as they that must give account, that they may do it with joy, and not with grief: for that is unprofitable for you. Pray for us: for we trust we have a good conscience, in all things willing to live honestly. But I beseech you the rather to do this, that I may be restored to you the sooner."

Verse 17. "Submit yourselves." This text repeats the injunction of verse 7, but in a little more definite form. We are here counseled to obey and submit. There can be no leader unless there are also followers; and as truly as it is the privilege of a leader to lead, so it is the privilege of a follower to follow. The cry is often for leaders; yet in some respects it is easier to find leaders than followers.

"Give an account." Leadership includes responsibility. Most leaders consider their responsibility as lying chiefly in getting things done, in getting as much work as possible out of a given number of people. God considers their responsibility from a different viewpoint. With God it is not how much work is done, but how those under the charge of leaders are prospering, how they are growing, how they are improving spiritually. God is more interested in the individual than in the mechanics of the work.

Verse 18. "Pray for us." Often these words are said lightly, and with little meaning, and are only a form.

But when a truly great soul says, "Pray for me," it is a cry for help that should not go unheeded.

"A good conscience." The apostle here tells us that his aim is to be honest, and have a good conscience. He feels his need of help. He is honest and desires only to do God's will. That such a man should ask others to pray for him shows a humble spirit.

Verse 19. "Restored." Paul was separated from the believers, and longed to be with them. Such is often the lot of God's servants. Alone, and separated from those they love, they long for restoration. With the saints of old, they long for a home, a city that has foundations, even the home of the saints.

Hebrews 13:20–25. "Now the God of peace, that brought again from the dead our Lord Jesus, that great shepherd of the sheep, through the blood of the everlasting covenant, make you perfect in every good work to do his will, working in you that which is well pleasing in his sight, through Jesus Christ; to whom be the glory for ever and ever. Amen. And I beseech you, brethren, suffer the word of exhortation: for I have written a letter unto you in a few words. Know ye that our brother Timothy is set at liberty; with whom, if he come shortly, I will see you. Salute all them that have the rule over you, and all the saints. They of Italy salute you. Grace be with you all. Amen."

Verse 20. "The God of peace." This is the apostle's parting salutation. He commends them to the God of peace, the God who brought again from the dead the great Shepherd of the sheep, through the blood of the everlasting covenant. This latter statement shows that the resurrection was a part of the everlasting covenant, a part of the agreement made in the councils of eternity.

Verse 21. "Make you perfect." The complaint against the old covenant and priesthood was that it made nothing perfect. The apostle now prays that God will make them perfect in every good work to do God's will. Having said this, he commends them to "Jesus Christ; to whom be glory for ever and ever. Amen. "

Verses 22–25. He closes the epistle with the hope that they will suffer his words of exhortation, also conveying to them the news that Timothy has been set at liberty. He hopes to see them shortly, if Timothy comes soon. He then asks them to salute their leaders and all the saints, and sends them greetings from Italy. His closing words are, "Grace be with you all. Amen."

. . . .

The author has now accomplished his task. He has shown Christ to be both God and man, one who is able to save to the uttermost, and also to sympathize with man in his struggles. He has presented Christ as high priest and mediator, now appearing before the face of God for us. However, Christ is more than an advocate; He is a captain who leads the way for men to follow. He has opened a new and a living way for us into the holies through the veil, that is to say, His flesh, and we may now with boldness enter there with Him.

To bring the reader to enter with Christ into the holy places, has been the aim of the author from the beginning. On earth the people never entered any part of the sanctuary. They worshiped a God whom they had not seen and could not see, and into whose habitation they might not enter.

In Hebrews, Paul presents an altogether new conception. The high priest on earth could enter the most holy only one day in the year, and he would certainly not presume to take anyone else with him. With fear and trembling he approached the sacred dwelling of God, and the people were greatly relieved when he came out alive, without having incurred the displeasure of God. It was a task rather than a pleasure to appear before God.

With Christ as high priest all this is changed. With joy He not only enters Himself but brings with Him the host of the redeemed, those who have here learned to follow the Lamb whithersoever He goeth. No one can fail to see that the privileges of the gospel far exceed those of the old dispensation.

The promise of something better occurs all through the epistle, as witness the repetition of "better" throughout: "better than the angels"; "better things"; "blessed of the better"; "better hope"; "better testament"; "better covenant"; "better promises"; "better sacrifices"; "a better and enduring substance" (possession); "a better country"; "a better resurrection"; "some better thing"; "better things than that of Abel." Heb. 1:4; 6:9; 7:7, 19, 22; 8:6; 9:23; 10:34; 11:16, 35, 40; 12:24. And chief of these "better things" must certainly be the privilege of standing in the very presence of God, not with fear and trembling, but with holy boldness, which is the heritage of God's children. Higher joy is not conceivable.

The author might well have closed his epistle with the tenth chapter, in which in verses 19 and 20 he brings his readers into the presence of God. But as he thinks of the many dear but trembling souls who doubt the possibility of their ever entering into such bliss, he adds some words both for encouragement and warning. It will not be through any merit of theirs that any will ever enter. It will be by faith only. And so he pens the eleventh chapter, that hopeful and encouraging chapter on faith. There the reader will find a list of persons all of whom finally gained the victory, though against great odds. How could any who had known Jacob have any hope of his ever reaching the kingdom? And what about David, and Barak, and Samson, and Rahab, and all the others? And their number is not yet complete, for "they without us" will not be made perfect. (Heb. 11:40.) Comforting words; glorious words. The number is not yet made up. It will not be perfect without us.

So let all take courage. God is waiting for the remnant to join those heroes who "obtained a good report through faith." There is room for all. May God give the reader, with all the saints, an abundant entrance into His kingdom.

Scripture Index

The Book of Hebrews

Subject Index

The Book of Hebrews

The Book of Hebrews

We'd love to send you a catalog of titles we publish
or even
hear your thoughts, reactions, criticism, about
things you did
or didn't like about this
or any other book we publish.

Just contact us at:

www.TEACHServices.com
1/800-367-1844